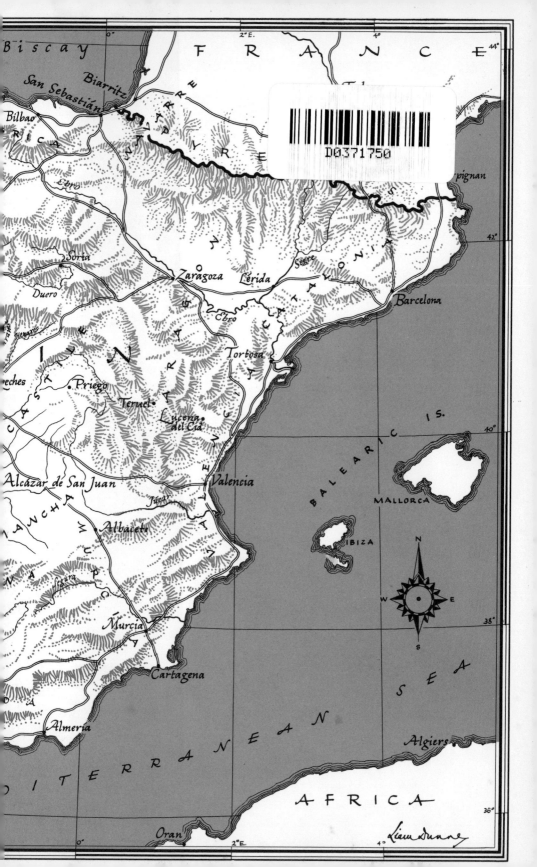

OR I'LL

By Larry Collins and Dominique Lapierre
Or I'll Dress You in Mourning
Is Paris Burning?

DRESS YOU IN MOURNING

LARRY COLLINS

AND

DOMINIQUE LAPIERRE

SIMON AND SCHUSTER
NEW YORK

"Don't cry, Angelita. Tonight I'll buy you a house, or I'll dress you in mourning."

—MANUEL BENÍTEZ, "EL CORDOBÉS"

to his sister on the day of his first
encounter with the brave bulls of Spain.

TABLE OF CONTENTS

Prologue

THE TOWN OF RONDA clings in precarious uncertainty to the rocky shoulders of a 654-foot ravine rising above the waters of the Guadalevín River. It is twenty miles from the Mediterranean Sea, near the southernmost tip of Spain, in the heart of that proud and hungry land called Andalusia. Ronda is known—both for the rapacity of its inhabitants and the remoteness of its perch—as a "nest of eagles." There, during the long years of peace in the sunset of Spain's Golden Age, when her galleons had brought conquest and the Cross to a world laid open by their adventuring prows, the noblemen of Ronda kept sharp the skills of war with a dangerous and sanguinary pastime. They killed wild bulls from horseback.

The site of their exercise was the riding grounds of the Real Maestranza de Caballería, the Royal Riding Circle. Its aim, in Ronda as elsewhere in Spain, was to inspire the highborn to valor and, in passing, to provide a spectacle for the poor who came to watch and drag the butchered bulls from the ring.

During one of those spectacles, at the beginning of the eighteenth cen-

8

tury, a noble and his horse were upended by a bull's charge. The noble was pinned to the ground under his mount, helpless before the horns of the bull he had intended to kill. As the bull poised to drive those horns into the nobleman's body, one of the village poor, hired to tend the Royal Riding Circle, leaped into the ring. Using his flat-brimmed Andalusian hat as a lure, he drew the bull away from the helpless rider. Then, to the awe and admiration of his noble employers, he continued to wave his hat before the bull's eyes, and fixing the beast's stare to its movements, he lured the horned animal past his body time and time again.

The poor man's name was Francisco Romero. He was a carpenter's assistant, and through those gestures of his Andalusian sombrero, Francisco Romero founded the ritual of the modern bullfight, a conflict between a bull, a dismounted man and the lure of a fluttering piece of cloth.

For thirty years from that day, Francisco Romero fought bulls on foot. He invented the muleta, the bullfighter's scarlet serge cloth, to replace his sombrero as a lure. By the time he died, he had become Spain's first *matador de toros,* and his improvised action in Ronda's Royal Riding Circle had changed forever the nature of the bullfight. He had transformed an equestrian art into the trial of a man on foot. The pastime of Spain's nobles, performed for her peasants, became a spectacle for her well-to-do, practiced for them by her poor and hungry sons. For the carpenter's assistant of Ronda died a wealthy man, and the harvest of his lifetime was the opening of a new horizon to his impoverished countrymen.

Ever since that afternoon in Ronda, the road away from hunger for Andalusia's poor youth has led past the horns of a brave bull in the fading glare of a Spanish summer day. Thousands have followed that road in the two and a half centuries since Francisco Romero laid it open with the movements of his Andalusian sombrero. For a very few, it led to wealth and fame beyond a poor boy's dreaming. For most, it led only to despair and suffering. For over four hundred of Spain's sons, it led to the grave.

This is the story of the painful journey of one man who walked that road.

CHAPTER ONE

Madrid:
A MORNING
IN MAY

"Ite, missa est—go, the Mass is finished."

For an instant, the words of the priest seemed to drift along the dark shadows of the church, suspended on the moist air like a wisp of incense flicked from a passing censer. Then, from the cluster of black-shawled women crouched in the half-light before him, came the reply, barely audible, the closing chorus of the sacred mutter of the Mass: *"Deo gratias."*

At those words, Don Juan Espinosa Carmona twisted his stout figure back toward the altar behind him and genuflected before the door of his tabernacle. Then, with gestures formed by a third of a century of habit, he began another ritual quite unrelated to the Mass he had just finished. For thirty years he had performed that ritual every Thursday and every Sunday from March to October and every day during this closing fortnight of May when Madrid celebrated the feria of San Isidro, its patron. He took two consecrated hosts from the tabernacle and snapped them into a silver compact the size of a pocket watch. Then he drew out a crystal vial of holy oil. With a final gesture, he locked both items inside a small black leather satchel into which he had already fitted a purple stole and a tuft of cotton.

A few moments later Don Juan knelt in prayer before a sputtering bank of votary candles lit by some of the black-shawled women for whom he had just said Mass. Above the candles, caught in their quivering amber light, the pale plaster face of the Virgin of Covadonga emerged from her half-darkened statuary niche. As he had done for thirty years on mornings such as this, Don Juan offered today a special prayer to the Virgin, beseeching her that he would not, in the hours to come, have use for the sacred vessels in the black satchel he clutched at his side.

His prayer over, he rose, blessed himself, and plunged into the street outside. There he turned left and pointed toward the Moorish arches of another temple rising in the sunlight before him a third of a mile away. It was the Plaza de Toros of Madrid, the bullring of the capital of Spain, the cathedral of an art as old and as Spanish as the Virgin to whom he had just paid reverence.

Don Juan was the chaplain of that bullring. He had begun his unique ministry as a young priest, wholly ignorant of the intricacies of the bull-fight. Now he was an elderly man, and the girth of his stomach popping open two of the buttons of his cassock gave graphic witness to his age. In the thirty years that Don Juan had exercised his function, he had become a passionate aficionado, and many were the cassocks he had worn threadbare against the bullring's concrete banks watching three generations of matadors parade past his square-rimmed spectacles.

The pleasures of Don Juan's uncommon charge were not without their price, however, and his stooped figure in the concrete ranks of Madrid's Plaza de Toros represented more than just a comforting symbol. Four times during that third of a century, Don Juan's olive oil of Granada, consecrated every year on Holy Thursday, had given solace to the last moments of a man dying young in a bullfighter's suit of lights.

Now, as he rushed through the warm May sunshine toward the bull-ring, Don Juan could feel, tucked into his cassock in a black cotton sack the size of a man's thumb, the seal of his office. It was the key to the tabernacle of the Plaza's chapel where, in a few moments, he would deposit the contents of his leather satchel. Wrapped around the key was a slip of red-and-yellow paper. It was Don Juan's season pass to Madrid's great bullring, the Plaza Monumental, popularly known as Las Ventas, and it was, on this May morning, the most precious document a Spaniard could possess. In exactly ten hours its official stamp and signature would assure Don Juan admission to a spectacle all Spain clamored to attend. It was to be the official confirmation of the elevation to the rank of *matador de toros* of a bandy-legged Andalusian orphan.

Not since the last fitful convulsions of the Civil War had an event captured the attention of the Spanish nation in quite the same manner as this one. To find its parallel in the recent history of the country's *fiesta brava,* her aficionados had to go back seventeen years to the tragic August day when Spain's last great idol, Manuel Rodríguez, "Manolete," died, gored by a Miura bull in the provincial city of Linares, stirring his countrymen in death as he had never been able to stir them in life.

No matador in modern times had provoked the frenzy, the mass hysteria, or the furious controversy that had attended the rush to fame of the youth whose art Don Juan would witness for the first time this afternoon.

He had come from nowhere. Just half a decade before this May morning, the only places his name was recognized were in the archives of half a dozen jails and on the juvenile delinquency rolls of the Guardia Civil post in his native town. Now, on the threshold of the most important bullfight of his career, that name was almost as well known in his country as that of the man who symbolized modern Spain, the Caudillo himself, Generalisimo Francisco Franco.

It was Manuel Benítez, "El Cordobés," and the young man who bore it had, on this 20th of May, 1964, just turned twenty-eight years old.

Madrid seemed to tingle with the excitement his corrida had aroused. The advertising panels of the city's double-deck buses carried a huge photograph of the matador drinking his personal brand of wine. His picture was pasted to almost every newsstand in the capital. Spanish National Lottery vendors invoked his name to bless their tickets with an extra ration of luck this morning. The drab gray walls lining the priest's route to Las Ventas were alive with bright splotches of color, bullfight posters, a blur of black and gold and scarlet promising, as they had done for generations, "six magnificent *toros* at exactly six o'clock in the afternoon, weather and authority permitting." To each was pasted a three-word announcement that summed up the excitement generated by the coming corrida, and reminded the pastor of Our Lady of Covadonga, as he marched past, of the very special privilege that would be his in a few hours. *"No hay billetes,"* it said: No tickets left.

*   *   *

That phrase, which the good priest might have noted with smug satis-faction, was not wholly accurate. There were some tickets left for the bullfight, exactly twenty-three hundred of them, 10 percent of the total available, held back under Spanish law for sale on this, the morning of the corrida. To get them, thousands of Spaniards were rioting around a two-hundred-yard-long alley named the Calle de la Victoria, only a few steps from the Puerta del Sol, the historic heart of Madrid and the geo-graphical center of Spain itself.

Their heaving mass menaced the plate-glass windows of the cafés, some of them no larger than a newspaper vendor's stall, that lined the alley. Those windows advertised each café's specialities in whitewashed letters: squid cooked in its own ink, baby eels, blood sausage thick as a man's forearm, pickled tripe. It was not, however, those delicacies that distinguished the cafés from the hundreds of others like them in Madrid; their distinction was in the single-mindedness of their decors. The walls, façades, even the ceilings of every café on the Calle de la Victoria were pasted over with bullfight posters, paintings and photographs, reminders of the fact that a sole and consuming passion united the men who fre-quented their premises.

With their stench of stale beer and soured wine, their sawdust-covered floors spattered with spit, shrimp shells and cigar stubs, those cafés were the bazaar stalls of the world of the bullfight. And, at No. 9 Calle de la Victoria, under a flyspecked blue-and-orange awning, was the institution that had made this smelly alley the capital of the corrida and had drawn this impatient mob to its cobbled confines. It was the office of the man-agement of Las Ventas.

Today's corrida represented to that management a financial windfall of unprecedented proportions. With the exception of the tickets about to be offered for sale, every seat in the bullring had been sold, not as single tickets but—to customers prepared to buy them—as full subscription tickets for every one of the sixteen corridas of the fortnight-long feria of San Isidro. Thus the management of Las Ventas had been able, thanks to El Cordobés, to sell out every one of the corridas of a San Isidro feria for the first time in its history. It was a stroke of good fortune worth well over two and a half million dollars.

To control the impatient crowd fighting for the few remaining tickets, the police had been forced to cut the Calle de la Victoria off to automobile traffic at midnight. Thousands of *Madrileños* had spent the night sleeping in doorways or priming themselves awake with coffee and cognac, awaiting seven o'clock, the hour at which the police had announced the ticket line could form. Office workers in shiny suits and worn ties slept beside factory hands in corduroy trousers. Scalpers, sure of a historic profit on the resale of every ticket they could collect, fought for space on the sidewalk with impassioned aficionados. Businessmen, generals and government officials sent office boys and chauffeurs to keep the all-night vigil in the street.

At daybreak an extra squad of police had joined those already in the alley, even though the city authorities had never felt obliged to send more than three policemen to control a ticket sale on Calle de la Victoria. Yet, when the first clear chords of seven rang out from Madrid's multitude of churches, the score of policemen on duty had been pushed aside by the mob bursting for the blue-and-orange awning over the Las Ventas ticket window and the promise of a place in its ticket line.

*　　*　　*

Two flights above those besieged ticket windows, a man drew apart a pair of beige cotton curtains and peered with unrestrained enthusiasm at the mob. The vest of his steel-gray suit was flecked with ashes from the cigarette he clasped rigidly between his lips. A field of freckles underlay the tan of his face, whose outlines were lost amid the jowls which drooped from his sideburns like a rooster's wattle.

No wild excess of *afición* would ever have driven him into a mob like the one surging below his window. He was a lawyer by schooling, a man who preferred to spend his Sundays weeding his country garden instead of watching a bullfight, a gentle humanist who cringed at the sight of blood.

Yet the impatient crowd milling along the Calle de la Victoria represented a singular personal triumph for Don Livinio Stuyck. Don Livinio was the impresario of the Madrid bullring. From this office he ran the activities not only of the first bullring of the world but of a chain of other bullrings, two bull-breeding ranches, and a stable of bullfighters. Almost one out of every three corridas held in Spain was conceived in his office, and his prodigious array of activities made of this quiet man, who shuddered every time he saw the sight of a bull's blood splashing onto the sand of one of his eleven bullrings, the most important impresario in that most Spanish of spectacles, the bullfight.

Nothing in his background had prepared Don Livinio to enter the strange profession of bullfight impresario. He was the heir to another Spanish institution, the Fábrica Real de Tapices, the Royal Tapestry Factory, founded by his Flemish ancestors summoned to Madrid by Philip V in 1721. The exquisite heritage of that factory now hung in the banquet halls and salons of the Escorial and the Prado and all the stately mansions of Spain. In that family factory, reeking of wool and dye, the young Don Livinio had had his own first brush with the corrida. For long boyhood hours he had stared at his family's collection of bullfight tapestries, woven by his ancestors from the patterns set out for them by the great Goya. But his *afición* had stopped there, and young Don Livinio went to the law.

One winter morning in 1941 two friends called on the youthful lawyer. They asked him to take over on their behalf the faltering management of the Madrid bullring. It was an institution Stuyck had visited only on rare occasions, when an extraordinary corrida had lured him away from the quiet of his country home. It was a "provisional" job, but Stuyck knew that "in Spain things that are provisional last; those that are permanent pass away fastest." He took it and now, twenty-three years later, still provisionally confirmed in his post, he continued to run the most important bullring in the world with the ordered reasoning of his legal mind.

During those years, this improbable impresario had staged over twenty-five hundred bullfights and sent out more than fifteen thousand of the noble bulls whose suffering so pained him to die under the swords of two generations of Spanish matadors. He had brought Manolete to Madrid, and helped to arrange the famous *mano a mano* fight of Antonio Ordóñez and Luis Miguel González, "Dominguín." But on this May

16

morning he was compelled to admit that never in all those years had a spectacle he had promoted unleashed the enthusiasm and emotion stirred by this strange defier of bulls and traditions called El Cordobés.

Don Livinio could not explain the phenomenon of this untutored Andalusian's success. Nor did he really care to. The fact of its existence was quite enough for Don Livinio's commercial soul. Along with three other men—a shy banker in Seville, a cynical octogenarian in Barcelona and an ex-horse wrangler in San Sebastián—he controlled the corrida. Among them, those four princes of the Spanish *fiesta brava* reigned over every bullring of any importance in Spain. Bullfighters, their managers, bull breeders, critics and aficionados all were beholden to their individual or collective whims.

Yet for almost two decades the spectacle over which they presided had been in decay. Spain, it was whispered, had lost its *afición.* Lassitude had crept up upon the corrida. An indifferent youth was drifting away to other pursuits. Since the death of Manolete, no matador had galvanized the crowds and guaranteed by the mere fact of his presence in a corrida the appearance of the phrase plastered this morning to the billboards of Madrid: *"No hay billetes."*

Then two things had happened. Television had come to Spain. And, at about the same time, a new Messiah with a muleta, this gangling youth who had provoked the riot under Don Livinio's window, had come marching out of Andalusia. With his unkempt hair, his angelic smile and his terrifying courage, he shook the *fiesta brava* to its foundations. His raw, untutored style, his almost contemptuous courage, provoked every emotion but indifference, and, carried across Spain by television, it stirred a mass hysteria never before built up around a matador. He had shaken the cobwebs from the corrida, and to the untrammeled delight of Don Livinio and his three colleagues, he had brought beating down upon the box offices of the bullrings of Spain an unprecedented wave of demand, a frantic scrambling for tickets of which the crowd outside the Las Ventas office was only the final manifestation.

Don Livinio had met the future idol of Spain for the first time at the gates of his bullring on a chilly morning in the late 1950's. He seemed to Stuyck "just another hungry kid from Andalusia with a dirty face, begging for a chance to fight a bull." Don Livinio saw hundreds of faces like his every year. They clustered around his office, his home, his car,

17

his bullrings, their owners all begging for the same thing, an *oportunidad,* a chance to fight a bull.

It was a futile pursuit. There were no *oportunidades* in the bullrings of Don Livinio. The places on his programs were saved for matadors of proven skill, not for hungry kids as apt to vault from the ring in fear as to kill a bull.

Don Livinio had turned to the youth before him and with a snap of his thumb flicked him a duro, a five-peseta piece. To Stuyck's surprise, he scooped up the coin and flung it back at him. "I don't want your alms," he shrieked. "I want a chance to fight bulls."

While Stuyck recovered from his astonishment, the boy thrust an angry arm toward the stands of Las Ventas, silent and empty in the winter sunshine. "Damn you," he cried, "someday you'll fill that ring because of me!" The impresario had laughed at his pretentious and pathetic gesture.

Now, five years later, that prophecy was about to come true. In a few hours the gates of Las Ventas would open before the gold-and-tobacco-colored suit of lights of the kid with the dirty face; the man whose charity he had scorned had spent three months trying to bring El Cordobés back to his arena, this time as the prime attraction of the most important feria in Spain's bullfighting season.

Just a month earlier, Stuyck had settled the last details of the fight with the manager who now spoke for the youth he had turned away from the gates of Las Ventas. In the tradition of the bullfight world, no official document would ever take note of the final details of their agreement. Stuyck had noted them instead in the red plastic notebook that contained all the records of his multimillion-dollar empire. There were three entries: the date of the fight, the ranch from which the bulls would come, and the matador's fee.

For the approximately thirty minutes he would take to dispatch two bulls from the world, the young man who had once refused Don Livinio's alms had been promised one million pesetas, $16,600, the highest fee ever paid to a matador.

*   *   *

It took less than an hour to sell the twenty-three hundred tickets set aside by law. When the sale was over, the Calle de la Victoria became an enormous black market. Voices muffled, their eyes flickering over the faces in the crowd for a prospective client or plainclothesman, scalpers slipped down the edges of the alley, reaping the rewards of their vigil in the ticket line. Prices soon climbed to fifteen times their face value. *Barrera de sombra* seats, ringside seats in the shade, commanded two hundred and fifty to three hundred dollars, more money than many Spaniards saw in a year. Factory workers pawned their watches for a bad seat high on the sunny reaches of Las Ventas; bank clerks sacrificed three months' salary for a modest place in the shade.

As the scalpers peddled their wares, the alley began to swarm with those intense and solemn men who dedicated their lifetimes to the corrida, the professional aficionados devoting themselves to the only pastime they held more sacred than the bulls: arguing. Invariably dressed in coats and ties despite the heat, panamas tugged down to shade their brows from the hot shafts of sunshine sinking into the street, they strolled from bar to bar as grave and ponderous in their quest of an appreciative audience as official mourners at an Irish politician's wake.

Their athenaeum was the Alemana, the German beer hall, a cool palace paneled in dark walnut, set in the Plaza Santa Ana. There, surrounded by pink piles of shrimp and reddish brown slabs of *mojama,* dried tuna, the aristocracy of *afición* gathered. Retired matadors, rich bull breeders, impresarios, distinguished bullfight critics, they sipped their beer in unhurried ease and, as they had done for decades, extolled the matadors of the past, disdained those of the present and despaired for those of the future.

Hostile to revolution in all its forms, even taurine, they had remained indifferent to the success of the unkempt orphan from Andalusia. He ignored the canons of an art they held sacred, and for that they scorned him. He substituted charlatanism for grace, they maintained, ignorant courage for skill, a vulgar appeal to emotion for dignity. They dismissed him as a passing clown, another one of the fleeting freaks regularly thrown up each decade or so by their *fiesta brava.* With baleful regularity they predicted his swift and merited return to the obscurity from which he had so recently emerged.

To the dignified and measured men in the Alemana, El Cordobés was more, however, than just a bullfighter whose art they condemned. With his uncut hair, his scornful laugh, his disdain for the rigid rituals of the

19

corrida, he seemed to sum up many of the currents astir in their nation and its youth, currents they neither condoned nor understood. The passions he aroused, they asserted, came from the masses, who were ignorant of the techniques of the bullfight; the crowd was reacting to the appeal of an idol rather than the gestures of an artist. He seemed the expression in the corrida of a quickening rise in mass values in all aspects of Spanish life, a rise threatening one day to overwhelm in vulgarity, mediocrity—and democracy—the watchtower from which their kind had so long imposed their graceful and rigid standards on Spanish society. Their disdain, however, did not prevent them all this May morning from brandishing tickets to the corrida of the young man whose art they scorned.

*   *   *

A quarter of a mile from the Alemana, on a sidewalk leading down to the entry of the subway station Sevilla, was another, less attractive adjunct of the corrida, an open-air market in broke and hungry toreros. Here gathered the unlucky and unemployed of the bullfight world: matadors too old, too clumsy, too unskilled to fight; men who in some distant bullring had caught the dread disease of fear and had spent a career trying to exorcise it, driven with derisive jeers from plaza to plaza down to this market of last resort, each trying to conceal his fatal flaw under a mantle of pride, still believing that somehow, someday, the impossible would happen and his skittery legs would at last stand still before the charges of a bull; banderilleros, plump and splay-footed now when they drove home their iron darts, dreaming, through the haze of their endless cigarettes, of the graceful promise of their lost youth; picadors, overtaken by age and alcohol.

Comforting their despair with the memories of their yesterdays, they waited for some miracle to open to them once again the road to those lost afternoons of light and triumph. Vain, that wait, for the only miracle these sidewalks offered was the occasional charity of a hundred-peseta note slipped into a proud torero's hand by a passing acquaintance, the unacknowledged alms with which to stem another day's hunger.

Most pathetic of all were the *maletillas,* the restless urchins of the corrida, wandering the pavements in battered tennis shoes and blue

20

jeans, their belongings hanging in bundles from their shoulders. Driven from their distant villages by hunger or ambition, they now begged for the chance to take their turn upon the sand of Spain's bullrings.

The horizons of their hope were limited. Occasionally a third-rate matador wandered by to replace an injured banderillero or patch together an improvised *cuadrilla.* To this marketplace came the representatives of the village impresarios looking for a youngster willing to kill a couple of bulls, for bus fare and a handful of pesetas, in honor of the local Virgin. The only glory they offered was a chance to fight in a *"plaza de mala muerte,"* a plaza of the bad death, lost in a country town without an infirmary or penicillin, where the only solace for a wounded torero was the calloused hands of the village midwife or the whispered Latin of the parish priest.

Today, in contrast to the bar of the Alemana, a very special excitement animated their world. They knew what the establishment of the Alemana chose to overlook: love of art may drive a man to bullring's ticket window, but it is hunger that drives him onto its sand. El Cordobés, standing this morning at the pinnacle of all a torero could dream of, was one of theirs. He had come off this sidewalk and the dozens of others like it scattered through Spain. He had shared the hopes, the humiliation and the hunger they knew. To the broken and scarred men, and still unblooded kids around the subway station Sevilla, El Cordobés' success was the miracle to which they aspired, the dream for which they kept going, against all reason, to the lost country villages and the *plazas de mala muerte.*

*   *   *

The interest stirred by the Madrid debut of El Cordobés was by no means limited to the capital of Spain. The entire nation awaited it with eagerness and impatience. In cities like Granada and Valencia where El Cordobés had known a special triumph, in the lost country villages through whose *plazas de mala muerte* he had passed on his long march to Las Ventas, today's corrida was regarded with a special pride.

Nowhere, however, was the corrida awaited with a fervor as intense as that gripping two sites by the Guadalquivir River: Córdoba, the ancient capital of the caliphs, and, forty miles from Córdoba, the town of Palma del Río, birthplace of Manuel Benítez. Córdoba, whose streets of white-washed buildings seemed haunted still by those dark sovereigns of the desert who had once ruled an empire from her gates, felt her history more intimately entwined with the *fiesta brava* than any other city in Spain. Here one hundred thousand mourners had paraded behind the coffin of Córdoba's local hero, Manolete. From Córdoba's Santa María slums had come a prolific and unending parade of matadors to stamp their marks upon the history of the bullfight. Four of them—Lagartijo "el Grande," Guerrita, Machaquito and Manolete—had so dominated the bullfighters of their generations that the city had canonized them as the Four Caliphs of Córdoba. Their names were enshrined in stone upon the seventeenth-century clock tower of the Iglesia de Santa María. To that church the old men of Córdoba came in daily procession to set their watches by the chimes of its carillon.

Córdoba had adopted with all the passion of its *afición* the unlettered peasant from its provinces who had chosen to bear its name into Spain's bullrings, and had built here his first home. One day his name, too, would probably be carved upon the stone clock tower of Santa María. It would be an ironic honor for a boy whose first introduction to the city of the caliphs had been as a prisoner in its jail, serving a three-month sentence for vagrancy.

For the people of Palma del Río, the matador's birthplace, this day was a moment of historic importance. It coincided with the opening of its annual four-day feria. Already, a good part of the town's eighteen thousand inhabitants swarmed through the striped tents set up for the occasion. Only the moist shadows of the parish church offered an oasis of silence in the happy tumult engulfing the town. Kneeling in a thin shaft of light sinking into the church from one of its stained-glass windows, Don Carlos Sánchez, Palma's pastor, looked up from his breviary. Behind him he heard the sound of furtive footsteps shuffling toward the altar. He turned, and as he did, a black-shawled figure glided past him toward a dollhouselike glass box set beside his sacristy door.

Inside that box, wrapped in a hand-embroidered robe of white satin and gold filament, clutching a silver scepter, was a statue of the Blessed Virgin of Bethlehem, the *patrona* of Palma del Río. She was the creation of an unknown nineteenth-century Córdoba sculptor. In the century and a half since his hands had wrought her pinched and delicate fea-

22

tures from the wood of a young acacia tree, all the hopes and miseries, the sufferings and aspirations of Palma del Río had been laid at her tiny feet. No ill was held too small, no hope too forlorn, for her intercession. She was carried through the cobbled alleys of the town to grace the bedsides of the sick and the dying; she was invoked to make the barren fertile or aid those broken in health by too frequent childbirth; to end a drought or stem a flood; to bless the newborn, or end in mercy the sufferings of the aged.

To the Virgin's feet the black-shawled woman brought a special prayer this morning. For Angelita Benítez, forty, a brother's triumphs were a sister's sufferings. Every time Manuel Benítez stepped into a bullring, a special pang of sorrow struck this woman who had raised him as a son. Angelita Benítez had spent her lifetime trying to keep her baby brother from the bulls. For her, the glorious moment the rest of the town awaited this afternoon represented a failure, her personal failure, in the one task she had set herself in life.

Alone with her fears in her festive town, she begged the *patrona* of Palma del Río to protect her brother this afternoon. A special nervousness accompanied her prayers. In a few hours, in front of the television set El Cordobés had bought her for the occasion, she would watch the rite that would confirm her brother in the profession from which she had sworn to keep him. It would be the first time Angelita Benítez had seen a bullfight.

*   *   *

A sister's protesting voice trying to call a brother away from the bulls had been only a despairing murmur beside the other voices beckoning him toward the corrida's glittering horizons. To that poor, proud and hungry young man who was her brother, those other voices had had an irresistible lure, a lure as old and as Spanish as Spain itself.

Indeed, to understand Spain, wrote the preeminent historian of the corrida, José María de Cossío, one must also understand the bullfight. So deep and numerous are its roots that no phase of Spanish life from art to industry and commerce escapes its stigmata. It is a cruel rite distorted by a false cloak of romanticism, a spectacle in which avariciousness is often taken for art. Yet for all that, for all its venality, its corruption and its fraud, the spectacle of which so many awaited a symbolic renewal this May afternoon was a constant and faithful manifestation of Spain's proud character.

Spain was a nation condemned by the Pyrenees to live her formative centuries forlornly alone. While Europe had spawned a Renaissance, she had been forced to forge a nation by driving her Arab conquerors from her soil. As her neighbors to the north grasped for the first prizes of mercantilism, she had assigned herself the more spiritual mission of Catholicizing the world, and had squandered an empire for the Cross. Her harsh, forbidding land stood higher, bore less water, and exacted, for each living thing it sustained, a greater toll of human sweat and toil than any other corner of Europe.

From that adversity and isolation had come a proud and ardent people, a people born to hardship, indifferent to suffering, possessing a fine disregard for death. Spain had sired Cervantes and St. Ignatius Loyola; she could offer the world both the quintessence of chivalry in Don Quixote and a synonym for cruelty, the Spanish Inquisition. She was a land of dark and stormy contrasts, of violence and exquisite tenderness; of physical passion and religious repression; all summed up so well in the very division of the bullring itself, *sol y sombra,* sunshine and shadow.

Only Spain, so close yet so far from the rest of Europe, this land of sorrow and suffering with its cult of honor, courage and death, could have spawned the ritual honoring today of its newest acolyte. With its brutality, redeemed by its fleeting beauty, its glorification of physical courage and disdain of death, the corrida was a living portrayal of the values Spain prized most.

The brave bull's fatal end was no less certain in the Spanish *fiesta brava* than it had been in the pagan sacrifices to which its origins might be traced. The nation that idolized courage and honor, however, offered the animal it was going to sacrifice the noble privilege of defending with all its savage force its doomed existence. The victim became, briefly, a measure against which Spanish man might try his courage, and the pagan sacrifice was infused with a new spirit that sundered its traditional dimensions by introducing into it the idea of danger. Now, before dying, the bull of mythology received the chance of maiming or killing the man who proposed to end his existence. It was a gesture worthy of the Spaniards' pride. And it made the *fiesta brava* something more than a sport or

24

a spectacle, the *plaza de toros* something more than a theater, and the bull something more than an accessory to man's vanity.

The first name to illuminate the rolls of the *fiesta brava* was that of Julius Caesar, reported by various historians to have fought bulls from horseback in Seville, Cádiz and the Colosseum of Imperial Rome. For seventeen centuries, until the historic intervention of the carpenter's assistant in the Ronda riding ring, the corrida remained the pastime of princes and nobles. In the decades that followed Romero's intervention, the institution born in the gestures of a carpenter's sombrero was transformed gradually from an anarchic combat into an ordered ritual with its own rules and traditions. Its heroes provided Spain a new mainstream of national idols, men like Joaquín Rodríguez, "Costillares," who posed for Goya; Rafael Molina, "Lagartijo," who killed 4,867 bulls in forty-two marathon years as a bullfighter; Manuel García, "El Espartero," eulogized in song as the "king of all toreros."

Those matadors marked out the milestones in her history, and in their own contrasting personalities seemed to capture the spirit of the generations that idolized them. In the years that preceded and encompassed World War I, Spain's *fiesta brava* was dominated by the man most often acclaimed the greatest bullfighter in history, José Gómez Ortega, "Joselito." The son, nephew, and brother of bullfighters, he had his picture taken with a sword in his hands at two, leaped unasked into a village bullring at nine, and began his professional career as a bullfighter at twelve. He celebrated his sixteenth birthday by killing six three-year-old bulls by himself and before he was twenty-one had been acclaimed as the greatest genius the *fiesta brava* had ever produced. In his poised elegance and the classic beauty of his gestures, Joselito seemed to sum up all the grace and style of the world dying forever before the cannons of 1914–18. So instinctive was his technique, so consummate his command of his art, that all Spain swore "no bull could ever catch Joselito." Spain was wrong. On May 16th, 1920, just two years after the eclipse of the world his elegance had symbolized so well, a bull named Bailador killed the idol Spain had believed immortal in the town of Talavera de la Reina.

His death left alone upon the pedestal the man with whom he had shared it for seven years: an ugly runt with a nervous stammer and a pair of stunted legs, a peddler's son from the Gypsy slum of Triana on the

25

wrong side of Seville's Guadalquivir River. His name was Juan Belmonte, and he drove those tortured legs into corners of the bullring where no man had dared to go before him. The crowds that applauded Joselito's cool beauty were awed by Belmonte's crude courage and rushed to watch him perform before he was impaled upon the horns of a bull.

No family ties, no inbred tradition, had aided his rise. He clawed his own way out of Seville's slums and with raw willpower forced a revolution upon the corrida. By the time he had finished, he had revised almost every one of its canons. He even snipped off the pigtail, the loathsome hank of hair that for generations had branded the bullfighter a man apart, and led the matador's invasion of the drawing rooms of Spanish society. As Joselito's elegance had summed up the grace of a dying age, so Belmonte's raw courage seemed to foreshadow the coming of a new one. It was the Spain thrusting out for justice and democracy, ringing with the demands of her trade unions, her Socialists, and her unruly anarchists, drifting already toward the tragedy of the Spanish Civil War. As for the reckless Belmonte, whose death in the bullring had seemed a foreordained certainty, he lived to die of his own hand at the age of seventy.

The third great idol to emerge in the twentieth century was Manuel Rodríguez, Manolete, who came upon the scene in the summer of 1939 in the aftermath of the Civil War. He had sad, black eyes and an angular face frozen into a melancholy mask. That face prompted critics to call him—after Cervantes—"The Knight of the Sorrowful Countenance." His bullfights were stark and somber tragedies, and in them a nation mourning half a million dead seemed to find the echo of the barely stifled sorrows in its own soul. For seven years his sad and solitary figure dominated the corrida, his reign coinciding with that anguished period in Spain's existence when, cut off from friend and foe alike, she suffered and starved in stoic silence. When Manolete died in the tragedy of Linares in 1947, a part of Spain seemed to die with him.

Now Spain had a new idol, the unruly vagabond from Andalusia upon whose corrida this afternoon so much attention was concentrated. And it was a new Spain that idolized him, a nation already profoundly different from the sore and wounded Spain that had buried Manolete in the cemetery of Córdoba.

26

It was the Spain of television, and of the most extraordinary tourist invasion the world had ever seen, over fourteen million people a year, almost one for every two Spaniards, streaming over the Pyrenees in an unending scramble for the sun, bringing with them in their Austins, Renaults and Volkswagens the seeds of the social revolution changing forever the isolated character of the Spanish nation. It was the Spain of American aid and economic takeoff, industrialization and migrating populations. Skyscrapers now stalked her skylines, and public housing developments marched out from her cities in gathering ranks, pushing their limits ever farther into the plains around them. The snarl of the motor scooter increasingly drowned out the clip-clop of her donkey carts, and the rasp of the jackhammer shattered the tranquil rhythms of her quiet neighborhoods.

Like a rash, her resorts had sprouted beaches with bars named St. Tropez, Soho, and Broadway, symbols of the once-disdained world beyond the Pyrenees, blaring out rock 'n' roll, peddling fish-and-chips, hamburgers, and steak-*pommes-frites.* Her once-deserted shorelines were speckled with a pastel profusion of garish new buildings inspired by Miami Beach and southern California.

It was the Spain of a new and restless youth—the youth that perplexed the dignified men of the Alemana bar—questioning its country's past, dissatisfied with its present, looking increasingly north toward the rest of Europe for the resolution of its future. Just as El Cordobés laughingly defied the centuries-old canons of his patterned art, so this modern generation surged impatiently against the pillars of Spain's rigid and structured society. They wore blue jeans and chewed bubble gum, let their hair grow like El Cordobés', danced the frug and rode motor scooters, read the once-forbidden works of Sartre, and questioned the religious dogma and the sexual mores handed down to them by their elders. Where, five years earlier, the Cardinal Primate of Spain had approved the publication of a text proclaiming that engaged couples holding hands in public committed a mortal sin, teen-age girls now flounced off to the beach in bikinis and gigglingly embraced their *novios* (fiancés) in the shelter of Madrid's darkened doorways. Like Brigitte Bardot in France, and later the Beatles in England, El Cordobés in Spain had become the symbol of this changing generation, the unintentional carrier of its virus to the farthest corners of his nation.

27

It was also a Spain beginning to stir from the long and troubled sleep imposed by the Civil War. The year before, an extraordinary event had taken place. Miners in the Asturias and steelworkers in Bilbao had sought to better their lives with an arm outlawed in Franco's Spain, the strike. Young priests, defying the clubs of the police and the official displeasure of their bishops, had come to the workers' side to offer their support and the moral caution of their presence. Similar events had taken place in Castile and Catalonia. In Andalusia, the Guardia Civil had been called out to discipline peasants agitating not just for more bread but for a greater share in the prosperity beginning to affect even their poor provinces.

Feeble testings of a still-implacable regime, those manifestations were indicative of the appetite of Spain's masses for a better and less fettered life than that offered them by the victors of the Civil War. It was not surprising that so many among them had made an idol of the unruly matador of Palma del Río. Manuel Benítez had been heir to a poverty as desperate as any in Spain, and branded by the sins of his Loyalist parents; yet he had escaped with his reckless courage the misery plaguing their lives. To many a Spaniard, the mercurial rise of El Cordobés was an echo of their own long-thwarted aspirations, his triumphs vicariously-lived victories over a common foe.

*   *   *

None of those considerations, however, none of the emotional frenzy building up for today's corrida from Málaga to Barcelona, had touched its principal participant. The young man who would shortly face the imperious demands of two brave bulls in the world's most prestigious bullring had ignored all the turmoil his presence had provoked in Madrid. He had chosen instead to hide away from friends and admirers on the fourth floor of the Hotel Wellington in a quiet residential quarter of the capital.

There El Cordobés passed this morning of the most important corrida in his life in a deep, untroubled sleep.

Four floors below the room in which the matador slept, a pair of worried-looking men picked their way across the crowded lobby of the

Hotel Wellington. Both were short. One was spare and bony, long strands of blond hair retreating back from his forehead, a set of gold teeth illuminating his quick and nervous smile. His name was Pepín Garrido. His companion, Paco Ruiz, was younger, a plump teddy-bearish sort of man. As he walked, he rose high off the balls of his feet, giving to his movements a sense of coiled speed like those of a cat stalking an unsuspecting bird.

A special air of respect accompanied the pair as they walked to the Wellington's elevator. They were banderilleros of El Cordobés. Half an hour earlier they had participated, at the corrals of Las Ventas, in the ritual of the *sorteo,* the drawing of the lots by which the bulls for the afternoon's corrida had been divided among the three matadors on the program. It was the result of that drawing which had fixed upon their faces this unaccustomed air of concern.

Twelve noon had just struck in the neighboring belfry of Our Lady of Covadonga when that ritual began with the appearance in the corrals of a stocky, middle-aged man surrounded by three policemen. His escorts cleared a path for him through the crowd of journalists, photographers and hangers-on blocking the railing overlooking the bull pens. There, indifferent and unconcerned, giving off a sour stench of sweat, urine and mashed grain, were six black bulls of the Andalusian bull-breeding ranch of Don José Benítez Cubero, the animals selected for the coming corrida.

They were big, dangerous animals and the stocky man studied them with a solemn regard. He represented in this corral the sovereign authority of the Spanish state, and his duties as a Madrid police commissioner had taught Mariano Bernardo de Quiros not to hold such authority lightly. The luck of another draw had assigned him, from among a pool of five police commissioners, the task of presiding over today's corrida.

This appraisal was, for President de Quiros, a formality. The evening before, accompanied by a team of veterinarians and a representative of Cubero's ranch, he had carried out the *"reconocimiento,"* the formal certification of the bulls' weight, age, health and condition of horns. He turned to his police escort and uttered the ritualistic phrase which opened the *sorteo: "Que pasen los toreros*—let the toreros pass."

With the banderilleros of the two other matadors on the program, "Pedrés" and "Palmeño," Paco and Pepín had set about the solemn business of dividing the six bulls into three lots of two bulls each, one lot

29

for each matador. The three teams of banderilleros whispered together in conspiratorial silence to pair the bulls into logical lots: the heaviest with the lightest, the one with the most dangerous horns with the one with the least dangerous. From their debatings came a decision to pair bull number 64, whose weak shoulder muscles gave a droop to his neck and promised an easier than average kill, with number 34, whose wide-spreading horns rendered an exceptional faena extremely difficult. Number 23, the lightest, went with number 17, the heaviest. Finally, number 25 was paired with number 77. These two constituted the most awesome lot. Each was heavy, high-necked and carried a head of sharply pointed outward-flaring horns. Appraising them, Gonzalo Carvajal, the experienced bullfight critic of the Madrid daily *Pueblo,* scribbled a sanguinary observation in his notebook. "Numbers 25 and 77," he wrote, "could kill a matador."

Paco Ruiz wrote down the pairings on three scraps of cigarette paper. Then he rolled them into three little balls and dropped them into the Andalusian sombrero of the *mayoral* who had brought the bulls to Madrid from the Cubero ranch. The *mayoral* clapped a second sombrero over his own and shook the three papers. One of the banderilleros of Pedrés, the senior matador, slipped his hand between the two sombreros' brims and drew out a paper ball. Palmeño's representative followed. Paco took the paper that was left over.

One by one, the three banderilleros unrolled their lots and announced to President de Quiros the numbers of the bulls they had drawn. Pedrés would fight numbers 23 and 17; Palmeño's man announced that his matador had drawn numbers 64 and 34. At his words, the dozens of spectators clustering around the three banderilleros saw Paco Ruiz's face blanch. His little roll of paper dropped to the floor beside him unopened.

As the Hotel Wellington's elevator rose toward the room in which their matador slept, the faces of Paco and Pepín were more composed but they were no less concerned. Soon they must announce to their employer that in this corrida upon which he counted so much, he must expose his hopes and his life to the horns of two black bulls bearing the numbers 25 and 77, the animals a newspaperman had written "could kill a matador."

*   *   *

In the hotel lobby below, another ceremony, this one unofficial but no less traditional, was taking place. With the disdainful air of an Arab prince distributing baksheesh to his retainers, Juan Antonio Insúa, the husband of one of El Cordobés' three sisters, slipped through the lobby, discreetly extending to a select group of men a small white envelope and a complaisant smile. The men singled out for his attention had one characteristic in common. They were all bullfight critics.

"Preparing the press" was the phrase applied to his actions in the euphemistic language of the corrida. In any other language it would have been called bribery. Each envelope contained two tickets to the day's corrida and, folded beside them, a bundle of banknotes. The thickness of each bundle was a function of the importance of the newspaper represented by the man to whom it was destined. In all, the contents of the little envelopes loftily distributed through the Wellington lobby by Juan Antonio totaled more than three thousand dollars.

This distasteful practice was by no means a monopoly of El Cordobés' entourage. *"Sobre,"* as this bribery was termed, for the envelope in which each bribe was passed, was an ingrained part of Spain's proud national *fiesta brava.* The practice touched its most loathsome depths in the countryside, in the *plazas de mala muerte.* There, young boys striving to form a reputation were often forced to surrender almost all their meager fees to the men who watched them risk their lives from the safety of their *barrera de sombra* seats, men on whose kind words the boys' youthful aspirations might depend.

Once his task was completed, Juan Antonio turned his mind to his own estate. The income of this former apprentice electrician had increased considerably in the years since it had been his good fortune to have Spain's best-paid matador as a brother-in-law. From his vest pocket he took a wad of tickets for the corrida and, in a corner of the lobby, began to sell them. It was a regular practice for Juan Antonio. The profits from these improvised little sales provided a steady and handsome supplement to the already substantial stipend he received from his brother-in-law.

*   *   *

In the sitting room of the sleeping matador's suite, a short, squat man, his wavy black hair a glistening mass of grease, tiptoed softly about his business. By virtue of that business he was the member of El Cordobés' entourage most intimately concerned with the matador's well-being. He had begun his working days butchering old cows in the municipal slaughterhouse of Córdoba. Now Paco Fernández held one of the most envied and exalted positions in the bullfighting world. He was the *mozo de estoques,* the sword handler, of his nation's leading matador.

From a large leather trunk he drew the gold-and-tobacco suit of lights that his employer had ordered for his coming fight. Gold and tobacco, Paco reflected as he folded the suit over an upholstered armchair, were his matador's favorite colors. He lifted his elaborately hand-embroidered parade cape from the trunk and spread it onto the sofa so that its sparkling gold-and-silver image of the Cristo del Gran Poder* cast its spell through the salon. Next he checked the three yellow-and-magenta percale fighting capes and the three red serge muletas with which his matador would arm himself in a few hours. Finally he honed a fine cutting edge onto each of the six handmade Toledo swords in El Cordobés' leather sword case, the instruments with which the matador had already put to death over six hundred bulls.

These tasks over, Paco turned to more spiritual occupations. He placed upon a small table a much-fingered image of San Rafael and a statue of Nuestra Señora de Belén the *patrona* of Palma del Río. In front of each he set a fresh votary candle. Just before he left this room for Las Ventas, El Cordobés would pause before these images for a brief prayer. Then he would light the candles. They would not be extinguished until his safe return from the plaza.

Paco drew himself up sharply. He had overlooked one last instrument of divine protection. He took it from a black velvet-lined box and placed it beside the two images. It was the gold medal of the Cristo del Gran Poder that El Cordobés always bore around his neck in the bullring. Stamped on the back of the medal was a bit of temporal information, a stark reminder that it was not just on divine intercession that the matador who wore it must rely in the hours ahead. It was the blood type of Manuel Benítez.

Now Paco's routine was almost finished. In the small refrigerator was a glass of orange juice which, with a pair of fried eggs, would constitute El Cordobés' sole nourishment of the day. That restricted diet was de-

* Christ of the Great Power

32

signed to ease a surgeon's task in an emergency. All that remained was to draw a warm bath and slip a new blade into El Cordobés' razor. When the bath was drawn, Paco would take the orange juice from the refrigerator, drop into it a vitamin pill, and tiptoe into the room of his sleeping matador. There he would lean down to the tousled head on the pillow below him and whisper the phrase with which the life of El Cordobés began on the day of a bullfight: *"Ya es la hora, matador*—The hour is come, matador."

Paco started the bath. As he did, he heard a sound rising over the splashing of the bath water. It was the tentative plunking of a guitar and it came from the next room. In a few seconds Paco heard the hoarse, rasping voice of his matador singing to himself in his half-darkened bedroom. He recognized the words of a song El Cordobés had learned in Mexico. It was called *"Tengo Todo el Dinero en el Mundo*—I have all the money in the world":

> *Yo conozco la pobreza*
> *Y aquí entre los pobres*
> *Jamás lloré.* . . .
> *Ay, qué me sirve el dinero*
> *Si sufro tanta pena?*
> *Si estoy tan solo?**

With those words, El Cordobés, the richest and most sought-after matador in history, sang himself to wakefulness on this, the day of the most important corrida of his life.

*   *   *

Not far from the flag-bedecked bullring where twenty-three thousand aficionados would soon acclaim the awakening matador, another man of the *fiesta brava* knew suffering and loneliness this midday. No anxious nation, however, would ever hang attendant upon his deeds.

---

* I am familiar with poverty
And here among the poor
I never cried. . . .
Ay, what good does money do me
If I suffer such pain?
If I am so alone?

Stretched out upon a white metal operating table, his features contorted by fear and pain, he represented the other face of Spain's festival of light and glory.

He, too, had dreamed that one day a bullring's flags might fly for him, that the magic of his name might fill the plazas with exulting crowds. He, too, had longed to see his picture upon the front pages of his nation's newspapers, to have a sword handler guard his valued sleep, to see a city's walls alive with posters proclaiming his rendezvous with "six magnificent *toros* at six o'clock in the afternoon."

But Robustiano Fernández had been to the *plazas de mala muerte,* and the dreams of this unknown banderillero were ending forever on this warm May day. His left thigh lay shredded open from his knee to his groin. The stench of gangrene mingled with the odor of ether in the room, the operating block of the Sanatorio de Toreros, the Bullfighters' Hospital.

His presence upon the hospital's operating table was the only stroke of good fortune to enter Robustiano Fernández's life in the past five days. Propped in the van of an old delivery truck, wrapped in a blanket soaked in his own sweat and vomit, Fernández had endured twelve hours of torture to reach it. Two hundred and forty-two miles he had come from his native Extremadura, the hard land, riding under a searing sun that turned the truck into an oven, its stifling air vile with the stench of his infected limb. So nauseating was that odor that Fernández's wife, weeping beside the driver, had had to stop every fifty miles to retch by the roadside.

Robustiano Fernández's ordeal had begun at a feria for San Isidro, too, another corrida five days earlier in a whitewashed village lost in the harsh and forbidding landscape of Extremadura. Fernández was not even a professional bullfighter. He scavenged scrap metal to support his wife and three tiny girls. In his creaking wooden cart towed by an aged donkey, Fernández wandered the cobbled alleys and barren hills of Extremadura, making his noisy way from village to village with the centuries-old cry: "I buy old metal, I buy old copper."

But on Sundays and feast days, Fernández gave flesh to the dream that warmed the long and lonely hours of his quests for old brass and iron. Then he put on a patched and faded secondhand suit of lights and under the name of "El Niño de los Metales, The Kid of the Scrap Metal," he went off to plant a few banderillas for some unknown matador in the village corridas of his province. He got a few pesetas and sometimes, after a good placing of a pair of banderillas, the richer reward of admiring applause. Above all, he got the stuff of another week's dreaming, and kept alive the hope that someday fate would take him away from those village corridas to the cities and the crowded bullrings, away forever from his scrap-metal cart and the bleak countryside of Extremadura.

Those village corridas in which he fought were as dangerous as any in Spain. The bulls were often huge, overage, vicious animals, the bulls more seasoned matadors had refused to fight. Their rings were a jumble of trucks, hay wains and donkey carts roped together in any available square. Their unruly and often drunken spectators clung to their platforms and scrambled around their wheels, at eye level with the bull, where any sudden movement could catch his eye and divert his attention.

Into just such a ring had Robustiano Fernández stepped in the village of Entrín Bajo, May 15. Three times his indulgent matador had allowed him to pass the first bull of the day with his cape. Each pass drew a raucous *"olé"* from the crowd. Delighted, Fernández had planted himself before the animal again and called him to his cape for a fourth and final charge. As the animal bolted toward the swinging cloth, some youngster crawling under the wheels of an oxcart had caught its eye. The bull swerved, and instead of plunging his horns into the swinging cloth, he ripped apart the thigh of the scrap-metal picker.

Fernández regained consciousness lying on a kitchen table in a house facing the plaza. Pushing up onto his elbows, he saw a little geyser of blood spurting from his left thigh, spreading a dark stain over the worn silk of his secondhand suit of lights. Beside him the village midwife tore up a dirty sheet and offered him all the medical care Entrín Bajo could extend. She twisted a tourniquet around his leg.

Then he was propped into Entrín Bajo's only taxi for the trip to the nearest hospital, in Badajoz nineteen miles away. Through that trip one image drifted in and out of Fernández's fevered mind. For seventeen years it had haunted every torero with a thigh laid open by a bull's horn. It was the image of Manolete dying in Linares, his life pouring away through a wound like his.

When Fernández arrived at the hospital, the young resident on duty realized the torero's most urgent need was outside his calling. He summoned a priest to give the scrap-metal scavenger Extreme Unction. Then, as best he could, he patched together with his inexperienced fingers the torn ends of his femoral artery and pumped over eight pints of blood into his body. Three days later gangrene set in, and Robustiano Fernández's life began to ebb away. Desperate, his wife and best friend had decided on the long journey to the Toreros' Hospital and the practiced hands of these surgeons who had spent a lifetime saving the lives and limbs of Spain's matadors.

Through his fever, Fernández now began to understand that those men were preparing to saw off his leg. As that realization laid hold of his delirious mind, a burst of horror flowed through him in a warm and sickening wave. His fevered brain held only one image, that of his wife Ángela begging him to give up the bulls. Now he was going to be a cripple, a twenty-three-year-old cripple with a wife and three tiny girls to feed.

Despair overwhelmed his young mind. Never again, he told himself, could he work. With only one leg he would never be able to hobble after his scrap-metal cart along the roads of Extremadura. With the energy of his despair, he half rose from the operating table.

"Oh God, oh God," he begged through his tears, "please don't cut my leg. How can I work? What will happen to my little girls? Oh God, my little girls, my little girls."

The doctor above him gently eased Fernández back onto the metal table. Dr. Máximo de la Torre had devoted his life to saving the limbs of men wounded by bulls' horns. His peculiar skill had won him the position of chief surgeon of the Madrid bullring and of this highly specialized Toreros' Hospital. As soon as this operation was over, he would rush to Las Ventas to stand guard over El Cordobés during the afternoon's corrida. Nobody in the world could better understand the despair of Robustiano Fernández than the soft-spoken fifty-year-old doctor preparing to saw off his left leg.

"Don't cry, *hijo*," he said. Tenderly he took the scrap metal scavenger's hand into his and drew it down until it pressed upon one of his own white-trousered legs.

"Feel," he commanded.

It was hard, as hard as the wood of which it had been made for twenty-five years, since the day he had lost his own leg after a battlefield wound on the Ebro front.

"Believe me, my son," he whispered, "to walk on two legs is a luxury."

*   *   *

It was four-thirty. By the hundreds, bullfight fans were already streaming toward the beckoning Moorish arches of Las Ventas. They rushed in babbling streams from the two subway stops flanking the Plaza de Toros, their voices high-pitched and excited, filled with that special air of anticipation that pervades a Spanish crowd on its way to a bullfight. Devoted aficionados, carrying in their hands or wallets admissions to the *andanada de sol,* the cheapest seats in the ring, they headed toward the sunny side of the plaza's steep cement banks.

In front of Las Ventas, the wide boulevard slicing from the heart of Madrid to the Plaza de Toros was a tangle of cars, buses and taxis. Caught in that angry mass, other, wealthier aficionados destined for the shadier reaches of the arena blessed themselves for their foresight in setting out early for the corrida. Around the bullring, black-market ticket peddlers sold the last tickets left for the corrida for sums large enough to meet all the earthly needs of a Spanish peasant and his family for a year. The traditional pack of petty vendors swarmed around the onrushing crowds peddling candies, caramels, chewing gum, lottery tickets, eyeshades. This afternoon many of them concentrated their energies on a special commerce. They hawked chains of colored postcards, felt dolls, key chains, pocketknives, coasters, eyeglass cases, all of which bore in some way the laughing face of the matador who had lured the anxious crowds to Las Ventas.

Only one concern marred the mounting excitement. It had built up latent and menacing all afternoon. It was the threat carried by the banks of rain cloud, gray and heavy, scudding down onto the capital from the Castilian plateau. Now, less than ninety minutes before the corrida was due to start, a rumbling burst of thunder rent those clouds and sent their first drops of rain onto the sands of the arena.

Don Livinio Stuyck watched with a special concern as those first drops, fat and ominous, splashed onto the windshield of his SEAT sedan. The impresario of Las Ventas was still ten minutes away from his *plaza de toros,* caught in the traffic jam of his own making. He had reason to be concerned. The men whose art filled the cement spirals of his bullrings

37

feared two natural hazards almost as much as the bulls they were paid to kill. One was wind, which could snatch away the protective folds of the muleta at some unforeseen instant and expose a matador's body to a bull's charge. The other was rain. Rain turned a bullring into a slick and treacherous morass that deadened a matador's surefootedness and could steal from his slippered feet the second he might need to escape a bull's searching horns. In recognition of those dangers, the rules of the corrida gave a matador the right to refuse to fight in rain or a high wind.

Don Livinio's philosophy about weather and the bullfight was more pragmatic. He was in favor of going ahead with a fight despite the weather. He had even run a bullfight in a snowstorm during the previous season. Practical considerations underlay his attitude. He was, by law, obliged to offer an immediate refund for every ticket of a canceled corrida. The cancellation of a corrida such as today's fight would represent a staggering loss to the management of Las Ventas. Besides, he realized that "the public knows it's more dangerous to fight in the rain. That gives the fight much more emotion."

Tense and worried, Don Livinio arrived at Las Ventas. Without a word to any of his employees he rushed through the crowds and out to the lip of the bullring. There he squatted on his haunches and, like a child on a beach, scooped up a fistful of sand and let it run through his fingers. It was wet and heavy, but, Don Livinio gratefully realized, it had not yet reached that glutinous consistency which could force the cancellation of the corrida. Bitterly, he cursed his lack of foresight in disdaining to buy a plastic cover for the ring. Then he looked up at the stands rising above him. They were packed. Some of the crowd sat in plastic raincoats or under umbrellas; others sat unprotected in their shirt-sleeves. They looked, Don Livinio thought, "as though they'd wait all night to see the fight start."

He shuddered. Probably half of them, he knew, had given up a week's, even a month's, salary to buy a ticket for this corrida on the black market. Scalpers never give refunds, and the public pressure to go on with this fight would be terrible. "If we cancel this fight," he thought, "they'll burn Las Ventas down in the riot they'll start."

"San Isidro," Don Livinio told himself, "has never let me down." Only once in seventeen years had he been forced to cancel a corrida during the annual feria honoring the patron of Madrid. With a frantic burst of piety, Don Livinio began "to pray to San Isidro and every other saint" he could think of for a break in the weather.

For once, the peasant saint turned a deaf ear to the pleadings of the impresario of Las Ventas. At five-thirty the black skies above Madrid split apart and sent a furious, drenching rain pouring down on the city.

*   *   *

The rain splashing onto the sand of Las Ventas struck an echo in every country village in Spain. Twenty million people, over half the Spanish nation, more than twice the number who had watched the funeral of Pope John, almost double the thirteen million Spaniards who had followed the funeral procession of John F. Kennedy, were clustered around television sets waiting to watch the confirmation of this peasant boy from Palma del Río as a *matador de toros*. That staggering audience, bound together for El Cordobés by a miracle of the electronic age, represented almost as many people as had witnessed personally all the other bullfights of the twentieth century combined.

Madrid, at five-thirty, was empty. Barely a car moved along its broad boulevards. Its shops were shuttered, its cinemas closed. Even the peddlers seemed to have disappeared. It was as though some massive airraid warning had swept clean the city's streets and sidewalks. The city was in front of a television set. Every bar and restaurant with a set was packed. Some sold places before their sets for as much as a hundred pesetas. A survey taken later revealed that an average of thirty-five people gathered around each of the sets in the city. In the capital's wealthy residential areas the soft, well-modulated voice of television bullfight critic Manuel Lozano Sevillano seemed to float from every open window. In the slums of Vallecas, Madrid's poor stood shoulder to shoulder in dozens of neighborhood bars waiting for a glimpse of the matador their pride held as their own but their pocketbooks would never allow them to see.

Hundreds of *Madrileños* had bought their first TV sets for the occasion. Television stores turned sets on and placed them in their shopwindows. The crowd in front of one, on the Avenida José Quintana, became so enormous its proprietor thought his show window would break under its pressure. When the crowd became so enormous it blocked even the

39

trickle of traffic moving along the avenue, the police finally ordered him to turn the set off.

Schools closed early. Hundreds of factories and stores, from the giant Pegaso truck factory in Madrid and the Renault auto assembly plant in Barcelona to tiny dress shops and offices, closed ahead of time to let their employees watch the corrida.

Just as it had in Madrid, highway traffic slowed to a trickle all across Spain, as motorists and truck drivers sought out village cafés to watch the fight. Lines of parked trucks and cars marked each roadside garage or restaurant equipped with a television set.

Thirty-five miles south of Madrid, in Spain's former summer capital of Aránjuez, a toothless old man turned on his set, rented for this occasion for a sum that surpassed his weekly salary. Three sullen faces stared at the set along with him from behind a barred window looking into his salon. They belonged to the three prisoners of the village jail of which Vicente Moreno had been, for forty years, the jail keeper. Moreno's gesture was a touching one. Just eight years earlier, he had inscribed opposite number 993 on the rolls of his prison the name of the young man whose presence he now so eagerly awaited on his rented television set.

Another, less distinguished, former guest of jailer Moreno squirted a last blast of air into the tires of a German tourist's car at the San Álvaro gas station in the city of Córdoba, 190 miles south of Aránjuez. He put the one hundred pesetas the German handed him into his coveralls and walked to the already crowded bar next door where he would use them to buy a few beers while watching the corrida. What very poignant regrets pierced that young worker's heart as he entered that bar, no man could ever know. Once, he had been the best and only friend of Manuel Benítez. They had grasped together after the fleeting mirage of the bulls, hoping to lift themselves out of the misery into which they had been born. Their restless feet had traveled, side by side, half the highways of Spain in pursuit of that mirage. Hurt and hunger they had shared, and Juan Horrillo's back would bear forever scars like those El Cordobés carried, from the beatings they had received together. But the bulls had chosen to bestow their blessings on Manuel Benítez, and Juan Horrillo had been left behind to spend his life living on the tips he could glean from the motorists passing through a Córdoba gas station.

A few miles away, life in the neighboring town of Palma del Río had

40

halted, waiting for the corrida to begin or be canceled. The town's three public television sets, in two cafés and a private club, had been surrounded by impatient spectators for hours.

Most of the rest of the town was gathered around the few privately owned sets in Palma. In a notable display of communal spirit, Rafael Nieto, the shoemaker, and Antonio Gonzales, the baker, had placed their sets in the streets where hundreds had gathered to watch. Don Carlos, the parish priest, invited his gardeners to join him before the set the widow of Don Félix Moreno, his wealthiest parishioner, had offered him to celebrate the Vatican Council. Doña Coza, the town midwife, whose active professional life in devoutly Catholic Palma put her in the town's highest economic bracket, watched by her private set. She had brought the matador, along with almost everyone else in Palma, into the world.

Angelita Benítez had spent the morning scurrying nervously around the patio of the house her brother had bought her, flapping her hands like a chicken. Now she sat in the place of honor before her TV set in the darkened salon, her friends and relatives gathered around her. As she awaited an initial glimpse of her brother in a bullring, Angelita Benítez realized that for the first time in her life she "was too scared to pray." Transfixed with terror, she stared at the screen before her, telling herself in simple wonder that if her brother was really going to be on that screen, "he must be the biggest man in the world, as big, almost, as Franco."

A world away from Angelita's darkened salon sat a man whose name symbolized to that peasant girl the very pinnacle of renown. In a drawing room of the four-centuries-old palace at El Pardo, under a ceiling depicting Apollo crowning the arts, he settled down in front of his television receiver. No affairs of state could keep General Francisco Franco from joining the rest of the nation watching Angelita's brother this afternoon. His hands folded over his little stomach, he prepared to offer the tribute of his attention to the triumph of this unlettered youth, the only Spaniard alive, probably, whose fame might rival his own.

*   *   *

In the tangle of cars still clogging the streets around Las Ventas, a black Chrysler with an old wicker hamper strapped to its roof tried desperately to inch forward. Motorists hooted at its passage. From the sidewalk, men applauded, women blew kisses, children waved. Inside, staring glumly at the rain streaking the Chrysler's windows, was the man responsible for all this tumult, the matador who was, his sister had thought in touching wonder, "almost as big as Franco." Trapped in this traffic jam, El Cordobés risked arriving late for the most important rendezvous of his career. He and Madrid had waited a long time for this meeting. Often, in the past four years, he had been criticized for his failure to fight in Madrid. On the streets of the capital he had felt the prick of many a taunt decrying his failure to appear in this most demanding of bullrings. And now the moment was here. The proud and pathetic boast of his youth had come true. Ahead was the most important *plaza de toros* in the world, every one of its seats filled with people who had come to see him, to witness his rendezvous with the bulls of Don José Benítez Cubero.

They would not, he knew, be an indulgent audience. Many among them considered him a clown who knew nothing of the art of bullfighting. A few minutes earlier, as he donned his suit of lights, his sword handler, Paco Fernández, had been struck by his sober air. Unlike most matadors, for whom the dressing for a corrida—a ceremony as public and as ritualistic as the dressing of a bride—was a somber and solemn moment, El Cordobés ordinarily spent those moments staring at the pictures in a *Playboy* magazine, playing his guitar or guffawing loudly with friends. Today, however, he had been silent and uncommunicative, apparently brooding on the trial ahead. Before leaving for the bullring, he had paused in front of his stained and wrinkled gallery of holy pictures for a long prayer. Then, all alone in his half-darkened hotel room, he lit the votary candles his sword handler had set out earlier in the afternoon. They would burn in an unseen vigil until his return.

Now the matador rode in despondent silence, his eyes fixed on the rivulets of rain running down the window beside him. The authorities, El Cordobés knew, might try to cancel the corrida. It was an action he was determined to prevent. Getting into the car, he had muttered to his banderilleros, "We'll fight on water skis if we have to. But Madrid is going to get what it came for."

Sitting beside El Cordobés, Paco Ruiz knew the depth of feeling behind those words. Earlier this day, El Cordobés had sworn an oath to him, one of those pompous and gory boasts that are so much a part of the matadors' language—and which the nature of their art makes so susceptible of fulfillment.

"Paco," he had told his banderillero, "this afternoon either I come out the great door *en hombros* or the infirmary door on a stretcher."

The black Chrysler jerked to a stop two hundred yards from the gates of Las Ventas, hopelessly trapped by the thousands of ticketless aficionados who had swarmed to the Plaza for the brief pleasure of watching El Cordobés ride into the bullring. Hundreds of other spectators waved from the balconies and rooftops around Las Ventas. Two blocks away, from a six-story-high scaffold, a group of masons waved a banner made of bedsheets in El Cordobés' direction. "Peña El Cordobés—El Cordobés Club," it read. Five years earlier the young man trapped in his black Chrysler had carried the hod to these masons preparing now to follow his triumph in the roar of the crowd rising toward their scaffold from the rim of Las Ventas.

Once inside, El Cordobés stepped from his car and pushed his way through a shouting horde of photographers to the door of the bullfighters' chapel. Even this sacred moment of solitude was marred by the mob. Despairingly, El Cordobés turned to the photographers: "One minute alone," he pleaded, "then you take any picture you want."

His banderillero, Paco Ruiz, barred the door to the chapel behind him. A few yards from the chapel, Mariano de Quiros, the police commissioner whose duty it was to represent the authority of the Spanish government in the bullring, stared sullenly at his watch. Before him the rain beat down onto the ring in unabated fury. It was five minutes to six. Only one ceremony invariably started on time in this nation that made a ritual of tardiness. Mariano de Quiros did not need to be reminded what it was. He had just five minutes to make the most public and perhaps most difficult decision of his life. He could cancel this corrida, disappoint twenty million people and risk a riot in the Plaza. Or he could order it to proceed and accept the moral responsibility of thrusting an unwarranted danger on the lives of three men.

Quiros walked to the chapel door. El Cordobés, surprisingly solemn, stepped out. *"Hombre,"* said Quiros, "will you fight in these conditions?"

Normally, such a decision would have rested with Pedrés, the senior matador on the program. Today, however, Quiros knew only one voice counted: that of the young man before him. El Cordobés answered him with a formality almost foreign to his irreverent nature: "For that have I come," he told the police commissioner.

"Then," Quiros said, "if you are really willing to fight, you must first come out and inspect the arena with me. Once you start," he warned, "I shall oblige you to fight until the last bull is killed."

El Cordobés, his two fellow matadors, and Stuyck and Quiros started into the ring. As they moved across the sand, the waiting crowd leaped to its feet. They waved umbrellas, hats and soggy white handkerchiefs. Along the *barreras,* people who had paid two hundred fifty dollars to sit in the downpour bellowed encouragement. From all the steep slopes of Las Ventas the public's howls beat down into the ring in hoarse, demanding waves of noise, one cry ringing out louder, more insistent, than all the others: *"Los toros, los toros, los toros!"*

In the center of the Plaza, the matadors and Quiros had to yell to hear each other over the roar of the mob. The sand was soaked and heavy, the ring dotted with puddles two and three inches deep. As the four men talked, the rain suddenly burst down in renewed fury.

Again the crowd howled, a new imploring tone entering its roar. Quiros knew at that instant he should cancel the corrida. "I felt the weight of all Spain on my shoulders," he recalled later. "Not just the mob in the Plaza. Not just Madrid. All Spain, all those people waiting by the TV. I knew as I stood there I should cancel the corrida. But there was that terrible anticipation, that terrible atmosphere. We were prisoners of his fame."

Again Quiros asked El Cordobés if he would fight. Behind the matador, his banderilleros hissed a beseeching "No." El Cordobés looked at the crowd. He knew he could not send those screaming people away without a corrida. "I will not leave until my bulls are dead," he said.

Quiros then turned to Stuyck. The impresario, who favored going ahead despite the weather, felt a nervous gnawing in his stomach. He knew this corrida should be canceled. If the rain abated, Quiros asked, could Stuyck's workmen shovel a new coat of sand over the arena? Stuyck nervously told him there was not enough sand to cover the whole ring.

"Then just fill the big puddles," El Cordobés said.

Yelling to be heard over the din coming down from the stands, Quiros announced his decision. He would suspend the corrida for thirty minutes to see if the rain stopped.

During those thirty minutes not a single spectator left Las Ventas. El Cordobés elected to hide from his enthusiastic admirers in a macabre hideaway, the operating room of Dr. Máximo de la Torre. Stuyck, poking his head into the infirmary, saw the matador laughing with his banderilleros. Watching him, the nervous impresario enviously assured himself that "he probably has his package he's hiding inside himself, too."

At six-fifteen, the rain eased up and a frantic squad of ring attendants began to shovel sand over the floor of the arena.

Ten minutes later, with the crowd already beginning an impatient chant, Quiros' assistant knocked at the infirmary door.

"The president invites the matadors to inspect the ring," he announced.

Once again the little group set out across the Plaza. Again the crowd sprang to its feet, letting off as it did another clamorous howl. This time, an angry insistent note had seeped into their rain-soaked voices.

Trailing behind El Cordobés, Paco Ruiz plucked at the elbow of his matador's jacket like a child striving for his father's attention. *"No se puede, Manolo, no se puede,* you can't," he begged gesturing at the slippery mud upon which they walked.

"Paco," El Cordobés answered, "you never picked cotton. Don't worry. My feet used to live in slime like this."

El Cordobés listened, without laughing, to the roar of the crowd. His sensitive ears could always hear "the people who came to make fun of you, the ones nothing will ever satisfy except your blood." He heard their voices now angry and insistent, jeering: "Fight, *fenómeno!*" He knew the fury that would descend on him if he refused to fight. He, too, like Quiros, was a prisoner of his fame.

"Let us fight," he told the police commissioner's assistant. A few minutes later the assistant returned. "The president," he said, "makes it clear that once the first bull has come out we will continue the corrida no matter how bad the conditions become. There will be no suspension."

"Tell the president," El Cordobés answered, "that I will kill my last bull in a rowboat if I have to."

Quiros, rain still running off his plastic raincoat, climbed to his presidential box. As he did so, an expectant roar burst from the crowd.

That roar reverberated under the concrete arches of the *puerta de ar-*

rastre where the toreros assembled for the *paseillo,* the parade across the ring which would open the corrida. Paco Ruiz arranged the folds of his matador's sumptuous parade cape sparkling with its image of the Cristo del Gran Poder. In these last seconds, Paco knew "the only expression on a matador's face was a forced, drawn smile, the "smile of the rabbit." El Cordobés rarely wore such a smile. He did not, Paco saw, wear one now.

Paco took his place in the procession and looked at his matador's relaxed, natural shoulders. He felt "an extraordinary sense of tranquillity." He knew the sensation ahead for El Cordobés. "Of all the *plazas* in Spain," thought Paco, "there is none like this one." Its steep banks sent a crowd's applause tumbling into the ring and, if it was strong, made a *paseillo* at Madrid's Plaza de Toros "the most impressive parade in the world."

High above them, Police Commissioner de Quiros looked at the four handkerchiefs dangling inside his presidential box. They were the instruments of his office: white to award ears or control the flow of the fight; green to reject a bad bull; red to jab such a bull with special banderillas; blue to honor a dead animal with a triumphant turn around the ring. Quiros picked up the white handkerchief and laid it on the wet balustrade before him. Across the ring, a trumpeter caught the signal and took his instrument to his lips.

As his first metallic notes drifted down the damp air, a roar rose from the crowd. The echoing waves of sound it produced shook the stillness under the *puerta de arrastre.* Paco Ruiz peered out beyond the dark outlines of the arch above them to the distant stands. Every single spectator he could see was on his feet yelling.

Ahead of Paco, the three matadors stiffened slightly. Each made a sign of the cross. El Cordobés turned to the men beside him. Softly, he spoke a last traditional phrase, a final invocation before the trial ahead: *"Que Dios reparta suerte*—may God divide the luck," he said. Then, with a slow, solemn pace, the three men started their long walk across the wet and dangerous sands.

CHAPTER TWO

Palma del Río: THE WAR YEARS

ANGELITA BENÍTEZ'S STORY

"I CRIED FOR MY brother Manolo the day he was born and I haven't finished crying for him yet. I was twelve years old then, I remember. It was a warm afternoon in May, just before the war. I was playing all alone downstairs in the dirt around the tree in the courtyard. I knew what was happening upstairs. There were already four of us, Encarna, Pepe, Carmela and me. I could hear my mother screaming. Then I heard the baby's cry. When I did, I hung my head against the tree and I started to cry, too. I didn't want him. He was someone else I would have to take care of because I was the oldest. He was another mouth to eat our food.

"In my house then there was only work and hunger. The only present anybody ever gave me when I was a girl was more work to do. You had to work because if you didn't, you didn't have something to eat. Sometimes you wouldn't have anything to eat anyway. Then all you would have was your hunger and your tears.

47

"I don't remember much about that time, but from what I remember, it was very bad. I didn't go to school very much. I went to the nuns' school next to the church a bit. When you worked, how could you have time to go to school?

"We didn't learn to read or write or anything like that. They didn't teach you that. I learned to sew a little bit. My name, Angelita Benítez—I learned how to write that. Sometimes on Sundays they gave you a piece of bread or lard, or maybe some oil. That was why I liked the nuns' school.

"Once, I remember, they gave me a pair of sandals. My sisters Encarna and Carmela and my brother Pepe and I, we never had sandals. We were barefoot. In the winter when it rained a lot there was mud everywhere, and it came up to our ankles. It was cold and then my mother would put our feet in water she heated on the fire to get them warm again. When I was eight or nine, I stopped going to the nuns' school. From that time on, I worked.

"Our house was on the Calle Ancha. All the houses on the Calle Ancha were the same. They were mostly one floor, sometimes two. All of them were whitewashed. You had to keep putting on the whitewash all the time with a pail of water and whitewash. The brush was made of twigs or sticks tied around a branch. It was very important to keep your house whitewashed on the Calle Ancha. People said things about you if you didn't.

"My mother always did ours. But because we were poor, she did it for other people, too, on the Calle Ancha and in Palma. My mother was a very good worker. When I was young, sometimes I carried the pail for her when she whitewashed other people's houses.

"There was no door to the house in the Calle Ancha. There was a curtain. After that was the courtyard where I was playing when Manolo was born. It was all mud, just mud.

"In one corner there was an orange tree with a few leaves hanging on it. I never saw an orange on that tree all the time we lived on the Calle Ancha. It was right beside the well. The well was just a hole in the ground but still we were lucky we had one. Water was scarce in Palma then.

"The rocks around the side of the well were covered with moss, very green and very slippery. There was an old pail with a rope around it that

48

we lowered into the well to get water. No one was supposed to drink the water from that well. It was so dirty that you couldn't see through it even if you just had one glass. It smelled so bad, that hole, I hated to lower the pail to draw up the water. That water was supposed to be just for washing. In those days everybody in Palma had to buy his drinking water from the donkey cart that came every morning. Some people still get it that way. It cost half a peseta a day for one jar then. That was a lot of money for us. Sometimes when my father wasn't working, we didn't have it and we drank the water from the well.

"There were four families in the courtyard. In one corner, under some tiles, was the stove where we all cooked. It was a piece of stone that had two holes cut in it and you burned wood underneath it. Each family took turns using it.

"We lived upstairs on the second floor. You got up on a ladder. There was one room, and one window on the street. We had an electric light but my father never turned it on. It cost too much money. There was a table and a chest of drawers and four chairs. My mother brought them with her as her dowry. She covered the table with a cloth she made herself. It was in many colors like the cloths of Toledo. My mother loved to sew, she could sew anything, point de Paris, things like that. I think she loved that cloth more than anything else in the world.

"My mother and father slept in the bed. Carmela, the baby, slept with them until Manolo came, because my mother was nursing her. That's the way it was then. You nursed one until the next one came. She nursed Manolo for two years until her milk ran out in the war.

"My father was a very serious man. He always had a very grave air, my father. He worked every day he could. He was a number-one worker.

"Like everybody else, he worked in the fields. He picked olives in the winter. Then he helped with the plowing. In those times they didn't always have enough horses and sometimes the men would haul the plow through the fields. When there was no work in the *campo,* he tried to find work on the roads. People went to different places in those days to look for work. Above all, they went to the plaza, the Plaza de Trabajadores (the workers' square). The *encargado* would come there every day early in the morning and pick out the men he needed, maybe for that day, maybe for two or three days or sometimes a week. Then the others could

49

go home or maybe they would go to the fincas themselves to look for work.

"When a man was a good worker, a number-one worker like my father, he didn't have to go to the Plaza de Trabajadores. The *encargado* came to our house. He would come so early it would be dark out. Sometimes I would hear him coming knocking on the doors of the Calle Ancha. Then I would hear him calling for my father to come out.

"Each time it was different. Sometimes they offered one day, sometimes a week, even a month. You never discussed. Everybody knew what the salary was, how many pesetas a day. So there was no need to discuss. You just went when they called you for work.

"They all left with the *encargado*. He usually had a horse and they all walked behind him. The work always began at sunrise and it ended when there was no more light. They always walked. They had nothing in those days, not even a bicycle. Sometimes it was near. Sometimes it was very, very far.

"They got four and then later five and a half pesetas a day, always the same. My father worked on all the big fincas. Don Félix, the Martinez, all of them, even the ones that were twenty-five kilometers [more than fifteen miles] from here if there was no other work. Don Félix Moreno had the biggest. He was the biggest man in Palma. Some people said he was the biggest man in Andalusia. He was the richest man we ever saw, Don Félix, but he'd kill a man before he'd give him an extra peseta. He's dead now. I won't say any more. It's better not to disturb the dead. But we hated Don Félix.

"In those days we didn't have many fiestas. Sunday was like every other day, you worked.

"When it was time to pick the olives, we all went. Each family searched out its tree and then you picked. My father and mother climbed in the tree and I picked the olives that fell on the ground. I used to pick almost one basket a day, and my father was very proud of me because the more you picked the more money you got. We used to sing to keep warm, it was so cold. I can't remember what we sang. I only remember you had to sing as loud as you could to stop freezing. My father didn't sing good. He wasn't a singing man. But he sang, too.

"Sometimes there was a fire in the field to get warm, but if you went there, you didn't pick olives. My father would call 'Angelita' and I'd have to go back and pick olives. When my father talked to me in those times it was to tell me to pick faster because the more you picked the more money you got.

"We worked from dawn until it was dark and you couldn't see any more. Everybody slept out there, sometimes for a week, two weeks, on the hay, in a big building on the finca. Each family had a corner.

"In the morning we had *migas*.* Sometimes you put bread and water in it and cooked it until it puffed up. Sometimes we had a glass of aguardiente to keep away the cold. The rich people had sausage for breakfast. For us to have bread—that was already something.

"At lunch maybe we would have lard and bread. We would sit under our tree and then my father would say '*Vámonos*' and we'd have to start picking the olives again. At night we had chick peas or a *cocido*—a stew —or maybe just lard and bread.

"That was how our life went, with the seasons. In September it was the green olives, in December the black ones. In the spring it was sowing and the plow. In summer, the harvest. In between was the hard time. Then, in the dry season, there was no work in the *campo,* and when there was no work, there was no food.

"So in the hard time my father went to work as a waiter in the café of Niño Valles. It was in the center of Palma. Poor people went there mostly. At night when he came home my father would pull the tips he'd made out of his pocket. People liked my father, and when they could they would give him a tip, a céntimo or two. My mother worked then too. My mother was a strong woman. She did everything, she whitewashed houses, she washed, she brought home sewing. The only time my father turned on our electric light was those nights when she was sewing.

"Every day of his life my father worked, every day. Sundays and feast days he was always at the café. He was no player of guitars, my father. Even then, before the war, I remember he looked like a worn-out old man because he worked so hard to keep us alive.

"In my house, we never talked about the bulls. My father didn't have much *afición* for the *fiesta brava*. Besides in Palma there was no *plaza de toros*. Sometimes on the walls you saw posters for bullfights in Écija or Córdoba, but only the rich people went there. The only thing we knew about the bulls was the animals in the fields of Don Félix.

* a soup, made of bread cut into pieces and sometimes dipped in oil.

51

"The one important day in Palma every year was the *patrona*, September 8. It still is a big fiesta here. In the morning everyone went to Mass and in the evening there was the procession. The men carried the statue of the Virgin out of the church on their shoulders. The statue was covered with flowers—geraniums, daisies, even lilies. Don Juan, the priest, walked at the head of the procession with altar boys swinging censers. Everybody carried torches and sang the hymn to the *patrona*. The procession went all through Palma and everybody watched, from balconies and windows. It was to bless the town. In the center of Palma where the rich people lived, it was the custom to hang an embroidered bedsheet from the balcony when the statue of the Virgin went by. They were lovely, made with flowers and designs of the Virgin. They were only used for that night, the procession, and for the wedding nights of the daughters.

"But that was only once a year, the *patrona*. The rest of the time, it was work. Sometimes at night when my father was away in the *campo* and the money was gone, I heard my mother crying to the *patrona* for help. But we never complained. Who could you complain to? By the time I was nine I had forgotten how to laugh. I was as hard as the earth of our Andalusia.

"I suppose that's why I was the way I was the day Manolo was born. I knew it was coming. To me, as I said, it was another one I would have to take care of because I was the oldest. My father sent me to get the Doña Coza, the midwife, that day. Manolo was born up there in the bed like the rest of us. I pretended not to hear the screams and the crying. After he was born, my father came and called, 'Angelita, come quick, it's a boy.'

"I refused to go. I hugged my tree and cried. My father came down and dragged me up the stairs. He was very proud, my father, because it was another boy. He had to push me into the room and pull me over to the bed. I looked down at my mother through my tears. She was crying too.

" '*Otra más en el mundo pa' dar de comer,*' she said. 'Another one in the world to feed.' "

SEÑORA VALLES' STORY

"I REMEMBER THE night. He was late for work. I can still see him coming in with a big smile. That I noticed right away. He was a serious man, not much of a man to laugh, so when he had a smile like the one he had that night, you noticed it right away.

"He came behind the bar and took down the bottle of aguardiente and poured a drink for my husband and me. 'I have a son,' he said, 'just now, a baby boy.'

"Well, señor, he already had four children and I can tell you in those days in Palma del Río, another one to feed was no reason to celebrate. But he, he was happy. He had a smile on him that made you think they'd had a miracle over there on the Calle Ancha.

"He was an honest, decent man. They were a good family, clean, and they didn't complain. The mother gave milk to my daughter when mine ran out. We used to see him first when he came to our bar for a glass of white wine to keep him warm while he walked to work in the fields. In those days work began out in the *campo* at sunrise. At three or four in the morning the men left, on foot. Some of them had twenty kilometers to walk through the darkness to get to work. Our café was in the center of the town then and we never closed. We served the workers a glass of wine when they left in the morning and another when they came back at night.

"He was no different from all the rest. I can still see him in his old cotton shirt and canvas trousers, his feet sticking out of his rope sandals, drinking all by himself before he went to work. He had a big mouth like his son, but even then he was already old with his cheeks sunk and his back bent. Somehow, he seemed to carry all the misery of our Andalusia on that stooped back of his. Like every other Andalusian, Benítez had a nickname. We called him 'El Renco': the limper.

"He inherited the name from his father. That poor man got such a beating from the Guardia Civil one day that he had a limp for the rest of his life. Later they called his grandson Manuel El Renco too, before he became El Cordobés. It was almost as though those clubs of the Guardia Civil had marked the bones of the Benítez forever.

"Later on, he came to our bar to work, as a waiter, when there was no

53

work in the fields. We paid him a couple of pesetas a day and his lunch. He made a little more on tips, sometimes more, sometimes less. He'd come to work at ten in the morning and stay until midnight. He was a hard worker, El Renco. His best friend was a man named Pedro Charneca, who was a waiter at the café across from ours. Charneca taught him how to be a waiter.

"In those days there were just a few cafés in the town. Ours was one big room. Everybody came to our bar except the big landowners. They had their own places to go like the Círculo de Amistad. We never saw them except when one of them rode by on a horse or maybe in a car.

"But everybody else came—carpenters, tradespeople, people like that. Most people drank at the bar. Some of them sat down and played dominoes or *tute,* a card game. In general, though, you could say our bar was for the workers. That's why they took it away from us after the war. We were the Socialists' bar. The anarchists came, too, but there weren't so many of them in Palma del Río. We were sort of the meeting place. We got *El Socialista* and *La Tierra,* the Republican papers, every night, and the workers came to read them.

"That began in 1931, when the Republic replaced the monarchy. We never served so much wine in here as we did that night. It was a great hope for us, the Republic. I even saw people kissing each other in the street that night. They thought it was all over then, the misery, the hunger, the rich landowners treating them like Arab slaves. They found out.

"I remember that night the new mayor sent a cable to Córdoba, to the governor, asking him: 'What are we going to do with the priest?' Can you imagine that?

"What people really wanted from the Republic, though, was land reform. Here in Andalusia all the good land belonged to a few families. Half of the whole province of Córdoba, the whole province, belonged to five percent of the people. In Palma there were three families: the Martinez, the Gamero Cívico and Don Félix. After them there was nothing. They owned everything here. They were gods. Everything worked for them—the priest, the Guardia Civil, the bank. Nobody could do anything against them.

"The worst was Don Félix. His name was cursed in my bar more often than the Devil himself. He was a small man, but he was tough and brutal with the workers his *encargado* hired in the Plaza de Trabajadores.

They called him 'Bismarck' because, I guess, he wanted to be like that German. He had the first car in Palma, a white Hispano-Suiza he bought in 1917. We used to call it the White Ass. Later on he changed it for a black Cadillac.

"He didn't use the car very much though. He liked to ride or drive himself in his horse cart. You couldn't count all the acres he had. All the land between Palma and Peñaflor, from the road to the sierra, was his. Thirty kilometers [eighteen miles], all the bottom land along the Guadalquivir. Everybody worked on his land: El Renco, the father of El Cordobés, all the workers here worked for Don Félix. They got nothing from him but broken backs and misery. Five or six pesetas a day they paid, those landowners. With that, señor, all you could do was let your family starve a little more slowly. And if you asked for more, it was finished. No more work. Those men they knew were agitators, the *encargados* walked by them each morning in the Plaza de Trabajadores like they were dead. And they might as well have been.

"You could see that one day trouble was going to come if the Republic didn't help. In July 1931 just after the Republic, we had our first trouble here. Some of the anarchist workers without houses burned down our *plaza de toros* one night. It hadn't been used for a long time. The *plaza* belonged to Julio Muñoz, who was a landowner from Córdoba. The anarchists were against the *fiesta brava*, so they burned it down and carried away the stones to build their houses.

"After that, things got gradually worse. The Socialists were the leaders here, and they finally got the anarchists and the few communists we had to all work together. They began to strike for a better life for the workers. They wanted better wages and work for everybody. Or at least they wanted a new system in the Plaza de Trabajadores. You see, the way it was then, the *encargado* picked whoever he wanted in the plaza, not the first one there or the ones who needed work most. It was unfair. If a man wouldn't vote the way they wanted, if they thought he wanted more money, they didn't pick him. When he got old or was sick, they didn't pick him either, even if his family was starving.

"They wanted to change that. They wanted to share the work so everybody would have some. The idea of the Socialists was that the *encargado* would say he needed fifty men, then they would say all right, these fifty go.

55

"So that way the strikes started. They refused the harvest. They let the sheep go off by themselves. There was fighting between the workers of the plaza and the *contratados,* the workers who worked all the time on the fincas. Sometimes the workers of the plaza went to the fincas to try to get the *contratados* to join them. The owners began to set up their own armed guards to keep them away.

"One night the workers went to demonstrate in front of the hacienda of Don Félix in Peñaflor. You know the answer they got from Bismarck? A volley of lead. Don Félix was so mad at the thought that these workers could dare drive right up onto his land and demonstrate under his window that he grabbed his rifle and fired on them. He killed one poor man, a worker who'd been going to his fincas for years, right on the spot.

"It was an enormous scandal. But Don Félix arranged things the way the landowners always did, so he was acquitted by the court in Córdoba.

"He claimed he was shooting in self-defense. That did change one thing, though. After that Don Félix spent less time here and more in his palace in Seville.

"The trouble kept getting worse. In 1936 they burned down all the churches here. There was the general strike in May 1936 just after El Cordobés was born. You knew terrible times were coming then.

"El Renco, El Cordobés' father, wasn't involved in all that. He had no political ideas. He was just an honest, hard worker. But you know how it is when troubles come. You have to be on one side or another. You have to stay with your own kind. His kind were the poor. When you're born poor in Andalusia, you're a poor man until you die. So he had to choose like everybody else, and once you start on one side you have to stay there, no matter what happens.

"He wasn't the only one caught like that; everybody in Spain was trapped the same way that summer."

ALONSO MORENO'S STORY

"MY FATHER WAS cut from the same hard wood as the olive trees that dotted his lands. He drove no man who worked for him as hard as he drove himself. He was up with the first light and his last act every day was a conference with his *mayoral* in his library after midnight. Sixteen hours a day he worked running those lands with all the energy of a conquistador of our golden century. At seventy, he still scorned his automobiles, and three horses a day he could wear out under his legs. By the time he died, he owned forty-five thousand acres and seven fincas. Between Palma del Río and Peñaflor, everything belonged to him. He was the biggest landowner between Seville and Córdoba and the second biggest in all Andalusia.

"He was a great man, my father. He was loved by many people and hated by some. But he was feared and admired by all. Originally our family came from Santander. We settled in Seville in the beginning of the nineteenth century during our troubles with the French. The name of our principal finca, La Vega, The Good Land, dates back to the Reconquest, and the Fourth Battalion of Castile camped in the *palacio,* our home in Palma del Río, on its way to the siege of Seville. One of our houses was once the Franciscan monastery from which the friars who first explored California set out. They took with them the seeds of the orange tree in our court, and it is from those seeds that the orange trees of California come.

"So as you can see, one way or another, our family and its possessions have always been intimately involved with the history of Palma del Río and Andalusia. This part of Spain owes a great debt to my father. He was one of the men who helped rouse Spain's agriculture out of the lethargy in which it had slept for centuries.

"My father was always passionate in his search for knowledge. By the time he was twenty-one, he spoke German, French and Italian. But from the day he got off the Seville Express in 1915 with a new diploma in his hand, agriculture was his passion. He went twelve hundred miles to get that diploma, to the French Agricultural Institute at Grignon, which is for things of the land what the Sorbonne is for things of the spirit. He had inherited just five thousand acres from my grandparents and he was determined he was going to make them the most productive five thousand acres in Andalusia. He bought the first tractor that had ever cut a furrow in the soil of Andalusia, in 1918. It was a Hanno and he kept it for twenty years. My father was so successful with his methods that he began to buy up other fincas in the region around Palma. In 1918 he bought for La Vega one of the most famous bull breeds of our *fiesta brava,* the Saltillo bulls of the heirs of the Marquis de Saltillo. It was

57

from those bulls that most of Mexico's brave bulls were descended, and they became the pride of my father.

"Despite all that, he remained a simple and severe man. In each of the haciendas he built on the properties he acquired, he installed an office. On whatever farm he happened to be, his day began and ended in that office. Every record of his forty-five thousand acres, every detail, the salaries of a thousand employees, his livestock records, his crop yields, his tractor mileage, everything, he wrote down in pencil himself in a little black notebook. Each year in September, on San Miguel's Day, he changed it.

"There were nine children in the family. Usually in the summer we lived at La Vega, the hacienda of our principal estate just outside Peñaflor. It was a big ranch house with ocher walls and green shutters. In the fall and winter we lived in Palma in our *palacio,* an old Moorish palace at the entry to the town. It was a lovely building with a little enclosed patio at its center with a fountain and a few trees. From the patio you could see the towers of our church, the Church of the Assumption.

"Whether we were at La Vega or the *palacio,* my father always insisted on a coat and tie for all of us at the table, no matter how hot it was. He said grace before every meal, and no one sat down until he and my mother were seated. There was always something about my father, his presence, that commanded fear and respect. For example, until the day he died, my brothers and I never dared to smoke in his presence.

"When people came to La Vega, we organized a little fiesta for them. There would be sweet melons, *serrano* ham, montilla. The workers would come and sing and dance the flamenco for us. Federico García Lorca visited us. Many French friends of my father, too.

"On Sunday we always went to Mass together as a family, in the summer usually to Peñaflor, in the winter at the Assumption in Palma. For formal occasions my parents went in their coach. It was drawn by four matched horses with a pair of uniformed coachmen to drive it. After Sunday Mass and the feast days when we were in Palma, my father received friends in the *palacio,* our cousins and the other landowners, for coffee and sherry. But after lunch he was back in his work clothes and off to his fields again.

"Our real social life was in Seville. We had a palace in Seville for

58

receptions and our urban life. When we were young, for example, we had our tutors at La Vega and Palma. Later we were schooled in Seville. The high point of our lives each year was the feria of Seville. The great pride of my father was the four coaches he displayed every year in the *paseo** of the feria. No other family in Andalusia had as many. Each was driven by a team of four horses. One was matched white, one gray, one black, one chestnut. Each coach—its harnesses and its footmen were in different colors for the four ranches of my father on which he raised his brave bulls. It took a day and a half to drive the teams down to Seville from our properties.

"My father was not a politically minded man. He was above all interested in his lands. He was a republican, a conservative republican, and he welcomed the birth of the Republic, just as everyone else did. But fundamentally, my father believed in order and discipline. Above all else, he believed in a man's right to be master of his own lands. My father had worked hard all his life for what he had; the one thing he could not tolerate was having someone else trying to tell him how to run his lands.

"Unfortunately, we have a long history of troubles here in Andalusia. They go back to before the First World War when the anarchists began to make trouble in Spain. Our peasants are simple people and not always very hard workers. Those anarchists' ideas came down to simple things they could understand. They thought they were poor because there were rich in the world. They thought if there were no laws, everybody would be naturally good. If they killed the rich, they thought, their problems would be solved.

"They fought progress. When my father brought tractors to his lands, they tried to sabotage them because they thought they put people out of work. That didn't stop my father from building one of Spain's first tractor factories.

"In the beginning, under the Republic, the strikes that began to start were timid and unimportant, over details. But as time went on, they became more violent and their demands more important. We went through a phenomenon we have lived through before in Spain. The left and the intellectuals speak to the people, seeking their support. They arouse them and then lose control of them once they are aroused. There

* procession.

59

are excesses, and then naturally there's a reaction from the propertied classes.

"That was what was beginning to happen in Andalusia. With the Socialists in the town halls and the Republic in Madrid, the Guardia Civil no longer filled its functions properly. Order broke down. There was no discipline any more.

"The strike leaders got so bold they began to invade the fincas and herd off a man's workers, even his domestic servants, at gunpoint. The first time they came to La Vega, forty of them in a truck, my father rode down to the gate with his pistol and dared them to come in. He said he'd shoot the first one who put a foot on his land. They left. Later they did come back, a delegation, to give my father a list of demands. One of them pulled a knife on him. My father shot him.

"The landowners like my father couldn't accept these invasions of their lands. So they began to arm their trusted workers into a militia to protect their property. In the villages, the Socialists began to arm their militia too.

"Things kept getting worse. The Guardia Civil had orders to avoid any confrontation with the people. They were told not to intervene and not to see much. So in 1936, after the elections, the result was the first wave of church burnings in Andalusia under the eyes of the Guardia Civil. In Palma they put half a dozen of them to the torch. That night some of those anarchists made the sign of the cross at the door before they went in to throw their torches on the altar. But that didn't stop the churches from burning.

"The situation became chaotic. Those months seemed to have been one long demonstration. There was always a yelling mob, an angry crowd, spilling around the streets of Palma arguing about something. My father decided it was too dangerous to keep us there and sent us to Seville. Most of the other landowners did the same thing with their families.

"The Republic voted all sorts of agricultural laws. They hit us with terrible taxes. They raised farm wages arbitrarily. They tried to force us to hire workers we didn't need. If there were men left in the Plaza de Trabajadores, they'd put them in a truck and drive up to the finca and tell you to hire them all—or they'd strike all your other workers.

"All that happened at a time crop prices had fallen apart because of the world depression. We had no liquid capital. For a man like my father, all the interference in his private affairs was intolerable, worse even than the death threats always being made against him.

"So to defend himself one day he fired all his workers in a single stroke and announced he wouldn't plant again until the government stopped interfering in his affairs. He took the train to Córdoba to tell the governor of the province he'd rather be shot than no longer be the master of his own lands.

"I think my father was really trying to create a scandal to force other landowners into action. The governor used a trick against him. He sent a technician from the agricultural laboratory of Córdoba to Palma to announce they'd found locusts on his land. Since locusts multiply very quickly, the governor ordered the lands of my father worked under the protection of the Guardia Civil.

"The government seized the lands of my father and issued a warrant for his arrest because he had refused to accept the decrees of the Socialists of Palma and the governor of Córdoba. It was the cruelest blow he ever knew.

"He went into hiding in Seville. Even we, his family, didn't know where he was. But nothing could drive him from his lands. Like some ghost, he disguised himself as a mechanic, a worker, a businessman, and in borrowed cars he'd come back to his properties at night to see how they were being run. His *mayorales* were loyal to him. It got so bad the militia set ambushes on the highway for him to try to kill him pretending they were arresting him.

"There was nothing really special about his case. It was like that everywhere. We were sliding into anarchy. Ever since the February election in 1936 when the Popular Front won 60 or 70 percent of the vote in Andalusia, you could see trouble was coming. The masses seemed to sense a day of rising was at hand. It was something, a conviction, that seemed to grow naturally that spring. They were just waiting for the word."

*   *   *

Twelve thousand people lived in Palma del Río in that spring of 1936. Their ancestors had been driven into the sanctuary of the walled town by

61

the uncertainties of life along a warring Arab-Christian frontier. In their retreat from the fields lay the seed of the economic ills now cursing Palma del Río. They had left behind their small family holdings of land. In the wake of the Reconquest, the Church and a few conquering cavaliers had seized all the lands they left beyond the city's walls. Later, in the middle of the nineteenth century, when the Church was stripped of its land, the impoverished peasants of Andalusia were unable to reclaim it. Instead, a new wave of families flocked south from Castile and Galicia to buy up the enormous estates into which Andalusia was now divided. Thus history had imprisoned Palma del Río in the cruel imbalance of a society composed of three landowning families supported by a tiny middle class.

Below them were the faceless cohorts represented by José Benítez, El Renco, plodding off each dawn to the estates beyond Palma's walls, men without even vegetable gardens of their own to cultivate. Neither their state nor their Church offered them succor. The boundaries of their meager lives were marked by hunger, fear and, finally, despair.

Palma's tiny middle class was composed of a notary public, a lawyer, a lady pharmacist, four doctors, a midwife, two veterinarians, six café owners, a handful of shopkeepers, five employees of the town hall, eight Guardia Civil members and two taxicab drivers nicknamed "Lefty" and "the Little Deaf Guy." The town had a parish priest, Don Juan Navas, and a dozen other priests and nuns for its convent school and its clinic. Finally, it had three prostitutes, one for each of its popular bars.

Life crept along in a chain of unchanging days, their passing marked only by the shifting seasons or an occasional religious feast. There were no strangers in Palma del Río. Even death was a neighbor. Here, as elsewhere in Andalusia, the church bell still tolled for the passing of a parishioner. As its mournful notes rang out, Don Juan Navas invariably scurried from his vestry toward the house of the dead, a white surplice flapping about his knees, his head bowed in prayer.

In Palma that spring there were, besides its two taxis and the cars of its landowners, two other private cars and barely a dozen motorcycles. Palma's doctors rode to their patients on bicycles. A trip by train to Seville or Córdoba was, for the town poor, so costly a journey that many never took it. The town counted half a dozen telephones and barely the same number of radios.

Beyond its crumbling Moorish walls, the bottomlands of the Guadalquivir, the reason for the town's existence, rolled down to the horizon in
rich green waves, their young tufts of wheat already combed by the first
hot breaths of summer drifting up from Africa. To the east, nine miles
away, the medieval spires of the castle of Almodóvar rose from a stub of
high ground, guarding the entry to the valley over which Palma del Río
held sway. To the north, the foothills of the Sierra Morena stumbled to a
stop along the Seville-Córdoba highway, frozen forever into the crude
and brutal forms into which some prehistoric glacier had pitched them.
Below them, between the highway and the railway, was the Guadalquivir
River, a muddy gulch the color of milk chocolate, flowing at a pace so
slow its motion was invisible and a leaf cast upon it seemed destined to
spend a century drifting down to Seville.

In the distance, the crests of the Sierra Morena pushed into the skyline
marking the outer limits of Andalusia and its frontier with the wind-
washed plateaus of La Mancha. Along the hillsides on both sides of the
valley stretched miles of olive groves. On and on they went, stretching
down the hills in rigid, regular lines, ageless sentinels that had watched
over centuries of Palma's springtimes.

It was a scene of untrammeled pastoral peace and quiet. A third of the
way through the twentieth century, the town and the country around it
seemed isolated from the world, as frozen into its past as the boulders of
the Sierra Morena.

Yet Palma del Río was not as cut off from the world as it seemed.
Like hundreds of other isolated Spanish villages and towns, Palma del
Río would soon prove its affinity with the world beyond the Pyrenees.
Unable to resolve with reason the social and political ills besetting her
Palma del Ríos, Spain prepared to forget them in the horror of civil war,
and in doing so, to abandon her fields and villages to their fate as the
testing grounds for the most terrible conflict in history.

*   *   *

Palma del Río's first taste of violence had come in the confusion that
followed the Popular Front's victory in the national elections of February 1936. They were destined to be Republican Spain's last elections,
and they climaxed five tumultuous years of republicanism.

Nationally, the Popular Front just failed to obtain an absolute majority of the popular vote. But in the improverished villages of Andalusia, its supporters won 60 to 70 percent of the ballots cast and town hall after town hall went tumbling into the hands of the Socialists and anarchists.

That victory in Palma sent the town's poor flooding into the streets in the same disordered mass that had greeted the birth of the Republic five years earlier. Again, the café of Niño Valles where El Renco worked spilled over with jubilant, cheering workers. This time, however, an undercurrent of bitterness flowed through their joy. On election night a mob of celebrating workers battered its way into the conservative political club of Don Félix Moreno and his fellow landowners. While the workers' wives and children looked on applauding, the mob burned that symbol of their ills to the ground.

Night after night, the same happy, disordered mass continued to run through the town sending the notes of the "Red Flag" and the "Internationale" echoing down its darkened streets. Nightly Don Juan Navas knelt before the altar of the Church of the Assumption and listened to the distant sounds of their revelry. The elderly priest knew well what traditions governed the vengeance of his impoverished countrymen in a land that had oscillated for generations between religious fervor and anticlerical violence.

On February 20, under the indifferent eyes of the Guardia Civil, that vengeance came. In a noisy, torchlit procession, the mob marched on the Church of the Assumption. From there it moved to the other churches of Palma: Santo Domingo, San Francisco and Santa Ana, and on to the convents of Santa Clara and La Coronada. At each stop, the priests and nuns were dragged from the chapels into which they had retreated in fear to pray. Statues were smashed, pictures slashed apart, broken strands of furniture heaped before each chapel's altar to provide the fuel for the pillars of flame that soon shot into Palma's darkened skyline.

Disorders similar to those in Palma del Río swept over Spain. Strikes, street fights, church burnings and political assassinations plagued the land and hastened its division into the extremes of left and right. In Extremadura, the peasants invaded the great estates, cut them into lots and distributed them among themselves to cries of *"Viva la República."* The terrified landowners abandoned their homes to flee to the cities, and in their flight hastened the land seizures they were hoping to avoid. The nation's economy jerked to a stop, its functioning paralyzed by strikes and the refusal of landowners and capitalists to honor the new regulations the Popular Front sought to impose on them.

Madrid was, on varying occasions, shackled by strikes of its café waiters, bus drivers, elevator boys, garbage collectors, construction workers, even of the attendants at its bullring. Seville was crippled by a hundred and seventy-five unresolved strikes in the month of April alone. Anarchist street gangs in Spain's cities erected roadblocks and imposed a "tax" of twenty-five pesetas on every passing car. Some workers, convinced a millennium of sorts had arrived, insisted on riding trains and buses free.

As elsewhere in Spain, the leaders of the Popular Front in Palma were forced to cede their power to younger and more extremist chieftains. In Palma, the twenty-four-year-old son of the town mattress stuffer grasped for the leadership. His name was as noble as his circumstances were humble. It was Juan de España, and his quick and angry tongue gave breath to the bitterness pent up in Palma's poor through years of squalor and repression.

In his first independent political action, Juan de España launched a general strike and marched his supporters onto the fincas near Palma, driving every worker, even teen-age domestics, off the properties at gunpoint. In the town, his followers extended their strike by appropriating what goods they could find in Palma's stores. Others ambushed as scabs the permanent workers of the fincas as they lugged home their *"hatos,"* the monthly sacks of chick peas and a few liters of olive oil paid out as a part of their salaries.

Palma's eight-man Guardia Civil watched impotently as disorder overtook the community; they had received no orders while these events were sweeping the town. At La Vega, Don Félix summoned his faithful foremen to a midnight meeting in his study. He gave them a few extra arms and a further injunction to defend his estate and his precious herd of a thousand Saltillo bulls. Then, a refugee from justice in this land he had ruled like a feudal sovereign, he disappeared into the night.

Thus, like the rest of Spain, Palma del Río edged toward chaos and civil violence. The brutal heat of summer fell upon the land. Around the town, the hot, dry winds licked the wheat fields, their golden expanse

65

flecked by the occasional scarlet burst of a poppy's petal. Soon another wind would rise to strike the little town stifling under the summer sun, and angry men would add their blood to the poppies' scarlet stains in the wheat fields of Palma del Río.

The inevitable conflict was at hand. Spain's military, prompted by her Church and the right, was ready to challenge her Republican government. For help, Spain's insurgents would turn to Nazi Germany and Fascist Italy, and her foundering Republic to France, England and the USSR. Soon, on the mournful plains of Castile and in the harsh sierras of Navarre and Andalusia, Europe's conflicting rivals would find the caldrons in which to test their arms and their ideologies. More than half a million Spaniards would die in the coming conflict and two million more bear its scars forever.

The spark to ignite the conflict was provided in Madrid during the hot and sodden night of July 12–13. There, at three o'clock in the morning, a military car of Asaltos, an auxiliary of the Guardia Civil, stopped in front of the fashionable apartment of one of Spain's most prominent right-wing politicians, a member of Parliament and a former Minister named Calvo Sotelo. Displaying for identification their official documents, they summoned Sotelo from his bed and ordered him to follow them. Sotelo was stuffed into the front seat of their car and raced off into the night at seventy miles an hour. The next morning his body was found sprawled at the gates of a public cemetery.

Sotelo's murder shocked and outraged middle-class Spain. Millions wavering in their opposition to the Popular Front government coalesced against it. And, for the plotters of the army, the hour had come. They fixed the date for their uprising. They chose July 17, 1936, at five o'clock in the afternoon, the hour at which by long tradition the corridas begin in the bullrings of Spain.

*   *   *

The urgent jangle of a telephone jarred the hot and sticky night. A sleepy figure lurched toward the noisy machine, a hand-wound instrument fixed to the wall of 1 Calle Pacheco, under a framed portrait of Manuel Azaña, President of the Spanish Republic. Painted in white on its black oval face was the number 49, which that phone carried in the telephone directory of the province of Córdoba. It was the number of the Guardia Civil barracks of the town of Palma del Río.

Sergeant Emilio Patón, chief of Palma's Guardia Civil, jerked the earpiece of the phone from its cradle. At the other end he heard the lieutenant upon whom he and all the posts in the river valley depended. He was calling from the mountain village of Posadas on the other side of the Guadalquivir.

The Spanish army in Morocco, the lieutenant announced, had risen against the government. The mainland garrisons were following them, and it was the Guardia Civil's duty to join the movement. The rising, he told the sleepy sergeant, would return discipline and order to Spain. He commanded Patón to place his Guardia Civil men on the side of the rebellion. Patón swallowed nervously. He was fifty-nine years old, a heavyset man who in just one year would retire from the service and return to finish his life by the tranquil, rain-swept shores of his native Galicia. He wanted nothing to disturb the studied routine propelling him toward that happy event. But Sergeant Emilio Patón, like so many other men in Spain that night, was trapped. Behind him his anxious young troopers, sensing the nature of the call, eyed him impatiently.

"*Arriba, España!*—Arise, Spain!" he shouted into the receiver.

It was just before midnight, July 17, 1936. With his words, the rallying cry of the right-wing Falange, the eight-man garrison of the Guardia Civil post of the Andalusian town of Palma del Río entered into rebellion against the Spanish Republic.

All along the Guadalquivir valley, throughout all of Andalusia, similar calls routed soldiers and Guardia Civil officers from their sleep and forced them to choose sides in the conflict breaking over Spain. The rebellion had begun in the Moroccan garrison of Melilla. From there it spread to Spain's two other major Moroccan garrisons. That evening the first mainland garrisons had joined the movement.

In Seville, fifty miles from Palma del Río, General Queipo de Llano spent the night with three aides and a handful of civilian plotters in the home of a retired major. He had arrived in the late afternoon in his official Hispano-Suiza in which he later recalled he had carried out "twenty thousand miles of conspiracy" while pretending to inspect customs posts. Now, with his tiny band of men, he planned to seize Andalusia's capital in the next few hours. Among his rapt and devoted little circle was a taciturn, squat civilian dreaming probably of the moment when this uprising would lead him back to his sequestered lands. It was Don Félix Moreno, the *señor* of Palma del Río.

In Madrid thousands of angry workers, alarmed by the uprising, spent the night in the streets, demanding arms and news. A prudent government refused them arms while Radio Madrid assured the nation "no one on the Spanish mainland has taken part in this absurd plot."

Palma del Río was no less agitated. Quite unaware that their Guardia Civil barracks had joined the rebellion, scores of workers jammed the Casa del Pueblo, listening to the news bulletins broadcast over Radio Madrid. José Benítez abandoned his post in Niño Valles' café to join them.

The town's economic life had been stopped for days. As elsewhere in Andalusia, its poor awaited only a command from their Socialist leaders in Madrid to institute a proletarian uprising and usher in the Socialist Nirvana for which they had waited so long. Once already Juan de España had led part of his mob on the town hall, demanding arms "to defend the Republic from its enemies." The Socialist mayor had refused because he had no orders; nor, in fact, any arms. Nevertheless, against the great day he was sure was coming, España had formed a militia of his own and set them drilling with sticks and pick handles. Among the men he had chosen for his first recruits was José Benítez, El Renco.

At dawn, anxious, beset by wild and contradictory rumors, his mob decided to follow the example of the workers of Madrid and make a second march for arms on Palma's town hall. But, like the government in Madrid, Palma's Socialist mayor remained reluctant to undertake an action as unpredictable in its consequences as the arming of the civilian population. A similar hesitation characterized the reaction of Republican officials throughout Spain to the first overt actions of the rebellion. Their vacillation would weigh heavily against the Spanish Republic in the hours to come. For the men who had vowed to overthrow them suffered no such failing.

*   *   *

Several hundred miles from Palma del Río, a man stood erect on the foredeck of a small fishing smack, watching the last few yards of Atlantic

Ocean that separated him from land slip past the gunwales of his boat. No hesitation fettered his spirit. His eyes remained fixed on the landfall just ahead and the object glinting upon it in the sunshine: a twin-engined British airplane waiting to fly him into the pages of history.

The voyage that had brought that airplane to this airfield in the Canary Islands had been as dramatic as it was devious. Its redheaded English pilot, Cecil Bebb, had been hired to fly a retired British army officer, a pair of attractive blondes, and an elegant Spanish newspaperman names Luis Bolín from London to Casablanca. The purpose of their trip had seemed obvious to pilot Bebb: a little fling by a pair of well-to-do roués far from the prying eyes of their wives and friends.

In Casablanca Bolín had abruptly left the party and sent the plane and his companions on to Las Palmas in the Canaries. Once there, Bebb found himself suddenly abandoned by the blondes and the retired artillery major as well. His isolation was short-lived, however. An army officer soon aroused him from a siesta in his hotel room and requested him to go to the cathedral of Las Palmas at 3:30. He would be asked to ride in a car. "Please accept the invitation," the officer had pointedly declared.

The "invitation" had led to a mountain villa outside the city, where the real reason for his flight was explained to Bebb. He was told he was to fly an important passenger back to the newsman Bolín, waiting in Casablanca. Until that passenger was ready to leave the Canaries, he was ordered to stay in the villa.

At four the next morning, Bebb was hastened from the villa to an air force barracks twelve miles from Las Palmas and then, just after noon, to the airport, where he had found his plane guarded by half a dozen soldiers, parked at the far end of the runway a few feet from the ocean's edge.

For an hour and a half now Bebb had waited under guard in his cockpit, hearing in the distance, from the center of Las Palmas, the sound of gunfire. He had been ordered to start his engines as soon as a fishing smack was sighted on the horizon.

He watched the boat chug to a stop a few feet from the low-lying breakwater rimming the edge of the landing strip. As it did, Bebb saw the short, mustachioed man in a khaki uniform standing at its rail lower himself into the water. At his side the man clutched a little leather satchel that gave him, Bebb thought, the air of "a traveling salesman off on a trip with his sample case." He plodded uncertainly up to the break-water, the knee-deep sea splashing over the trousers of his uniform.

Watching his awkward arrival, Bebb asked himself if it was to meet this ordinary little man that he had flown so many devious miles from London's Croydon airport.

The man's first gestures answered his question. After a few quick words in Spanish to the officer guarding the plane, he climbed into Bebb's cabin. Two young officers followed him.

"To Casablanca, please," ordered the youngest among them.

As soon as they had reached their cruising altitude, Bebb's unknown passenger stood up and performed his first act of this historic trip. He took off his wet uniform and put on a gray flannel suit he drew from his little leather satchel. Then he gathered up, one by one, his passport, his identity card, and his personal papers and flung them out the window of the plane. As those documents went fluttering down toward the Atlantic Ocean six thousand feet below, he turned toward a quizzical Captain Bebb and emerged from the anonymity with which he had just so carefully cloaked himself.

"Excuse me," he said in accented English. "How do you do? I am General Francisco Franco."

*　　*　　*

In Spain, the rebellion toward which Franco was flying spread with startling speed. Andalusia had risen first. By noon the center of Seville was in the Rebels' control. Córdoba was won by sunset. So were Algeciras and Jérez. Granada wavered. Only Málaga, its army garrison cowed by the Spanish fleet, remained loyal to the Republic. In Africa the last opposition to the rising was stifled by nightfall.

But if Andalusia's cities had fallen to the rebellion, the countryside had remained loyal to the Republic. The frantic warnings of Radio Seville, issued with the Rebels at its doorstep, had aroused village after village between Seville and Córdoba. Palma del Río's turn came at midday.

Once again the workers from the Casa del Pueblo, José Benítez marching proudly with them, had stormed toward the town hall, demanding the right to search the town for arms. Again, on instructions from Córdoba, the town's Socialist mayor refused them permission. This time their leader, the mattress stuffer's twenty-four-year-old son, Juan de España, would not be turned back. Calling to the mob to follow him, he stormed the town hall.

Once inside, he dispossessed the mayor and announced from the building's balcony that Palma del Río was now governed by a Revolutionary Committee of which he proclaimed himself the chief. As his deputies, he appointed his brother-in-law and a twenty-one-year-old mason.

The first action of Palma's new leader was to order his followers to scour the town for arms. From house to house his improvised militia went, ripping up mattresses, overturning cupboards, digging up the suspect tiles in the patios of the town's shopkeepers and other middle-class citizens. As the afternoon went on, a haphazard pile of old and battered arms began to rise in the town square. There were a handful of carbines, dozens of shotguns and hunting rifles, a smattering of pistols.

España meanwhile ordered the vaults of Palma's two banks, local branches of the Banco Hispano-Americano and the Crédito de España, broken open. Guarded by an escort toting old pistols and hunting rifles, his men carried the bank notes they found in them to the town hall. There the treasure of Palma del Río was heaped on an unsteady table in an office adjacent to España's. Two of his militia stood guard over the pile of bank notes, while from the doorway their companions gawked at this crude mound of money—enough, it seemed, to provide for the needs of all Spain.

España himself led an expedition on the estate nearest the town, that of Pepe Martínez. Like the other great landowners of the region, Martínez had fled to Seville. He had left behind, however, his black eight-cylinder Packard. España promptly requisitioned it for his personal use. Then, as an afterthought, he proclaimed Martínez's hacienda his new revolutionary residence.

Later, in the town square, he distributed to his followers the heterogeneous mass of arms seized during the afternoon. José Benítez was among those who received them. For the first time in his life the quiet waiter of Niño Valles' café held a firearm in his hands. Like dozens of his fellow Palmeños, Benítez had no idea how to use the weapon assigned him. Laughing like children with new toys, they cluttered the square in front of the Casa del Pueblo, trying to find out how to make those weapons work.

The arms of José Benítez and his associates were not, however, for amusement. At dusk Juan de España ordered an attack on the town's Guardia Civil post. There he hoped to lay his hands on Sergeant Emilio Patón's supply of modern carbines and his stocks of ammunition.

Palma's eight rebelling guardsmen had been joined at dawn by a handful of civilians, all noted for their right-wing politics, all certain their names appeared on the list of townspeople earmarked for execution by Juan de España. They included the clerk of the town hall, the town's carpenter and the three Romero brothers, proprietors and operators of Palma del Río's leading barbershop.

All day they had barricaded their headquarters with sandbags and stones while the *calles* outside rang with the happy cries of the rampaging militia. Now in the fading afternoon sunshine, Sergeant Emilio Patón and his men in their black patent-leather hats waited for the opening shot in the assault of a vengeful town.

It came from the belfry of Our Lady of the Assumption, Palma's half-ruined parish church. There a militiaman pushed past an abandoned crane's nest and fired into the courtyard of the besieged barracks. His well-aimed shot struck one of Patón's men in the head. The guardsman stumbled to the ground, Palma del Río's first victim of the Spanish Civil War.

Furious, his fellow guardsmen sent a burst of fire sweeping over the houses around them. Juan de España's militia prudently drew back. They would not conquer their rebelling Guardia Civil tonight; the modest whitewashed barracks would resist for days to come the furious assaults of Palma's populace.

That evening the jubilant militia packed the café of Niño Valles. The center of their attention was the cafés newest addition, an instrument over which José Benítez and his fellow waiter stood guard. It was one of Palma's rare radios, confiscated during the afternoon in the home of the town's leading veterinarian, Miguel Prieto. Day after day the people of Palma would follow on the veterinarian's radio the tragic progress of the civil war sweeping over Spain.

Now a voice echoed from it through the crowded café of Niño Valles. It came over Radio Madrid, and for three years its strident tones would stir the defenders of the Republic and serve as the symbol of their resistance and their hopes. It was the voice of Doña Dolores Ibárruri, aflame with the impassioned words that would win her notoriety around the world as "La Pasionaria." Tonight she spoke to the women of Spain. "Fight with knives, with burning oil!" she screamed. "Better it is to die standing proudly than to live on your knees!"

Then, as the workers in Niño Valles' café cheered, she hurled out for the first time the defiant words that would become their rallying cry and that of a dying Spanish Republic: *"No pasarán!*—They shall not pass!"

* * *

No raucous radio's blaring marred the quiet of the dreary hotel room. The only sound its occupants could hear was the regular beat of the surf smashing and washing over the sands of the beach just below its shuttered windows. His shirt-sleeves rolled up, his tie undone, Francisco Franco quietly ate a cheese sandwich with the journalist, Luis Bolín, who had plotted so carefully to get him from the Canary Islands to this Casablanca hotel room.

Here they waited for a telephone call from Tangier that would fix their final destination and the place where Franco would take command of the rebellion breaking over Spain. Alone in their room, its shadowy corners lit by one flyspecked light bulb dangling from the ceiling, the two men talked their way through the hot night. Franco, only a few hours from the awesome and bloody responsibilities which would soon be his, seemed to Bolín extraordinarily somber and composed. The conflict ahead, he predicted, would be a long and bloody one.

"We shall lose Madrid, Barcelona, Valencia and Bilbao from the start," he said. "Málaga and Granada too, probably. Maybe we'll have Seville.

"The other cities of Spain," he sighed, "we shall have to pluck one by one like olives."

Then, to a jolted and discouraged Bolín, he added, "But we shall win. We have a faith, an ideal and a discipline. Our foes have none of these."

Just before dawn their call arrived from Tangier. It ordered them to the Spanish Moroccan city of Tetuán.

Halfway through the trip, Franco opened his valise and changed back into his uniform, its trouser legs still damp from his brief stroll in the Atlantic the day before. Then he sat down and spent the rest of his journey staring moodily out the window.

73

By seven o'clock the long voyage was over. Franco's plane taxied to a stop in front of the headquarters of Tetuán air base, its façade scarred by the fighting that had ended only a few hours earlier. With a few brusque words to the men waiting for him, Franco rushed into the city to take command of his rebellion. There, a few moments later, Bolín sat with him in the office of Spain's High Commissioner to Morocco while he received a summary of the situation facing him.

They were interrupted by a message from the nearby naval base of Ceuta. Spanish Navy ships entering the harbor, it said, were refusing to answer the rebelling army command signals. It was, Bolín knew, the worst news Franco could have received. He had hoped those ships might convoy his rebelling army to the Spanish mainland.

Franco thought for a moment. Then he issued his first direct order of the rebellion. "Signal once more," he said. "If they don't answer, open fire."

At almost the same moment, in Madrid's Defense Ministry, the besieged Republic's newly appointed Minister of War, Luis Castillo, too, issued his first order. He ordered all Spain's loyal provincial governors to distribute arms to the people.

It was Sunday, July 19, 1936. With those two orders, issued five hundred miles apart, the Spanish people were propelled irrevocably into an arena as large as their nation for their long and bloody corrida, the Spanish Civil War.

*　　*　　*

Yet, for the poor of Palma del Río, that conflict began not in bloodshed but with a banquet, the longest, happiest banquet of their lives. Not even their boldest anarchist prophets could have foretold a material abundance as grand as that which now befell them. Many among them would remember these days of Palma's "Red Terror" as the only time in their lives they had gone to bed with their stomachs full.

Among the first orders of Juan de España had been a proclamation that all the food, oil and grain in the warehouses of Palma's great estates would be seized in the name of his Revolutionary Committee. For the next forty-eight hours his followers swept clean the granaries of those fincas. They brought their contents back to the town, in burro carts and on foot: long lines of men toting burlap sacks, happily carrying away the wealth of the estates to which they had so often plodded in misery and economic subjection.

Their plunder was stored in the charred shell of the convent of Santo Domingo. To it was added the stock of all the shops in Palma whose owners were suspected of disloyalty to the Republic. The townspeople named their unlikely cornucopia an "Economato," after a chain of labor cooperatives that had taken root in Spain's cities just before the war began. Each morning, the town game warden marched through Palma's streets, tooting his horn to announce the opening of the "Economato," calling out Palma's poor to share in the daily distribution of its treasures.

From these days the memory of one delicacy above all would stand out in the years to come in the minds of Palma's poor. It was a delicacy many of them had never tasted before and would never taste again: red beef. Unable to avenge themselves on Don Félix Moreno himself, the men of Palma del Río fell instead upon his most treasured possession, his Saltillo bulls.

Each morning a team of Juan de España's militia rode out into Don Félix's pastures to kill a day's supply of bulls for the town. Their matador's sword was an old carbine carried by an anarchist worker named Manolo El Ecijano. He turned to his task with such vengeful zest that his companions soon assigned him another nickname, that borne in the bullrings of the province of Córdoba that spring by a young matador. They called him "Manolete."

So abundant was "Manolete's" daily delivery of dead bulls that the stomachs of Palma del Río's poor, shrunk by years of privation, were unable to consume all the mounds of meat spread before them. Soon the town was choked with a surfeit of meat. Yet, day after day, "Manolete" and his men rode back into Palma, towing behind them a hay wain spilling over with the great black carcasses of another load of Don Félix Moreno's precious bulls. These townspeople who had spent a lifetime in ignorance of the taste of beef could now digest only the choicest steaks and chops of the carcasses of Don Félix's treasured animals. The rest they tossed uneaten into the Guadalquivir.

Each dead animal represented to Don Félix more money than the workers so happily consuming it could earn in years of punishing labor on his lands. Small wonder, then, that so many Palmeños savored in each

75

morsel they tasted not just a new eating experience but a little personal vengeance on the man who represented so much of the misery in their lives. They ate those steaks boiled, or fried in streams of olive oil, or roasted over open fires in the *calles* of the town. The Palmeños ate until, quite literally, they could eat no more. In the years to come, the memory of those nights would torture a famished Angelita Benítez and she would see again her mother boiling the steaks her father had brought home for his family.

For others in the town, those who did not share the political convictions of Juan de España, these were memorable days, too, days of fear and terror. When España's men were driven away from Don Félix's ranch house by his faithful and well-armed retainers barricaded inside, they captured and publicly executed three domestic servants from his Palma del Río *palacio*. Two of the town's rare Falangists were shot in the first hour of revolutionary jubilation. One, a doctor, was shot on his doorstep after being lured outside on the pretext that his services were needed for a sick man. The second, a young druggist, was shot in his bed before the imploring eyes of his mother.

The basement of the town hall was turned into a provisional prison by Juan de España. The parish priest, Don Juan Navas, led the parade of prisoners into jail. They included two doctors; Palma's lawyer; its two veterinarians; the only landowner the angry militia had been able to find, a small farmer named Rodrigo Díaz; and the president of the town's Catholic Action movement, Palma's lady pharmacist, a woman named Lucía Blanca Ortiz.

In the besieged Guardia Civil barracks, Sergeant Emilio Patón and his men, completely cut off from all news, held out day after day. While their triumphant besiegers feasted on the steaks of Don Félix's bulls, the guardsmen killed their horses and ate them raw, trying to slake their tortured thirst with the animals' blood.

Finally, out of ammunition, dying from thirst in the brutal heat of summer, they decided to surrender. Sergeant Patón performed his last act as a member of the Guardia Civil. For the first time in his life he raised the white flag of surrender. Hooted and jeered, dragging their wounded along with them, Patón and his exhausted guardsmen marched off to join Juan de España's other prisoners in the town hall cellar.

While Palma feasted, Queipo de Llano's Nationalist forces finished the conquest of Seville and began to turn their attention to the project the general promised nightly in his ramblings on Radio Seville, the "liberation" of the countryside between Seville and Córdoba.

Each day at dawn, his columns set off from the plaza in front of Seville's cathedral, burial place of Christopher Columbus. They were a ragged collection of regular troops, Falangists, Guardia Civil men and dispossessed landowners trying to get back to their estates. They fell each day upon a different village, driving its Loyalist defenders into the hills, killing those foolish enough to stay behind. Proclaiming the village "liberated," they returned to Seville at sunset to celebrate their triumph.

In the van of those columns was Don Félix Moreno, whose brave bulls were roasting in the streets of Palma del Río. Gradually the vengeful columns crept along the Guadalquivir until they reached the surroundings of the little community happily living its brief hour of Socialist glory. Peñaflor, the next town up the valley from Palma, fell to the Nationalists August 16. Two days later, Écija, eighteen miles south on the main road between Seville and Córdoba, fell, too. With their capture, two of the three approaches to Palma were in Nationalist hands.

Each advance of those Nationalist columns prompted its flow of refugees, friends and kinsmen of the Republic's defenders, fleeing before Queipo's threatened vengeance. They stumbled into Palma del Río by the hundreds. They lurched along the Calle Portada, Palma's main street, parading their misery past the whitewashed houses of the shocked and terrified townspeople. There were old men and women, collapsed in hay wains or wheelbarrows, tugged along the cobbles by their exhausted offspring; infants clinging to the necks of their worn and haggard mothers; the sick, swaddled in rags. Some came in burro carts or wagons. A fortunate few rode bicycles. Most shuffled by on foot, their rope sandals ground to shreds from their march.

They slept in the streets, clutching in their tired arms the few possessions they had saved from their abandoned homes. The town shared with them the contents of its "Economato" and the meat from Don Félix's dwindling herd of bulls. In unbelieving terror, the Palmeños listened to their litany of the massacres carried out by the Nationalist troops in each town they had seized. For Palma del Río, their arrival heralded the fact that the feasting was over and the fighting was about to begin.

Palma had become the last Loyalist stronghold in the river valley. To the Nationalists it was now known as "Palma the Red." Juan de

77

España's militia began to barricade the city for the assault they knew must soon come. Its flame-scarred church towers became lookout posts. Men chopped down centuries-old olive trees to barricade the entries to their walled town. The houses near them were turned into strongpoints. Palma's wall, which had faced the cavaliers of the Reconquest, was lined with chains of sandbags to meet a new generation of conquerors. Over and over again, men shouted to each other the Loyalist slogan carried down the alleyways of the little town on the hot summer wind: *"No pasarán—*they shall not pass."

Soon, from beyond the drab walls to the south and west, the first sound of firing began to drift up to the town. For forty-two Palmeños that sound was a tocsin, a knell that summoned them forth from Juan de España's prison in the cellar of the town hall. Chained together in groups of four, they were marched to a truck and carted off to Palma's cemetery, a white-walled enclosure set in a field of waving wheat just beyond the town gates. There they were unchained and ordered to dig a trench in an unoccupied corner of the graveyard.

As the night sky softened with the first gray lights of dawn, the executions began. Sergeant Emilio Patón, the man who had dreamed of retiring to the shores of Galicia, was first. Then, one by one, his policemen followed. Ángel Romero, the town barber, and his brothers were next. Only one prisoner was missing: Lucía Blanca Ortiz, the lady pharmacist, who had been imprisoned for her work in Catholic Action. Her sex had won her the right to a private execution and burial place by the banks of the Guadalquivir.

Before each burst of fire, Don Juan Navas, the parish priest, stepped to the edge of the pit and murmured a hasty absolution to his condemned parishioners. Soon the common trench was filled with forty bodies and Don Juan was alone with his captors. He closed his breviary, bowed his head in a rapid prayer and then stepped in his turn to the edge of the pit. He turned and raised his eyes to the firing squad before him. Behind him the early morning sky was now milk-white and the black cassock draping his erect figure stood out like a dark tree trunk against the lightening horizon. A voice called to him from the circle of poised figures.

"Don Juan," it said, "we are not killing you because of what you've done. You were always good for the town. We're killing you for what you stand for."

The priest sighed. "My poor sons," he said, "blood shall beget blood.

78

In a few days you too shall perish here for your crimes." With a sad and heavy gesture, he offered the last blessing of his life to these men gathered to kill him. Some of them, forgetting for an instant the mission that had brought them to the graveyard, made the sign of the cross along with him. Then their shots rang out and Don Juan's body toppled into the pit.

*　　*　　*

The "liberators" column formed in the porticoed Plaza Mayor of the town of Écija, eighteen miles south of Palma del Río. Its commander clutched in his hand a French Michelin road map with which he planned to find his way to Palma the Red. Écija's municipal hearse was the column's ambulance. Its water was carried by a tank truck still bearing the name of the oil company from which it had been requisitioned. Behind it came a patched-together parade of the world's auto industry: Model-A Fords, Chevrolets, Fiats, even one majestic old Duesenberg.

The troops hung from farm trucks, delivery vans and hay wagons, some of those vehicles already steaming like locomotives in the August heat. They were headed by three hundred regular soldiers. Supporting them was a patched-together collection of Écija's civil guards, Falangists and Requetés, their uniforms as disparate as their politics. They straggled along on bicycles, on muleback, on foot, in Falangist blue forage caps, scarlet berets, khaki work shirts, or sometimes no other identification than an armband twisted around a biceps. As they left Écija, their women scuttled after them throwing flowers, kisses, or goatskins of wine.

Behind the column, riding off as proudly as if they were parading at the feria of Seville, were three of Palma's great landowners, the Martínez brothers and Don Félix Moreno. Erect and proud, an enormous pistol jammed into his belt, Don Félix rode off to avenge his brave bulls. Five centuries after El Cid, a Palma feudal lord had set out upon the road to the reconquest of his particular corner of the Spanish nation.

*　　*　　*

The fingers of the lookout tightened around his collapsible spyglass. From his sentry post in the belfry of Palma del Río's Church of the Assumption, its brick base blackened by the flames of the Popular Front,

79

carpenter Adolfo Santaflor had just spotted the first trucks of the Écija column twisting up to Palma in a cloud of dust. The carpenter laid aside his spyglass and grabbed the heavy cord dangling from the bell above him. With strong and steady strokes, Santaflor began to ring out the bell that had so often summoned Palma to Mass or marked the passing of a parishioner. Now its heavy gong marked the passing of the proletarian paradise that Juan de España had so briefly installed in the little town below.

A few moments later, bright bursts of orange flame began to spread out from a dozen points along the base of Palma's Arab wall. Through their field glasses its Nationalist assailants could see the townspeople, torches in their hands, scampering along the foot of the wall. As their first defensive gesture they were setting fire to the unharvested wheat fields stretching out toward the attacking column from Palma's gates. In a few moments those isolated bursts of flame became a low-lying wall of fire, eating its way over a year's supply of Palma's bread as it swept toward the attackers. Startled, the civilians in the attacking column began to panic.

Their commander realized he would have to use his professional troops to capture Palma. A second column of volunteers had joined his, cutting Palma to the west. He invested the town cemetery, two hundred yards to Palma's east, leaving one exit from the town in the Reds' hands: its arching Roman bridge over the Guadalquivir. Then he ordered his soldiers to prepare to seize the town after darkness.

ANGELITA BENÍTEZ'S STORY

"WHAT I REMEMBER most about the war is the night the men left, the night my father went away. That day there was fighting in the town. We thought Palma was being bombed, but it wasn't, it was just thunder. I remember my mother made us stay in the house. Outside you could hear the shooting. Manuel, the baby, and Carmela wouldn't stop crying. Once my mother went out to find my father. When she came back she was crying. I thought she was crying because my father was dead but she was crying because she didn't know what to do.

"A lot of the people were leaving. They were leaving because the people from the other villages said the army would kill everybody who had been for the Socialists. If you had been with the people at the Casa del Pueblo, they would kill you, they said. They said there were *regulares,* the Arab soldiers, and they killed people with their knives. One woman told my mother that in Lora del Río they nailed a baby to the door. She got all her news from the charcoal man who listened to Radio Madrid at the Casa del Pueblo. I don't know if it was true, but that was the kind of thing people said in those times.

"Maybe my mother wanted to leave. But how could my mother leave? Manolo was just born. The baby Carmela couldn't walk. So my mother couldn't leave. She had to stay. Maybe that's why she was crying that night.

"Everybody was running around the streets. They were all yelling at each other. Nobody knew what was happening. There was no electricity in the town that night, only candles.

"I woke up sometime in the night. It was dark, and I could hear the sound of feet running along the alley outside. I heard men pounding on the doors in the *calle,* calling everybody to come out, yelling 'They are coming, they are coming.' The sound of the men pounding on the doors kept coming up the *calle* closer to our house. Then I heard people yelling in the patio below us and someone threw open our door and yelled, 'Renco, come.'

"My father got up and put on his leather jacket and his work shoes. He kissed each of us. He picked up Manolo who was his last son and hugged him. To me he said, *'Ya vuelvo,* Angelita, I'll see you again.' Then he went out.

"For a long time I could hear the sound of the men running in the *calle.* Then the sound faded away and I couldn't hear anything any more. The only sound left that I could hear was the cries of my mother sobbing alone in the darkness."

*   *   *

The last footfalls of Palma del Río's fleeing defenders faded away into the night. The little town, naked now before its attackers, wrapped itself in a foreboding silence like some flower folding up its petals at the first chill of evening. Nothing moved. Palma's maze of cobbled streets was empty. The houses rising so abruptly from those streets seemed to huddle together, fragile and forlorn, their whitewashed brilliance softened to a blue-gray in the moonlight, their latticed wooden shutters drawn and barred. Abandoned to its fate like so many other Spanish villages and towns during this August of 1936, Palma waited the arrival of its new rulers.

It would be a sharply reduced Palma that would greet them. Of the community's twelve thousand inhabitants, barely four thousand remained behind this night. The rest had made the decision Angela Benítez had refused to make. They had fled. A string of shadows shuffling off through the sweltering night, they jammed the Roman bridge leading over the Guadalquivir toward the Sierra Morena and the safety of its Loyalist-held villages. Each clutched a handful of belongings knotted up in an old skirt or a burlap rag. Whining children pulled at their mothers' skirts. Women toted their infants on their backs like knapsacks. A handful of elderly men marched with the column, limping along in dignified and stoic silence. The privileged few creaked off in donkey carts, their frail vans bending under their hastily assembled loads.

Suddenly the insistent honking of an automobile horn rang out from behind the silent column: the car's swift advance forced the refugees to stumble aside to the ditches beside the road. Those already on the bridge threw themselves against its stone parapet to let the black form brush past. As its silhouette disappeared into the darkness, a sullen murmur rose from the refugees on the bridge. It was the Packard of Pepe Martínez. Inside, riding off to safety in comfort, was the young man who had so proudly appropriated it thirty-nine days earlier. Juan de España, too, was fleeing the town over whose destiny he had briefly presided.

The first Nationalist troops cautiously picked their way into the deserted town along the Calle Ancha, sliding like spiders along the whitewashed buildings rising from its cobbles. Wary of the silence and lack of resistance, they edged tentatively toward the empty town hall, its walls still bearing the slogans of Juan de España's revolutionary reign. Once there, they realized Palma del Río had been abandoned by its defenders. They broke into a noisy celebration. The rest of their column, alerted by their shouts, poured into Palma behind them.

A handful of pale and haggard Palmeños hailed their arrival: the community's rightists who had escaped Juan de España's proletarian revenge by hiding for weeks in cellars or in closets. The rest of the town huddled behind shuttered windows, cowering in their dark and silent hovels, waiting to find out what punishment Palma's liberators would reserve for them. Their wait would not be long.

A black and dirty automobile rolled into town behind the mob of armed civilians flooding down Palma's streets. Its principal occupant sat slumped against its back seat, his eyes red with fatigue and anger, plotting perhaps the answer to the question haunting so many Palmeños.

The car slowed to a stop in front of Palma's town hall. Its occupant abruptly sat up, then leaped to the sidewalk. An angry curse echoed through the little town hall square.

"My bulls," rasped a furious voice. "They killed my bulls. I'll kill ten of them for each one they slaughtered."

Don Félix Moreno had come home to Palma del Río.

Two teen-age civil guardsmen kicked in the wooden door with their feet. "Your husband," they shouted at Ángela Benítez. "Where's your husband?" The frightened woman sat whimpering on her bed, her children cowering around her. She shrugged her shoulders in a despairing reply, almost the only reply she was capable of giving. "He's gone," she mumbled.

For the next hour the frightened Benítez family could hear other doors being banged open all along the Calle Ancha. Armed civil guards and Falangists were swarming through the town, smashing down its closed doors and driving out the men who had not fled Palma; these were escorted to the town hall for identification.

On the Calle Portada, a few yards from the Benítez family home, José Sánchez, a twenty-year-old farmhand on leave from the army, and Juan Olivero, a tailor's assistant, joined the herd of men being prodded toward the town hall. By midmorning there were almost six hundred of them packing the town hall square and the *calles* feeding into it. The civil guards drove them into one long line stretching from the square to the edge of the town. Sánchez and Olivero found themselves side by side near the head of the line. Like most of the men around them, they had no

83

special crime with which to reproach themselves. They had consumed with delight their allotted share of the steaks from Don Félix Moreno's bulls. They had watched without protesting as the flames had destroyed Palma's churches, but they had not fought in Juan de España's militia nor had they participated in his brief rule. The men who had were already miles away, fleeing along the banks of the Guadalquivir. Thus it was with relatively easy consciences that the two men waited out the morning quietly reviewing the events that had shaken Palma del Río in the past few hours.

Their chatter was interrupted by a sight that stilled for a moment their idle talk. Two soldiers carrying a machine gun marched down the column toward the Church of the Assumption. A minute later, a second, far more terrifying sight reduced them to silence. At the far end of their column Olivero and Sánchez recognized the red and angry face of Don Félix Moreno.

Don Félix was slowly stalking his way toward them, working his way up the line of cowed and trembling men. In his right hand he carried a wooden switch, which he swatted nervously against his trouser legs. He stopped before every face in the line, studying for an instant the terrified stare of each of these men, all of whom had, at one time or another, bent their backs to his foremen's commands. Occasionally he paused. Then, with a flick of his switch, he thrust a worker from the line and ordered him into a second, shorter column building up behind him as he advanced. The Martínez brothers, the town's other landowners, followed him, repeating the process.

Too terrified now to talk, Olivero and Sánchez followed Don Félix's progress up the line. Each time his angry stick drove one of their friends into his second, sinister column a burst of anguish spread through the two simple men. They could not imagine what punishment Don Félix had reserved for the victims plucked abruptly from the line. Their minds had room for only one thought: a desperate desire that his vengeful switch pass them by. His stubby figure drew abreast of theirs. His quick, angry eyes flickered for an instant over their faces, searching for some sign only he could read. Then he passed on, and his switch chose instead to drive Sánchez's neighbor into the lengthening column behind him. Olivero's breath slid from his lungs in relief. Sánchez muttered a hasty prayer of thanks to the Virgin whose statue he had helped burn a month earlier.

Finally it was over. Don Félix shouted a command and the men driven from the main column by his switch were marched off under an armed guard. With grief Olivero and Sánchez watched them disappear; they were comforted only by their relief at having escaped Don Félix's vengeance.

"God save them," Olivero whispered to Sánchez. Now, he thought to himself, "they're going to give us armbands like those they're wearing."

He was wrong. Olivero and Sánchez had misunderstood the mathematics of Don Félix's vengeance. The men chosen for the second line were marched into the town hall, identified, issued armbands and told to return home.

As the last of them disappeared, Don Félix turned his attention back to the far longer line from which they had been taken. Again he stalked past Olivero and Sánchez, counting with his stick this time the men in the line before him. He stopped at fifty. Smacking his switch against the biceps of the fiftieth man, he barked *"Al corralón*—to the corral."

Flanked by armed civil guardsmen, the fifty men thus counted off were marched through the Town Hall Square and down a little alley running toward the Church of the Assumption.

Their guards marched the group up a narrow flight of stairs. There they were herded through a passageway running along the rim of Don Félix's winter palace. It led to a second flight of stairs, this one descending into the *corralón.* As they emerged from the passageway, the prisoners could see straight ahead, rising over the *corralón's* whitewashed walls, the red stone tower of the Church of the Assumption. Running parallel to its rim was a fragment of Palma's once proud Arab wall, its edges a decayed and rounded heap of dirt and stone speckled with bright-blue *azulejos.* The *corralón* itself was empty except for one corner. There, guarded by two soldiers, its barrel trained on the wall opposite, was the machine gun Olivero and Sánchez had noted disappearing down their column an hour earlier.

"The first twenty-five," yelled Don Félix. At his words, the civil guards fell on the first men straggling down the steps into the enclosed square. Prodding them with rifle butts and kicks, the guards drove them up against the whitewashed wall, covered by the waiting machine gun. In those seconds of noise and confusion, these men who had been driven from their homes to be identified at the town hall suddenly understood what was about to happen to them. Some screamed. Some burst into tears or hurled themselves, sobbing for pity, at Don Félix's feet. One fainted; he was carried across the courtyard by a civil guardsman and propped up into a sitting position against the wall. Olivero and Sánchez, at the top of the stairway leading down to the *corralón,* stared in dumb terror at the sight below. Sánchez heard one man yell, "Don Félix, Don Félix, not me! For the love of God, I've done nothing wrong." Moreno stepped up to him and stared at the speaker's face.

"Your father was a good man," he spat at him. "You, you're rabble. Die."

Another, younger voice shrieked to him, "Godfather, godfather, save me! Get me out of here!" Don Félix moved over to the voice's teen-age owner. He was indeed his godson, one of the many he had sponsored under Andalusian tradition, the offspring of his field workers. Looking at this youth he had held in his arms as an infant, Don Félix snarled an abrupt accusation at him. "You worked for the anarchists," he said, and walked away.

Don Félix stepped back from the line of men against the wall, some shocked to silence, some sobbing, some shouting to him for forgiveness. He turned to the soldiers crouched behind their machine gun.

"Fuego," he ordered.

The clanging metallic roar of the machine gun beat against Sánchez's ears. His head shook with its reverberations. He watched the gun pick its way along the wall from left to right. It moved very slowly, chest-high, its bullets tearing puffs of white mortar from the wall exposed between its victims. He saw them fall, these men whose sweat and sorrow he had so often shared, their bodies twitching in disjointed movements as the machine gun's cartridges tore them apart. Then it was over. The echo of the machine gun hung for an instant on the still, stifling air of midday. From the heap of men at the base of the wall a new sound rose to join it, the pathetic groans of the dying. Some of their bodies jerked their way toward death with a few last convulsive fits of energy. Sanchez saw an officer kick his way through that pile of bodies, firing a rapid *coup de grâce* into each form that moved or from which rose a last dying protest.

When he had finished, Don Félix turned to the remaining twenty-five huddled on the stairs.

"The rest," he commanded.

Petrified by the shock of what he had just seen, Sánchez was too terrified to talk or resist. He found himself being shoved by a civil guardsman toward the bullet-pocked wall against which his friends had just died. Then, behind him, he heard a voice. It was Olivero's.

"Don Félix, Don Félix," he cried, "I'm your cousin. Save me." Moreno turned toward his voice. Olivero shouted out his name. He was indeed a distant kinsman of Palma's great landowner, too distant for Don Félix to have recognized him in the lineup but close enough to arouse his charity. With a swat of his switch, Don Félix ordered Olivero from the line.

Sánchez watched his companion give him a last agonized look, then turn and run back to safety up the steps they'd just descended. Behind him a rifle butt thumped against his shoulder blades and sent him tumbling forward. Lurching toward the wall, he almost fell over the still-bleeding bodies at his feet. As he turned to face the machine gun, his mind, frozen with fear until now, began to function again. He realized he had in his pocket a piece of paper that might save his own life: his leave orders from his regiment. He burst away from the wall and flung himself at the officer who a few minutes before had put a bullet through the heads of so many of his friends.

"I'm a soldier," he cried, waving the paper at the officer. "Save me!" The officer examined his orders. Recognizing them as valid, he told a civil guard to take Sánchez to the town hall. Once out of the *corralón,* Sánchez, his state of shock now thoroughly broken, bolted away from his guard, vaulted a wall and sprinted into the fields beyond. Seconds later, falling exhausted at the base of a eucalyptus tree, he heard the first sharp reports of the machine gun that had been meant to kill him.

Few were those who shared with Olivero and Sánchez the blessing of a last-minute reprieve from Don Félix's vengeance. Ángel Gómez, a farm worker, the father of four children, recognized the man behind the machine gun as he was being driven to the wall. It was his brother. "Pablo, help!" he cried.

The brother, taking advantage of the confusion, helped him escape. A second farm worker, Manuel Díaz, was saved on his way to the wall by the *mayoral* of the ranch on which he worked. The *mayoral* realized Díaz had been mistaken for his anarchist brother. Once outside, Díaz was rearrested by Falangists looking for that brother and sent back to the *corralón.* Three times he was driven before the machine gun of Don Félix's firing squad. And three times he was saved by his foreman.

Soon the disordered pile of corpses sprawled in front of the *corralón's* wall was so thick that the executions had to be suspended. The men waiting to be shot were ordered to clear the bodies of their dead comrades from the patio floor and load them onto trucks. In a grotesque caravan the trucks carted the dead down the Calle Ancha, past the Benítez home, to the white-walled cemetery of San Juan Bautista, lying at the end of an alley of eucalyptus trees half a mile from Palma's gates.

As those trucks coughed and sputtered down the Calle Ancha, women peered from behind their shuttered windows, watching in horror as the piles of corpses disappeared toward the cemetery. As the trucks swayed past their windows, some of them glimpsed the lifeless forms of husbands or sons stacked among their ghastly cargoes.

Alarmed, the women began to rush to the town hall square to plead for the lives of their men. They were driven back by the Guardia Civil. Those who protested were seized and pulled into the town hall, where their heads were shaved. Some, recognized as the wives of anarchists or strike leaders, were offered a more novel punishment: they were forced to eat bread soaked in castor oil "to purge them of their republicanism."

After all the bodies of the first wave of victims had been carted from the *corralón* to the cemetery, the executions began again. This time a priest was at hand. Unable to confess eacn man separately, he offered a general absolution as each lot of prisoners was forced up against the wall of the *corralón*. By now, none of the men waiting outside had any illusions about receiving armbands from their captors or having their identities checked. The scenes that accompanied their execution became so painful that the Spanish soldiers manning the machine gun had to be replaced by Moroccans.

Some prisoners fought with the guards. Others shrieked their innocence at Don Félix and his fellow landowners. A few had to be clubbed half senseless by their captors before they could be dragged to the wall. There, already dying, they were jacked up like broken cornstalks to await the machine gun's volley. All afternoon the executions continued until the blood splashing the surface of the *corralón* had melted its hard earth into a dark mud, an atonement in kind for the blood of each Saltillo bull killed in the pastures of Don Félix Moreno.

At sunset it was over. The last angry echo of the machine gun died in Palma's cobbled streets. In its place, a heavy, agonized silence settled upon the town. The entire population seemed paralyzed with horror at what had happened, too numb, even, for tears of mourning. Its poor, like the Benítez family, clung together in terror in their darkened homes.

Only in the cemetery was there activity that night. There, on the same hallowed ground where barely four days earlier Don Juan Navas had prophesied to Juan de España's firing squad that "blood shall beget blood," a group of prisoners labored by lantern light. They shoveled the dirt back into a trench thirty feet long and seven feet wide. Stacked in that hole in uneven rows were the victims of Don Félix's machine gun, the sad vindication of their parish priest's dying prophecy.

A few feet from their common trench, at the outer limits of the flickering orange light cast by the gravediggers' lamps, was the white silhouette of a family mausoleum. Three generations of Morenos slept behind its slender peristyle. Twenty-seven years later, Don Félix himself would come to take his assigned place in the mausoleum, and begin his eternal rest in his town graveyard beside the victims of his wrath of an August afternoon. No one would ever know how many men lay in the trench beyond his family mausoleum. The machine gunners of the *corralón* had not stopped to count their victims. Later years would estimate their numbers at between two and three hundred men. One thing, however, was certain: few of Palma's revolutionaries were among them. They were the town's dumb and downtrodden, numbed by their labors, the men who had marched blindly behind Juan de España's red banners and stayed behind to pay for his hopeful follies. In the terminology of the *fiesta brava* whose bulls he had sought to avenge, Don Félix Moreno had "killed the *mansos*," the castrated steers, the ignorant and ineffectual shepherds of the enemy he had sought.

Thus the little Andalusian town of Palma del Río was liberated. For a generation to come, Palma del Río would be scarred by the brutal slaughter of this summer day. The savagery that stalked her streets in August 1936 was by no means, however, her special privilege. Rare were the cities and villages of Spain spared similar sufferings in the cruel summer of 1936 when the Spanish people lost their reason.*

* For Palma del Río, with its population of 12,000 people, the loss of perhaps 350 of its sons in the opening weeks of the war was not out of proportion with the losses endured by the Spanish nation as a whole during that same period. Probably 75,000 people, among them almost 8,000 priests, monks and nuns, were killed by the Loyalists between July 18, 1936 and early September. The number killed by the Nationalists in those weeks of vengeance is more difficult to establish. It lay, probably, somewhere between 75,000 and 100,000.

In Palma, the passions of July and August abated with the first cool breath of autumn. The front stabilized about sixty miles to the east and the north of Palma, and life in the village returned to something approaching normality.

Living was, however, extremely precarious for those families in Palma in which a breadwinner had died, or disappeared with the militia of Juan de España. There was little work, and that little was not shared with women like Ángela Benítez of the Calle Ancha, the wife of a Loyalist partisan. For Señora Benítez, with four children and her four-month-old infant Manuel to feed, life in Palma soon became untenable. By September the family was on the edge of starvation. The only work Ángela Benítez could find was an occasional house to whitewash or bundle of laundry to beat clean upon the banks of the Guadalquivir. She was without news of her husband, unaware of whether he was still alive or already a victim of the storm shaking her nation. Finally, on an evening in late September, what protection Providence had offered ran out for Ángela Benítez. That night her five crying children consumed the last scrap of food she possessed.

To save her situation, she abandoned Palma del Río and made her way north to the Sierra Morena, the ridge of mountains separating Andalusia from the Mancha. A treasure trove of minerals lay under the Sierra Morena's arid flanks. Those minerals and a terrain ideally suited for defense made the Sierra Morena a natural battleground for Spain's warring armies. For three years Franco's legions and the Republic's brigades would struggle along that skyline north of Palma del Río for the Sierra's mines, for the narrow-gauge railways spiraling down its flanks, and for the desolate mining towns huddling on its slopes.

One of those isolated communities was called Pueblo Nuevo del Terrible. It sat upon the richest deposit of anthracite in the south of Spain, a vein first laid bare by the scratchings of a hound dog known as *"Terrible,"* whose name had been given to the town by its grateful citizens. At the end of September 1936, the front stabilized at Pueblo Nuevo del Terrible's doorstep. Captured by Franco's forces after a bitter fight, the town, and a strange pillar of rock capped by an Arab tower on its outskirts, constituted a troublesome wedge in the Republic's lines. Day after day, the Republic's artillery and aviation bombarded the town. Yet it was to Pueblo Nuevo that Ángela Benítez brought her hungry brood in her desperate search for work. Once there, she pushed aside whatever political sympathies she might have had and took the only job she could find. She went to work as a scullery maid in the officers' mess of a Nationalist artillery regiment.

There she and her family lived in a pair of stone huts, huddled side by side on an unpaved road behind the town. One of the huts had already been partially destroyed by a stray shell. Neither had any glass left in its windows. Only one member of the family had a bed. It was the baby Manuel. He was fitted into an old wooden crate found on the premises. The rest of the Benítez would spend their nights in Pueblo Nuevo sleeping on a dirt floor.

Ángela Benítez's first weeks of service were harsh and painful ones. She was alone in a strange town, separated from her parents; she did not know whether her husband was alive or dead. She often cried herself to sleep in the chill stillness of the Benítez family's newest hovel.

Her two eldest daughters, Angelita and Encarna, soon joined her in the kitchen. For Angelita, the long, punishing hours in the regimental mess were just a continuation of the life of drudgery that had been hers for some time. For Encarna, they marked the end of childhood. She was six years old. In a few months her girlish hands would rival those of her mother in the thickness of their calluses and the roughness of their skin.

Each night, the two girls plodded back and forth between the kitchen and the mess, meekly setting before the officers the food prepared for them by their mother. Often, between courses, they listened in childish awe as their employers reviewed the fighting of the day and the part their guns had played in it. Sometimes their mother, sliding shyly to the door of her kitchen, listened too. The triumphs those men recounted between morsels of Ángela Benítez's cooking were almost exclusively concerned with their efforts to shell a unit of Loyalist soldiers, the Republic's 141st Brigade, off a ridge just north of the town. Those Loyalists defended the two French 140-millimeter cannons, nicknamed "Felipe" and "La Leona," that regularly devastated the supply columns moving into Pueblo Nuevo. Daily, as autumn ran to winter, the guns of the artillery regiment Ángela Benítez served tore apart the Republican positions, sending a regular flow of dead and wounded to the Loyalist rear. Like every other woman in Pueblo Nuevo, Ángela Benítez prayed regularly

91

that her employers' guns would silence "Felipe" and "La Leona," and stay the stream of Loyalist shells menacing her life and that of her infants playing in their stone hovel on the outskirts of town.

Happily, Ángela Benítez did not realize the ironic reality that underlay her wish. Unknowingly, she and her family were a sad and specific example of the divisions civil war had drawn through the heart of Spain. At the other end of the trajectory of the guns whose cannoneers she nourished, among the soldiers of the Republic's 141st Brigade, was a new recruit, her husband José Benítez.

As the Benítez family settled into its new life in the beleaguered community of Pueblo Nuevo, the war that had forced them there settled, too, into a new pattern. Franco's hopes of a quick victory had depended on the rapid capture of Madrid. On November 7, twenty thousand Nationalist troops, backed up by Italian and German armor, attacked the capital. Its barricaded streets were defended by an enormous but underarmed and poorly trained mass of workers shouting the battle cry of La Pasionaria: *"No pasarán*—they shall not pass." The city's defenders wavered, fell back, then held again. After twenty-four hours of violent combat, help arrived. Singing the "Internationale," the first of the Republic's storied International Brigades marched through Madrid to take its place on the barricades. Frenchmen, Germans, Poles, Englishmen, Slavs, Italians, Americans followed to add their accents to those of the Spaniards shouting *"No pasarán."*

Franco's attack failed, and its failure ended the first phase of the Civil War. The war lost the mobility that had marked its opening months, and it settled instead into a slow, exhausting struggle.

Both sides looked abroad for help to break the deadlock facing them. Franco turned to Germany and Italy. The Republic looked first to France and England, only to be thwarted by the policy of nonintervention. Thus frustrated, the Loyalist government was forced to rely on the Soviet Union and Europe's Communist parties for help.

The combatants' calls for help turned the Civil War into an international conflict. Men and materiel poured into Spain to reinforce both sides. With them came the professional artisans of warfare, determined to use Spain's agony as the testing ground for the tactics and machinery they had molded for the conflict they knew must soon engulf Europe.

The influx of foreign aid to both sides did little, however, to alter the stalemate into which the war had fallen. As the weeks turned to months, and the months to years, it remained what it had become at the end of 1936: a slow, painful, costly war of attrition.

For the family of Ángela Benítez, the long and wearing months of the war at Pueblo Nuevo were not, despite the family's proximity to the front line, unbearable ones. They were marred by the terror of errant artillery shells and the void created in the family by the absence of José Benítez. But they had brought the family an unexpected compensation. They had enough to eat. The leftovers from the officers' mess in which Ángela and her two eldest daughters worked provided the family a source of nourishment Palma del Río could never have offered.

Every night before leaving the mess, Ángela Benítez performed a little ritual. She wrapped up in an old newspaper the scraps which would sustain her three youngest children through another day: a few crusts of stale bread softened by a brief immersion in a bowl of olive oil, a few cold potatoes, a piece of lard, an occasional twist of sausage. Sometimes a certain bluff soldier from the regiment she served would slip a square of chocolate into Ángela Benítez's palm as she wrapped her nightly bundle. She brought it to her children in triumph, as though that modest gift might efface all the sufferings of their young lives.

Her jovial benefactor was, during those somber days, a figure of considerable importance in the regiment. He supplied the officers' mess. His name was Rafael Sánchez, "El Pipo," and for El Pipo the war was a very good deal.

EL PIPO'S STORY

"Look, in a war, there are guys who are made to be heroes and guys who look out for their own skin. Me, I'm one of the second kind. I wasn't cut out to be a hero. Patriotism and all that, these ideas always seemed childish to me. Not that I don't love my country. I do. I wouldn't live anyplace else. But from that, to go out and get your head shot off, *poff,* like that, with a flower popping out of your gun and a big smile on your face, there's a big difference, believe me, a big difference. So when all of a sudden I found myself a gunner in the third battery of

93

the First Heavy Artillery Regiment, I said to myself, 'Rafael Sánchez, this war isn't for you.'

"Besides, just looking at those lousy Italians fighting with us made me sick to my stomach. So one day I went to see the commander. I said to him, 'Look, Major, it's all very fine to make war, but to make war well, you've got to eat and drink well. You, you take care of the war. Let me, Rafael Sánchez, take care of the food and drink.'

"He thought about it for a few minutes, then he said to me, '*De acuerdo*. But if it doesn't work well, I'll shoot you.' As he said that, he made a little sign to let me know what he meant. I said, 'Don't worry, Major.'

"Still, it was a risky deal. But as we say in Andalusia, I had broad shoulders. My father was the King of the Shellfish in Andalusia and I'd known the score for a long time. In 1920 my father bought a little seafood shop in Córdoba, on the Calle de la Plata. That shop became famous for its shellfish. My father had begun selling ice cream from a cart on the streets of Córdoba. Then he decided to sell little baskets of raw shrimps instead. One day he got this bright idea to cook the shrimps before he sold them. That idea made him a rich man. That's how he bought his shop in the Calle de la Plata.

"From the time I was a kid, my father taught me about business. It didn't take much teaching. Business was in my blood. By the time I learned how to count, I was working behind the counter of his shop. The shop worked so well we opened up a second one at Bélmez, a mining town in the Sierra Morena near Pueblo Nuevo. We called it 'El Puerto' like the shop in Córdoba. We started to sell wine, sherry, lemonade there too. It worked so well we began to open up other shops all through the Sierra Morena, in Peñarroya, Monterrubio, Cabeza de Buey, Pueblo Nuevo del Terrible.

"I ran the whole thing myself. In an old pickup truck I wandered up and down those mountain roads, checking up on the business, keeping the shops stocked with alcohol and shellfish. I put someone from the family in charge of each shop until we had so many I started to run out of brothers, cousins and uncles.

"When the war began, I had a regular empire. It covered all of a part of Andalusia. All those revolutions, the changes of regime, the troubles we had in Spain in those years, didn't stop people from eating and certainly not from drinking. But the war, that was something else. The war meant bombing, people robbing you, getting killed, things like that. Still, I was lucky. The army I was mobilized in occupied all the towns in which I had shops during its attack in the summer of '36. I'd seen trouble coming, and I'd stuffed those shops with everything I could get my hands on. I figured if I could just find a way to get around, then I could make a fortune. That's where my idea of supplying the battery mess came from.

"I can tell you the First Artillery Regiment ought to have been proud of gunner Rafael Sánchez, El Pipo. For two years not a canteen, not a mess of the regiment, ever ran short of wine, sherry or aguardiente. In my old pickup truck—the same one I had before the war, only camouflaged this time with khaki paint—I set out on those roads again. I drove from town to town through all those places I knew so well, keeping our units supplied.

"Naturally, at the same time I kept an eye on my own business. I changed the seafood shops into bistros where our officers could eat and drink and have a little fun. Those cellars I'd stocked before the war began to pour out all sorts of things you couldn't buy anywhere else. So you see, in the middle of all that madness, Rafael Sánchez had kept a clear head. The war could have gone on for ten years. I had it all figured out.

"There was only one thing I hadn't counted on. It hit me, I'll always remember the date, December 15, 1938. I was sleeping that night in Pueblo Nuevo. Just before dawn a whole series of explosions shook me out of bed. I groped around in the darkness for my clothes, but each time I stood up I thought the earth was shaking apart under my feet. Everybody was yelling at everybody else. I'd seen some bombardments but nothing like that, believe me. Outside, people were running around like chickens. In those few minutes our whole little world had fallen apart.

"I couldn't figure out exactly what was happening. Then I heard our commander yelling, 'They're attacking.' 'They' were the Reds.

"That news really hit me hard. It was like waking up from a dream. The Reds hadn't attacked like that for a year. Maybe, I figured, they're going to overrun us. That would mean we'd have to give up all the villages where I'd installed my little empire of bistros. I still had plenty of stocks stored in those bistros, maybe ten million pesetas' worth. If the Reds found them, they'd be destroyed or stolen. Me, I'd be ruined.

95

"But Rafael Sánchez wouldn't have been the man people said he was if he didn't know how to triumph over adversity. I said to myself, 'Rafael Sánchez, either you get those stocks or the Reds do.'

"I jumped into my truck, still half dressed despite the cold. I raced off right through the middle of the bombardment for Peñarroya where I had one of my biggest bistros. I figured that was the one the Reds would get first because it was closest to their lines. Going out of Pueblo Nuevo, I ran into a group of soldiers stringing telephone wire. One of them was a good friend of mine. He was a skinny kid all bone and angles. You'd never know it to look at him, but in civilian life he was a bullfighter. He'd just begun then as a *novillero,* and nobody knew who he was in those days, but I knew he had a great career ahead of him. His name was Manolete.

" 'Hola, Rafael,' he yelled, 'where are you going?'

" 'Peñarroya,' I said.

" 'Are you crazy? There's nobody left there,' he said. 'We're retreating. We're going to blow up our guns.'

"Well, it was going to take more than that to stop me from going after that stuff.

" 'Come on,' I shouted to Manolete. 'Instead of acting like a jerk and putting down that wire that's never going to go anyplace, come with me.' I explained to him what I was going to Peñarroya for. Well, I can still see him with that strange smile of his looking up at me. He was thinner than ever and the sleeves of his uniform were too long. They hung down to his knuckles. He dropped the wire he was unrolling and got in beside me.

"Twenty minutes later we were in Peñarroya. The city was completely empty when we got to my bistro El Puerto. Nothing had been touched. The Reds hadn't arrived yet. Tough luck for them. That cellar was crammed with sherry, anise, cognac, beer. Half a million pesetas' worth we took out. That night we unloaded it in the cellar of my shop in Córdoba.

"After that, Manolo and I did the same thing every day until we'd cleaned out the cellars of every one of my bistros that was in danger. It was one of the real miracles of the war I managed to save just about all of my stocks.

"By the time we'd cleaned out all those cellars, the Reds had been stopped anyway. Then they were pushed back into the sierras. You could see the Republic was finished. They were just falling apart, like that. You could see the war was just about over.

"Six months later, on the second of July 1939, I was in a *barrera de sombra* seat at the Real Maestranza in Seville watching my friend take his *alternativa* from the great matador, Chicuelo. That summer, in my new Studebaker President, I followed Manolete from ring to ring, riding along the road to glory with him. I was rich. For me, the good life was just beginning."

*　*　*

Pleasure, however, is a fleeting thing, and the good life of ex-gunner Rafael Sánchez lasted but a summer, the time to squander in the footsteps of Manolete the fortune he had amassed in the war-torn villages of the Sierra Morena. Nevertheless he would build other fortunes, which he would cast away with equal delight, for Rafael Sánchez was a man of many resources. The last and most important of these fortunes he would amass a quarter of a century hence from the courage of the infant son to whose mother he had offered, in the mess of Pueblo Nuevo del Terrible, the occasional charity of a tablet of chocolate.

*　*　*

Rare, however, were the Spaniards for whom the war ended with prospects as pleasant as those facing the former supply specialist of the First Heavy Artillery Regiment. As Rafael Sánchez had so astutely observed, the Republic had begun to unravel. First, the International Brigades paraded out of Barcelona, marking with their departing footsteps the almost total isolation of Spain's dying Republic. They left in a rain of flowers and tears, sped to the French frontier by a last stirring speech of La Pasionaria.

"Go proudly," she called to their fading figures. "You are legend. You are history. We shall never forget you."

Ten thousand of that foreign legion, a quarter of those who had found their way to Spain, stayed behind, embraced forever in the soil of the nation they had sought to defend.

Defeat now followed defeat for the Republic. On January 26, 1939,

Barcelona fell. Two months later, after two years, four months and twenty-one days of furious resistance, Madrid was captured. As Franco's first troops marched down its broad avenues, the Nationalists who had hidden during all the long months waiting for this day crowded the capital's balconies and sidewalks. Over and over again they chanted an ecstatic phrase, an exultant reply to the words that had so often haunted their hiding places: *"Han pasado, han pasado*—they have passed."

With Madrid's fall, Franco's victory was only hours away. The last Republican government fled Valencia. The front simply dissolved as thousands of Loyalist soldiers threw away their arms and started trudging back to the villages they had abandoned in haste three years earlier. On March 31, 1939, Almería, Murcia and Cartagena, the last cities in Loyalist hands, fell to the Nationalists. They represented, those cities, the last olives that Franco, in a humid Casablanca hotel room, had predicted, his forces would have to pluck one by one. That evening an aide slid quietly into General Franco's office to announce that his Nationalist armies had occupied the last of their objectives.

"Very good," said Franco, without looking up from the work spread out before him on his desk. "Many thanks."

The Spanish Civil War was over.

*　　*　　*

Approximately six hundred thousand Spaniards had died in the conflict and two million more were wounded or mutilated. Half a million homes were destroyed or damaged. One hundred and eighty-three towns were devastated, two thousand churches burned, a third of the nation's livestock slaughtered, almost half her railroad equipment destroyed. Worse still was the moral and spiritual price Spain would pay for those three years of warfare. Decades would be required to heal the hatreds that conflict had buried in the Spanish soul and to erase the psychological heritage of a fratricidal war whose ferocity surpassed that of most international struggles. Nor would the victors hasten the moment of reconciliation with any display of charity for the vanquished. A hundred thousand Spaniards would be shot in the weeks to come, and two million more shunted off to jails and concentration camps.

Now the millions of Spaniards displaced by the war threw themselves back upon the roads over which they had fled as refugees three years earlier. For many, that long trek back home would end before a devastated doorstep, and for others, the desperate search for a missing relative on the threshold of an ill-marked grave.

*   *   *

Ángela Benítez, too, started back to Palma del Río. Trembling with cold, huddling in the open van of a truck, she watched with emotion as the shell-scarred rooftops of the town in which she had spent three years of her life faded behind her. In her arms she cradled her youngest son, Manolo, so accustomed to the rigors of their life that at the age of three, as his sisters recalled, he had "already forgotten how to cry."

For Ángela Benítez, this return to Palma del Río was almost as much of a voyage into the unknown as her flight from the town had been three years before. Like so many other women wandering over the roads of Spain, Ángela Benítez did not know what awaited her in her hometown, or whether the husband who had left her side in the summer of 1936 was alive or dead.

Haggard, dirty, half starving, hobbling with still-fresh wounds, the men came home. Some came on crutches, with empty sleeves dangling from their shoulders, or broken faces, testimony that those Palmeños had left pieces of themselves behind, before Madrid, along the Ebro or in the Sierra Morena. They came riding in the vans of passing trucks, on foot, in the rare trains that shuttled through Palma's station. Broken and beaten men, those survivors of Juan de España's militia stared with anxious eyes at the beckoning roofs of the town before them. For many of them, that comforting glimpse of Palma's tiled rooftops would be the only view they would have of their hometown.

The Guardia Civil met every train stopping at Palma. At the city's outskirts they checked everyone coming back to the town on foot or by truck. Those whose names figured on their list of "enemies of the regime" were immediately arrested. Twice a day an aging bus carried the men thus seized to Córdoba. There they were given a summary judgment. Those whose alleged crimes appeared to be substantial were condemned to death by a military tribunal. They were shot the same night

99

they were judged, lined up against the wall of the city's Miraflores prison. The rest were sent to spend their strength in the work camps which Franco's Spain had created to punish and rehabilitate its former foes.

José Benítez, the quiet waiter of Niño Valles' café, was fortunate. His name did not figure on the Guardia Civil's list. He was allowed to go home to his wife and children on the Calle Ancha. There was a joyous reunion, but there would be few joyous tomorrows to follow it. Forty-eight hours after José's return, some zealous informer rectified the oversight on the Guardia Civil's list. He too was arrested and cast into one of the endless prison convoys heading for Córdoba's prison. José Benítez would never come back to Palma del Río, nor would he see again the infant son whose birth on the eve of the Civil War had brought a fleeting moment of happiness to his poor life.

Many others would not return at all, not even for the brief forty-eight hours Providence had accorded José Benítez. The list of the dead and executed, posted to the doors of Palma's town hall, daily grew longer.

Palma's living had little time or strength, however, to long mourn their dead. After the horror of war another trial fell upon Spain, famine. Cut off from the world by the outbreak of World War Two, obliged to surrender to her German and Italian debtors a substantial share of her shattered economy's slender yield, Spain was driven to her knees by a final curse, drought. For two years, as if the nation labored under some Old Testament judgment for the spilling of fraternal blood, that pitiless drought shriveled the fields of Spain and brought the Spanish people to the edge of starvation.

As everywhere else in Spain, those in Palma del Río who suffered most were the very young and the very old. For the very old there was little solace beyond that which memories might provide. The young in Palma, at least, had one source of relief for their misery. They had a benefactor. His name was Don Carlos Sánchez. He was a priest, the prewar pastor of the Church of Santa Clara, now the successor of Don Juan Navas, who had been shot by Juan de España's men in the town graveyard.

DON CARLOS SÁNCHEZ'S STORY

"EACH DAY, I tucked a few pieces of candy into my cassock. Then I took a brass Mass bell from the church. Like a Pied Piper, I set out walking through the *calles,* ringing my Mass bell. The kids would hear the bell and come out from wherever they were hiding, some of them afraid of me, some as bold as baby bulls. I gave them what candy I had, and I talked to them. Every day I went out like that, walking up and down the alleys of the town, ringing my bell and looking for the children. They lived like savages, like packs of little rats.

"Most of them were children of the Reds and they had heard so many bad things about the Church and about priests that in the beginning they were afraid of me. This saddest problem from a human standpoint was the children whose parents had disappeared, or the children who'd been abandoned by the roadside during the flight in 1936 because they couldn't keep up with their parents. We had dozens like that. They just grew up here without ever knowing who they were or where they came from. Somehow, they survived the war, begging, stealing, sleeping in the fields or hiding in the houses of people who had run away.

"When I came back to Palma, I was told to take care of them. I was told to get them into a school and out of the streets and the fields. The first problem was finding them. So day after day I wandered through the town with my brass bell and my candies, taking a census of our stray children.

"When I had located them all, I had to find a place to put my orphanage. I decided to use the old Convent of Santa Clara. The Reds had burned the convent in 1936, but these old stone buildings are strong, and its walls and ceilings were still good. I got some of the older children and we cleaned it out. We shored up the timbers that had been damaged by the fire and whitewashed the walls and ceilings.

"I made an oven so we could bake our own bread whenever we could find wheat. Then I went to Córdoba and I got the provincial governor to promise me an allowance of fifty céntimos a day for each child. Our terrible problem was food. The fifty céntimos a day I had to feed the children was hardly enough for a field mouse. The famine was upon us. The two staples of our diet were chick peas and bread, and they were the

101

hardest things of all to find. To find just a handful of wheat, I had to walk for hours. I looked everywhere then, everywhere I could, for enough food to feed my children for even one day.

"If I had any money I'd try to buy what I could on the black market. Most of the time, I would hang a burlap sack over my shoulders and walk from village to village begging for my children.

"Sometimes I would ask a miller if I could sweep the floor of his granary. I would dump whatever I could get that way into the sack. Sometimes I would go to the farms where the farmers were beating out the grain from the wheat stalks. I would ask them to let me sweep up the floor of their threshing platform when they were through.

"Occasionally I'd take a couple of the older boys with me to help carry the sack. Once in a while, when I had some money and I expected to bring something back, I'd take an old two-wheeled donkey cart. I didn't own a donkey to go with it. The boys and I would tow the cart ourselves, tugging it along the dirt roads from farm to farm.

"Somehow, we survived. In the morning, I tried to give the kids a cup of *café con leche* and sometimes a scrap of bread to dunk in it. At noon we tried to have mashed chick peas or bean soup that I thickened with flour if I had it. At night we gave them whatever we could find. When we couldn't find anything, well, we just gave them the only other thing we had, a prayer to recite.

"I had about six hundred children all together. Perhaps seventy-five of them were orphans and lived with us. The rest came in the morning and left in the afternoon. The nuns and I taught them what we could.

"One day Ángela Benítez came to me. I already had one of her children, Carmela. The others worked. She was pulling along a little boy who was pouting and dragging his feet.

" 'He can't eat, Don Carlos,' she cried. 'Take him. Maybe you can do something with him. His name is Manolo.' He was a shy boy who tended to slouch and drag his feet along behind him. They already called him El Renco—the limper—after his father and grandfather. Snot seemed to run down his face from his nose like water from a faucet, and it just hung there unless one of my nuns came along to wipe it off.

"From the beginning, you could see he was popular with the other kids. In the morning, at the exercise period, I'd hear them giggling; 'El Renco's here!' they'd say. Then I'd look down that line of little faces peering up at me until I came to his with that stream of snot always falling down from his nose and a wide, funny smile on his face.

"I often thought how good God was to let those children smile. They didn't have much to smile about in those days. The reason Manolo couldn't eat was that he was already half starved and those hunger pains gave him such a set of stomach cramps that eating was a torture for him. Dear God, we had many like him then. We have always been a hungry nation, but those years—they were the hungriest and hardest years of our lives."

*   *   *

Those years would later be known, in the memory of those who suffered and survived them, as *los años del hambre,* the years of hunger. Every facet of man and nature seemed to conspire to produce the terrible, searing hunger that stalked the villages of Andalusia in the years of 1940 and 1941. Day after day, a blazing sun rolled across a blue and barren sky scorching the countryside until Andalusia's fertile fields seemed to choke for lack of rain.

The area's primitive irrigation systems had been put out of action by the war, and her farmers had to watch in helpless rage as the waters that could have saved their crops flowed unchecked down the Guadalquivir from the Sierra Morena to the sea. The untutored vengeance of the Red militia that had seized the area around Palma del Río in 1936 had been turned on any hint of mechanization in the region's great estates. Tractors, combines, threshers—all had been smashed to ruins wherever they were found, by men convinced they were part of the cause of their unhappiness. Those destroyed could not be replaced. There were no replacements. And now there was no gas for the few farm vehicles that had escaped. Nor were mules and farm horses available. They had been slaughtered by the thousands during the war to feed Spain's warring armies.

The parched earth had to be split apart by men dragging plows that were meant to be pulled by horses and oxen. Even men were lacking, idled in Spain's new prison camps or sacrificed forever in the conflict that had just closed. Without machinery, without fertilizer, without even enough willing arms, Andalusia's agriculture had, in the words of one

103

landowner, "reverted to the Middle Ages" in those postwar years.

Only the olive trees, hardened by the droughts of distant centuries, continued to produce. But their fruit, harvested under the eyes of the Guardia Civil, was all assigned to the state food organization. The organization in turn realloted a minuscule share of the harvest to local olive pressers to meet Palma's ration requirements.

As they had done for centuries, the misfortunes of Andalusia struck most cruelly at those least prepared to endure them, her landless peasants. During those years the average daily wage, when her drought-stifled estates were hiring workers, was five pesetas a day, a pittance that rendered even the black market in olive oil totally inaccessible to Palma's poor.

They turned in desperation to other expedients. On the Plaza de Abasto, the town's covered marketplace, a new commodity soon became a staple item in their diet. It was grass, wild grass cut during the night along the banks of the Guadalquivir. It was prepared by being boiled in a big kettle. To that green and glutinous mass the fortunate added a drop or two of oil or the leg of a stray dog or cat, until the day came when there were no more cats and dogs wandering the streets of Palma del Río. So widespread did the consumption of grass become during those years that a police survey in Córdoba in 1941 turned up 357 grass peddlers in the city's marketplace. Nor was grass the only staple furnished by the open spaces of Andalusia. *Tangadina,* a kind of hard and bitter wild cauliflower usually reserved for mules and horses, and *cardo,* a sort of thistle, also found their way into the cooking pots of the poor. Acorns were ground up and used to produce a brew consumed in the place of coffee. Dried leaves and the shavings of potato peels replaced tobacco.

Almost daily the mournful toll that marked the passing of another Palmeño rang out from the charred belfry of the Church of the Assumption. Familiar now was the sight of Don Carlos Sánchez hurrying down some cobbled alley, bringing to the bedside of the dying the only substitute he could offer for the food and medicine they lacked: the miracle-working statue of Palma's *patrona,* Nuestra Señora de Belén, mounted in the little glass box before which so many generations of Palmeños had prayed.

The mortality rate reached its high point during the winter and spring of 1940–1941. Hunger claimed so many victims during that period that,

104

to cover the extent of the famine, the clerks in Andalusia's town halls began to ascribe deaths from starvation to "pneumonia."

ANGELITA BENÍTEZ'S STORY

"YOU CAN NEVER understand if you've never been hungry. The hunger we had in those days after the war—sometimes even now I cry when I think about it. Then that was all you could do for it, cry. You cried when you went to bed at night because there was nothing for you to eat, and you cried in the morning when you got up because there was still nothing to eat. Your stomach hurt you so much you couldn't stand up straight. People fell down and died, just like that, in the streets of Palma then. You could see them lying there with their bellies all swollen up. They died because they had nothing to eat, but their stomachs were all swollen up as though they'd eaten too much. We had a lot of pain in our lives, but nothing, ever, like those hungry times after the war.

"My mother and I had to take care of the family. Encarna took care of the young ones while we worked. My mother found a new house for us in the Calle Belén near the Calle Ancha where we lived before we went to Pueblo Nuevo. It didn't cost as much as the other one because it didn't have a well. You had to go to get your water from the river in a jar.

"All day long my mother worked. She worked as many hours every day as my father did before the war. She did whatever work there was. If there was work in the *campo* she went to the *campo*. If it was time for the olives, she picked olives. If she could find washing to do, she washed. Sometimes she worked for fourteen hours like that, kneeling on the rocks by the river, washing. When she came home, her hands would be red and swollen and covered with cuts and her knees would bleed from kneeling all day.

"My mother was a pretty woman. She was small but she was very lively. She was a very strong woman, my mother, and she was never sick. But she wore herself out trying to keep us alive after the war. When I think of her in those times she was very thin. Her bones stuck out all over her body and her hair turned to gray. Her skin seemed to get that color, too, all gray. She was just made of pain and hunger.

"Finally a time came when there was no work at all in Palma. We had no money and we had nothing to eat except some grass. So my mother decided to take us to a place where my grandfather was working as a caretaker outside Palma. We walked out there. It took us all morning because the younger children were too weak to walk fast. My mother cooked for her father there and did his washing for him. We picked the grass and the *cardo* from the *campo* around the place he lived, and my mother boiled it all together in a kettle on his stove.

"One day while we were there at my grandfather's my mother got sick. She felt bad and she couldn't get up. She'd always been so strong but that morning she couldn't get up. Finally she did and she fell down. She fainted. They laid her down on her bed and this time she couldn't get up any more. Each time she tried she fell back down on her bed.

"My grandfather decided we had to take her back to Palma. He brought her back in a cart with an ox from the farm. We put all the things we had in beside her and we walked back to Palma behind the cart with my mother in it.

"In the morning she was worse and I went to get the public doctor, Don Rafael from the social security, the one you didn't have to pay. He was the only one we could have because we were poor. But in those times there were so many sick people in Palma Don Rafael wouldn't come. He said he would come the next day if my mother was still sick. He didn't come then either.

"Finally he came the sixth day. My mother was much worse. She had the fever and was so weak she couldn't raise her arms any more. Now I realize she had simply worn herself out trying to take care of us, trying to keep us all alive. There was just nothing left of her any more, it was all gone. But then, at that time, I thought she was just sick.

"Don Rafael looked at her for a long time and sighed. He asked her some questions, then he gave me a piece of paper. You took the paper to the town hall and you gave it to them. Then they gave you medicine for the paper and you didn't have to pay. It was aspirin. In those days that's all there was, there were no antibiotics or penicillin or things like that. There was just nothing, nothing not even in the big cities, not even in Madrid.

"That night, around five o'clock, my mother got worse. She was lying in her bed gasping for breath with a fever. We all stood around her bed looking, the children and Tía Carmen and Tía Antonia. The room smelled awful from her being sick. It was very hot that night and it smelled rotten in the room.

"We lit the candles I got from the church and we all said the rosary. My mother knew she was dying then. She was crying a little bit, not much because she was too weak to cry much. She could hardly talk any more. She kept whispering over and over, 'What's going to happen to my children? What's going to happen to my children?'

"She kept looking at us, at each one of us standing around her. Manolo was so small then, his head hardly came up over the edge of the bed. He was crying, too, but he didn't know his mother was dying. My mother looked at me and cried. I don't think she suffered then, but she was so worn from overwork and exhaustion there was nothing left inside her. It was all used up. She slid her hand down the bed to where I was. She took my hand. There was no force in her hand any more, that hand that had worked so hard. I had to hold it or it would fall.

"After a while she whispered to me, 'Angelita, Angelita, I give you your brothers and sisters. You will have to be their mother now.' A few minutes after that she was dead, and all that was left of her was that tired look on her face. She was thirty-six.

"In the morning they brought the coffin from the carpenter's shop. I kissed my mother a last time. Then my uncles closed the box. They carried it out to a donkey cart they had brought with them, and they took my mother away."

*   *   *

That afternoon, as the rigorous customs of Andalusia demand, Angelita Benítez whitewashed the house of the dead, the one-room hovel on the Calle Belén in which her mother had died. Then she went to her grandmother's house to fetch her brothers and sisters, Encarna, Pepe, Carmela, and Manuel, the youngest, who had turned five just two days before his mother's death.

Angelita was seventeen. She was alone now in a starving world with a promise to keep, the one she had made to her dying mother, a promise summed up by the four children at her side.

That night, as Angelita sobbed out her sorrow, her uncles went to the civil registry of the town hall of Palma del Río. There, as required by law, they recorded the death at six o'clock in the evening of May 7, 1941, of Ángela Clara Benítez, age thirty-six. To their simple declaration they appended one last phrase, an epitaph to Ángela Benítez's life of misery: *"No tiene testamento."* The deceased left no will.

CHAPTER THREE

Madrid:
THE
BRAVE BULL

THEY CALL THEM the Gates of Fear. Twenty million people now fixed their gaze upon the gates' wooden beams and rusted
hinges. Every head in Madrid's packed Plaza de Toros was twisted in
their direction. The long black tube of a television camera lay trained
upon them, offering to an eager Spain a symbolic curtain about to rise on
the drama so many anxiously awaited. The rusted doors opened directly
onto the sand of the Las Ventas bullring. Behind them, in a dark and
humid passageway, waited the six brave bulls of Don José Benítez Cubero, ready to test the courage of the men who would challenge their
right to that rain-soaked sand.

El Cordobés kept his eyes, too, fixed on those wooden gates. The parade was over now. The first bull to bolt from them would be his, an
honor imposed upon him by the fact he was confirming with this corrida
his ascension to the rank of *matador de toros*. He was concerned. The
rain that had nearly forced the cancellation of the corrida continued to
splash into the ring. A few seconds earlier he had felt it damp down the
flowing movements of his seven-pound fighting cape as he twisted it

through a series of practice *verónicas*. Now, beneath the soles of his *zapatillas,* his bullfighter's slippers, as thin and sensitive as a ballet dancer's, he could feel the slick and uncertain surface of the bullring floor.

Behind him, the excited cackle of the crowd had stilled down to that nervous murmur that always preceded the entry of the first bull into the ring. From somewhere in that crowd a rasping voice rang out. "You long-haired clown," it called, "now they'll show you up for the freak you are!" El Cordobés was used to that kind of insult. It confirmed that nothing he could do, not even his decision to fight in the glutinous half mud before him, could temper the hostility many Madrileños bore him.

Bitterly he spun around and scanned the black wall of umbrellas above him, searching for the voice's owner. Like so many matadors, El Cordobés despised those people piled rank upon faceless rank in the stands above him, the howling crowd that had made him an idol and might someday drive him to hang himself in despair upon the horns of a bull. It could do that, this demanding, fickle, often ignorant mass for whose benefit the rite of the bullfight was performed. "It is the public that gores, not the bulls" was an old bullfighters' maxim.

El Cordobés turned back and fixed his eyes again upon the Gates of Fear. A pair of horsemen, black velvet capes flaring out from their shoulders, galloped toward them. They were the *alguaciles,* the bailiffs of the bullring, anachronisms in their costumes of Philip II, symbolically bearing the keys that would throw open those shuttered wooden doors.

For El Cordobés, as any matador, these were the long and lonely moments, when no man escaped the creeping fingers of fear. Immobile, waiting, their inactive bodies gave their brains the time to think. Some spanned these moments with prayer. Others took inventory of their plans for the trial ahead. El Cordobés sought to protect himself with a vacuum, making "an enormous effort to think of nothing." No amount of experience, no amount of professional knowledge, eased those instants of anguish. In the twilight of their careers, with the deaths of thousands of bulls behind them, Spain's most seasoned bullfighters still felt fear. The young man standing at the rim of Las Ventas had already fought and killed over six hundred bulls; but like the generations that had preceded him before those wooden gates, he, too, felt that eternal apprehension that made the matador underneath his bold suit of lights a very human man.

He had no idea what kind of animal those gates sheltered. He had never seen him. He did not know his name. All he knew of him was written in chalk on a blackboard over the gate: his weight, 1,161 pounds, more than half a ton; and the number, 25, he bore upon his flanks. That and the fact he was obliged to kill the animal thus sparingly described within a time limit rigidly fixed by law.

Somewhere above him a lone trumpeter rose and sent out the clear, high call that summoned the waiting animal to his fate. The moment for which El Cordobés' sword handler had called out *"Ya es la hora"* was at hand. Slowly the rusted hinges of the Gates of Fear began to creak open.

"I was not afraid," El Cordobés later remembered, "I thought of nothing. I leaned my chin on the edge of the *burladero* and tried to stare down into the black hole the doors were uncovering. At that moment there was a great stillness all over the ring."

The bull burst from the yawning black hole in an explosion of savage fury. Startled by the sudden rush of light, he plunged straight out onto the empty sand. As he thudded past the swinging *toril* gate, he was already hurtling forward faster than a racehorse at full gallop.

So swift was his headlong dash into the ring that the blue-and-white ribbons of the Cubero ranch, attached to a small dart driven into his neck, stood out straight behind him like pennants in a high wind. At that splendid sight, a respectful murmur rose from the concrete stands of Las Ventas.

The bull was glistening ebony with barely a dapple of white to mar the blackness of his body. He held his head high above a thick, powerful neck. Halfway down his neck, the *morillo* that would give his horn thrusts drive and power already bristled in a black mound, a sure sign that the beast who carried it was alive with rage.

His horns thrust from his heavy skull in a broad U, each almost a foot long, each plunging straight forward with a slight upward sweep at its tip. As they should be, they were *astifino,* fine, slimming down to the sharpness of a knitting needle at their points.

They could uproot a tree, those horns, splinter a railway tie or disembowel a man. Behind them there was force enough to toss a horse and rider into the air—and the deftness to spear a falling leaf. The bull could use them with the swiftness and precision of a switchblade fighter in a barroom brawl.

Behind them was a savage instinct honed by centuries of breeding to seek out and destroy any object challenging the animal who bore them. In thirty minutes inside this ring, the bull would have learned so much of the game in which he was an unknowing partner that it would be impossible to kill him by the classic rules of the bullfight. "A bull," proclaims a Spanish saying, "learns more in half an hour than a man in a lifetime."

In a sprint he could outrun a racehorse; and he could swivel his massive bulk around with the grace and agility of a cat. He bore as little relation to a domestic bull as a tiger does to a tomcat. He had been bred for nothing else but these coming moments of bravery and brutality. Their issue, for this superb black animal, was fatally foreordained. But it was not a wholly unequal combat. This bull was the product of a bloodline of animals that had killed and maimed thousands of the humans who had chosen to challenge their horns, among them six of Spain's ten greatest matadors and two of the three most important bullfighters of the twentieth century.

The animal braked to a sudden stop in the center of the ring, looking for a target for his anger. Tossing up his head in a gesture of wild defiance, he resembled for just an instant those images of his ancestors scrawled upon the caves of prehistoric man. He was, millions of Spaniards might think, "a bull born to die well."

None of the spectators would take greater satisfaction in that thought than a frail man in leather chaps and a shoulder-hugging bolero jacket standing on a wooden platform just over the passageway from which the bull had galloped into the ring. Beneath the soles of his Andalusian riding boots he could feel the vibrations stirred by the tossing of the five bulls still penned behind the Gates of Fear. Francisco Galindo had delivered those bulls into this last sanctuary of their short and savage lives. He was, in a sense, their shepherd.

He was the *mayoral,* the foreman, of a Spanish bull-breeding ranch. For thirty-five years Galindo had devoted himself to the bulls that carried the sky-blue-and-white colors of Don José Benítez Cubero into the bullrings of Spain. He recorded their births in his labored and elaborate hand in the frayed leather logbooks of the Cubero ranch. He stood witness at the ceremony that pointed them toward either the slaughterhouse or the bullring. And he faithfully followed them all on their last journey from the Andalusian pastures in which they had been born to the hour of their death on the sand of some distant *plaza de toros.*

The bulls had given him the only moments of glory Galindo had lived.

In Valencia, in June 1950, after Julio Aparicio and Miguel Báez, "Litri," had cut twelve ears, six tails and four hoofs from his bulls in an extraordinary *mano a mano,* the crowd had risen to give the little *mayoral* an extravagant ovation. In 1958, in the sherry capital of Jérez de la Frontera, he had lived the apotheosis of a *mayoral's* career. His bull Compuesto displayed such extraordinary courage that his life was spared, and Galindo was carried in triumph from the *plaza* on the shoulders of a delirious crowd.

And now he was to witness the death of another of his animals before the greatest assemblage of spectators in the history of the corrida. Silently he prayed that this beast's manner of dying be worthy of his noble heritage.

To Paco Ruiz, El Cordobés' *banderillero de confianza,* fell the task of offering a first challenge to the bull's waiting horns. His job was a routine one. It consisted of giving the animal two or three quick passes to test his reactions and the manner in which he used his horns. Normally it was a task devoid of real danger. Today this wet sand made even Paco nervous, and he cursed the fate and the matador that were sending him off to test a bull "like Jesus Christ walking on water."

He licked his lips. The rain running off his forehead mixed with his sweat to leave a salty taste on his tongue. He blinked hard to shake off the tiny drops of water clinging to his eyelashes. Then, slowly flaring open the folds of his magenta-and-yellow cape, he stepped from behind his *burladero* and called to the bull.

The animal lowered his head and, thrusting off his hind legs, drove toward Paco's gently flowing cloth. Wet sand shot up from his hoofs like dirt thrown from a spinning car wheel. Galindo, the *mayoral,* noticed he kept his hoofs close together and well under his body as he ran. That meant this bull would be an exceptionally surefooted and agile animal. As for the matador, a second's hesitation, a fumbling for footing on these wet sands, Galindo thought, and he was going to be caught on his adversary's horns.

Paco Ruiz had no time to remark such a fine point of the animal's behavior. He was to discover it in more practical fashion. The bull shot across the sand separating them. With a tearing thrust that could be heard in the stands, he dove after the banderillero's waving cape, almost ripping it from Paco's hand.

Just as Galindo had predicted, the animal pivoted around with breathtaking speed. He was driving back onto Paco before the banderillero could set himself for his charge. Desperately Paco jerked his cape about, agitating it with all the force in his wrist. The bull this time was leaping at him from the left, from less than four yards away. In one ghastly second of awareness, Paco saw that the bull was not taking the lure of his cape. That black, rushing mass, those dull brown eyes, the horns that could punch a hole as big as a baseball in his lungs, were streaking instead for his body.

He had time only to utter a hasty *"Madre,"* then instinctively draw his cape forward and closer to his body. It was a desperate effort to force its folds into the bull's line of vision and realign his charge. In a black blur the bull swept past. For a second, Paco felt the warmth from its sweating hide lap against his face like a sudden blast of hot air rushing from an open furnace. In the next instant he felt something much more disturbing: the tip of the bull's left horn flicking open the embroidered edge of the jacket of his own modest suit of lights.

El Cordobés, his chin still firmly fixed on the edge of his *burladero,* noticed that gesture, too. His experienced eyes had seen the pass as though it were a slow-motion film. They had picked out a movement many in the crowd missed, a leftward swerve by the bull followed by a vicious, upward jab of his left horn. It indicated, probably, that the animal favored his left horn as a human being may favor his left hand. It would make this fight a very difficult one, for that tendency rendered particularly dangerous one of the corrida's loveliest passes, the *natural,* which brings the bull's left horn across the matador's body. El Cordobés did not worry about that possibility, not yet. Now his mind was absorbed by only one thought, his own first brush with the animal waiting for him in the middle of the ring.

He spat into his hands and rubbed his palms together. It was an instinctive gesture, a Gypsy trait he had adopted because he felt it gave him "confidence, like running my hands through my hair."

Grasping his cape, El Cordobés stepped out from behind his *burladero,* brushing past his retreating banderillero as he did. Now it was his turn to test the bull. "He's fast, my God, he's fast," gasped a shaken Paco, "and for God's sake keep that left horn away from your gut."

That same warning was being silently voiced by another man, nearly three hundred miles from Las Ventas, settled comfortably before a TV set in the hacienda of his bull-breeding ranch. Don José Benítez Cubero could feel the damp breaths of his retainers, ranged in respectful ranks behind his black leather armchair, warming the nape of his neck. Around him in the shuttered grayness of his sitting room were the trophies of other great afternoons in the history of his *ganadería,* the stuffed heads of the bulls whose bravery had brought particular honor to his name and his colors. To that glassy-eyed gallery of death Don José hoped to add this afternoon another head, that of one of the two animals a draw had chosen to confirm the courage and skill of a young man born just fifteen miles from the gates of his finca.

Don José's experienced eyes, too, had spotted the leftward thrust of his first bull's horn. Like El Cordobés, he knew it might simply be an indication that the bull favored his left horn. Nearly all bulls had a "master horn" that they favored. If that tendency was pronounced, an experienced matador could correct it during the fight by selecting passes that would force the bull to use his other horn.

Don José's concern was far more serious than that. He feared his bull's erratic swerve might have been provoked by faulty vision in his left eye. It had seemed to Cubero that his bull's leftward movement had been a lunge of his entire body rather than just a hooking of his head. That, if it were true, would be a serious matter. Upon the bull's vision depended the entire structure of the bullfight, for it was to his eyes that the lure of the cloth was directed. If his vision was bad, his response would be erratic and unpredictable. No bull, Don José knew, was as dangerous as an animal that did not see properly. The greatest matador in Spain's history, Joselito, had been killed because he had forgotten for a split second that the bull he faced had faulty vision.

Don José drew another cigarette from his pack, and the scratching of his match broke the quiet of his sitting room. The bull breeder inhaled deeply and muttered, under his breath, a hasty prayer. He had hand-picked the animals for this corrida himself. God grant, he fervently begged, that they do nothing to besmirch his proud name before the watching eyes of half his nation.

* * *

Outside the shuttered stillness of Don José's salon, the relentless heat of Andalusian summer already weighed upon the land. The high whitewashed walls surrounding the ranch house cast back the sun's rays in a blinding whiteness. Their shadows sliced like an uneven scar down the cobbled alley leading to the hacienda of his ten-thousand-acre ranch, Los Ojuelos.

Just fifteen miles to the east, along the straight and sluggish course of the Guadalquivir, was Palma del Río. Off to the north, on the other side of the hacienda, was a ridge of low, bald hills, a green and fecund welt in winter, burned down now to a pale amber. Along their crests and flanks drifted Don José's six hundred animals, gliding noiselessly through the scorched high grass in their never-ending quest for forage and water. They grew free, held as far apart as possible from human contact, every instant of their brief, unfettered life a conscious preparation for that moment when, in some bullring far removed from these ranges, they would give combat to a dismounted man. Every year seventy of them went out from these fields to die under the swords of Spain's matadors.

*   *   *

A full moon splashed its pale silver light along the pastures. From the north, the biting wind driving down from the Sierra Morena flattened the high grass. Instinctively the herd of brave cows clustered together in a compact mass, protecting themselves against the cold.

Yet, despite the cold, one wide-horned cow split apart from the herd and lurched up a gentle incline toward a clump of trees. Her name was Impulsiva. She tumbled to the ground at the top of the rise, falling under the branches of a paradise tree, so named because, the Andalusians believe, its leaves were patterned from angels' wings. There, by the light of the full moon, under the wind-whipped branches of her paradise tree, Impulsiva fulfilled the destiny she had been assigned on the ranch of Don José Benítez Cubero. She dropped a bull calf onto the soil of Andalusia.

Francisco Galindo, the *mayoral*, found her at dawn, still under the paradise tree, her bull calf already wobbling around her on his shaking legs. No animal is more dangerous than a brave cow with a newborn, and Don José's *mayoral* approached no closer than he had to, to get the information he would need to record the birth and its date, December 17, 1959, in Los Ojuelos' archives.

Later, when he did, he performed the first official act in the life of the bull now facing El Cordobés on the sand of Las Ventas. He assigned him a name. He chose Impulsivo, after his mother.

Impulsivo's violent heritage was evident in the young bull from the first hours of his existence. As soon as he could stand and run, he was prepared to charge any creature coming within his range. At the age of five days, with his withered umbilical cord still trailing from his belly, he was ready to greet with a violent butting of his head any human foolish enough to try to caress him.

With the other animals of the herd serviced by the seed bull that had sired him, Impulsivo drifted for almost a year through the high grass of Don José's ten-thousand-acre ranch, stamping out the springtime of his brief life in the same sort of green and sprawling *campo* in which El Cordobés had roamed in youth.

With autumn came Impulsivo's first contact with man and the beginning of his life as a brave bull. It was in the traditional ceremony of the *herradero,* the branding. With the burning of the initials of the ranch onto the flank of each animal, Impulsivo's generation of bulls received the title deeds of its nobility and took its place in the long line of brave animals sired on the ranchlands of Don José Benítez Cubero.

Midway through the young bull's second springtime, Don José and his *mayoral* decided the time had come for the most important event in the annual cycle of a bull-breeding ranch, the *tienta,* the testing of a new crop of young bulls for bravery.

It began with a long, exasperating, difficult operation, a forced migration of the young bulls away from the pasturelands in which they had been raised. A primitive, inexplicable force attached them to their pastures. It was the first manifestation of the concept of *"querencia,"* a bull's instinctive attachment to a particular piece of terrain. They felt secure within those pastures, prowling about inside some invisible but rigid boundaries known only to the reasoning of their savage natures.

Later they would display that same notion in the bullring. There, instinctively, a bull would choose some piece of ground as his and draw an imaginary circle around it, some invisible frontier separating him from the rest of the world. That undefined piece of sand called his *querencia* would become the most dangerous spot in the ring for the matador because any violation of its invisible limits would provoke the bull's sudden attack. Ignorance of that immutable geography, or the failure to draw a bull from that refuge before working him, had led many a matador to injury or death on the horns of a bull he had believed subdued.

The aim of Don José's vaqueros was to use the bulls' predilection for a particular piece of ground to set up the psychological conditions necessary for the test of their bravery. For four days they were kept in a distant field. Then, this time in a joyous stampede, they were herded back to their familiar pastures.

That calculated uprooting reinforced the bulls' natural notion of *querencia,* which now became the yardstick against which their bravery was measured.

Once again they were driven from their familiar surroundings. This time their destiny was a closed corral a few miles south of their pasturelands. There, one by one, the young bulls were cut apart from the herd and released.

As each animal spurted free, a group of mounted vaqueros rode down on him, cutting his path and forcing him away from his nearby pastures, his *querencia.* Furious, disoriented, the bull twisted and zigzagged, trying to find a way back to familiar surroundings. Finally the panting young bull stopped in an open field to which the vaqueros had driven him. They melted away and left him alone facing a single horse and rider. The horseman was so positioned that, to attack him, the bull would have to charge away from the path that would lead him back to his *querencia.*

It was a moment of suspense, the decisive instant of the *tienta.* Don José and his *mayoral* Galindo watched intently from horseback from a little knoll a few yards away.

When Impulsivo's turn came, he responded unhesitatingly to the call of his savage blood. Ignoring the lure of his *querencia,* he hurled himself at the horse and rider, thrusting his shoulders against the outthrust pic held in the vaquero's hand. Twice he threw himself against that steel blade, almost overturning the vaquero with his second charge.

Don José watched with satisfaction. Beside him, Galindo, the logbook of the Ojuelos ranch spread across his saddlehorn, waited to note down his employer's judgment of the animal's reaction to the test.

Don José gave to Impulsivo his highest praise: *"un toro muy bravo*—a very brave bull," a verdict that set the young animal firmly upon the road to the sand of Las Ventas. Twelve of the forty-eight other animals tested with Impulsivo received that same high praise. Thirty were cited as *"bravo."* Six were assigned the degrading adjective *"manso"*—cowardly —a judgment that condemned them to a summary execution in the slaughterhouse.

Impulsivo's performance won the young bull the right to another fifteen months of uninterrupted tranquillity. During those months his weight swelled to almost nine hundred pounds. His horns sprouted to full length, making him a dangerous, vicious animal quite capable of killing a man.

Then, in the autumn of 1963, Don José took the first step in the inexorable series of actions that led Impulsivo down to the *toril* gates of Las Ventas. Don José was a bull breeder of sufficient stature to be certain he would sell each year a lot of six animals to each of the major ferias of the bullfight season. Every fall, prowling through his pastures on his stallion Neguir, he chose with Galindo the best of his animals for those ferias. Then he divided those he had selected into six-animal lots that were as uniform as possible. The best lot of each generation of bulls he marked off in his mind for the most prestigious fair of the season, Madrid's San Isidro.

The process took almost a week. When it was over, Galindo noted down the numbers of the animals they had chosen for each of the ferias. At the top of the list selected to carry the blue-and-white ribbons of the Cubero ranch at the 1964 San Isidro was number 25, Impulsivo.

A few weeks later, Impulsivo and the five bulls selected to die with him were taken forever from the pastures in which they had so long roamed free. Their universe was now restricted to four acres of fenced-in corral. There, like prisoners quartered in some elegant Death Row, they were destined to live out the last months of their brief lives, consuming daily over twenty pounds of prepared feed. That diet would make them, by spring, monsters of well over half a ton each.

Eight days before the corrida, the six San Isidro bulls were driven into six detachable cages fixed to the platform of a trailer truck. When the last bull was loaded, the truck's consignment was weighed on a special scale. Don José watched with satisfaction as the needle on that scale climbed to the figure of 3,139 kilograms, well over half a ton per animal.

119

It was one of the heaviest lots of bulls his ranch had ever sent to a bullring.

Mayoral Galindo climbed up into the cab beside the driver to accompany the six animals on their journey. Slowly, under Don José's watchful eyes, the truck swayed out of his corral and down a long dirt road to the Guadalquivir, carrying the six bulls away forever from the Andalusian pasturelands that had nurtured them.

Their first stop was in the suburbs of the capital. It was the exhibition yards of the Madrid bullring. There, with the other bulls selected for the San Isidro feria, they spent six days exposed to the inquiring eyes of the capital's aficionados. That respite, and the attentive care of *mayoral* Galindo, allowed them to gain back the weight and strength they had lost on the trip to Madrid.

During that final week, *mayoral* Galindo never left the bulls' corral. He slept on a straw mattress tossed on the floor of the room in which their grain was stored. His vigilant surveillance was designed to prevent any tampering with the animals to render them less dangerous, and therefore more amenable, foes. There were many ways to do it. Their shoulder muscles could be weakened by being battered with sandbags; their feed could be doped; or their horns could be shaved. It was to prevent such abuses that Galindo was assigned to watch over the animals during their sojourn in Madrid.

At six o'clock on the evening before the corrida, the animals were formally examined by President de Quiros and two veterinarians employed by the Spanish state. Certified acceptable for combat in the bullring, the bull Impulsivo, number 25, and the five animals with him were herded back into their wooden cages and reloaded onto their trailer truck. This time their terminus was the Plaza de Toros of Madrid and the destiny for which Impulsivo had been born under the branches of a paradise tree on a windy December night.

*   *   *

Now Impulsivo was alone in that bullring with a 150-pound man whose only weapons were the control he could exercise over his nerves and a seven-pound cotton cape.

For his first jousting with Impulsivo, El Cordobés decided on a dramatic and dangerous gesture. He trotted deliberately to the center of the ring. It was, for a matador, the most dangerous spot in the arena. Here he was as far away from help as he could possibly be. Should Impulsivo's horns catch El Cordobés there, vital seconds would tick by before his banderilleros could reach him and draw the bull from his fallen figure. Those seconds could mean the difference between a bruise and a serious goring, for a matador's worst wounds often came not from the first blow that toppled him to the ground but from the ones that followed when he was sprawled helpless under the bull's horns.

That danger, on this rainy afternoon, was even greater than usual. The wet sand below El Cordobés' feet increased the risk of an accidental fall. They would add seconds, too, to the journey his banderilleros would have to his side. He was making a spectacular and calculated appeal to the twenty-three thousand spectators in Las Ventas and the millions more watching on television, an effort to stir their sympathy at the very outset of the fight.

Their reaction was immediate. As he unfurled his cape and fixed his feet into the soggy sand, an appreciative murmur lifted up from the crowd. Impulsivo took the lure of his cape with the same startling speed he had displayed in charging that of Paco Ruiz. Clutching tightly at the cork bulbs sewn into the collar of the cape, El Cordobés effortlessly swept its folds before Impulsivo's horns, setting the rhythm of its retreating cloth to the speed of the animal's charge. He did not, on this first pass, try to draw him close to his body. He was testing and measuring the animal.

The matador swiftly shifted his stance and, snapping his cape with his wrists, called the animal to him again, this time from the left side. Again Impulsivo catapulted past, closer on this pass so that El Cordobés, too, felt the heat thrusting from his hide as he swept by. As he went, El Cordobés could hear the first smart *"olé"* come cracking down from the stands above.

Again he swiveled his body around, retreating a step to put more distance between himself and the bull's shortening charges. The animal stiffened, hesitating for just an instant, then drove once more for the cape. This time, confident and taking him from the right, El Cordobés pulled the onrushing horns of his ponderous skull to within inches of his body. Another *"olé,"* this one louder and more certain, rang out from the stands.

Impulsivo spun about, faster now, and threw himself back at the cape.

El Cordobés changed to a different kind of pass. As Impulsivo charged, he dropped his left hand from the cape's collar and with a sudden, sharp twist of his right wrist sent the cape swirling about his hips, its folds flaring out in a horizontal plane until, behind his back, he was able to grasp its collar once again with his left hand. He timed that quick gesture so that he was in a sense jerking the lure from the bull's focal plane at the instant he careened past, thus exposing his own body to the bull for the first time. For one lovely instant the cape seemed frozen about the matador's hips, all its folds spread out on the air like the delicate magenta petals of some enormous flower.

Impulsivo stopped his bursting series of charges, panting for breath, baffled by the sudden disappearance of the object of his fury. Overhead the clear, metallic notes of a trumpet announced the passage to the next phase of the bullfight, the entry of the picadors.

El Cordobés folded his cape over his arm and strutted slowly away from his dazed and momentarily numbed adversary. As he did, a warm, appreciative burst of applause came tumbling down on him from the concrete benches of Las Ventas. Sure now that this controversial young man was going to offer them an admirable spectacle, the crowd forgot for a moment the rain, the mud and their long exasperating wait. His untidy hair spilling down to his eyebrows, his gold-and-tobacco suit of lights already flecked with mud and sweat, El Cordobés returned their applause with an open, easy grin.

That smile lasted only the time it took him to march back to the edge of the ring. There it disappeared. He had learned something in those few minutes when he drew the bull past his body, something the clamoring spectators did not see. He had discovered a flaw in the seemingly perfect makeup of the bull Impulsivo. It was a flaw not unlike that which had been responsible for the death of the incomparable Joselito, the finest matador his nation had ever known.

"My God," he gasped to his banderillero, Paco Ruiz, "he doesn't see a damn thing with his left eye."

CHAPTER FOUR

Palma del Río:
THE YEARS
OF HUNGER

THE CINE JÉREZ sits in the center of Palma del Río, its unlit, hand-lettered marquee gazing down upon its principal square. The movie theater shares that place of honor with the town's two banks, its leading store and its only restaurant. It is no coincidence that it occupies so coveted a spot. For thirty-one years, from its first showing in 1931 until the miracle of television reached down into Andalusia, that movie theater was the only source of entertainment available to the people of Palma del Río.

With its warped plywood seats, its two-peseta benches whitened like the pews of the parish church with the hand-carved initials of half the town and its walls smelling of damp cement, the Cine Jérez was a palace of wonders for thousands of Palmeños. Mary Pickford and Douglas Fairbanks, Ginger Rogers and Fred Astaire, Clark Gable and Vivien Leigh, had all flashed across its scratched old screen. The Eiffel Tower and the Moulin Rouge, the rice paddies of Japan and the skyscrapers of a land their ancestors had helped to discover—all were cast before

123

Palma's wondering eyes by the Cine's aged and faulty projectors. To the people of this isolated town, the Cine Jérez was much more than a movie house. It was an eye on the unknown, a glimpse—the only one many Palmeños would ever have—over the Sierra Morena looming beyond the Guadalquivir. Here, once a week, when the lights went out, the world came to Palma del Río.

One winter night in 1950, those lights went down on a film that had crowded the little movie house to capacity. The mayor was there. So were Don Rafael, the doctor; Sergeant Mauleón, the chief of the Guardia Civil post; the notary public, the pharmacist. Pedro Charneca, the fat waiter who had been the best friend of Manolo Benítez's father, the proprietor now of a café of his own, was on hand. The bull breeders of the region and their *mayorales* were present. Even Don Félix Moreno was there, lending with this rare appearance in the Cine Jérez a special luster to the evening about to begin.

At the rear of the theater, among Palma's poor, squirming on their two-peseta benches, a pair of unkempt fourteen-year-old boys giggled at the sight of Don Félix's head profiled in the audience before them. They had reason to giggle. It was thanks to the sale of a sack of oranges stolen from Don Félix's trees that Manolo Benítez and his inseparable companion, Juan Horrillo, had been able to pay their way into the Cine Jérez.

One by one, the flyspecked light bulbs of the theater went out. With the high, clicking whir of a sewing machine, the Cine's ancient projector started into motion. As its beam of light illuminated the screen, the impatient sound of scraping feet indicated the eagerness with which the crowd awaited the picture.

Yet no Hollywood star, no special spectacle, graced the amateurish Spanish film fixed upon the Cine's projector. That did not matter. It was its subject that had crowded this theater, and for two hours that subject held the diverse audience of Palmeños in silent satisfaction.

It was a legend that the film projected in the Cine Jérez that night, a legend as firmly embedded in the folklore of Andalusia as the tales of El Cid, Cortés and Pizarro. It was the story of a poor boy fleeing his poverty by following the bullfighter's trade, earning his passage away from hunger with the public display of his courage. In this case, the hero of the legend was a product of the slums of Seville named Currito de la Cruz.

His belongings slung over his shoulder, an old cap perched on his head and a smile on his face, the film's hero tramped from village to village, looking for a bull to fight. He hopped the freight trains, slept in barns and the open fields, until finally fortune smiled on him and the gates of the bullring swung open before his cocky little figure.

Nothing could have been more banal than that story. Yet the crowd in the Cine Jérez followed its predictable course with rapt attention. One common denominator bound that disparate group together. It was their love for the *fiesta brava.* In Palma, as in so many other communities in Spain, only the *fiesta brava* could have drawn together in common enterprise representatives of every level of society, from landowner to middle-class shopkeeper to landless peasant. Huddled there in their darkened theater, watching those scratched images slide past, they understood and they believed. For, in fact, it was true. Courage before the horns of a bull as displayed by Currito de la Cruz was still the best key with which to open the gates of Spain's rigidly structured society.

Physically, barely a dozen yards separated Don Félix Moreno's plywood seat from the two-peseta benches of Palma's amateur orange thieves, Manuel Benítez and Juan Horrillo. Socially, that distance was a chasm so enormous that almost nothing their young minds could conceive this winter evening could ever bridge it. Almost nothing, that is, except the example unfolding before them on the screen of the Cine Jérez. Currito de la Cruz's story might be just another hackneyed version of an old legend, but it was a legend that remained as true in Palma del Río on this windy evening of 1950 as it was the day it was born in Ronda's mountain fastness two hundred years earlier. In the age of the atom bomb and the airplane, the surest way across the gulf separating Don Félix's plywood seat and the benches in the rear was still the one being demonstrated by the imaginary Currito de la Cruz and his scrap of scarlet cloth.

Of all the eyes fixed on the screen of the Cine Jérez, none bulged wider with wonder at the spectacle than those of Manolo Benítez and Juan Horrillo. They discovered a new world on that screen. Until this night the corrida had been for them an abstraction: a game they sometimes played in the *calles,* the faded shreds of a bullfight poster on a wall, or the black shadows of the bulls gliding through Don Félix Moreno's pastures.

Now suddenly, in this stuffy movie house, it was before their eyes. It was bleached clean of its suffering and squalor. Only the glitter remained. It was, for the fourteen-year-old Manuel Benítez, an overwhelming experience. Huddled there in the darkness, Manolo could actually feel the hunger that sent Currito de la Cruz down those long roads looking for a chance to learn the bullfighters' art by fighting a bull in some forbidden pasture. Instinctively he saw himself walking down the same roads, leaving, like Currito, his fate and his town behind him.

He listened spellbound to the applause, the shrieks of joy, all the screams, as he watched the images of Currito's first successes. Looking at the film's hero sparkling in his suit of lights, dominating the black mass of a bull, he told himself that that was "what glory must be like." The life of a bullfighter, it seemed to the boy on the two-peseta bench, was "the easiest life in the world."

His jaw agape, Manolo watched in awe as the imaginary youth whose hunger had been so akin to his own moved through the world his courage had conquered for him. His life seemed to be an endless round of banquets; of hotels with bathtubs steaming with hot water, enormous beds; of people surrounding him, pressing things upon him, calling him by his name; of plump men in sombreros smoking cigars and pretty girls snapping their fingers through an endless flamenco.

Above all, the success of the slim young man in a suit of lights had won for him the ultimate trophy of material well-being. To the simple and frustrated orange thief of the Calle Belén, that physical possession marked the frontier dividing the very rich from the rest of the world. Currito de la Cruz had a car. It was an enormous black Chrysler, and in it he roamed the highways to San Sebastián, Burgos, Barcelona and Madrid, places that seemed to the boy in the Cine Jérez that night almost as remote and romantic as the Indies must have once seemed to the sailors of Cádiz.

It was all there, as hackneyed, as trite, as unreal and romanticized as a bullfight film could be. And when it was all over, and the lights went on after a final triumphant burst of glory for Currito de la Cruz, Manolo Benítez was slumped in wonder on his bench.

Finally he got up and headed back with Juan Horrillo to their tawdry world. They walked home together, indifferently kicking stones down the streets before them. They were brooding and silent, haunted now by a new image that would follow them for years to come.

126

At the door to the shack in which his sister Angelita had struggled to raise him in the decade since his mother's death, Manolo turned to Horrillo. "You'll see," he vowed, "one day my belly will be as full as his."

The next day he took his first step toward the fulfillment of his prophecy. He stole the blanket from his sister's bed. With it he made the first muleta of his life.

ANGELITA BENÍTEZ'S STORY

"THE FIRST THING I had to do after my mother died was to go to the prison in Córdoba where they kept my father, to tell him she was dead. It was my job to go because I was the oldest. I took whatever I could find with me, some black bread and some oranges. I was dressed in black for my mother. The visiting days were the same then, always the same, so my father was expecting my mother that day. When they called out our names and I stood up in that black dress, he understood right away. He said, 'Oh,' very quickly, like that. For a long time we just sat and stared at each other. We were strangers. My father hardly knew me. For him I was just a black messenger of death, some stranger who had come to tell him his wife was dead.

"My father started to cry, just a little, without any noise. I cried, too. He was crying for his wife, my father was, but me, I was crying for him. I remembered him so different from before the war. He was strong then, and still young. That day in the prison, his face was old and gray. He was huddled over, and his chest was sunk in. He coughed a lot. He hardly knew who I was and I was the oldest, the one who was his favorite.

"After that I tried to go see him every week. I brought him something of whatever there was, an orange or some olives or a potato. We never talked much. There wasn't much to say. Most of the time we just sat and looked each other through the bars. One day when I came, my father told me they were sending him away from there. He said they were sending him to Málaga to work on the roads. Málaga is on the sea, a long way from here. We were very sad together because Málaga was far, too far to go to visit him. When they sent him away, that meant I would not be able to go see him any more. We looked at each other for a long time. Finally they rang the bell and I had to go. I kissed my father through the bars. He

127

said, 'Adiós, Angelita,' like always. That was all. When I came back the next week, he was gone.

"The months went by and there was never any news from him. Then, one day, a letter came. It was very short. I still have it.

" 'Dear Angelita,' it said, 'I am very sick. They are going to let me go because I am so sick. I am afraid that I am going to die. Please come and take me home. I want to come back to Palma to die with my children and be buried beside my wife.'

"I was his favorite but I couldn't go. How could I go? I had to work to feed the small ones. My sister Encarna was working in Córdoba then and she went. They got as far as Córdoba and my father couldn't go any farther. He was too weak. He was coughing and spitting blood. Some people helped Encarna carry him to the hospital, but at first they wouldn't let him in. They said, 'We don't have beds for the dead.'

"Finally they put him into a big room, the ward for the people with no hope. It was just a place to keep them until they died. Every day during the siesta Encarna went to see him. One afternoon, on the day of the Virgin of the Pillar, he was very bad. He couldn't even sit up in bed any more. He was choking on his blood because he was too weak to cough. He said to Encarna, 'It's over. I'm going to die now.'

"She ran out to try to find a doctor but none of them would come. They told her he was finished. When she had to leave to go to work, she told him 'Adiós, Papá' and ran out of the room without looking back. That night they called at the house where she worked and told her our father was dead."

*   *   *

The cemetery of the city of Córdoba lies just outside its gates, along the main road to Seville, looking back upon the moat and the crenellated rim of the caliphs' ancient ramparts. Like most of the graveyards of Andalusia, it is walled. The interior is planted with jasmine and cypress trees, sad and stately guardians of its cobbled alleys, their branches thrusting upward as though in supplication for the eternal salvation of the Spaniards buried below.

It is known to the city's believers as the Cementerio de Nuestra Señora de la Salud, the Cemetery of Our Lady of Salvation. To the less reverent it is known as the cemetery of the bullfighters. Three of Córdoba's great matadors, Largartijo, Guerrita and Manolete, are buried there. Like Arab princes, they rest in the munificence of their marble mausoleums, dominating even in death the poor and despairing masses around them, those masses from whose poverty their blood and courage had bought them an escape.

Encarna Benítez hurried past their handsome sepulchers toward the most forlorn corner of the cemetery. Not even in death would José Benítez go home again to the city he had longed to see one last time. His daughter's left hand folded over a greasy packet of peseta notes, 375 of them. That sum represented for the fifteen-year-old Encarna slightly more than six months' wages. Too poor to take her father's body home to Palma, too proud to leave him to charity's impersonal hands, Encarna had borrowed that sum from her employer to offer her father a modest parting gift, the cheapest funeral available in Córdoba.

At the farthest corner of the cemetery she found a shallow hole freshly shoveled into the raised dirt terrace of common graveyard 4. It was the hole that would receive her father's coffin. Encarna looked into the hole below her for a long time. She was a woman, and the unbending rituals of Andalusia would not allow her to follow her father's coffin to this cemetery. She made the sign of the cross over the open hole. Then she turned and fled to the gravekeeper's cottage.

There she counted off a wad of her precious notes and handed them to the graveyard keeper. They represented ten years' rent on that hole over which Encarna had just uttered a last prayer. With weary indifference the man inscribed in his register the name of his newest ward, José Benítez; and his age, 45, the latest occupant of plot 54, graveyard 4. Then he made a second notation, this one after the name of an unknown Córdoba woman, Dolores Payul. She had been, until just a few hours earlier, the occupant of plot 54. The graveyard keeper's words were a blunt reminder that even eternity could be a fleeting thing for the poor of Andalusia. "Exhumed after ten years for lack of payment," he wrote. "Reburied in the common trench."

A few moments later the funeral procession left the hospital's improvised morgue, a damp, stone-walled storeroom next to its kitchens. It consisted of a priest and four *sepultureros,* gravediggers who, for a few pesetas, bore the poor and friendless to their graves.

129

Encarna watched them go, following each movement as though to freeze forever upon her memory this last glance of her father her society allowed her. Slowly the unmourned coffin moved away until it disappeared down the alleys leading to the city gates.

Then, as it passed under those gates, Encarna, arms askew, her black shawl streaming behind her, ran frantically after the disappearing coffin. In defiance of Andalusia's customs, she had decided to accompany her father to the graveyard's forbidden precincts because "in all Córdoba there was no one who knew my father, and I could not let him go to his grave like that all alone, without even a friend to mourn him."

ANGELITA BENÍTEZ'S STORY

"I CAN'T THINK of those days after my parents' death without crying. There are tears on my cheeks that are still wet from the times I cried then. We had no friends. We lived with our hunger. It was always there beside us, our hunger, like the dream of a crane I had as a young girl, a big crane who was in the room and who was going to snatch me up in his beak. It was like that crane, our hunger, always ready to snatch us up.

"There was nobody to look after us but God and ourselves. Nobody helped us, not even my grandmother who lived across from us. I don't blame her. It was natural. She had her own troubles, too, because it was a very bad time for everybody. You know what it was like, in Spain, after the war. It was terrible to try to find something to eat because there was nothing to eat anywhere, not even in Madrid.

"We sold everything from my mother's dowry, bit by bit, everything except the bed and two chairs. We had to, to buy food when I couldn't work. We lived in the same house, the one where my mother died. Everybody slept together on the bed except Manolo. He was small, so we pushed the two chairs together and he slept on them.

"Every day I walked around looking for work. I went everywhere. I went to Don Félix's fields in the potato season to run my fingers through the dirt looking for potatoes the pickers had missed. Don Félix let you keep half of what you found. When the potatoes were gone, I'd have to go somewhere else to look for work. Sometimes it was the corn. Sometimes it was the olives again, but this time I was old enough to have my own tree.

"Somehow I found work most of the time. When you're as hungry as we were then, you find work. Because if you don't, you starve. We ate once a day to save our food. We ate at night, some chick peas or some rice or some bread and water. You put whatever there was with the water and made your soup.

"In the dry season, the bad times came. Then, sometimes, there was no work, no matter what you did, sometimes for a month, even more. Then there was nothing. We went to bed hungry, hoping in the morning there'd be something to eat somewhere. Sometimes we'd get a swallow of coffee or a sweet from Don Carlos. It hurt Manolo the worst, because he was the youngest. When he cried because he was hungry, I gave him something to eat if we had it. If we didn't, I let him cry.

"I had no money then to buy clothes. All we had was rags. We kept them all, everything we owned, in a pile on the floor of our house. Every morning each one of us picked what he needed from the pile. When the pile got too small, I went out and begged for more. All our days were the same, just work and hunger. You never knew what day it was, sometimes not even what month. You just knew how hungry you were.

"The worst time was Christmas the year after my father died in 1947. Everybody wants to do something for his family on Christmas. I wanted to do something for mine. I wanted to buy something for them. I used to dream of the meat we'd eaten from Don Félix's bulls. I wanted to buy some meat like that for our Christmas. The young ones, Carmela and Manolo, didn't even know what meat like that was. Every day I walked by the market and I looked at the meats hanging there, wondering if I could save enough money to buy some for Christmas.

"But there was a drought that year and there was no work. When Christmas came we had nothing to eat at all, no meat, not even any chick peas, nothing. We locked ourselves into the house all alone. We sat on the bed together crying, holding on to each other. We were like snails, sliding down into their shells, trying to hide ourselves and our misery from the rest of the world."

*　　*　　*

Shortly after that Christmas, the Benítez family split apart. It would be years before they would be reunited: Pepe, the eldest son, was taken away to live with his grandparents. Encarna fled to Madrid looking for work as a maid. She took with her a vow she would keep for the rest of her life. It was never to return to the town in which she and her sisters had suffered so much.

Their departure eased the burdens Angelita had to carry. She had only the two youngest children, Carmela and Manolo, on her hands. Manolo was still, as Don Carlos Sánchez had noted, "a dirty-faced kid with a big grin, and snot running out of his nose like water from a faucet." But he was bigger now, stretching gingerly toward the moment when his bony body would at last fill the baggy shirt and pants he snatched each day from the Benítez family rag pile. His badge, his most treasured possession, was a worn and lice-filled black-leather workingman's cap, which he had taken from some neighbor's rubbish bin. Its size bore no relation to the dimensions of his head. It was so big his fist could fit between its rim and his skull. Its visor, falling to his eyebrows, cut the horizon of his world by half. It made him look ridiculous, like a boy playing Jackie Coogan in his father's cap. But to ten-year-old Manolo Benítez it was the unconscious symbol of his individuality, the seal that set him apart, however slightly, from the gray and faceless mass around him. He wore it everywhere—even, if his sister's attention wandered, to bed.

He had his own corner of the family bed now, the place abandoned by Encarna upon her departure for Madrid. He was a lean and wiry boy, his body burned down to muscle, bone and skin by years of chronic hunger.

Despite his malnutrition, he was tall for his age. His mouth was outsized, stretching into a gaping hole when he laughed. He walked with the indifferent, ambling gait that had hung upon him the Benítez nickname, El Renco. Occasionally he punctuated his moody silence with a roaring burst of laughter that seemed to break the sober surface of his nature like a porpoise splashing up into a calm sea.

Angelita often worried about her brother's future. In those moments, she wished him a destiny quite in keeping with the poor horizons of her own life. She wanted him "to be what our father had been, a good honest worker in the fields."

Her brother would never follow that road traced out by Angelita in her maternal naïveté. Already he was escaping her control. Whenever her disciplining eyes were turned elsewhere, he was off, scampering into the dirty *calles* that circumscribed his world. The wooden bench to which he was assigned in Don Carlos' orphanage was noted more for the absences of its occupant than for his attendance.

Those brief hours when he fled from the commanding hands of Angelita and Don Carlos' nuns were the only childhood Manuel Benítez would know. One day, coming back to the family hovel from a long afternoon in his alleyways, Manolo found Angelita collapsed on the family bed, her head hidden in her hands, "crying to God to help us because there was nothing for us to eat."

That sight stunned him. Never before had his sister's strength failed them. His responsibility was clear. It was time for him to turn his childish hands to the task of helping to feed his family.

He began on a sultry afternoon not long afterwards. An old grain sack in his hands, he slipped into the Guadalquivir and dog-paddled his way to the opposite bank. Without waiting to dry himself, he headed toward the orange groves of Don Félix Moreno. There he picked out a well-concealed tree and industriously filled his sack with oranges. That night he offered them to Angelita, the first provender he had brought to the family dinner table.

His forays into the fields around Palma continued. Soon he had an accomplice: the boy named Juan Horrillo, who was to become his closest friend. He was shorter than Manolo, and hunger had pushed the bones of his rib cage taut against his skin. He had quick dark eyes and a shrewd intelligence that made him the natural leader of the pair. They consecrated their tentative friendship of the *calles,* foraging their way through the fields alongside the Guadalquivir. Soon they were inseparable.

Their childhood fled past, its hours divided between their expeditions to the potato fields and orange groves around Palma, their restless wanderings through its *calles,* and those reluctant moments when, shamed or beaten into submission by their families, they sat upon the wooden benches of Don Carlos' school.

Manolo's new activities hardly fitted into the modest ambitions his sister cherished for him. The knowledge, however, that a little more food would find its way into their bare hovel each day was a blessing sufficient to mute the pangs of her already overtaxed conscience. In any event, whatever he did mattered little. Whether he roamed the fields or wore out his smock on the benches of the orphanage, the prospects the future held out for him, and the others in Palma like him, were the same.

They could dream, Manolo and Juan, of the proud authority of a policeman's coat, of the romance of the truck driver's life, of the far remoter adventure of the corrida. Those dreams were not going to alter their futures. No policeman's coat was going to grace their shoulders, no lumbering truck await their adventuring hands. They were going where their fathers had been, and their grandfathers before them, to the fields at the edge of town to break their backs and their health in the service of Palma's landowners. Manolo Benítez was going with them, too, to labor in those fields from which he now so gaily plundered an occasional sack of oranges.

That future was still for him just a vague horizon he yearned in his inarticulate way to avoid. But until that winter night in the Cine Jérez when his wondering eyes discovered the world of Currito de la Cruz, he had had no goal, no ideal, beckoning him elsewhere. In those closing moments of boyhood, only one hazy ill-defined ambition had made an occasional appeal to his imagination. He had wanted simply "to be a somebody," a creature his untutored mind regarded as "a man with a cigar, and a car and a panama hat"—and who lived as far away from Palma del Río as possible.

*   *   *

On the morning he stole his sister's blanket, Manolo Benítez's knowledge of bullfighting was, for all intents and purposes, limited to the sanitized and stereotyped images he had seen on the screen of the Cine Jérez the night before. The desire that had seized him was a common one, one that captured at some time or another the imagination of almost every young and hungry male in Spain, every awkward adolescent longing for acclaim. It was akin to the dream of a Negro slum kid aching to beat his way with his fists to a place in the white's man sun, or an Indian miner's boy in the Andes dreaming of the day his magic feet would electrify a crowded soccer stadium.

Manolo Benítez's chances of realizing his dreams, once they had confronted the realities of his life, were so infinitesimally small that had he been aware of them that winter morning he stole his sister's blanket, he

134

probably would never have set out to chase them. But he was not aware, and so he began.

He soaked the blanket for hours in a bucket of *punia,* a cheap brick-colored dye, until it came out a rusty brown, its folds so stiffened by the dye that they cracked at each movement like sheets frozen by the wind. During one of his forays in the countryside, he found the ideal weapon for his fantasies. He picked it from a mound of rubble by the Guadalquivir. It was a rusting Civil War bayonet, abandoned there by one of the men who had come to attack his town in the summer of 1936.

"To become a bullfighter, you become first a bull." For generations the sidewalks and back alleys of Spain's communities have been animated by youngsters putting that simple maxim into action. With noisy shouts, they play at the corrida the way other boys play football or basketball, charging each other's muletas to learn the basic gestures of the torero's trade. In Palma the young who played at that game gathered every day by the walls of the burned-out shell of the Church of Santo Domingo. Their leader was a gaunt cripple of nineteen named Luis Rodríguez. Like the youths who swarmed around him in the roofless ruins of the church, Rodríguez had felt the call of the bulls. To those youngsters he exuded a special awe, for he had once worn the suit of lights. He had fought without picadors, as an inspiring *matador de novillos,* three-year-old bulls, in the portable bullrings brought on occasion to the villages around Palma. He had in fact killed three such animals. The fourth had nearly killed him. The bull had ignored the crude, unskilled gestures of Rodríguez's cape and chosen instead to sink a horn into the teen-age matador's knee. When the horn came out, there was hardly a ligament or cartilage left intact in that knee. Now a hopeless cripple, Rodríguez hobbled through the *calles* of Palma, gleaning alms here and there to keep alive. In the warm afternoons he came to the ruins of the Church of Santo Domingo to impart his limited and defective knowledge to this handful of boys who wanted to take their turn on a bullring's sand—and to daydream, perhaps, of triumphs he might have had on such afternoons in sunlit arenas far from this charred church.

Forsaking now the classroom of Don Carlos Sánchez for the new catechism of Luis Rodríguez, Manolo and Juan set out to learn the gestures of the corrida. Day after day they jammed their fists against their ears, thrust out their index fingers and ran at each other's improvised muletas. In between those charges, Rodríguez tried to teach them what little he knew of the bullfighter's passes, how to control the bull's speed, to lead his charge, to turn him safely away at the end of a pass.

For Manolo the afternoons in the shadows of the burned-out church were boring and frustrating. He longed to see an animal charging his cloth, not the curly head of his friend Juan Horrillo. Only the bulls could teach him what he had to know, and the bulls did not hold classes in Palma's *calles*.

There was a traditional road leading toward the confrontation Manolo longed to have with a live animal. It passed through the miniature bull-rings of the great breeders like Don Félix. Several times a year in those rings, the ranchers tested their female calves for bravery. On those occasions they let youngsters recommended to them practice their passes. With half a dozen passes with a live animal, a boy could gain as much knowledge as he could learn in hours in Luis Rodríguez's improvised classroom.

Abandoning their crippled schoolmaster, as they had earlier abandoned Don Carlos' classes, Manolo and Juan set out to try their hands in the *tientas* around Palma. With his ever-present cap jammed down over his ears, his shirttail hanging out, his sister's blanket knotted up on the tip of his Civil War bayonet, Manolo looked like some Hollywood caricature of a hobo as he plodded toward the gates of Palma's bull breeders. He and Horrillo quickly learned that it took more than goodwill to get into those *tientas*. It took the friendly recommendation of someone already inside. Those recommendations were not lightly given, and it soon became clear to Manolo and Juan that this was not their way to the experience they sought.

There was, however, another way to find the bulls. It was at night, by the light of a full moon, in the pastures where they roamed. It was the way of Currito de la Cruz, and Manolo quickly realized that it would have to be his way, too. There was nothing new about it. Brave and desperate Spanish youths had resorted to it for years. Even Juan Belmonte had taken his first steps toward the *fiesta brava* that way.

It was, nevertheless, both blatantly illegal and extremely dangerous. Every year an undetermined number of kids were killed doing it, some shot by overzealous vaqueros for trespassing, others gored and left to die alone in the weeds of some trackless pasture.

The practice was roundly condemned by all associated with the corrida. The whole premise of the bullfight is that it is the first confrontation between a bull and a dismounted man. A bull loses his innocence only once, and if he has been fought in the fields, he will remember the lesson he learned there when he gets to the bullring. His horns will go for the man instead of the cloth, and the bullfight will become a fiasco. Such a bull is a public disgrace to the man who bred him. To protect their animals, breeders exercise a special watch over their pastures when the moon is full. December, January and February are the worst months. The moonlight in Andalusia is clearest then, and the menace to the animals greatest. Yet protecting them is an extraordinary difficult job. The ranches sprawl over dozens of square miles, and trying to catch an intruder in them is an enormous game of hide and seek in the night.

For the intruder, the price of getting caught is high. At the least, it is a brutal beating. But the risk of that beating is only the price of admission to the far more dangerous game they have come to play. For all the risks he takes, a matador in an arena still has certain safeguards around him. The boy in the moonlit pasture has none of them. There is no banderillero hovering nearby prepared to take the bull away from him with his cape, no surgeon prepared with his penicillin and his operating table to treat a wound. Help is miles away, across an expanse of fields often unmarked by even a goat track. Underfoot is the uneven terrain of a pasture, its grass often coated with a slippery cover of dew. He works by the uncertain light of the moon, his gestures impeded by that inadequate knowledge he has come to increase. It is a fittingly dangerous apprenticeship for a notably dangerous craft.

Several months after the passage of Currito de la Cruz on the screen of the Cine Jérez, on a wind-chilled February evening, a pair of shadows slipped down to the edge of the Guadalquivir. On the opposite bank, beyond a grove of orange trees, began the *dehesa,* the enormous, rolling domain of the bulls. For miles, down to the first slopes of the sierra, those immense spaces belonged to the man who had avenged the blood of his bulls with the blood of his fellow citizens. Patiently, proudly, Don Félix Moreno had rebuilt his herd of Saltillo bulls until now by the dozens they roamed his ranges once again. Nothing was more natural than that Manuel Benítez and Juan Horrillo should have chosen these pastures of the *señor* of Palma del Río for their first forbidden venture into the world of moonlight bullfighting.

They had hesitated some time before coming. In practice, that enterprise had suddenly seemed a good deal less easy than it had appeared on the screen of the Cine Jérez. They wrapped their clothes into a bundle and slipped into the icy water. Downstream they could see the metal skeleton of a bridge, the only bridge providing access to the pastures they sought to enter. A pair of Guardia Civil men, their cloaks turned up against the wind, patrolled its entry. Unsteadily, their feet picking the riverbed for a rock on which to anchor themselves, the two boys struggled through the chest-high water. They reached the other side gasping for breath, their bodies shaking uncontrollably from cold and fear.

For a long time they huddled under an orange tree, waiting for the moon to rise over the sierra. When it appeared, they set out, crouching as low as they could so their silhouettes would not catch a vaquero's eyes. At every sound—a grasshopper's whir, a bird's cry, the thump of a bullfrog—they froze, their ears straining for the distant clump of a vaquero's horse.

Suddenly their ears caught the noise of a new and foreign sound. It was the sound for which they were waiting, the muffled tinkling of the bell of a steer. Like a buoy bell marking a shoal, that sound marked the presence of a part of Don Félix's herd. Slowly, cautiously, the two boys picked their way through the damp grass toward that sound. It grew louder. As it grew louder, Manolo's fear and excitement built up, too, until his heart seemed to batter his rib cage and fear crowded even the hunger from his stomach.

Then, suddenly, the bulls were in front of them. They were barely fifteen yards away on a flat piece of ground atop a gentle rise. There were about a dozen of them. They were, perhaps, two-year-old animals, but to those petrified youngsters looking at a bull close at hand for the first time, they were the largest and most terrifying creatures they had ever seen. The shadows and the gray, uneven moonlight blurred their outlines and distorted their already frightening dimensions.

Manolo recovered first. The moment for which he had been longing was at hand. He gently unfolded the blanket he had stolen from his sister's bed. Silently he spread it apart with the two sticks given him by Adolfo Santaflor, the carpenter who had sounded the alarm from Palma's church tower the day the town fell to the Nationalists. Then, with his bayonet dangling from his left hand, his improvised muleta from his right, he began to tiptoe prudently toward one of the animals, who was lagging slightly behind the others. He forced from his mind the thought that that animal had the strength to spear him like a pig with one thrust of his horns. The instant was too good for reflections such as that. He was about to savor the privilege denied him by Palma's breeders at their *tientas,* and to savor it on the soil of one of them, a man he had been brought up to hate and fear.

Alive with the exhilaration of suddenly finding himself in front of a brave animal, Manolo grasped after what shreds of Luis Rodríguez's instructions his excited mind would deliver to him. Ten yards from the bull, he stopped. He stood up straight, arched his back, and stiffly hung the improvised muleta before him. Nervously, he shook the scrap of cloth. From his dry throat came a high-pitched uncertain call: "Hey, *toro!"*

The animal raised his heavy black head and fixed his dull eyes on the cloth. Manolo forced himself to lock the joints of his knees to still their trembling and tightened still further the taut muscles of his stomach. He repeated, his voice firmer this time, his summons to the bull before him. Horrillo, crouched on his hands and knees at the base of a scrub oak tree, watched the scene in terror. Again Manolo shook out the folds of the blanket and, profiling as had his hero Currito de la Cruz, awaited the bull's charge.

At Manolo's second call, the animal shook slightly as though preparing to burst toward his lure. Astonishingly, he did not. He turned instead and trotted back to his herd.

Manolo stood there watching him go, too stupefied by the sight to make a movement of any sort. That moment was one of the most extraordinary revelations of his life. He had barely been able to push his feet in front of the bull. Yet that proud heir of the Saltillo strain had fled before the movements of his dyed muleta. A near-hysterical self-confidence filled him and the fear flowed out of his limbs in one rush of feeling. Years later, an idol of the corrida, he could still recall his boyish awe at that moment and wonder if a different reaction from the bull might not have sent him scurrying back forever to the *calles* of Palma del Río.

In fact, the animal's inexplicable departure had nothing to do with fear. The two would-be matadors had, in their haste for combat, forgotten to set up the conditions needed to make a bull charge. A bull's charge is a defensive gesture. He attacks when he feels menaced and insecure away from his herdmates. Reassured by the presence of his herd a few yards away, Don Félix Moreno's animal had felt no need to attack the cloth Manolo had offered him.

For a bull to attack in the open fields, he must first be cut off from his herd and driven, sometimes for miles, until he is psychologically ready to fight. Spent by the emotion of their first encounter with a bull, Manolo and Juan were too tired for such a chase now.

They stretched out under the moon-splashed branches of a wild olive tree and fell asleep. When they awoke, dawn had broken over the *campo* and their herd of bulls had disappeared over some distant hill. Their initiation into the world of Currito de la Cruz would have to await another night.

When it came, it began with a chase, a wild, breathless scramble over the blue expanse of the *campo*. Only the sounds of their own heavy panting, the whine of the crickets and the hoofbeats of their bull marred the silence of the moonlit night. Using their darting bodies as lures, Manolo and Juan drew their young bull on and on until finally, caught up in the game, the animal forgot the growing distance between him and his herd.

At last the chase stopped near a grove of willow trees miles from the spot at which Manolo and Juan had spotted the bulls. It was three o'clock in the morning. Their bull suddenly sensed his isolation from the comforting presence of his herd. He lifted his enormous head upwards, thrashing his horns back and forth against the night sky.

Manolo stared at him. For twenty-four hours, emboldened by the adventure of the night before, he had lived in a state of tense excitement like that of a child to whom a special toy has been promised. Now that toy was before him. "He's mine, he's mine," he whispered to Juan. Horrillo studied his friend. Manolo seemed "suddenly like a madman. His body was quivering and trembling with excitement." Without a word, Horrillo retired to the edge of the willow grove, leaving Manolo alone with his bull.

There was no sound in the pasture. It was so quiet Manolo could hear each tired, panting breath of the bull before him. The bony contours of his black hide blended into the darkness, giving him a terrifying illusion of size. Only the dull light in his eyes and the horns standing out against the dark like the gray-white limbs of a skeleton seemed real to Manolo. More confident this time, he stretched apart the folds of his sister's blanket. Shaking it lightly, he advanced on the dark form. The shadow stirred. With a rush the bull swept at him out of the semidarkness. Manolo clutched the dew-slicked grass with the toes of his bare feet. He fixed his eyes on the bull. Slowly, as he had been taught to do, he drew the muleta along before the bull, past his thighs, and into the void behind him. And it happened. Just as he had been told it would, just as all the rules proclaimed, the black mass slid past his shaking body, following the command of the muleta. Manolo was elated. He spun, and before the bull could go back to the shadows, he drew him back again, then again and again. And each time the bull came past, the delirious boy saw the miracle of the muleta work. An exalting, jubilant sense of triumph swept over him. On and on he went, spinning the bull around, turning him, twisting him at his will until it seemed to the watching Juan that "he was in a trance." Juan stared astounded at the sight: Manolo's sweating body sparkling in the moonlight, the bull's black form spinning around him, until it seemed to Juan that the two bodies must be rubbing against each other.

Finally Manolo stopped and slipped away from the bull. Exhausted, he tumbled to the ground next to Juan. He propped his shoulders against a tree trunk, his head thrust back against its bark, gasping for breath, his body still heaving with excitement and emotion. Over and over again his panting voice repeated one word, a word that summed up, for this teen-age boy, the transcendent moment he had just experienced:

"*Fenomenal . . . fenomenal . . . fenomenal . . .*"

Whatever doubts about bullfighting Manolo Benítez might have had were resolved by that first moonlight encounter with the bulls. The pattern of his life changed. He belonged to the *campo* now. His infrequent visits to the orphanage of Don Carlos Sánchez dwindled in number and length until his place on the wooden bench became permanently vacant.

The priest watched him go with regret. The boy with the runny nose had a bright mind. With luck, Don Carlos thought, he might have done something with that mind. Not much, he knew; the Benítez family's means were too limited for that, and the months left before work would summon Manolo from the classroom forever were too few. But he had

141

hoped to give that mind some parting gift, something that might lighten the dismal years ahead, something to help him raise himself, however slightly, above the total poverty into which he had been born.

And yet the priest understood the lure that was pulling the boy away from his classroom. He was himself an aficionado. More important, he had been to the Benítez hovel often enough to know the squalor and misery in which the family lived. Don Carlos' life had been spent trying to give poor men a cause for hope, but life had taught the good priest to understand despair. He knew well what emotion drove youths like Manolo Benítez into the pastures in search of the bulls.

Anyway, there had been no stopping Manolo. He was out the side door of the orphanage, across the dirt play yard and into the river before the nuns knew he was gone. The scholastic souvenirs Manolo took with him from those years at the orphanage were few. He could count a bit, read but not write his name, recite by heart a few prayers and some of the simple homilies thrust upon him by Don Carlos' nuns. He left, the priest would wistfully recall, "knowing five vowels and little else."

For Manolo Benítez, the exhilaration of his first moonlight encounter was soon forgotten in the pain and brutality of those that followed it. Rare were the animals that proved as willing subjects for his muleta as his first bull had been.

Manolo and Juan now sought out brave cows rather than bulls for their midnight corridas. It was a gesture of respect for the rule that decrees a bull must not be fought before he reaches the ring. Most of the cows in Don Félix's pastures had already been passed, either during their *tientas* or at night in these same pastures by some other urchin. The animals knew the rules of the game they were about to play, and they made Manolo and Juan pay in pain for every lesson they gave.

The boys' nights in those moonlit pastures became punishing ordeals. In winter and early spring, they were tortured by the cold. The icy waters of the Guadalquivir almost paralyzed their lungs as they struggled to swim the river. Later, the wind lashed their wet rags against their skin, scraping them over their goose pimples until their flesh became raw and sore to touch.

They went barefoot, running in the dark over thorns and thistles, squashing their way through mounds of cows' dung. They shredded open the soles of their feet on flint rocks, stubbed their toes or twisted their ankles on unseen mounds and holes.

Then there were the animals. Sometimes it was a blunt blow to the pit of the stomach that battered the breath from the boys' lungs. The flat surface of the animal's horns smashed against their rib cages and jolted their kidneys. They jarred their backs and wrenched their knees in their falls; sometimes they smashed their heads on stones lying in the pasture, staggering to their feet dizzy and nauseated, to be slammed down again by an onrushing animal.

There were nights, Juan Horrillo would recall, when no gesture seemed to work, when the animals hit them so much that "there wasn't a pimple on our bodies that didn't hurt." On other occasions the animal they had driven from its herd proved to be so vicious that they fled in panic from its horns. Once Juan remembered watching an animal smash Manolo until he could no longer stand. On his hands and knees, his partner dragged himself away from the cow to a clump of wild mustard. There he retched, then collapsed, half conscious, into the weeds wet with his own vomit.

The minor wounds they received in those ordeals they ignored, sopping up their blood with a twist of their ragged clothing. For the others they had one remedy. Manolo was the first who needed it. One night a young cow picked open three inches of his thigh with her horn. Juan dragged him to the cover of a cluster of trees. He gave him a stick to bite on, so no scream of pain would alert a prowling vaquero. Then with his fingers Juan massaged into the pulpy edges of the wound the only antiseptic they had, the contents of a bottle of vinegar. Manolo fainted with pain for the first time in his life.

And so, month after month, their agonizing apprenticeship went on. Time and time again they drove themselves back into the moonlit pastures to receive another battering from Don Félix's animals, hoping to discover in the blows they received the knowledge they needed to fight a brave bull. And each morning they dragged themselves back along the road to Palma, tattered figures in their filthy rags, crusted with dirt and dried blood, lurching to their hovels to collapse exhausted and await another night, another moon and another painful lesson.

143

ANGELITA BENÍTEZ'S STORY

"I WANTED MY brother to be somebody. I wanted him to stay with Don Carlos and learn to read and write so he could become someone better than us. Pepe, his brother, was already no good. I couldn't stand to see my baby brother be like that. Like my father, I wanted him to be a number-one worker, a serious man the people respected. I didn't want him to grow up to be just another peon hanging around the Plaza de Trabajadores begging Don Félix's *mayoral* for some work.

"But he had to have his bulls. I don't know where he got that idea. He didn't get it from any of us. Nobody ever talked about the bulls in my house. I wouldn't let them. My father had never gone to the bulls, so why should he? But, no, he had to be different, my brother Manolo. He had to have the bulls.

"It all started after he stole our blanket. He stopped going to Don Carlos' school then. He'd come home at night with his clothes all dirty and the kids shouting that he had been off to the bulls again.

"I beat him. I beat him as hard as I could. He'd never cry or say he was sorry. He just went off into the corner like a hurt dog. He'd promise me he'd never go back to the *campo* again. He'd stay home for three or four days. Then he'd go back. It was always the same. Those dirty clothes smelling of cow dung for me to wash, all torn apart for me to sew up. I'd beat him some more, and nothing would happen.

"He'd say to me, 'Don't do that. I'm going to be a bullfighter and buy a car' or 'I'm going to be rich. You'll eat again,' or 'Don't worry; I'll be somebody when I'm a bullfighter and your daughter will marry a marquis.'

"Nothing ever changed him. It was always the last time. He was always going to go back to school for me. I wanted that for him so much. Just to have one of us in the family who could read and write a little. Our parents could have been proud of that. But nothing ever worked. I never believed those things he said. I never believed in his bulls. I just prayed to the Virgin every night to take him away from them, to bring him back to me and make him a good man like his father, not a bum.

"Finally, when he wouldn't go to school any more, I told him at least

144

to go out and work like everybody else and help get some food for us. It was no use. He wanted to be the bullfighter and a great person. I would have preferred him to be a smaller person now and a worker then. It got worse and worse. He began to sneak away at night and then come home and sleep all day. Sometimes when I came home at night I found blood on the bed from where he had been hurt.

"Once I came home and he was lying there with a terrible hole in his leg. There was blood all over our bed. I got the only thing I could, a bottle of alcohol to pour in it. It must have hurt him terribly but he didn't say a thing, not one word. I was the one who was crying. I was crying because I hated to see my brother wounded like that, and because I wanted the alcohol to hurt him so much he'd never go back to those bulls again.

"I hated the bulls of Don Félix in those days the way I never hated anything else in my life. My father and the other men like him, they worked like dogs so Don Félix could be rich and have his bulls. All our suffering of the war, it was Don Félix who gave that to us because we ate his bulls. Half the *pueblo* he killed for those damn bulls. And now, his bulls were trying to kill my brother. There he was, all hurt and bleeding from Don Félix's bulls. It was like Don Félix himself was chasing us in our miserable house.

"Oh God, I never understood. I never understood why my brother had to go to the bulls."

*   *   *

The bar was on a corner of the Plaza de los Martiros at the end of the dirt road Manolo and Juan followed walking back to Palma from the *campo.* Outside, a mat of desiccated palm fronds supported by four bamboo poles splashed a small square of shade before its door. Huddled under it were half a dozen frail wooden chairs and a pair of tables, all crammed into the little patch of shadow like a clutch of pedestrians crouching in a doorway to get out of a rain squall. A Coca-Cola cooler, its fire-engine-red paint beaten down to a dull brick color by the sun, rusted apart unused against the wall, a reminder, in this land where ice was more precious than wine, of progress's occasional extravagances.

The interior was barely larger than a modest-sized bedroom. It was divided in half by the bar itself, a chest-high slab of cement. Once that slab had been painted brownish red, the color of the wooden barriers that enclose a bullring. Only a few pale splotches of that original hue now remained, scattered over the gray surface like blemishes marring an unhealthy skin. The top was raw gray cement, pocked and grainy under the fingertips, an eloquent comment on the scruples of the mason who had mixed it. The floor was littered with cigarette stubs, dirt from the square outside, sugar-cube wrappings. Here and there, souring in the heat, lay the half-eaten remains of one of the bar's *tapas* (snacks), each covered, like a warm cow dropping, with its little crown of buzzing flies.

So primitive an establishment required a special reason for its existence. That reason stood behind the bar. It was the establishment's owner, Pedro Charneca, the man who once had been the best friend of Manuel Benítez's father.

Fortune had chosen, among all the destitute citizens of Palma del Río to bestow her blessings upon Pedro Charneca. Charneca's obesity had absolved him from military service in 1936. He had spent the war at the little café where he worked as a waiter, serving with a fine impartiality the Republican militia of Juan de España and their Nationalist successors. Like all the rest of Palma's poor, Charneca had known the dread agony of hunger in the months after the war. Then one lovely day, in 1940, a scrap of paper had changed Charneca's life. It was a winning ticket in the Spanish National Lottery. That ticket was worth ninety thousand pesetas, a sum so enormous that in Palma only people like Don Félix Moreno were able to comprehend it.

The day he heard he had won, Charneca threw aside his waiter's apron and moved to the other side of the bar. He had been a poor man all his life. Still, he was wise enough to know that no one is lonelier than a rich man. Every day at sunrise he stationed himself by the side of the road over which Palma's field hands shuffled off to work. Whenever one of his friends went by, Charneca would say to him, "Where are you going? To work? How much are you going to make? Five pesetas? Here, here's five pestas. Don't go to work. Come drink with me." When he had collected a dozen or so friends, Charneca would waddle off with them to a nearby bar quietly to drink away the day.

He lived like this for almost a year. Then he decided to change his environment and go to Seville. He spent just over a year there living, quite literally, in the city's bordellos. When the year was over, he had three thousand of his ninety thousand pesetas left, and the awe and gratitude of a sizable part of Seville's prostitute population. As drained of emotion as he was of cash, he took his memories and his money and went home to Palma. There, with the last shreds of his winnings, he opened his squalid little bar.

Charneca's friends did not forget his generosity in his moment of glory. They came to his bar to take a morning glass of wine before leaving for the fields or to talk together at night. Soon Charneca's bar became in a sense a postwar version of the bar of Niño Valles in which Manuel Benítez's father had worked as a waiter.

It also had an additional reason for its existence, a reason rooted in the personality of its proprietor. Charneca had two consuming passions in his life: white wine and the brave bulls. He was the acknowledged leader of Palma del Río's aficionados. Here in his flyspecked and dusty little bar the glory and the glitter of the *fiesta brava* had its principal outpost in Palma del Río.

Behind the bar, just over the chalked list of Charneca's debtors, hung the mounted black head of the first bull killed in Madrid's bullring in 1874. Ensconced there under the bull's glassy eyes, his hammy forearms reposing on his bar, Charneca ruled over the *afición* of Palma, oracle, authority and statistician of all that was the corrida.

Charneca's jowls fell off his cheeks in heavy rolls, pulling down the corners of his mouth with their weight. When Charneca talked, it was in a mumble that barely moved his lips, as though the effort of displacing all that facial weight hanging upon his jaw simply wasn't worth the trouble. Nonetheless, when Charneca talked about the *fiesta brava,* Palma listened. Well could he boast, "Whenever anyone in Palma wants to know anything about the bulls, they come to see me."

So complete was his devotion to the corrida, in fact, that it had won him a peculiar distinction: that of having the biggest telephone bill in Palma del Río, the biggest, perhaps, in the whole province of Córdoba. Charneca had installed his telephone at considerable expense and only after incurring a good deal of suspicion in the town. In Palma the telephone was, after all, an instrument generally reserved for those whose social classification was considerably higher than that of a barkeeper.

During the *temporada,* the bullfighting season, he used that phone constantly, telephoning over the length and breadth of Spain each night for the results of the day's principal corridas. When he had received them all, he chalked them up on a blackboard he proudly hung outside the door to his bar. No newspaper in Spain, he boasted, announced the result of a day's corrida as quickly as Pedro Charneca's blackboard bulletin. It was a staggering luxury, for the telephone tolls it demanded devoured the profits of the bar and condemned Charneca's establishment to its slow but certain physical decay. But it secured beyond all challenge his position as an authority on the bulls, and that, for Charneca, was more important than a new coat of paint for the structure in which he held forth.

All day long he would stand there behind his bar, his eyes slowly glazing over with a watery film produced by his tumblers of white wine, serving drinks to his friends and discoursing on the bulls. Like some Greek Orthodox monk on Mount Athos venerating his holy icons, Charneca had hung on the wall beside him his most precious possessions, there to rekindle his faith should ever his spirit falter. They were reproductions of twelve portraits of Manolete, in each of which he was performing a different pass; they were set in identical wooden frames, all taken from a 1942 calendar advertising Pagoda León manzanilla wine.

It was natural that Manolo Benítez should begin to drop by Charneca's little citadel of the corrida. Charneca did not notice the first time he came. He just seemed to be there all of a sudden, looking as though he had always been there, standing silently in a corner, staring at the pictures of Manolete. He was dressed in rags, Charneca noted, "because that's all they had in that family, rags."

He began to come regularly, early in the morning, his face usually dirty, his clothes torn. Charneca knew perfectly well from looking at him that he had been in the *campo*, fighting illegally at night. Manolo would stand there and stare at the pictures for ten, fifteen, twenty minutes without a word. Then, as quietly as he had come in, he would drift away.

Dozens of youngsters did that. Charneca's bank of pictures was a kind of shrine for the town's teen-age aficionados. But most of them, Charneca had noted, liked to boast about the likelihood of their doing the same thing someday. This one never said a word.

One morning Charneca was alone in the bar when Manolo came in. As the boy stared up at Manolete's pictures, Charneca leaned his heavy chest across the bar and spoke to him.

"Listen, kid," he said, "if you want to make money and be a torero, that's what you have to do: stand quiet like that with your feet together when the bull goes by."

Manolo stared at Charneca with gratitude, too stunned and shy to respond. The fat ungainly man who had been his father's best friend pushed a plate of pork *tapas* across the bar to him.

"Take one," he said.

From that brief exchange a friendship was born between the fat man and the teen-ager. It was a friendship that the boy would need in the years to come.

*　*　*

The meticulously whitewashed building with the green shutters at the head of Palma del Río's Calle Pacheco had, in fifteen years, undergone astonishingly few physical changes. The flower boxes under the wrought-iron grilles screening its windows still blossomed with clusters of bright red geraniums and pink azaleas. Inside, the hand-cranked telephone that had summoned Sergeant Emilio Patón and his Guardia Civil to rebellion and death still hung in its place on the wall.

Only the portraiture had changed—and, of course, the personnel. In the place once occupied by the picture of the Republic's President Manuel Azaña now hung a stern and formal color portrait of General Francisco Franco, his full stomach encircled by a burgundy sword sash. And, behind the white wooden desk at which Emilio Patón had dreamed of retiring to the mist-bound seascapes of Galicia, sat a new man. His name was Rafael Mauleón. He was a squat man, with heavy curling shoulders and biceps as thick as a butcher's. The skin of his face seemed as hard and cracked as a puddle of mud baked dry by the sun. Its color, however, was a bright red, a tint that reflected Mauleón's chronic high blood pressure and his devoted, daily consumption of a quart of raw red wine. That shading had won him, among the citizenry of Palma del Río, the nickname of "El Colorillo," the equivalent of "Tomato Face."

It was a name uttered with little affection or familiarity. Rare are the policemen anywhere in the world as little loved by their fellow citizens as Spain's Guardia Civil. Instruments of repression at the service of king, communist and dictator, their name had become synonymous in Spain with brutality and the dispassionate suppression of the poor for the nation's rulers, whoever they might happen to be. The severe regulations of their organization insured their effectiveness. No member of the Guardia Civil was ever allowed to serve in the region in which his own or his wife's family lived. Familiarity and intimate association with the town's people of the areas which they policed were rigorously forbidden. And their assignments frequently were rotated to prevent any special ties of affection from binding them to a particular village or town.

Rafael Mauleón, "Tomato Face," had come to Palma del Río from a mining village in Asturias. It had been a difficult assignment. Civil disorder among the hard and bitter miners of Asturias had been as frequent as it was rare in Palma. More often than not, when Rafael Mauleón's men had opened fire in the hills around his mountain village, someone had fired back. His brutally effective performance in slowly imposing order in those hills had won him a promotion and his transfer to the more tranquil neighborhood of Palma del Río.

To maintain the peace in Palma and its environs, Mauleón had at his disposal twelve men, six horses and two dogs, a force quite adequate to maintain the peace in a community whose problems rarely went beyond a barroom brawl between a pair of hot-tempered Palmeños or an occasional wife-beating. Palma del Río represented to "Tomato Face" and his men a stable, ordered existence. Regular and uninterrupted now were his wine-filled lunches and the siestas that followed them. "Tomato Face" had no intention of allowing circumstances or individuals to interrupt his pleasant existence in Palma or to oblige him to return to an assignment such as the one he had left behind him. Its continuation depended heavily on the benevolent regard of Don Félix Moreno. Don Félix's personal relationship with the governor of Córdoba province was such that with a telephone call he could have effected Sergeant Mauleón's transfer to Asturias from which he'd come.

The sergeant was notably careful to cultivate a good personal relationship with the *señor* of Palma. Once a year, on New Year's Day, his green uniform freshly pressed, his black patent-leather hat polished to a radiant ebony hue, he rode to La Vega to join the more important citizens of the town in a ceremonial glass of wine and a toast to the order, peace and prosperity of the New Year.

To the growing regret and irritation of Sergeant Mauleón, the order and peace of a year in the early 1950's began to be interrupted with increasing frequency. The black wall telephone beside his desk began to

sound with distressing regularity bringing complaints in an epidemic out-
burst from all the great landowners of the region. But to Sergeant
Mauleón's discomfiture, most of the calls came from the ranch house of
Don Félix Moreno. At first they were relayed by one of his foremen. But
finally it was the angry voice of Don Félix himself that ordered Sergeant
Mauleón to the telephone. His pastures, he complained, were being regularly violated by teen-age hoodlums intent on fighting his bulls. He
angrily ordered Mauleón to put an end to those incursions.

That demand, Sergeant Mauleón realized, was not one to take light-
heartedly. He was enough of an aficionado to know what an insult to
Don Félix's honor it would be if one of his bulls should be ordered from
a bullring because it had been fought before. He well knew how much his
reconstituted herd of Saltillo bulls meant to Don Félix. As much as the
tranquillity of Don Félix's *toros,* it was the peaceful life of Sergeant
Mauleón himself that was being threatened by the hoodlums prowling
Don Félix's pasture.

"Tomato Face" vowed to become the implacable foe of those ma-
rauders—a vow that was to place the beefy sergeant in opposition to an
improbable, if not altogether unworthy, set of enemies: a pair of teen-
age boys. For Manolo Benítez, the road to fame was about to open with,
as its first milestone, the inscription of his name in the police records of
his nation.

A new sound now rang through Don Félix's pastures, mingling with
the tinkle of the steers' bells, the moan of the wind off the sierras and the
whine of the cicadas. It was the quick hoofbeats of the Guardia Civil's
patrolling horses. "Tomato Face" was as good as his word. He was determined to bring peace back to the pastures. Every time a full moon
broke over Palma, he sent his men off to the fields in search of the intruders plaguing Don Félix's herd.

Their early efforts were not notably successful. The first time a pair of
mounted Guardia Civil men surprised Manolo and Juan caping a young
cow, Manolo scooped a stone from the ground and flung it at the leading
guardsman's horse. It struck the animal in the head. With a shrill neigh
of pain, the horse bucked, spun about, and bolted off into the darkness.
The second guardsman hesitated, then galloped to the aid of his companion, letting the pair escape.

Their second meeting with the Guardia Civil was, from their standpoint, even more successful. They found a horse left tied to a tree by a guardsman who had decided to sneak up on them by foot. They untied the animal, which went galloping off before the policeman's furious eyes. Shortly thereafter, "Tomato Face" himself decided to join his men in their full-moon patrols of Don Félix's pastures. He rode off armed with one of his most treasured personal possessions. It was a hand-carved oak stave, a couple of inches thick and about three feet long. "Tomato Face" had two such staves. He valued them so highly that he had given them pet names, the names of two of his personal heroes, men whose bullfight-ing exploits had galvanized Spain just a few years before. He himself had carved and burned those names down the faces of the sticks. They were "Manolete" and "Arruza."

The sergeant's perseverance finally earned its reward. One summer night a pair of his guardsmen came galloping out of the darkness on Manolo and Juan as they played a brave cow. "Tomato Face" rode up in triumph behind them.

He got down from his horse. Smacking his stave against the palm of one of his hands, he advanced on the terrified youths. A pair of guards-men jerked Manolo upright by the wrists. "Tomato Face" went to work on him, bludgeoning his back, his buttocks, and his legs with the blows of his club. Manolo's screams echoed across the darkened pasture, spurt-ing out in pain as each thump of "Tomato Face's" stave stamped onto his flesh the name of one of the men he had come here to emulate. Then it was Juan's turn.

When he was finished, "Tomato Face" climbed back into his saddle and, giving Manolo and Juan a last warning to stay out of Don Félix's pastures, rode away.

Their discovery in Don Félix's pastures posed for Manolo and Juan difficulties that went far beyond the pain of "Tomato Face's" beating. Now they were identified as the hoodlums who were disturbing the peace of Don Félix's bulls. That knowledge, added to their already unsavory reputation as petty thieves, marked them as incurable delinquents for the men of the Guardia Civil. The guardsmen, rather than wasting their eve-nings prowling Palma's pastures, now often waited for a complaint from one of the town's breeders, then headed directly for the hovels of Manolo and Juan.

A torn shirt, a bruise, or a spot of blood on a bedcover was all a guardsman needed to drag the pair off to the Guardia Civil barracks for another beating by "Tomato Face's" pet staves. Sometimes the Guardia Civil didn't even bother looking for some sign of their nocturnal corridas. They gave them a beating anyway, convinced of its therapeutic value.

The Guardia Civil now attributed to Manolo's and Juan's hands any unresolved petty thievery in Palma. Sadly, Charneca, the barkeeper, watched the Guardia Civil men "beating the boy around like an old rug for every orange that was missing from a tree in Palma." On the Guardia Civil rolls in their Calle Pacheco barracks, Manolo was already condemned with a notation destined to follow him through the rest of his life. It came after the entry for "Public and Private Moral Conduct" in the standard dossier compiled on every Spaniard by the vigilant Guardia Civil. "Constantly stealing fruits and vegetables in the fields," it read; "mistreats the animals and property of others. Considered a chronic delinquent."

Despite the beatings, Manuel Benítez and Juan Horrillo kept going back to their moonlight rendezvous with the animals of Don Félix Moreno. They had no other choice if they were to pursue the dream, now so remote, that had inspired them one winter's evening in the Cine Jérez. The months glided by until one day three years after their first encounter with "Tomato Face," when disaster overtook them again. It occurred, naturally, in Don Félix's fields. They had been prowling his pastures for three days and three nights, fighting by night, hiding in the weeds and underbrush by day. They had lived on a handful of oranges and the few edible weeds they could find on the *campo*. On their third night they were caught caping a cow by the Guardia Civil.

Exhausted and half famished, they were driven back to Palma, prodded along in front of their captors' horses like a pair of Roman prisoners. "Tomato Face" and his staves were waiting for them at the Calle Pacheco. The sergeant beat the boys until they could no longer stand up. When he had finished, he ordered them locked in his stables. Never would Juan forget their first gesture when they found the strength to lurch back onto their feet. They hurled themselves at the feed troughs of the Guardia Civil's horses "like a pair of starving dogs." Shoving aside the horses' heads, they clawed up the scraps of oats left in the trough and stuffed them into their mouths.

153

They stayed there, locked up in those stables, for ten days. The sole rations "Tomato Face" provided them were those they shared with his horses: oats and water. They continued to eat like animals, scooping their oats from the horses' troughs by the fistful. For drinking water, they plunged their mouths into the same rusty buckets used by the horses. At night they sought out the corner of the cobbled stable that seemed least steeped in urine and horse dung, scattered straw over it, and went to sleep. By day they squatted sullenly in the open yard of the stables.

They had been there for just under a week when one day Horrillo saw a loaf of bread bounce onto the cobblestones at his feet. An instant later a red-orange coil of chorizo sausage smacked onto the stones beside the bread.

Stunned, the pair looked up. They could see nothing on the bare wall above them except a pair of dark and empty windows twenty feet above their heads.

Every day thereafter it happened. Sometimes it was an orange, a piece of cheese or a carrot. But always, each day, at some unpredictable moment those mysterious gifts came tumbling to their feet.

Finally, a day or two before their release, Horrillo discovered who their unseen benefactor was. He happened to glance up at the wall of the Guardia Civil barracks at the instant a chunk of bread was arcing down toward them. Beyond it, in the open window, he caught a glimpse of Sergeant Mauleón's wife. Shocked by her husband's brutality, she had seized the moment offered by his absence on patrol to throw his teen-age prisoners a few scraps from his own kitchen.

Even that brutal sojourn in Sergeant Mauleón's stables failed to keep Manolo and Juan from the *campo*. Furious, under unrelenting pressure from Don Félix, "Tomato Face" decided on a more lasting solution to his problem. In the spring of 1954, shortly after Manolo Benítez turned eighteen years old, a bagful of fruit was plucked from a fig tree near the convent of Santa Clara. "Tomato Face" ordered Manolo arrested for the crime. This time he sent Manolo to begin his adult life serving a three-month sentence for vagrancy in the Miraflores prison in Córdoba, where his father had wasted away so many of the last months of his own life.

Angelita hoped in vain that her brother's stay in Miraflores prison would turn him away from the bulls. No sooner had he come home to the

Calle Belén than he was off again with Juan Horrillo. This time, however, the pair decided to escape "Tomato Face's" vigilant patrols by finding new pastures to conquer beyond those lying at the outskirts of Palma del Río. They would wander off for two or three days at a time, trying their luck in ranches farther down the Guadalquivir valley. As mysteriously as they had left, they would wander back, dirty, famished, often bearing the still-fresh sores of some midnight encounter with a bull. Gradually their absences grew longer.

"One day," Angelita recalled, "it seemed that they had gone for good. It started like all the other times. I came home from work and they had disappeared in the clothes they were wearing without one word to anybody. Days went by, then weeks and months, and I never had one word from Manolo. I never knew where he was, or what he was doing. I didn't know if he was in jail or in a hospital or in his grave. Every night I went to see Ana Horrillo, Juan's mother, and asked her if she had any news.

"Ana Horrillo knew how to read, and every night she bought a newspaper. I don't know where she ever got the money to do that, I think she almost had to stop eating to buy it. Every night she read it because she thought there might be news about them in there. She didn't read the bullfighting columns to see if they'd had any of those big triumphs they were always talking about. She read the accidents and the arrests to see if they were dead or in jail. The only news we got, though, we got from a truck driver in the village, who said he'd seen them walking along the road outside Huelva.

"Seven months went by like that, seven months when I didn't know if my brother was dead or alive. Then one night I heard him scratching at the door. I opened it and there he was. He said, 'I'm hungry.' All he had brought me home from those months was an empty stomach, a head full of lice and his clothes all covered with cow dung to wash."

JUAN HORRILLO'S STORY

"THERE IS NO road, no field, no village square of this sunburned land of Andalusia that did not know our wandering feet. For months we wandered up and down our land, through every one of its valleys and its plains, to its mountains and its sea, looking for adventure. There is not a bull breeder in Andalusia, not even Don Eduardo Miura, whose pastures we did not know, whose animals did not pass before our capes.

"We wandered free like the eagles. Sometimes we hitchhiked. We rode in trucks of grain, lumber, cattle; once, even, we sat in the middle of a load of goats. Sometimes we walked for days, begging a piece of bread or sausage from the farmhouses we passed. We stole the fruit from the trees and the vegetables from the fields, and we learned to sneak into a chicken house and strangle a chicken with our fingers before he could make a sound.

"Sometimes we rode the trains. On the passenger trains we hid in the lavatories or climbed onto the roof when they came to get the tickets. We knew the freight trains like railroad men. We knew where to hide, how to find an open car, how to catch them. We knew the times they left and the places they went. We even had our favorites like "El Pescador," the fish train, that left Cádiz for Madrid each night at ten with the seafood for the capital. We knew this Andalusia like we knew the *calles* of our Palma del Río.

"Sometimes we slept at night in the fields by a fire. Sometimes we found an old stone hut or shack and slept there. Sometimes a farmer let us into his stables or his hayloft. We worked when we had to, a day here, a day there. We begged when we could, spreading our capes in a village square with a sign that said we were hungry bullfighters. A tomato, an egg, a peseta or a few coins—the people dropped them there on our capes for us.

"We learned to live with the fields. We ate acorns and fir nuts, wild asparagus, sorrel and *cardo*. In the worst times we ate the grass the bulls ate. We knew what herbs to crush and spread on our wounds to stop the bleeding if the bulls got us. In the winter when the bad weather came and we caught cold, we learned to burn eucalyptus leaves and breathe in the smoke to cure ourselves. It was the season of our adventures. Manolo Benítez was learning to be a bullfighter and I was his soul."

*　　*　　*

The fruits of those adventures were bitter. Through the Gypsy slums of Seville's Triana they marched, over the marshlands of Huelva, past the seaweed-hung walls of Cádiz. They tramped the Arabic alleys of

Granada, the desolate spaces of Extremadura, the vineyards of Jérez. They were just two of dozens of others like them, emaciated figures seared by the sun to the dark hue of the soil, stumbling along through the same whitewashed villages and dangerous fields, all of them pursuing the same miracle in a land whose miracles had long since vanished.

They were called *maletillas* after the bundles of belongings they carried slung over their shoulders. Like Manolo and Juan, like the imaginary hero, Currito de la Cruz, they pursued the mirage of the bullring. No corner of Andalusia was without them. In that land of clacking castanets, of the flamenco, of the lace elegance of the mantilla and the cool waters splashing in tiled patios, they were the other face of the image Spain held up so enchantingly to her visiting tourists, the reminders of Andalusia's unrelenting and abiding poverty.

Halfway through the twentieth century, while her neighbors marched toward a prosperity without precedent, Spain, and particularly Andalusian Spain, remained frozen in the postures of the past. At a time when the Guardia Civil of a country town could concentrate its energies on a couple of wayward youths yearning for a better life, Spain awaited the production of her first automobile. Television was still unknown. Three quarters of her homes had no toilets and less than one in five had running water. Agricultural production had just returned to its pre-1936 level.

As a result, there were thousands of youngsters like Manolo and Juan wandering Spain, too, in those mid-fifties. The roads they followed led, however, to Madrid, Bilbao, and Barcelona, and beyond them to the coal mines, the steel mills, the factories of Western Europe. Half a million of them would flow away from Andalusia's soil, driven out by hunger and a landholding system so archaic that four thousand men, two percent of Andalusia's landowners, reaped two thirds of the harvest of her soil. By the thousands they clustered in the damp, fog-shrouded steel towns of the Ruhr, in the soot and soullessness of the Saar's coal-mining communities, dreaming of the sunshine and the Spain they had left behind for the dignity of a weekly pay packet in a foreign factory.

Those roads were open to Manolo and Juan Horrillo, too. They offered a far more certain escape from their hunger than the illusory promise of the corrida. But those two, and the scores of other *maletillas* who roamed the highways with them, were a minuscule, dissenting minority of Spain's wandering youth. They wanted it all, these youngsters, not just

157

the weekly assurance of a pay envelope. The land to which they sought admittance was a land of men in panama hats and cigars who rolled up to the front gates of the estates of Don Félix Moreno and his peers in their own proud automobiles.

They hounded the cafés where the small-town impresarios arranged their occasional corridas, imploring for a chance to show some public their skills. They clustered at the gates of the fincas at *tienta* time, begging for a chance to play a calf before the breeders' distinguished guests. And always at night they crept into the fields to fight by moonlight, to learn the patterns of another pass, to extract from one more animal a little more of the limitless lore of their art.

The world they were trying to enter was one of the most inbred, most closed societies in existence. Courage and ambition alone were not enough to buy admission to its ranks. Friendship was needed, and the aid of someone already inside. Access to that world was natural to a Domingúin or an Antonio Ordóñez. Sons of matadors, they were born inside its perimeters. They had only to present themselves at the gates of a finca to be invited in to display their skills. To Manolo Benítez and the hundreds of faceless young men like him, the gates of those fincas were firmly closed. The testing of a brave cow was a serious business and the breeders did not let just anybody participate in it. To draw a young Miura cow to the picador's horse was a signal honor; it was not accorded lightly. The ranchers extended such privileges to adolescents already known to them or those recommended by men whose judgment they trusted.

Sometimes they included a boy who pressed a frayed and stained calling card into their hands. Those cards might come from another rancher, once mildly impressed by the bearer's skills, a retired manager or a second-class matador; they were passports into the world of the corrida issued by one of its citizens. The *maletillas* who had them cherished them more than a thousand-peseta note. Often they could not even read the few words scribbled on them. But they carried those dirty, thumb-worn scraps of paper with the same ardor they bore the medals of local Virgins around their necks. The cards were, for those youths, the keys to the gates of opportunity. They could occasionally win for them the chance so regularly denied Manolo and Juan.

For the two young Palmeños there were only the leftovers. Sometimes, uninvited, they leaped into the ring anyway. On such occasions the recognition they won was generally a beating administered by one of the rancher's vaqueros. Once in a great while a rancher would let them perform a pass or two on an inept cow destined for the slaughterhouse, or an animal that no one else had succeeded in passing. Those were the only *oportunidades* offered to Manolo Benítez and others like him.

Yet they all hoped that one day, in some *tienta,* one of those "fat men in panama hats with the big cigars" would recognize the gold of genius in their gestures and summon them from their anonymous little pack of *maletillas.*

In the *tientas* in which Manolo Benítez managed somehow to perform, however, no one stepped forward to offer him help. No well-fed face called to him from behind the *burladero* of a breeder's private ring. Years from the first revelation of Currito de la Cruz, after two years of fruitless wanderings across Andalusia, he was as far from that dream as he had been the moment he stepped out of the Cine Jérez into the cold of a winter evening. His fingers had never even touched the tassels of a suit of lights. He had never killed a bull. He had never earned a peseta with the gestures of his cape. All he had gained from those years was the scars of his beatings and the memories of the lessons the bulls had taught him by moonlight.

He and Juan were destitute. They were despised by their townsmen, despaired of by the only humans for whom they cared, dreamers who no longer had a reason for their dreaming. Finally, after a last uneventful *tienta* in a last unremembered finca, Manolo and Juan gave up. They turned their wandering feet around and began the trek back home to Palma del Río with their empty stomachs, their heads full of lice, and their clothing covered with cow dung. Once there, Manolo Benítez made the gesture he had vowed he would never make. He went, as his father had done, and his grandfather, to ask work from the *mayoral* of Don Félix Moreno.

* * *

A pair of eyes as blue as two freshly laid robin's eggs set José Sánchez apart from the dark-eyed Andalusian world around him. Barely a strand of hair had fallen from his head in over fifty years of life. It all still lay there in curling rolls, as totally white as the fur of an albino kitten, contrasting brilliantly with the mahogany stain of his perpetually sunburned face. He was a proud, handsome, hardworking man, and every day of his hardworking life José Sánchez had spent in the service of Don Félix Moreno. He was his *mayoral,* his senior employee, the custodian and foreman of his vast estates.

He was regarded by his fellows with a mingling of respect and resentfulness, fear and dislike. So total was his devotion to the man whose bulls he guarded that Sánchez had barricaded himself in Don Félix's abandoned ranch house at the outbreak of the Civil War, ready to defend his employer's property with his life.

If the social distance Sánchez's position placed between him and the men he hired in the Plaza de Trabajadores was appreciable, however, the economic gap between them was notably less so. Sánchez lived in a one-story stone shed two miles from Don Félix's ranch house on the opposite side of the Guadalquivir River. Half of the shed Sánchez shared with the mules and horses assigned to his care. Its floor was beaten earth. There was no electricity and no water. The bull pastures were the toilets for Sánchez, his wife and six children. Water they hauled to the shed from a well a few hundred yards away.

Inside the shed the family had one enormous room. It served as kitchen, dining room and living room. Beyond it were the luxuries of Sánchez's existence: three bedrooms. The stone-and-mud walls of the main room were hung with the few memorabilia of Sánchez's life: portraits, withered and brown like dying autumn leaves, of his mother and father, of himself during his military service and on his wedding day; a well-thumbed Virgin; and Sánchez's most treasured possession, a signed photograph of Alfonso XIII offered to him by the monarch during a visit to the Moreno ranch in pre-Republic days.

Sánchez knew well the reputation of the gangling youth he found standing at his doorstep one evening in that hot summer of 1955. The last time he had seen him, he had been slumped in the stables of the Guardia Civil, his body still covered with the bruises left there by "Tomato Face's" clubs. Then he had silently expressed the hope that those clubs had cured forever the boy's desire to prowl Don Félix's pastures. He had had a pang of regret, too, for it was his custom to punish the intruders he caught in his pastures by locking them in his stables to scour them clean. Had he caught Manolo half the times he had fought in his fields, he reflected, he would have had the cleanest stables in Spain.

Now, cap in hand, Manuel Benítez, the son of José Benítez, a good and honest worker, was asking for a job in the fields he had so often prowled at night.

Sánchez only half believed Manolo's vows to reform and give up the bulls. He decided, however, it would be better to lock up the wolf inside the fold than to have him roaming free outside. He agreed to hire him.

To his surprise and gratification Manolo turned out to be an exceptionally good worker. The wolf, however, grew restless in the fold. Manolo's back may have been bent over hoeing Don Félix's cotton; his eyes were drawn irresistibly to those open ranges beyond the cotton lands where his bulls beckoned. His good intentions dissolved. He headed back to the fields at the first chance.

Almost immediately Sánchez realized someone was getting into his domain again. His suspicions fell naturally on his newest field hand, but each time he was accused, Manolo produced an alibi. If he had proved elusive on his earlier forays into Don Félix's fields, he seemed to be totally uncatchable now.

"He could run the fastest and hide the best," Sánchez was forced to admit. "The finca was so damn big that if he wasn't fighting in one part of it, he was fighting in another. I could never catch him. He was the ghost of the *campo.*"

With each passing of the moon, Sánchez's fury mounted. The tactics and ambushes he and Sergeant Mauleón plotted together to catch the intruders grew more complex and more subtle. He swore regularly at the family dinner table that with his latest trap he would finally catch the ghost of the *campo.* And just as regularly he and his vaqueros rode home at dawn empty-handed.

Many frustrating months would pass before the unhappy *mayoral* would discover the reason for his consistent failure to catch Manolo. There was, indeed, a wolf within his fold, but not the one he suspected. It was, instead, a person whose presence graced his family dinner table. It was his eldest daughter, Anita, a graceful dark-haired girl who was the pride and comfort of his advancing years. She was betraying her father every night the full moon rose over Palma.

ANITA SÁNCHEZ'S STORY

"I MET HIM at the Feast of the Virgin, September 18. He had just started working in the fields for my father then. He was ugly and he had a funny way of walking and of talking. He had already been in jail for chasing the bulls in our fields and stealing figs from somebody's fig tree. Everbody said he was just a thief and a bum and that one day he would go back to jail and stay there for the rest of his life. But he was warm and simpático. I couldn't help it; I liked him right away.

"I didn't dare say much to him at the Feast. My brothers were there. He was below our social class and they wouldn't have let me talk to him much. Then a few days later my father found a footprint in the mud not far from our house, on the path leading to the bull pastures. My father was sure Manolo was always going into his fields at night to fight the bulls. So when he saw that footprint, he and one of his vaqueros went down to where Manolo was picking cotton. They dragged him back to the footprint and my father made him put his shoe in. I could hear Manolo from our house, yelling that anybody could have a foot as big as his. Then they began to beat him. I could hear them shouting, my father and the vaquero, and even, sometimes, the sound of their sticks hitting him. Then Manolo began to scream. Finally, my father and the vaquero rode away and left him alone.

"A little while later I went to get water at our well. It was an old dried-up riverbed about three hundred yards from our house. The water dripped out of an iron pipe stuck into the old river wall. Manolo was sitting there under the pipe washing himself. He had his shirt off and his back was covered with blood. They had hit very hard, my father and his vaquero. I went back to the house to get him some medicine. There wasn't much, some alcohol and some cotton.

"I bathed his cuts with alcohol and he did his best not to cry out and let people know we were there together. My father would have beaten me the way he beat Manolo if he had found me there with him.

"Afterwards we talked for a while. He didn't talk much. He told me right away, 'Voy a ser torero—I'm going to be a bullfighter.' He kept saying that. I told him, 'You can't become a bullfighter without a manager to help you. Nobody can.'

162

"He looked at me. 'I don't need anybody, you'll see,' he said. 'Anything can happen. Planes can land on the sea.'

"The well became our secret meeting place. It was our frontier. My father wouldn't let me go any farther away from the house than that. Manolo couldn't come any closer to the house without getting caught. There was a flat gray rock just above the pipe. It was just big enough for the two of us to sit on. We'd sit there in the sun and talk, and eat gooseberries we picked from the bushes in the riverbed. He was always the same. He was always telling me how he was going to be a great bullfighter and triumph all the time.

"He was usually working in the cotton then, and I'd send my younger sister out to whisper to him the time we could meet by the well. That way I didn't attract my parents' attention. Sometimes I'd leave a note for him under the rock. He couldn't read. He'd take it to somebody who could. He'd have him write an answer. Then he'd sneak back and leave it for me in the same place. He put a stone on our flat rock to tell me a message was there. Every time I saw that stone, my heart would start to beat fast.

"I knew my father was always trying to catch him fighting the bulls in our fields every time there was a full moon. Manolo used to sneak away after work and hide in the fields until darkness came. Then he came down to the well. After my father left, I lowered some food on a string from the kitchen window. As soon as my mother was sleeping, I climbed out my bedroom window, got the food and ran off to the well. I whistled three times, that was our sign, and he came out of the darkness. While he ate, I told him where my father had gone. That way, Manolo could always go to some other part of the finca where they couldn't catch him, and fight his bulls in peace.

"The only other time we could see each other was on Sundays in Palma del Río. We used to go to Mass at noon at the Ermita (the Hermitage), the shrine to the Virgin on the hill over the Guadalquivir. It was one of the few times my parents weren't always watching me or keeping me busy working. The whole town would stroll off to Ermita together. I would drop back behind the family and Manolo would sneak up to me. Usually he was laughing and playing the clown.

"Then one morning in May he came up to me there, and he was very serious. He told me he wanted me to be his *novia,* his fiancée. I blushed because I was afraid somebody might hear him. I knew my parents disapproved of him so much that if they ever found out I was his *novia,* they would never let me see him again. And me, I wanted to see him again. I wanted to be his *novia.*

"That Sunday, at Mass, during the consecration, when no one was looking, I bent over and took the medal of the Christ of the Great Power that my father had given me for my first communion from around my neck. After Mass when we were walking back to Palma, I lagged behind again. I slid up to Manolo and took his hand. I pressed the medal into his palm. 'I'll be your *novia,*' I said. Then I turned and ran back to my parents."

*   *   *

Manolo Benítez was twenty that spring; Anita Sánchez was fourteen. To the life of the former inmate of Miraflores prison, the dark-haired Anita brought "a touch of purity." In later years, when movie stars and models besieged the doors of his hotel suites in Spain and South America, he would recall her as "the only girl I ever really loved." Inevitably, Sánchez discovered their idyll. Few things could have angered Don Félix's proud *mayoral* more than the knowledge that his favorite daughter was seeing a young man he considered a worthless delinquent. The fact that Sánchez did not have a toilet in his stone shed did not stop him from having social aspirations for his daughter. Angrily, he forbade all contact between Anita and Manolo.

His edict was ignored almost before its echoes had died in the Sánchez household. Anita and Manolo continued their covert meetings by the rusting waterpipe in the dried-out riverbed that lay at the frontier of their youthful affections. At night Manolo often prowled the open fields around the Sánchez house, hoping for a glimpse of Anita through a window. Sometimes, leaning against the trunk of a laurel tree, he would stare for hours at the outlines of the shed profiled against a starlit sky and "listen to the sounds coming to me from inside, imagining what Anita and her family were doing there." Those happy, idle reveries could have their brutal awakenings; on occasion, Sánchez's dogs caught his odor in the night and came snarling across the fields after him, their slashing jaws adding a new set of scars to a flesh already marked by the clubs of the Guardia Civil and the bulls of Don Félix Moreno.

Thwarted in his ambitions, beaten back into the rut from which he had been trying to escape, frustrated even in those first awful yearnings of love, nothing seemed right in the life of the bitter orphan of the Calle Belén. Yet his life was not without its small triumphs. That year he leaped unbidden into Don Félix's bullring during the ranchers' annual *tienta.* His features carefully concealed by an enormous cap, Manolo drew a series of creditable passes from the stubborn calf before him.

"Holá, Don Félix," he shouted to Palma's grand *señor,* "this one's for you."

Impressed, Don Félix shouted back, *"Chico,* if you go on like that, the bulls will help you eat."

Suddenly Manolo's little display was interrupted: the calf slammed against him, jarring his cap from his head. For a second he stood there in the middle of the ring, unmasked before the surprised and angry eyes of José Sánchez. The *mayoral* announced to Don Félix that any skill this hoodlum was displaying he had acquired illegally in the Moreno pastures. Don Félix's face reddened. He ordered two of his vaqueros to take Manolo behind the bullring and give him a beating that would teach him some respect for private property.

There were, however, some *"olés"* awaiting Manolo. Suddenly he was offered the chance he had yearned for so long. His benefactor was a most unlikely figure. It was Don Carlos Sánchez, the parish priest.

DON CARLOS SÁNCHEZ'S STORY

"WHEN YOU ARE the parish priest of a town like Palma, you learn to be ingenious. You have to. There's much to do here and not much to do it with. Any way of raising money for the parish is a good way. I knew about Manolo's wanting to become a torero. We all did. It was the town's little joke those days. I decided to do something about it. 'If Manolo wants to be a bullfighter,' I asked myself, 'why not organize a little corrida and earn some money for the church?'

"We hadn't had a corrida in Palma since the day the anarchists burned the bullring down. Before I could announce the news, though, I had to get some bulls. Matadors you can always find. It's the bulls that are difficult. It costs a lot more to get a bull than it does to get a matador to fight him. I went out to see Don Félix and I convinced him it was his Christian duty to sell me three bulls at a good price. He promised me three three-year-olds that he hadn't been able to sell, for twenty-one thousand pesetas. So I announced that that year we would celebrate the feast of the *patrona* with a bullfight for the benefit of the parish's good works.

"We decided to hold the fight in an open field just beyond the wall of Don Félix's *corralón* where it joins the old Moorish wall behind the church. I got the young people to make the ring by driving stakes into the ground in a rough circle. Everybody would just stand around with their elbows hanging over the stakes. We put a rope behind it to separate the people who had paid from the ones who were just trying to see for nothing. Then I announced that we would sell tickets to adults for fifteen pesetas and to women and children for five pesetas.

"That's all anybody talked about in Palma for days. Of course, as soon as Manolo heard about it, he came to me and asked me if he could fight. I selected him, Juan Horrillo and Alonso Sánchez, the youngest son of Don Félix's *mayoral,* as my three matadors. I knew that half the town would come to laugh at Manolo, but he—he took it very seriously. Three days before the fight, he came to the church. In a very serious tone, he asked me what *apodo* he should take for the fight. He didn't like El Renco, he said, because it wasn't dignified enough for a bullfighter. I asked what he was picking for Don Félix that fall.

" 'Beans,' he said.

"So I told him, 'Call yourself El Niño de las Habas—The Kid of the Beans—because that is what you are, a bean picker.' "

* * *

As Don Carlos had hoped, half of Palma del Río turned out for the *patrona's* bullfight. It was a happy, raucous crowd, laughing noisily, passing bottles of wine from hand to hand. Half-drunken men draped themselves over the poles surrounding Don Carlos' bullring like soldiers leaning from the windows of a troop train. Don Félix Moreno was there, smiling benignly at the crowd from his perch atop his horse carriage drawn up alongside the ring. Charneca, the barkeeper, was nearby, his face shaded by an enormous panama hat. In one hand he clutched a bottle of white wine, in the other a handkerchief with which he mopped his sweating face.

Sergeant Mauleón, properly solemn as befitted the occasion, marched among the crowd bestowing upon his wards a faint—and usually unreturned—smile. Shortly before five, the excitement mounted with the arrival at Palma's *plaza de toros* of the afternoon's three matadors. Manolo's suit of lights for this festive occasion was the work clothes in which he had been harvesting beans an hour earlier. The trio shared one "cape," an old shepherd's cloak. In deference to their lack of experience —and in recognition of the state of Palma's medical establishment— Don Carlos had decreed there should be no kill.

As grim and determined as any matadors preparing to stride across the sand of Seville or Madrid, the three field hands surveyed the improvised cages before them and waited anxiously for the entry of the first animal. Juan and Manolo speculated nervously together on the possibility that they had already encountered that beast in some corner of Don Félix's *campo*.

The hour of six began to strike from the belfry of Our Lady of the Assumption overlooking the bullring. As it did, a black-robed figure emerged from the belfry's stairwell. Although Spain's rules of clerical behavior made it improper for Don Carlos to attend his own bullfight, ecclesiastical considerations were not going to keep him from watching it. With a mumble of apology to the cranes nesting there, he settled down in the bell tower to watch his corrida from the special vantage point it offered.

As the last stroke of six sounded, the corrida began. Proud and dignified, the three matadors marched into the ring and doffed their cloth caps to the fight's president, Palma's iceman. Watching the first bull rush from his pen, Anita Sánchez closed her eyes and muttered a hasty prayer to the Virgin. It was, from Anita's standpoint, a supplementary gesture. She had already gone barefoot for three days to invoke the Virgin's blessing and protection for Manolo this afternoon.

The fight was a noisy, happy performance bearing little resemblance to the stately ceremony of the corrida. One of the bulls showed an overwhelming reluctance to fight. Spectators kept jumping into the ring to join the matadors in passing the two that would charge. Drunks distracted the animals by slapping their palms against the bullring's poles or waving their hats at them.

It was a howling success for all concerned except the day's three matadors. They soon understood they were just accessories to the crowd's childish good humor. When the fight was over, a group of steers led the bulls off to the slaughterhouse. That evening, after the bulls had been hung and weighed, Don Carlos collected the price for their sale as meat.

The *patrona's* bullfight had earned the parish purse of Our Lady of the Assumption the appreciable profit of slightly more than a thousand pesetas. Before slipping that sum into the folds of his cassock, Don Carlos offered each of his matadors a 100-peseta note for his performance.

That wrinkled bill was the first money Manuel Benítez had ever earned before the horns of a bull. Years later, when he had earned millions of them, he would still be able to recall the ecstasy with which he had caressed that soiled slip of paper—and the use to which he put it. At dawn, as much of a pariah as ever, he would be back picking beans in Don Félix's fields. But that evening he laid claim to a luxury he had never before dared seek. He asked Anita Sánchez to the movies at the Cine Jérez.

Even in Palma, the social dispensations the corrida bestows upon its heroes could have their brief effect. In recognition of Manolo's role that afternoon, her father let her go.

*　　*　　*

The fame for which Manolo had longed in Don Carlos' improvised bullring would soon be his. The quality of that fame, however, and the circumstances prompting it, were far removed from those that had stirred his youthful imagination. He was caught by his old enemy, "Tomato Face," creeping up the banks of the Guadalquivir with a sack of stolen oranges slung over his shoulders. Juan Horrillo was caught with him.

Sergeant Mauleón handcuffed them together. He hung the sack of oranges around Manolo's neck in a public proclamation of their crime. They were barefoot, shivering with cold, dressed only in the wet underpants in which "Tomato Face" had found them crawling up the riverbank. With a brutal whack of one of his hand-carved oak staves, he sent them stumbling forward. He drove them like that, half naked, through the streets of Palma del Río. At each corner his alcohol-corroded voice summoned the town to the sidewalk to witness their degradation.

Down *calle* after *calle* they went, over the cobbles Manolo had dreamed he might be carried on the shoulders of his admiring peers as the conquering Niño de las Habas. The eyes he had hoped to fill with awe peered at him from doorways and hastily opened shutters, contempt replacing the respect he had so wanted to inspire. One aged woman puckered up her dry lips and spat at them. Marching down that gauntlet of scorn did something to Manolo that "Tomato Face's" club had not been able to do. He wept, with shame.

Just before they reached the Guardia Civil barracks, Manolo caught, among the faces lining the sidewalk, a glimpse of the one person he had hoped would be spared the sight of his disgrace, Anita Sánchez. Her eyes remained fixed on his for an instant. Then she turned and ran away. Wiping his tears with the back of his free hand, Manuel Benítez bitterly swore to avenge the degradation he had suffered this afternoon with an act Palma del Río would never forget.

* * *

The light of another full moon coated the cobbles of the Calle Pacheco with its glistening light. Inside his barracks a sleepy Sergeant Mauleón reached for his jangling telephone. The good sergeant had devised a tactic to insure the tranquillity of his rest on these moonlit nights. He had installed a series of informers along the routes Manolo and Juan were obliged to follow on their way to Don Félix's distant fields. To his fury, "Tomato Face" heard the voice of one of those informers warning him that Manolo and Juan had disappeared into the night. He summoned his guardsmen from their sleep and saddled his horses. Then, with all the seriousness of a sheriff's posse out to head off the rustlers at the pass, his troop went jangling off to the *campo*.

In a distant corner of these fields, well ahead of their pursuers, Manolo and Juan stared in awe at the sight outlined in the moonlight before them. It was the enormous bulk of an animal as big, it seemed to Juan, "as an American car." It was one of Don Félix's treasured seed bulls. For years he had been a lord of those fields, transmitting to his offspring the centuries-old heritage of the Saltillo caste.

"Tonight," Manolo whispered to his terrified companion, "we fight him."

It was the most memorable evening Juan Horrillo would ever spend in anybody's bull pasture. In the shadows, the bull's massive 1,600-pound form stretched out until he seemed to Juan to disappear back into the shadow. Yet it appeared to Juan that Manolo swung him back and forth as though his heavy head were chained to the old blanket he held in his hand. In the silence of the fields, Juan could hear only the rush of the bull's hoofs across the grass and the grunts of Manolo as he swept by. He watched half paralyzed by fear, wondering if he would ever have the courage to lure the bull away should the animal overturn his friend. But Manolo remained on his feet. To the spellbound Juan, it seemed that "God's hand was on Manolo's shoulders" that night.

Suddenly Manolo pulled away. He rushed back to Juan.

"This one I kill," he said.

He grabbed from Juan's hand the Civil War bayonet they had discovered on the banks of the Guadalquivir. Its rusted blade had served them for everything except the function for which they had intended it. Neither youth had ever killed a bull. Now Manolo prepared to live for the first time in his life the "moment of truth," the most dangerous instant in the bullfight, and to live it with the outsized animal before him, his massive head unbowed by any picador's thrust. He had practiced the gesture a thousand times. He stood a few feet from the bull, his toes clutching the damp grass to steady himself. He raised his sword in his right hand, sighting down the uneven blade in the half-light, past the head and the waiting horns to the spot the size of the palm of a man's hand into which he must drive it. With his left hand he dangled his sister's blanket at his feet, moving it just enough to hold the bull's eyes to its folds.

He raised himself to his tiptoes. Then, half closing his eyes, he leaped at the bull. In one blind, wild gesture, he flung the bayonet into the beast's mass. Its tip held for an instant, then slid down into the bull's soft flesh, seeming almost to suck Manolo along with it into the depth of the animal. The bull lurched uncertainly, already coughing blood. He swayed unevenly about the pasture, slowly dying from Manolo's uncertain thrust, bellowing his fear through the night. Then he stopped and Manolo rushed to his side. He threw his exulting arms skyward in the triumphant victory sign of the conquering matador. As he did, ten thousand dollars' worth of seed bull tumbled dead at his feet.

Juan, his faithful companion of these moonlit corridas, broke the spell with the only gesture appropriate to the occasion. He ran to the bull and yanked the sword from its back. With furious strokes he hacked the bull's ears from his skull. Proudly, he offered the two bleeding chunks of flesh to his partner.

Manolo tucked the still-warm ears inside his shirt and the pair started back to Palma. At the edge of town Manolo turned from their usual route home. Beckoning Horrillo to follow him, he headed toward the railroad station. Manolo had a ceremony he wanted to perform there, a defiant mocking gesture toward Don Félix, toward "Tomato Face," toward the whole town that had shamed and humiliated him.

Nearly bursting with glee, he clambered up onto the wooden bench in front of the station. There, in the first gray light of dawn, he hung the ears of Don Félix's seed bull onto the most public place in all Palma del Río, the railroad-station timetable. He jumped down and surveyed his work. Then, laughing hysterically, he and Juan fled, leaving behind their black and boastful trophies, a few last drops of Saltillo blood trickling down the listings of the Seville-Córdoba trains.

* * *

It was midmorning when one of his guardsmen laid the dried ears of Don Félix's butchered bull on "Tomato Face's" desk, and explained the circumstances in which he'd found them at the railroad station surrounded by a circle of chuckling Palmeños. The sergeant was appalled. He and his men had ridden home at dawn, tired but confident that Manolo and Juan, aware of their presence, had not dared to venture into the open fields.

The call he dreaded was not long in coming. Palma's outraged landowner vowed he would personally oversee "Tomato Face's" transfer to another corner of Spain if he did not take action against the murderers of his seed bull in twenty-four hours.

With an unerring sense of purpose, "Tomato Face" strode off to the Calle Belén. He found Manolo asleep, still wrapped in the bloody shirt in which he had carried his bull's ears back to town. It was all the evidence

"Tomato Face" wanted. He rounded up Juan and marched his two chronic delinquents back to the Calle Pacheco.

This time he did not bother to beat them. The sergeant decided instead to end his problems and secure his personal tranquillity with one definitive action. He decided to cast these two delinquents he had been unable to reform on other, more distant authorities. With a stroke of his pen he banished Manuel Benítez and Juan Horrillo from the town in which they were born. They were to leave Palma del Río by sunset, he ordered, and they were not to return without the written consent of his Guardia Civil barracks.

There were few people in Palma del Río to whom Manolo wanted to say goodbye. He went to see Charneca. "I'll either become a torero or go to France," he told him. "But one way or another, when I come back to this miserable town, it'll be in a car."

Angelita wept. It was a final disgrace for her, the confirmation that she "hadn't known how to raise him," that she had failed in the promise she had given her dying mother. She gave him the few pesetas she had and the address of his sister Encarna in Madrid. Then she let him walk away alone, his cloth cap in his hand, because she was "too ashamed to go to the railroad station with him."

Pride prevented Manolo from saying goodbye to the one person in Palma he really wanted to see before leaving. He had not seen Anita Sánchez since his public humiliation at Sergeant Mauleón's hands.

This afternoon of his exile coincided with a local feast, and as Manolo and Juan walked to the railroad station, the *paseo* was already forming on the Avenida General Franco. The young of Palma, wearing costumes for the occasion, were beginning to stroll up and down the avenue. The boys and girls, who by custom walked in separate groups, exchanged shy, tentative glances through their masks.

Anita Sánchez was among them. Her costume was a worn bedsheet girdled with a piece of rope. Her head was covered by a brown paper bag which she had painstakingly made into a mask. Anita knew of Manolo's banishment from Palma. Her father had announced it with unconcealed satisfaction at midday. It was in hopes of catching a final glimpse of him that she was here with her two younger sisters.

Finally she saw his dejected figure slipping through a group of giggling youngsters. She walked past him. He did not look at her. She was furious until she realized he had not recognized her under her paper mask. She turned and walked back. Timidly she lifted the bag from her face.

They spoke again. She asked Manolo where he was going to go. He told her they would take the train to Córdoba. From there, he said, he would hitchhike to Madrid. Anita promised to write to him. Then she drew from under her sheet the gift she had brought with her, hoping for this moment. It was her photograph, the only one she had, marking—like the medal Manolo wore around his neck—her first communion.

The pair started to walk together. Suddenly, impulsively, Anita made a bold gesture. It was one that would stamp her publicly, for her father, her brothers and all the gossiping town, as his *novia*. She took his hand and, holding it firmly in hers, marched beside him toward the station.

She watched the boys board the train. As it left, she stood on the open platform watching them go, a forlorn little figure standing by the railroad tracks in an old bedsheet. Then she pulled her brown paper bag back onto her head and walked away. As she passed the Seville-Córdoba timetable, its figures still stained by her *novio's* last defiant gesture in the birthplace he was leaving behind, she stopped. With a swift gesture she ripped a piece of the bloodstained paper from the wall and tucked it inside her bedsheet. Then, her head high, she marched back to the *paseo*.

173

CHAPTER FIVE

Madrid:
THE
CORRIDA

SHRILL AND MOCKING, the noise spurted from thousands of pursed lips. It poured down from every corner of Las Ventas, from the last row of *tendidos* to the umbrella-lined circle of *barrera* seats around the ring, a whistling wail that was as accepted a part of the bullfight as the trumpet's call or the crackling gaiety of a pasodoble. It marked the entry into the bullring of a pair of mounted men. As they passed into the ring, one swung right, the other left. Their horses' right eyes were patched over with blindfolds and their flanks hidden under thirty-three pounds of quilted cotton canvas. The riders were only a little less grotesque. They wore big felt hats, their brims curled upwards, embroidered bolero jackets and cream-colored chamois breeches. In their right fists they clutched the symbols of their trade, called *picas* or *varas,* eight-foot-long wooden poles capped by four-and-a-half-inch spikes tapering abruptly to blunt points one inch long. They were picadors, the pariahs of the bullring.

Brutal, bloody, graceless, the task they were about to perform was an

174

ugly intrusion into a spectacle that pretended its end was beauty. It was the most criticized, the most disliked, and, perhaps, the least understood act in the ritual of the bullfight. Anglo-Saxons sickened watching it, shocked by the suffering, real and imagined, it imposed on the picadors' horses. Spaniards suffered with them, not for the pain it brought to the horses but for the abuses it all too often directed at the bull.

Essentially, the picadors' job was to force a lowering of the bull's head and horns by jabbing the points of their pics into the lump of muscle, the *morillo,* with which the animal carried them. That reduction of the bull's power was vital if the matador was to work successfully with him with his muleta. Furthermore, it was necessary to allow a proper kill at the end of the fight. If at that instant the bull carried his head and horns at their normal height, it would be virtually impossible for a matador to go in for his kill over the horns as demanded by the regulations of the bullfight.

Beyond that, the picing provided the measure of the bull's bravery, the illusive, fleeting quality upon which the fight was based. The instrument chosen for the test was, in fact, a larger version of the goad with which, three years earlier, Impulsivo had been set irrevocably upon the road to this bullring. Now he would be called to leave upon that spike that had spared him the slaughterhouse a last imprint of his courage, the gesture which would be, in a sense, his epitaph in the long annals of the corrida.

All the attention of the crowd was fixed on Impulsivo, poised in the center of the ring, his massive head pointed toward the hulking form of El Cordobés' senior picador, José Sigüenza.

$$* \quad * \quad *$$

Once the jeers that had marked their entry into the bullring had seemed the loveliest sounds José Sigüenza's ears had ever heard. It was nineteen years earlier, on a hot July afternoon in the *plaza de toros* of San Roque next to the granite slopes of Gibraltar. José was just eighteen years old then, and opening before him, for the first time, were the gates of a bullring. The chamois trousers of his borrowed picador's costume were patched and baggy. His embroidered jacket flopped loosely about his shoulders. On his head the wide-brimmed *castoreño,* the picador's hat, hung over his ears with the listless air of an old rowboat foundered in six

175

inches of water. Yet José thought himself that hot afternoon as splen-
didly dressed as any scarlet-jacketed noble riding off to the hounds. So
excited had he been that he wanted to "kick the horse and go charging
into the ring at a gallop."

That moment had represented the culmination of all his youthful
dreams, the realization of Jose's one aim in life. Where most young Spaniards aspired to be matadors, José's own aspirations had pointed him
elsewhere. He had always wanted to be the man on horseback.

His birth had destined him for quite a different task, that of a docker
as his father was, as his grandfather had been, on the wharves of Algeciras. By the time he was fourteen he was a full-fledged docker staggering
under the crates his boyish frame hauled from the ships unloading at
Algeciras. But the young stevedore daydreamed of other tasks for his
swelling muscles. One day he retrieved from the debris-littered wharves a
magazine whose cover was adorned with the portrait of the man who
would become his idol, his guide in his flight from the docks. His name
was Rafael Andrada. He was a forty-five-year-old Sevillano and he was a
picador. So precise were the placings of his pic that he bore the nickname
of "El Artillero," the gunner.

Soon El Artillero's portraits papered the wall over the straw sack on
which young José Sigüenza slept. He began to spend his Sundays and
holidays working as a laborer in the plazas around his home, hitching up
the dead bulls to the horses that dragged them from the ring, smoothing
out the sand, and guiding into the plazas the mounts of the men whose
functions he coveted. Finally on that July afternoon in 1945 the impresario of San Roque had asked him to fill in for an ailing horseman. Totally confident of his untested capacity, José put on the picador's costume and, for the first time, settled onto a horse.

There was no glory for him that afternoon. But then glory was not one
of the compensations of the calling he had chosen. He displayed, however, an attribute much prized in a picador, stolid competence. That
competence won him further invitations to work as a picador in the third-
class corridas of his province. Gradually José learned to handle his horse
properly, to apply with quiet skill the strength built into his frame by the
hard hours on the wharves of Algeciras. Three years later José left the
docks forever to take up the wandering life of a bullfighter's *cuadrilla*.

Now the first picador of the first matador of Spain, the former docker stood at the very pinnacle of his craft. He was among the most esteemed and respected members of his union. He held, in fact, the position that had been El Artillero's when he had pasted his boyhood idol's photo to his wall. No aficionado would ever ask for his autograph. No giggling band of girls would ever scamper after his fleeing footsteps when he left the front door of his hotel. But he was, nonetheless, a preeminent member of the most envied and romanticized fraternity in Spain.

For four months out of every year he wandered Spain like an impatient vagabond, bullring after bullring drifting past his eyes in a numbing parade until sometimes José did not even know the name of the town in which he was performing. During the long, hot nights of summer, he crossed and recrossed the parched plateaus of his nation, his bruised body jackknifed into the worn jump seat of the Chrysler that served the *cuadrilla* of El Cordobés, when the plaintive wail of a flamenco drifting up from the driver's radio was the only sound in the black stillness of the car. He slept as best he could, slouching against the seat in front of him, his head resting in his arms. Sixty thousand miles José covered like that every year, rolling on and on through the black and sodden nights while the rest of Spain slept. The eccentric schedulings of their matador's corridas could take them from Málaga in the south of Spain to France's Arles, then back to Badajoz on the Spanish-Portuguese frontier, 870 miles in less than seventy-two hours. The companions of their lonely nights were columns of trucks hauling their produce across Spain, their gray hulks punctuated occasionally by the whizzing image of a foreign sports car plunging south in search of the sun. Sometimes during those endless nights it seemed to José that the only thing real in his life was "a pair of headlights rolling on and on down a highway that never seemed to end."

Each autumn, when it was all over, José's jousting with the bulls had earned him more than seven hundred thousand pesetas. To gain such a fortune, the stevedores of Algeciras would bend their backs for a decade. Scrupulously he carried the sum back to Córdoba where, for four months, his wife and his young son had awaited his return.

Like a sea captain home from a long expedition or a traveling salesman returning from a business trip, José the picador fell comfortably into a bourgeois and routine existence. His apartment was a model of cleanliness and ordered living. Its slippery floors invariably gave off the flat, slightly rancid smell of the wax with which his wife polished them daily. The paths along which José was expected to walk over them were traced out in old rags, removed only on Sundays or for a visitor of note. Only a souvenir brought back from a season in Mexico or an occasional photograph of José in action reminded visitors of the occupation of the head of the household.

José's wife was a quiet, self-effacing woman who had never seen a bullfight and never intended to. Side by side, the couple passed their winter evenings in front of their most glittering possession, an enormous German television set. And each spring when the bulls began to run, José got up from his easy chair and his ordered life and set out once again to make his living thrusting the force of his 224 pounds down a steel-pointed wooden stave driven into bulls like the one called Impulsivo now poised for him on the wet sands of Las Ventas.

José's standing orders were to pic his bulls as rapidly as possible. Today José had a special consideration in mind. El Cordobés had warned him to get the picing over with quickly. The matador wanted to give the Madrid public a demonstration of his skills in front of animals that were still strong and dangerous. He would certainly call for an end to picing before the four pics permitted by the rules had been placed. It was a crowd-pleasing gesture, and José knew that El Cordobés had no intention of missing it. A special responsibility weighed therefore on José. He had to protect his matador from both the bull and his own ambitions. He had to work swiftly and cleanly. But he had to be certain the one or two pics he would place were deep and punishing. Otherwise he would deliver to his matador an unnecessarily dangerous animal.

His pic held in his right hand, his left drawing the reins of his horse firmly to him, José studied the animal being led toward him by the lure of El Cordobés' cape. Impulsivo's enormous bulk gave him pause. Big bulls were the bane of picadors. Size usually meant strength, and the stronger a bull was, the more likely it was he would be able to topple horse and rider with his charge. This bull, José thought, was very likely to send him sprawling into the sand.

Beneath his thighs José could feel the trembling of his mount, awake now to the danger that was only a few yards away. He lowered his pic until it pointed out almost at right angles to his horse. He raised the pole so that it passed under his armpit, solidly pinned against his rib cage by his biceps. Before him, El Cordobés, with a brusque movement, snatched his cape away from the oncoming bull. That gesture exposed Impulsivo, frustrated by the flicking cloth his horns had not been able to catch, to a familiar sight: another four-legged creature like himself.

Impulsivo swerved from his course, and with a swift, brutal movement hurled his black mass at José's horse. At the instant his bristling *morillo* grazed the tip of his pic, José jammed his weight onto his flat Andalusian stirrups and drove his lance into Impulsivo's hide with all his force.

An oozing of blood marked its entry. All José's strength, however, had no perceptible effect on Impulsivo's charge. With a grunt the bull sent his horns smashing into the quilting protecting the horse. The thrust of his charge momentarily lifted the horse off the ground. For an instant José feared he and his horse would be hurled against the barrier by Impulsivo's charge. His pic was now almost vertical, jammed solidly into the black mass writhing below him. Twisting right and left in furious bursts of strength, Impulsivo's horns sought out the horse's underbelly. His own blood was now streaming down his black shoulders, and as that stream thickened, a new chorus of catcalls rose from the crowd.

El Cordobés signaled José with a quick gesture of his hand to release the animal from his pic. But like a pair of boxers locked in a clinch, the two adversaries were unable to break apart. Despite his wound, Impulsivo continued to tear at the canvas that covered José's horse. That courageous display won for Impulsivo a burst of admiring applause. Finally El Cordobés, advancing to within a few feet of the bull's horns, caught his attention. Impulsivo abandoned his assault and with a grunt plunged toward the matador's beckoning cape. With a series of quick movements, the matador led him away from the horse and fixed him immobile in the middle of the ring to catch his breath. Then El Cordobés indicated to his picador that he was largely satisfied with his first pic. He wanted the second to be shorter and less punishing.

José barely had time to take note of those instructions before he saw El Cordobés was bringing the bull back to him. With a spinning jerk of his cape, El Cordobés again snatched the lure away from Impulsivo's eyes and left him staring once more at the familiar creature he had just attacked.

The searing, unexpected pain of the first pic will occasionally make a bull pic-shy and reluctant to charge the horse a second time. Not so Impulsivo. He hurled himself forward again. This time with an intuitive snapping of his head as he came, he caught José's descending pic and deflected it so that it slid off to one side of the *morillo*. His rush unchecked, Impulsivo slammed into the pads protecting the horse.

The crowd howled in delight. Impulsivo smashed his horns into the quilt as José, caught off balance, tried desperately to hold him back with his badly placed pic. Off balance, unable to contain the bull's charge, José thought of only one thing: how to keep himself upright in his saddle. Savagely, Impulsivo dug his horns into the quilting, searching out the horse's underbelly. José felt the weakened horse beginning to buckle under him. Sensing the same thing, the crowd roared. Impulsivo jammed at the horse's belly again, lifting the frightened animal off his feet. In an instant, horse and rider seemed certain to topple into the wet sand of Las Ventas.

*   *   *

Three hundred miles to the south, a sound broke the tense silence of the men gathered around the television set at Seville's Los Corrales bar. It came from an elderly man slumped in a despondent lump against one of the worn green benches of the café. It was a great catarrhal "argh," violent enough to shake the phlegm loose from the most congested of throats. It was, the men around him knew, the sign that Antonio Cruz was concerned. And, indeed, he was. He was worried about the horse on the verge of stumbling to the ground under Impulsivo's vicious charge. It was his horse.

Antonio Cruz was Spain's leading exploiter of one of the corrida's most loathsome and lucrative commercial by-products. He was a horse contractor. He supplied every major bullring south of Madrid with the horses used by the picadors during the bullfight. So preeminent was his position in his field that he was known throughout Spain as the Alcade de los Caballos, the mayor—or the boss—of the horses.

The skin of the fingers on Cruz's right hand was one continuous nicotine stain the color of burnt almond, the result of half a century of chain-smoking hand-rolled cigarettes. His face was invariably glazed with a stubble of white beard. His lips curled over his toothless gums in a taut circle, leaving him only a puckered little line for a mouth. An old felt hat, its aged brim twisted into a rolling series of curves like a sheet of warped plywood, rested on his head during most of his working hours and some of his sleeping ones as well. His round stomach pressed against the front of his trousers like an enormous hard-boiled egg, and once he was settled onto his café chair at Los Corrales, Cruz's first act was to unbutton the top of his trousers, permitting his stomach to flow freely into his lap, thus revealing an extraordinary expanse of underwear. For sixty of his eighty years he had made his living sending horses into the bullring, and for twenty-two of them his office had been the worn café bench on which he was now sitting.

Like so many of the men who lived on the periphery of the bullring, Antonio Cruz had begun his association with the corrida as an aspiring matador. One summer day in 1905, he had found himself begging a bull-fight from the impresario of a provincial bullring in San Juan del Puerto near Huelva.

Bullfighters, the impresario informed him, he could get every day. What he needed was horses, and in particular horses for his Sunday cor-rida. Eager, and short of funds, Cruz promised to get them for him. Sunday, proud and triumphant, he showed up at the bullring of San Juan with thirty horses trailing behind him.

The impresario looked at him in dismay. It had never occurred to him to take Cruz seriously. He had already procured his horses on his own. So impressed was he, however, with the young matador's zealousness that he offered him a contract to furnish horses for his three other rings during the rest of the season. Cruz pondered for a moment, then termi-nated forever his unpromising bullfight career. He never put on a suit of lights again.

The economics of his new business were quite simple. He was obliged to have thirty-six horses on hand for a fight with fully grown bulls, twenty-four for one with *novillos*. He received in return a flat sum of four thousand pesetas a corrida. That fee was immutable and was in no way affected by the number of horses he lost each day in that era before the canvas quilt had been devised to blunt the bull's attacks, when the horse's death in the ring was as inevitable as the bull's.

Cruz bought his horses wherever he could find them for three to four hundred pesetas an animal. He got them at the slaughterhouse gate, at

181

horse fairs, from Gypsy horse thieves. When he traveled from bullring to bullring, he took the country roads, buying old horses out of the fields in which they were working.

Success, for Cruz, rested on his ability not to lose more than one horse per bull. If he lost more than ten horses in a corrida, it was a disaster, for that meant that, at four hundred pesetas a horse, he had worked his way through his fixed four-thousand-peseta fee for the corrida. And if one of his horses could survive the assault of one bull and be bludgeoned back into the ring a second time, Cruz could "make a fine profit."

Achieving that was his primary occupation during the corrida. His first-aid treatment to keep his gored animals alive for a second appearance in the ring was brief and rudimentary. He "stuffed their guts back into their bellies with a fist," then "sewed them up with a needle and twine." If any lingering piece of anatomy pushed its way through his hurried stitches, Cruz snipped it off with a pair of scissors. He took a very special pride in his skills in impromptu horse surgery. "No vet ever touched my horses," he could later boast. "I did it all myself. I really understood horses."

Cruz's most disastrous season was 1925. That year he lost 694 horses in ninety-seven corridas. His worst day was August 15, 1923, in the city of Badajoz, where in a corrida featuring Juan Belmonte he lost eighteen horses to the bulls of Don Pedro Coquilla. That toll left him with far fewer than the minimum number of thirty-six horses he was required to muster for the next day's corrida. As his stock of reserves was a hundred and fifty miles away, Cruz took the only course open to him.

Stuffing his pockets with peseta notes, he set out to prowl the streets of Badajoz in search of horses. His first he found on the outskirts of the city towing a Gypsy caravan: a clamorous mass of crying children and clanging pots and pans.

He rode off bareback on the horse after paying "a robber's price" for the animal. Behind him he left the Gypsies, their caravan stranded in a daisy patch, the children crying louder than ever, the pots and pans silent, the men slowly re-counting the packet of pesetas he had paid for their horse.

But on that sweltering August night there were no more itinerant Gypsy caravans in the outskirts of Badajoz to deliver up their aged nags to the "Alcade" of the horses, no farmers willing to deed a beaten plow horse to the bullring. Dejected and despairing, Cruz rode back to the bullring on the Gypsies' horse. Leaving him in the corrals, he started back to his hotel in a hansom cab. As he reached into his peseta-filled pocket for the fare, a flash of inspiration swept over him. He leaned forward and whispered to the driver an offer to buy his horse out from between the drive shafts of his cab. To his surprise, the man agreed.

Filled with fresh enthusiasm, Cruz began to stalk his way across the city, moving from cab rank to cab rank in search of horses. When he found a seller, he unhitched the horse from his cab on the spot. On and on he went with his growing string of horses, leaving behind him in the streets of Badajoz a trail of abandoned hansom cabs, their empty drive shafts pointing upwards in the night, reminders that Antonio Cruz had passed by.

When he found his seventeenth and final horse, he commissioned the cabby to drive him to the bullring before surrendering his animal. Comfortably settled into the seat of the cab, Cruz rode back to the *plaza de toros* in triumph, his sixteen freshly acquired horses clopping along behind him, his commercial honor safe once again.

All that had ended with the introduction of the canvas covering for the horses in 1928. The popular legend that the mattress was hung over the horse to mask his injuries from public view and allow him to die privately in the corrals was nonsense. Cruz's animals now serviced seventy-five to a hundred corridas per year. This man who had sent thirteen thousand horses out to die in bullrings—more than Napoleon had lost marching to Moscow—was now even able to offer the artisans of his fortune the luxury of a death in a slaughterhouse. Some of his horses survived six or seven seasons in the ring.

The horses had been kind to Antonio Cruz, a good deal kinder, probably, than the bulls would have been. He rode to his daily rendezvous at Los Corrales behind his chauffeur in an air-conditioned Mercedes. He lived in an elegant modern villa just outside Seville and owned a summer house on the Costa del Sol. The empire he directed was at this moment earning him more than it had ever done before. That was a reflection of revived interest in the corrida and the debt he, too, owed to the young man now trying to lure a bull from the flanks of one of his horses.

Cruz was particularly anxious that this horse withstand Impulsivo's attack. A few seconds before this pic, a glance at his notebook had shown Cruz this was a five-year-old horse he had bought only a few weeks earlier. It was the horse's fourth corrida, and his loss now would be most uneconomic.

Nervously, Cruz reached into the pocket of his suit coat and drew out the black pouch in which he kept the tobacco for his hand-rolled cigarettes. That pouch was a special talisman. He had carried it for almost forty years. Embedded in it was a gold medallion representing a wounded horse. It was one of Cruz's horses killed in the Seville bullring April 18, 1925, and it was from that horse's hide that Cruz's pouch had been made.

*   *   *

El Cordobés rushed to his beleaguered picador's aid. Waving his cape at Impulsivo's head, he tried to draw the bull away from the wobbling horse. Impulsivo refused his lure and continued to bury his horns in the folds of the mattress protecting the horse's flanks. Above him, José had finally sunk his pic into the *morillo* and tried now to relieve the pressure on his horse by thrusting all the strength he could muster down his pic. The crowd roared its approval of Impulsivo's furious courage.

Finally, fatigued by his fury and wounds, Impulsivo responded to the invitation of El Cordobés' cloth. He carried his head "a little less proudly now," El Cordobés noted, as Impulsivo dove into the folds of his cape. As he swept past, he gave his massive head another violent jerk upwards and to the left. In bullfight slang, those sudden jabs were called "swings of the censer," from the movement the priest gave to his incense-filled vessel during benediction. El Cordobés considered them particularly dangerous because "they caught you at just the moments you weren't looking for them." And in the case of Impulsivo, he had every reason to believe those gestures came from the faulty vision of his left eye.

Despite that ugly tendency, El Cordobés decided to take a calculated risk with the bull, one he knew would win him the quick approval of the crowd. Lifting his black *montera* from his head, he spun on his heels and sought out the figure of Police Commissioner de Quiros in his presidential box high above him. El Cordobés extended his *montera* to him in a supplicating gesture.

Paco Ruiz, his *banderillero de confianza,* saw the movement of his

184

matador from the corner of his eye. It meant El Cordobés was asking the president to end the picing with what Paco knew was only one valid pic in this awesome animal. Paco gasped. His matador, he realized, "was taking a terrible risk fighting a bull that didn't see right, that had been barely punished by the pic."

"Manolo, Manolo," he screamed, trying to make himself heard over the crowd's approving applause, "not yet. One more, please, he needs one more."

It was too late. Paco's last words were drowned by a new sound, the blare of trumpets calling the picadors out of the ring. Whatever the risk, El Cordobés was condemned, by his own gesture, to finish this fight with a half-blind, underpiced animal.

*   *   *

Their task finished, José Sigüenza and his fellow picador rode out of the plaza. As they disappeared, a new mood overtook the crowd, this one indulgent, as instinctively receptive as the previous one had been reproachful. It heralded the opening of the second act of the corrida, the placing of the banderillas, an action almost inevitably associated with grace and beauty.

That that action should so please the crowd and particularly the uninitiated among it was ironic. Of all the actions of the bullfight, it was perhaps the most useless, the pain it inflicted on the bull the most gratuitous. Theoretically, the jabbing of those metal-barbed wooden batons into the bull's back, just beyond the hump, could correct an animal's tendency to hook to one side in his charges, and tire still further the neck muscles already weakened by the picador's jabs. Both assertions were debatable. The brutality of the picador, so loathsome to the crowd, was a necessity; the elegance of the banderillero, which so pleased it, was probably irrelevant.

For Paco Ruiz and Pepín Garrido, as for most banderilleros, the graceful gestures of their trade constituted an act of profound humility, a daily ritual reminding them of the central failure of their lives. They were men who had resigned themselves to being forever second. That resignation was the hallmark of their craft. Almost every man who ever served as a banderillero had aspired first to be a matador. To thrust two barbed sticks into the neck of a bull and sprint away is one thing, however; to stand quietly before him and kill him with a sword is another. The first requires skill and grace, the second skill and courage.

In some remote bullring, in some moonlit pasture, these men had discovered within themselves a fatal flaw that barred to their hands the command of the matador's muleta. They lacked the courage to stand still before the horns of a bull. And so, to remain within a world they loved but could not conquer, they had consented to place themselves at the service of a man who had the courage they themselves lacked.

Almost every phase of their life was stamped by the hallmarks of its subordinate nature. The nickname assigned them in the slang of the *fiesta brava,* "peones," summed it up with coarse eloquence. In many *cuadrillas,* the banderilleros were never invited to eat at the same table as their matador. They traveled apart, in aging vehicles lumbering along the highways, while their matadors sped through the night in the best cars their bank accounts could command. No gold braid was allowed to sparkle from a banderillero's costume; black or silver was the color traditionally reserved for their modest suits of lights. During their matador's triumphant journeys around the bullring, they walked one pace behind him, humbly picking up the flowers tossed at his feet by an exulting crowd, the only crumbs of glory the corrida assigned them.

The very action they performed could be, skillfully done, an act of breath-catching elegance, yet even the satisfaction of evoking that elegance was usually denied them. The first maxim of the banderillero's trade was to do nothing that would draw attention to himself. Attention was something to be monopolized by his matador. A banderillero's job was to be quick, competent, and self-effacing. He was expected to thrust home his sticks with dispatch, professionalism and a total lack of brilliance. Dispatch was, this rainy afternoon, the quality their matador most wanted Paco and Pepín to display.

El Cordobés, eyeing them from his position along the *callejón,* snapped to Paco, "The banderillas, quick."

Paco grabbed the pair of red-and-yellow sticks offered him from behind the barrier. When the corrida was over, those sticks would be sold to souvenir hunters for over three hundred dollars apiece. He clutched them in the fist of his left hand. Quickly he spat onto the thumb and forefinger of his right hand, then lubricated the sticks' points with his spittle. With a nod to Pepín, he stepped into the ring and advanced toward Impulsivo.

Thirty feet from the bull, Paco stopped. He held a banderilla in each hand, its blunt end pressed against his palm with the circle of his fingers. Slowly he raised his outstretched arms, like a conductor raising his baton, until they stood out like wings from his chest, the banderillas pointed in and straight ahead toward Impulsivo's inquisitive eyes. With a snap of his wrists, he smashed the batons together, sending out a dry clash to draw Impulsivo's attention.

Paco watched Impulsivo's immobile form, looking for the first warning of his charge. When it came, he too began to run, toward the bull, slowly at first, then gathering speed as Impulsivo advanced, moving to the right in a narrowing quarter circle. As he ran, Paco silently cursed the heavy, wet sand sucking at each of his fleeing footsteps. With a supreme summing up of his will, he forced his eyes to stare beyond the onrushing horns to the dark corner of Impulsivo's hide where he would jab his sticks. That was one of the rules of his trade: never look at the horns. If you did, Paco knew, fear could freeze your feet and you couldn't go on running toward the bull.

Of all the members of El Cordobés' *cuadrilla*, Paco was the farthest removed by birth and upbringing from the world of the *fiesta brava*. He had not seen his first bullfight until he was nineteen years old and then only because his father had almost dragged him into Seville's majestic Real Maestranza bullring to see one. Paco had other things on his young mind than the corrida. He had graduated from high school at sixteen. He had a good job as a clerk in a business news agency. He was attending night school to further his education. So auspicious had his first months of employment been that his employer had promised him a raise and a job as a reporter for his twentieth birthday.

And yet something happened to that serious young man on the sunny spirals of the Maestranza that April afternoon. It was, perhaps, the sort of miracle Spaniards so often ascribe to the bullfight but rarely believe. In any event, years later, Paco Ruiz himself would be unable to describe the sentiment that had overtaken him that spring day. It was as though he had been "struck by the grace of God." Leaving the bullring, he turned to his father and announced, "Papá, I'm going to be a torero."

The astonished man burst out laughing.

Papa Ruiz laughed too soon. Tormented by whatever aspiration it was that had struck him that day, Paco quit night school and his job and marched into his father's butcher shop announcing he was ready to do something his father had urged him to do for years. He would, he said, enter the family business. Paco's father was skeptical. Finally he told him, "All right, but you start the hard way." The hard way was learning how to cut up animals at the family's assigned station at the Seville slaughterhouse.

That was exactly where Paco wanted to go. In Seville, as almost everywhere else in Spain, the slaughterhouse served as a kind of trade school for apprentice toreros. It was there that a youngster could learn to kill a bull. The boys bribed the butchers to stand aside and let them take their places in the slaughtering line. Thus several generations of toreros had learned to use their swords properly on the dumb steers destined for the dinner tables of Seville.

Paco's education in the slaughterhouse went quickly. With a rusty sword purchased in Seville's flea market, he had soon hastened over a hundred steers to Papa Ruiz's shopwindow. On his day off, Paco haunted Seville's bullfighting cafés, looking for a chance to show off his skills in a *tienta.*

Papa Ruiz soon became aware that his son's publicly announced desire to become a torero was not a joke. He determined to rid him of his foolish ambitions once and for all with a classically simple parental stratagem. He located the organizers of an underfinanced corrida in a nearby village. For the sum of two hundred pesetas he bought his son a place in the *cartel* for the village bullfight and, along with it, the privilege of killing one of the three "bulls" of the day, an aged cow named Romerita. Papa Ruiz counted on Romerita to give his inexperienced son such a painful introduction to the corrida that he would forget forever his aspirations to be a matador.

Things failed to work out quite the way Papa Ruiz had planned. Paco was brilliant. The delighted citizens awarded him both of Romerita's ears and her tail, and took him on a triumphant tour of the village on their shoulders. Poor Papa Ruiz was speechless. He was quite unaware of his son's clandestine activities in the slaughterhouse. He was convinced instead that this had been the first time his Paco had stepped in front of a brave animal. Where a few moments earlier he had deplored his son's ambitions, he was now suddenly convinced that he had sired a genius of the *fiesta brava*. Instead of an idle dreamer, he now saw his son as the successor to Manolete. All the way back to Seville he ran up and down the aisles of the train, showing off Romerita's ears, boasting that his son would soon be the toast of the Spanish nation.

Encouraged by his proud father, Paco was able now to devote all his time to becoming a bullfighter. He fought in a series of village corridas in Andalusia. He appeared on a beginners' program at the Real Maestranza. He celebrated his twentieth birthday with his first fight with picadors. He was gored, but he returned to the ring.

His rapid little rise reached a culmination of sorts when he fought on a regular program of the Real Maestranza where, just six months earlier, he had witnessed his first bullfight. He was excellent. That winter, with his press clippings and a newly hired manager, Paco set out for Madrid and laid siege to the offices of Don Livinio Stuyck. His efforts were a success. On March 2, 1950, he made his debut as a *novillero* at Las Ventas. It was a most inauspicious occasion. Paco performed indifferently. Worst, his modest resources had forced him to "prepare" the press in an indifferent fashion. The critics repaid him in kind. His notices ranged from indifferent to scathing.

Paco fired his manager and set out on his own. For four years Paco, in the slang of the *fiesta brava,* "ate the mad cow." Broke, unknown, without a *cuadrilla* or a manager, he wandered over Spain, seizing any chance he could find to fight. He fought as a last-minute replacement, without picadors, in crossroad towns, for the insignificant fees of two or three thousand pesetas. In between fights, he haunted the offices of Don Livinio Stuyck with his little sheaf of press clippings, begging for a chance to redeem himself.

Paco was not a bad bullfighter; nor was he a good one. He was something worse: he was mediocre; and he inspired only indifference in the crowds before which he performed. The career that had begun so swiftly took four painful years to die. The end came in Málaga when a loathsome half-blind bull from the ranch of Pablo Romero was so ungracious as to refuse to die for Paco. Paco chased him around the ring, hacking away at him with his sword like a butcher in the Seville slaughterhouse. As he scampered after the seemingly immortal animal, the crowd showered him with cushions, cigar butts, orange peels, Coca-Cola bottles and oral abuse. Three times he heard the trumpet issuing an *"aviso,"* a warning from the president to kill the bull. And still "the damned animal wouldn't die." Finally the bull was taken away alive and Paco was hounded from the plaza in disgrace.

He became a banderillero, and for ten years Paco had passed from *cuadrilla* to *cuadrilla,* his fortunes rising and falling with those of his matadors.

For four of those years he had worked with El Cordobés, becoming his *banderillero de confianza,* a role which set him apart from Pepín Garrido and Mariano García, the matador's two other *peones.* Paco shielded El Cordobés from the crowd and his admirers. He screened the lines of people who wanted to meet him. He watched and worried over his health, reprimanded him when he drank too much, served as intermediary between the matador and Spain's impresarios. They wenched together, and to Paco fell the task of informing each succeeding young lady that the matador had passed on to other fields.

In the bullring, he advised El Cordobés on the idiosyncrasies of each bull he faced. From his post at the edge of the ring, he cautioned him in his moments of seeming madness. No one suffered more during those instants than Paco, his fingers tightly folded over the cape with which he might have to rescue his matador in an emergency. With El Cordobés, Paco had lived the most exuberant joys and terrible fears of his life. Swept along by his matador's triumphant rise to the very summit of his profession, Paco had lived vicariously through El Cordobés' success the sweet hours of glory his own ill-fated career had denied him.

The moment Paco had sought in his deliberate collision course with Impulsivo was at hand. The bull was before him, barely six feet away, his head already lowered for the thrust that could impale Paco on his horns. Paco pulled his extended arms inwards and upwards until they formed a V rising at a 45-degree angle above his head. He drew his feet quickly together like a Prussian clicking his heels in salute. At the same instant, he rose up off the balls of his feet and lunged forward, driving his arms down in one quick, smooth motion. The metal points of his banderillas cut into Impulsivo's hide with a dry "pop" clearly audible at the edge of the bullring. As he threw them in, Paco used the momentum of his gesture to swing around Impulsivo's right horn in a tight semicircle that landed him close to the bull's flanks, behind and just out of range of that menacing horn.

Impulsivo stopped short at the burst of pain inflicted on him by the banderillas, locking the joints of his forelegs together to bring his rush to a halt. He snorted and jerked his head frantically upwards as though he were trying to pluck Paco's banderillas from his hide with his horns.

Paco watched him from the corner of his eye, able to observe for the first time the results of his handiwork. He was pleased. He had placed the banderillas as he should have, well behind Impulsivo's neck where they would not get in the way of the sword thrust that would kill him in a few minutes, barely two inches apart, up on the right crest of his shoulder and not down on its flanks.

His eyes still warily trained on Impulsivo, Paco sprinted back to the safety of the *burladero.* A polite wave of handclapping warmed his return. Stepping breathlessly behind his *burladero,* Paco noticed Manolo a few feet away, quietly studying Impulsivo's movements. These moments during the placing of the banderillas were the matador's last chance to study the peculiarities of the animal confronting him.

Once he had placed his banderillas himself. In his hands, the act just performed by Paco had an entirely different dimension. Sometimes he had called the bull while sitting on the *estribo,* the wooden step rail that ran along the inside of the barrier circling the ring. Sometimes he had broken his banderillas in half, chopping them down until they were no bigger than long cigars. So dangerous had some of his actions been that the spectators had actually stood up and begged him to stop. But he had not stopped—until the moment a bull put seven inches of horn into his intestines in Granada one afternoon and very nearly killed him. Since that day, El Cordobés had left the placing of his banderillas to his subalterns.

Now Pepín prepared to take his turn with Impulsivo. This afternoon, the risks in the placing of the banderillas would be his. Banderilleros always worked to the left or the right of a bull. Paco worked to the right. Pepín placed his banderillas on the bull's left, a fact which meant that today he would have to pass over Impulsivo's menacing left horn as he placed his sticks. The banderillero's trade was not an excessively dangerous one; but it was not rated highly by the actuarial tables of Spain's insurance companies, either. Pepín's thirty-six-year-old body bore the scars of seventeen wounds given him by the bulls in twelve years as a torero. Five young children depended on him for their well-being. That fact inspired him to an understandable prudence in the exercise of his peculiar vocation.

His face distorted by a grimace, his legs vibrating with an imperceptible trembling, Pepín started to work his way across the sand toward Impulsivo's waiting figure. At this instant Pepín's mouth was always "as dry as a pile of old bones." He ran his tongue anxiously over the roof of his mouth. Too nervous, even, to murmur a prayer, Pepín paused before the bull and provoked his charge with a clattering of his banderillas. As Impulsivo came, Pepín broke into a trot, describing, as Paco had done, a quarter circle toward the oncoming bull, this one to the advancing animal's left.

With an enormous effort Pepín forced himself to look past the horns rushing toward him to the black hump of muscle swelling behind them, its surface pitted by the two pulpy pockets of flesh cut open by José Sigüenza's pic. There he focused on the red-and-yellow banderillas already placed by Paco, flapping in cadence with Impulsivo's onrushing strides.

Pepín accelerated. As he did, he slipped, one of his knees buckling under him for an instant. A half-stifled gasp rose from the crowd. Pepín straightened up again and with furious little steps mashed his way over the clinging sand toward Impulsivo. He miscalculated by a split second the instant of their collision. Instead of using a graceful downward plunge to place his banderillas, Pepín was forced to lunge at the bull like a soccer goalie diving for a ball. As he pirouetted away, Impulsivo's left horn chopped upward at his fleeing figure, almost stroking the vest of his suit of lights.

The new burst of pain drew a furious reaction from the bull. Instead of continuing his forward rush, he swiveled around and set off in pursuit of Pepín. As he did a figure emerged from every *burladero* around the ring, frantically flapping capes in the bull's direction to divert him away from Pepín. The banderillero, slipping and panting on the wet ground, felt the animal overtaking him in his race to the safety of the wooden barrier, still twenty yards away. The crowd, sensing his misfortune, leaped to its feet.

Suddenly a savage shout rang out. Impulsivo turned his massive head

Flamboyant Idol of a Changing Spain

Spain's great matadors have been milestones along the course of her history. Today, the idol of the nation that once worshiped Joselito, Belmonte and Manolete is Manuel Benítez, "El Cordobés," born on the eve of the Civil War, son of a Loyalist soldier, raised in a poverty as desperate as any in Spain. His flamboyant style both in and out of the bullring and his disdain for the classic canons of his art and the conventions of an older society have revolutionized the corrida and made him the symbol of a nation in which the traditions of an isolated past are fast yielding to the tides of the modern world.

LUCIEN CLERGUE

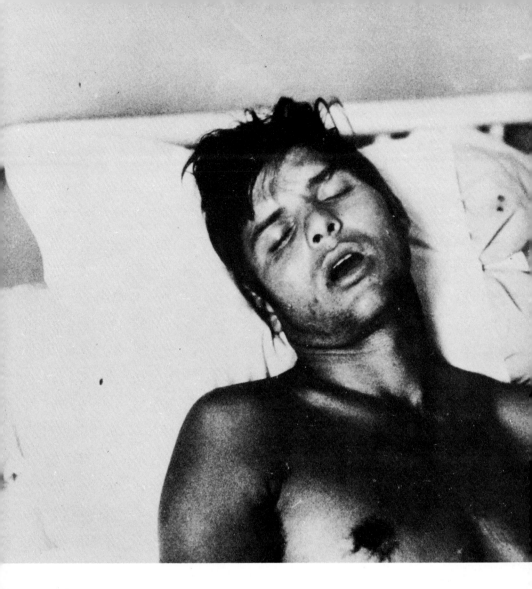

The Ransom of the Bulls...and the Price They Ask

Thousands of young Spaniards have sought to flee their hunger and their misery by following the road that leads past the horns of a brave bull. Most of them have found at its end only pain, despair and ignominy. Twenty-one times the hard voyage of El Cordobés down that road has ended on a hospital bed like the one above. But it has also delivered him from the hovel (right, upper photo) in which he was born and left him with a fortune so prodigious his accountants cannot calculate its exact value. Among his newest acquisitions is the hotel in Córdoba (right, lower photo) from whose penthouse suite he can look down on the jail in which he spent his first night in the city whose name he now bears in the bullring.

The Faces of a Bitter Childhood...

Angelita Benítez: El Cordobés' eldest sister, left with four children to raise on her parents' death in the bitter aftermath of the Civil War. Her attempts to keep her family from starvation were equaled only by her determination to keep her brother from the bullring. It was to her that Cordobés remarked minutes before his first official fight, "Don't cry, Angelita. Tonight I'll buy you a house, or I'll dress you in mourning."

Don Carlos Sánchez: The parish priest of Palma del Río in whose orphanage Manuel Benítez received a few scraps of knowledge and a few crusts of bread to slake his ferocious hunger. It was he who gave him his first chance to appear in a charity bullfight organized in honor of Palma's patron saint.

Don Félix Moreno: The great landowner of Palma del Río. His fields (for two generations of Palmeños, a bitter vineyard in which to harvest a few pennies an hour) served, by moonlight, as the first illegal testing ground for El Cordobés' skills.

Pedro Charneca: Palma del Río's foremost admirer of the bullfight, and its leading bartender. He alone in a hostile Palma del Río believed in the possibilities of the young delinquent who regularly came to stare at his most prized possession, a series of portraits of Manolete taken from a calendar advertising manzanilla wine.

Rafael Mauleón: Nicknamed "Tomato Face," he was the chief of Palma del Río's Guardia Civil detachment and the implacable foe of young Manuel Benítez. Unable to control the youth's petty thievery and his nocturnal forays into Don Félix's bull pastures, he finally expelled him from the town.

...and an Orange Thief's First Taste of Glory

Despaired of by his sister, scoffed at by his fellow Palmeños, Manuel Benítez' first glimmer of triumph came, as he had hoped it would, waving the trophies of a bullfight. The fight was an informal affair, organized by the parish priest in honor of the feast of the Blessed Virgin. Cordobés fought under the name of "El Niño de las Habas" because he was harvesting beans at the time. For a suit of lights he wore his dirty workclothes, and the results of the fight were soon forgotten in a town that had already condemned Manuel Benítez to oblivion.

In 1956, like thousands of his countrymen driven from their villages in misery and hunger, Manuel Benítez came to Madrid in search of "an opportunity." The goal he sought, however, was not a laborer's shovel or a factory worker's machine but a chance to fight a bull. Refused that chance by bullbreeders and impresarios all across Spain, he decided on a bold gamble. He leaped into the most celebrated bullring in Spain, hoping to steal a few passes from a bull and win with a reckless display of courage the chance that had eluded him. His "espontaneo" ended in ignominy. No sooner had he landed in the ring than he was tossed by the bull (above).

PORRAS

The Despairing Gesture of a Desperate Youth...
and Its Ignominious End

Then, bruised and dazed, his trousers half falling off, he was led out to the only "opportunity" Madrid was prepared to offer him, a visit to its jail.

PORRAS

PORRAS

The chance that had so long eluded Manuel Benítez finally came in a meeting with Rafael Sánchez, "El Pipo" (left), a former shellfish tycoon turned bullfight manager. In one wild summer, El Pipo's commercial acumen and his torero's reckless courage transformed both their lives. While Pipo lured the crowds with his publicity stunts, the new sensation of Andalusia enthralled them with his terrifying courage.

A Promoter's Magic...

MARTIN

DUSSARAT

ROBERT DALEY

and His Torero's Untutored Courage

OLIVER

ROBERT DALEY

A Somber Matador and the Bull That Awaits Him

The guitar he always carries poised behind him, El Cordobés wears a grave expression that reflects the tension prevailing in his hotel room as he prepares to put on his suit of lights. Below, he pauses for a prayer before leaving for the arena. On the right, the bull Impulsivo, like El Cordobés himself a product of the sun-scorched plains of Andalusia, that awaited him on his first appearance in the bullring of Madrid on May 20, 1964, the occasion of his confirmation as a *matador de toros*.

Four Devoted Men in a Matador's Service

José Sigüenza (left) is El Cordobés' senior picador. Stolid, unsmiling, workmanlike, Sigüenza is the highest paid picador in Spain. He fashioned his 224-pound frame working as a stevedore on the docks of his native Algeciras. Today, despite his bizarre calling, José's life is a model of middle-class respectability.

Paco Fernández (second from left) is the matador's sword handler. He came to his calling from a strange starting point, the slaughterhouse of Córdoba. He is the matador's man of all work. He sets out his suit of lights, sharpens his swords, guards his sleep, washes out his blood-stained muletas, arranges the candles and holy pictures before which El Cordobés prays on the afternoon of a bullfight.

Andrés Jurado (third from left) is El Cordobés' chauffeur. He has covered perhaps half a million miles at the wheel of the matador's Mercedes delivering him to the bullrings of Spain and France. A special curse is attached to his job: he rarely gets a chance to see his employer perform. While El Cordobés fights, Jurado prepares for their trip to the next bullring.

Paco Ruiz (right), El Cordobés' senior banderillero, is his closest friend and adviser. He fusses over his health, chides him when he drinks too much, hurries on his departing female guests, advises him on the bulls he faces, stands ready to run to his aid in moments of danger or to applaud his passes, like the one at the right or on the following page, photographed during El Cordobés' Madrid debut.

ROBERT DALEY

CANO, AGENCIA J

Madrid, May 20, 1964: Triumph...and Disaster

This extraordinary series of photos records the triumphant faena that began on the previous page and ended with El Cordobés' near-fatal goring by the bull Impulsivo. Twenty-two days later, confirmed as the idol of all Spain, Cordobés fought again.

SUAREZ, AGENCIA J

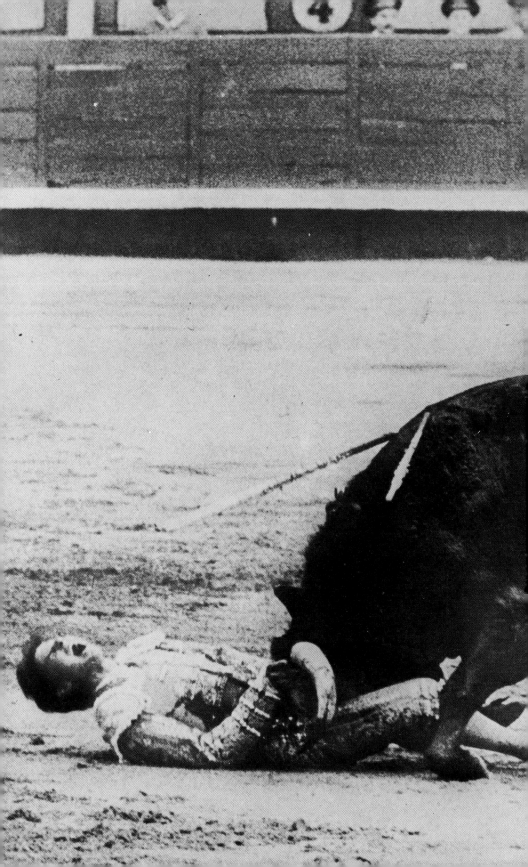

JOSÉ MARÍA LARA

The Many Faces of an Idolized Matador

Playing the guitar, dancing the flamenco, administering his properties, El Cordobés lives with the same extraordinary zest and energy he displays in the bullring. Today, the lonely orphan of Palma del Río is continually surrounded by his court of nearly 250 hangers-on, who depend upon him for their living.

LUCIEN CLERGUE

JOSÉ MARÍA LARA

An Ironic End to a Young Spaniard's Flight from Poverty

Symbol of a new Spain, the Spain of tourists and television, the miniskirt and the Common Market, traffic jams and American aid, low-cost housing and cheap credit terms, the Loyalist soldier's son who became a millionaire bullfighter represents to many of his countrymen a reflection of their own hopes for a better life. Paradoxically, El Cordobés' own triumph over his beginnings is symbolized by the tableau in this photograph, showing him with his nation's aging dictator and his wife. For El Cordobés, it is the supreme accolade of Franco's Spain, and for the Caudillo standing with him a tacit acknowledgment of what the matador stands for today in his restless nation.

The Price of Success: Sweat, Strain and Suffering

To stand before the horns of a bull and risk one's life as a hungry young man is one thing; to do it for a living with eight million dollars in the bank is another. El Cordobés' punishing trade has left its marks. Laid end to end, the scars the bulls' horns have left on his flesh would stretch three times around his waist. His face bears the signs of the strain and the tension that come from facing the bulls and the demanding crowds day after day, year after year. Increasingly, now, it is the image (at right) of worry and exhaustion that Cordobés wears instead of the exuberant smile of his early years in the bullring.

ROBERT DALEY

ROBERT DALEY

And Always Another Rendezvous with a Brave Bull in the Dying Sunlight of a Summer Day

LUCIEN CLE

in the direction of that imperious burst of noise. There, dancing violently before his eyes, was a magenta-and-yellow cape. In a swift, graceful gesture, he swiveled away from Pepín and dove at the cloth. Having caught the bull's attention with his shout, El Cordobés now lured him away with his cape's hypnotic folds. Impulsivo churned past him, and El Cordobés, with a flick of his wrists, sent the bull toward the folds of another cape offered by a second banderillero rushing up behind him. Pepín vaulted over the barrier to the safety of the *callejón.* As he did, a polite round of applause rewarded El Cordobés' rescuing gesture.

The matador smiled. Once again he lifted his *montera* from his head and gestured toward the distant box of President de Quiros, signaling that he was ready to waive the third and last pair of banderillas. He was ready for the final act of this bullfight. He stepped nonchalantly back to the barrier. He took a last gulp of water from the clay jug before him, rinsed his mouth, and spat the water onto the sand.

The clear notes of the bugle rang out again, announcing with their metallic echoes the beginning of the last phase of the bullfight, the moment for which everything that had taken place in this ring had been only a preparation: the act that must inevitably end in the death of the bull Impulsivo.

El Cordobés took his sword and his carefully folded muleta from the hands of his sword handler. His long journey to this great bullring was over. He sighed a prayer and slipped from his *burladero,* ready now to try in his turn to create before the greatest audience in the history of the corrida what Ernest Hemingway had called the "emotional and spiritual beauty that can be produced by a man and a bull and a piece of scarlet serge draped over a stick."

As he stepped back into the ring, an anguished voice called to him from behind the *callejón.* It was Pepín. Frantically he shouted a last warning at his exulting matador, but in the rising clamor El Cordobés' entrance had brought from the crowd, his words were lost like a shout drowned in the wind.

"The left, my God, Manolo, look out for the left!" he cried.

CHAPTER SIX

MALETILLA

IT WAS 2 A.M. A bitter wind off the Castilian plateau chilled the capital of Spain, its gusts tearing the last leaves from the plane trees lining the stately Paseo del Prado. At the southern end of that broad avenue, the huge Plaza de Carlos V was deserted. Only the bracelet of gaslights along its rim and the ghostly glimmer of the watch lights filtering from the massive frame of Madrid's Provincial Hospital softened the darkness of the lonely square.

Swaying under its load, a dilapidated farm truck picked its way across the plaza into the freight depot of Madrid's Atocha Station. Two stiff and sleepy figures scrambled down from the pile of orange sacks heaped in its open van. For Manolo Benítez and Juan Horrillo, the journey into exile was over. Their feet now rested on the pavement of Madrid. It was, in a sense, a privilege, a privilege barely a hundred of their fellow townsmen had ever known. To thousands of Andalusians like the two youngsters shivering in the freight depot of the Atocha Station that cold night in 1956, the dark and uninviting skyline stretching out before them represented the only salvation possible for the outcasts of their poor and undernourished land. Heaving their little sacks over their shoulders, the outcasts of Palma del Río marched off in their canvas sandals to conquer the capital of Spain.

MANOLO BENÍTEZ'S STORY

"MY FIRST MEMORY of Madrid is being kicked in the ass by a cop. We were half asleep in a doorway, where we had lain down to get out of the cold. I felt this terrific pain. Then I heard a voice yelling, 'Get up, get up.' I rolled over and I caught another kick—in the ear. I opened my eyes. There was a cop standing over me. The Guardia Civil had thrown us out of Palma and here the first person I saw in Madrid was a cop.

"He made us go with him to the police station. They asked us for our papers and the thirty pesetas you had to have so they couldn't throw you in jail as a vagrant. We didn't have thirty pesetas and we were afraid to show them our papers because they showed that the Guardia Civil had thrown us out of Palma. I explained that we were toreros looking for an *oportunidad*. I waited for the beating to start. That's the way it would have been in Palma—a beating, and then they'd lock us up for a while. What I didn't realize was that in Palma there was no one else like us. In Madrid there were hundreds. The police didn't have time to bother with us. They yelled, '*Anda!*' and threw us out of the station. We went back to our doorway and went back to sleep.

"After that first welcome to Madrid, we decided we'd better have a battle plan. We didn't go to Madrid just to lie around freezing in some doorway. What we had to have was someone to help us. The trouble was we didn't know anybody. And Madrid—Madrid's a big place. How do you find someone who's going to help you in a place like that?

"Finally I said, 'Let's go see Dominguín.' He was the biggest matador in Spain, the *número uno*. He was rich. It seemed to me he was the one to get to help you. Who else would you go to when you didn't know anybody in Madrid? We asked the owner of a café where he lived, and Juan and I started to walk to his house.

"My first impression of Madrid was an enormous shock. I was like I was knocked out. I was dizzy. It was so big I couldn't believe it. They don't teach you to understand things as big as that in school. Every time I crossed the street, I almost got knocked down. *Grande,* I kept thinking, *qué grande.* All those people running around, all those buildings, all those cars. In Palma when you saw a car, everybody ran up to look at it. In Madrid that's all there was, cars.

195

"The other thing I remembered was the food. It was piled up in the windows, *calamares, serrano* ham, peppers, sausage, everything you could ever eat. Juan and I just looked and looked. I think I got sick just from looking at all that food. Every time we moved on, we had to kick each other to get going.

"Finally we got to Dominguín's house. It was an old building with carvings around the door. We walked right up and rang the bell. A maid in a white apron opened the door. We explained to her that we were toreros and we had come to get the help of the maestro; we wanted him to help us get an opportunity to fight somewhere.

"She told us to wait and closed the door. A few minutes later she came back. She told us the maestro couldn't do anything for us.

"We were sad. We were scared, too, because Madrid seemed so big and we didn't know where to put our feet in the city. Juan suggested our battle plan should be to go to the Plaza de Toros. There, he said, there was more chance that we would find somebody who could help us.

"We took the subway. It was the first time in our lives we'd been on the subway. We asked at the door where the Plaza de Toros was. At the Las Ventas station, they said, you get off at the Las Ventas station. We got on the train. All of a sudden, we had a big panic. The stations started to go by and we understood you had to be able to read the signs to know where to get off. Neither of us knew how to read. Finally Juan asked the man next to us to tell us where to get off.

"When we came up the steps, we could see Las Ventas before us. I recognized it right away from the pictures in Charneca's bar. We just stood and looked at those red brick walls. It was the promised land.

"When we got down to the sidewalks around the Plaza, we saw a terrible thing. That was when I understood why the cops didn't bother to beat us up. There were dozens and dozens of aficionados just like us there. They were everywhere. They came from every part of the world, from Barcelona, from San Sebastián, Cádiz, Bilbao, everywhere, even cities I never heard of. They were all looking for the same thing we were, an *oportunidad*.

"The watchman let us go in to look at the ring and I looked at the empty seats that seemed to go all the way up to the sky. The only thing I wanted in the world then was to be there in that bullring with all those seats filled with people cheering for me.

196

"On the way out, someone said, 'There goes Don Livinio Stuyck.' I ran up to him and told him I wanted a chance to fight in his bullring. He tossed a duro at me. I threw it back to him. I said I wanted an *oportunidad,* not his money. But he walked away. After he walked away, I picked up the duro.

"Later we went to a café to use the money for some *calamares* and white wine. We decided it wasn't going to be any easier to get someone to help you in Madrid than it was in Andalusia and our battle plan had better be to get some money.

"I had two sisters in Madrid but I didn't want to beg from them. In Palma, Charneca gave me the name of a man who had a café in a place outside Madrid called Vicálvaro. He would give us something to eat until we got a job, he said.

"It was a filthy, lousy place, just the same as Palma. Life there was the same as it was in Palma. You stand around in the Plaza de Trabajadores to get picked for work in the fields. Ten pesetas a day they paid, just like Palma. It was the sugar-beet season, so we dug beets.

"At night Juan and I slept in the cemetery, in the shed where the gravediggers kept their shovels. We didn't have enough money to sleep anywhere else. There were some cypress trees next to it and a big stone cross for the people killed in the Civil War. It was a terrible time. We were dying of hunger, dying of cold in that cemetery, dying for the sun of Andalusia. Our dream then was just to get a job on one of the new buildings they were building around there. They paid thirty pesetas a day. Whenever there was no work in the fields, we went around looking for work there. So did everybody else. Madrid was filled with guys like us then, looking for a job on a building."

*　　*　　*

Manolo Benítez's and Juan Horrillo's emigration from Palma to Madrid in 1956 was forced, but it symbolized, nonetheless, a fact of life in their nation in the decade of the nineteen-fifties. Three million others like them, one Spaniard in ten, left their homes in that period, forced elsewhere in a desperate search for work. By the thousands they had, like Manolo and Juan, poured into Madrid. Those reluctant emigrants clustered in a series of ramshackle encampments outside the capital, their squalid settlements

197

ringing Madrid like a scar tissue. The huts were thrown together of wattled sheets of rusting metal, packing crates, cinder blocks stolen from construction sites, and were sold for a hundred dollars or two by speculators anxious to make a quick profit on those unfortunate refugees from Andalusia and Extremadura. For a generation of Spain's poor, those settlements, thrust upon her cities by her overburdened land, became way stations through which all had to pass en route to the modest life they had come to conquer.

Two decades after the opening of the Civil War, Spain was in 1956 a backward nation, fettered by outdated traditions, its intellectual and social horizons foreshortened by an oppressive Church, its economy hobbled by bureaucracy and incompetence, its political life stifled by a rigid regime.

In 1956, Spain would export slightly less than she had done in 1935, the year before her Civil War began, and barely one third of what she had exported in 1928. Her road system was only slightly more developed than Yugoslavia's. An astounded U.S. Air Force discovered that the Strategic Air Command B-47's stationed at three air bases in Spain could consume more fuel in an afternoon than the entire Spanish railway system was able to transport in a month.

Her state-directed economy had become a graft-ridden monster run for the benefit of the faithful of 1936–1939. Almost two hundred million dollars' worth of goods, a third of the nation's imports, would be smuggled into Spain that year. Army officers in uniform rode back and forth across the border in trucks, forbidding customs guards to search their bulging cases of smuggled radios, typewriters, wristwatches, and phonographs.

Almost eight million of Spain's thirty million people were officially classified as illiterate. There were barely a quarter of a million cars in the country, one for every 120 Spaniards, compared to the ownership ratio of 1 to 11 in neighboring France. Eighty-five percent of Spain's wage earners were paid less than $850 a year. Spain still had no domestic production of washing machines, refrigerators or sewing machines.

The nation lived in rigorous, self-imposed isolation from her northern neighbors. No Spaniard could leave his country without an exit visa; no European could enter Spain without an entry permit. Spain's controlled press extolled daily the "insurmountable" differences setting Spain apart from the lands that lay beyond the Pyrenees. The use of foreign names of bars, restaurants, cafés, cabarets or movie houses was strictly forbidden. Franco's government tolerated no hint of opposition, and the Caudillo himself could remind his countrymen that "we did not win the regime we have today hypocritically with some votes. We won it at the point of a bayonet with the blood of our best people."

The Spanish woman lived in a restricted world that had disappeared three decades earlier in the rest of Europe. No woman dared smoke on the streets. An Argentine girl was arrested in Madrid for wearing slacks on the Gran Vía and fined for "creating a scandal on the public way." The two-piece bathing suit was illegal in all Spain and some resorts still required men to wear tops to their bathing costumes. On the Catalonian coast, women of Catholic Action stoned female tourists in shorts or slacks and tried to burn a hotel where unmarried foreign couples shared the same rooms. The Cardinal Archbishop of Seville lent his authority to such actions by stopping his car and personally upbraiding two English lady tourists for wearing sleeveless dresses in the streets of his archdiocese.

Censorship standards were rigid and ridiculous. The list of writers whose works were banned began with Karl Marx and ran on for pages, through Jean-Paul Sartre, Albert Camus, Simone de Beauvoir, on to James Joyce, Ernest Hemingway and John Dos Passos. Film censorship forbade any hint of adulterous relationships. The works of Spain's greatest living artist, Pablo Picasso, were proscribed and his name was banished from the press.

The Catholic Church, reinstalled by Franco's government in its position as Spain's state religion, made its attitude felt in every phase of Spanish life. Darwin's teachings were banned as heresy. Catholic catechism still taught that it was "generally" a mortal sin to read a Socialist newspaper. Protestant and Jewish religious services were prohibited outside private homes. Neither faith's members were allowed public religious weddings or funerals. Thirty thousand Protestant Bibles were seized by the Minister of Information in 1956, an action which drew an angry protest from the President of the United States.

Yet under the archaic and frozen surface of Spanish life, the seeds of change were setting out their first uncertain roots. Television came to Spain in 1956 with all its terrible and wonderful potential for bringing

199

the world to the doorsteps of the nation's remotest villages. That summer 1,400,000 tourists would visit Spain, returning home to inspire others with tales of a sunlit paradise where a hotel room might cost a dollar a day and a three-course meal seventy-five cents. Spain, which had watched the United States pour sixteen billion dollars of Marshall Plan aid into Western Europe without diverting a penny to her shores, had finally had her first gulps at that golden fountain. Impatiently, she now awaited the first results of that catalyst of underdeveloped capitalism, economic aid.

The first among them was perhaps the disordered clutter of construction sites ringing Madrid: the sites Manolo Benítez and Juan Horrillo haunted looking for work. No employment they could have found, in fact, could have typified better the era opening up in the capital of Spain in that winter of 1956. Madrid stood at the threshold of a building boom that would profoundly alter the city's character in the coming decade. Already the first precursors of that construction spree pushed their lonely silhouettes against the horizon, forerunners of a forest of brick and concrete that would soon dwarf the steeples which had been for so long the symbolic guardians of Madrid's skyline. Those first gray walls, those uncertain scaffolds, were only the harbingers of change, however, not change itself. For Spain, for Madrid, as indeed for Manuel Benítez, the new era was still a long time away.

*   *   *

It was with pick and shovel that Juan and Manolo took the first step toward that distant change. They found the jobs they had searched for so desperately on the construction sites around Madrid. With their new wages, they abandoned their graveyard for a workers' flophouse where, for twelve pesetas a night, they rented straw sacks in a room filled with two dozen others like them. They had enough money for a daily bowl of stew and an occasional beer. That was about all.

Nonetheless, after a few weeks of exile, Manolo's fierce ambitions were more frustrated than ever. He understood perfectly well that his new life on a construction gang was not going to lead him to the world he had discovered in the Cine Jérez any faster than Don Félix's fields had done. "I had come to Madrid to wear a suit of lights," he recalled, "not to carry a hod in a construction gang."

Pocketing the few pesetas they had managed to save, Manolo and Juan quit their jobs and struck out again.

This time their restless footsteps carried them down the course of the river Tagus, toward the great citadel city of Toledo, from which Christian Spain had marched off to the Reconquest. Their first stop was Aránjuez, where Manolo earned a sentence of ten days in jail for jumping into the town's bullring during a corrida in the hope of winning with his unsolicited demonstration a more orthodox opportunity to display his talents. While he sulked in Aránjuez's one-room jail with two petty thieves, a wife-beater and six undernourished chickens for company, Horrillo worked sweeping out the stables of a nearby inn. Each night, bearing a few scraps of food for his companion, Juan showed up at the prison door and solemnly persuaded the toothless old jail keeper to lock him up for the night with his friend. When Manolo was released, the young men resumed their wanderings over the endless melancholy spaces of New Castile dotted with a score of bull-breeding ranches. They stumbled along from ranch to ranch, sometimes begging at the front gate for a chance to fight in a *tienta,* more often providing their own chance at night in the open fields. They lived on apricots stolen from the groves carpeting the river valley. By day they plodded along the back roads, their bundles bobbing from the poles thrown over their shoulders. They shared their hot and dusty roads with goatherds, Gypsy caravans, and the endless lines of swaybacked little mules staggering down to Toledo with their loads of jute and clay water jugs.

Finally they wandered up to Toledo itself. It was the end of July, and a brutal sun pounded the countryside around the city in a seeming affirmation of the Spanish proverb that "when God made the sun, He hung it over Toledo."

For a week Manolo and Juan wandered the shadowy streets threading Toledo's crowded neighborhoods. They spread out their capes in the plazas where the Inquisition had raised its first stakes, begging an egg, an orange, a slice of bread, a worm-infested potato. At night they slept at the foot of the Alcázar under the benevolent gaze of a one-legged night watchman assigned to stand guard over those shell-pocked stones that were the grave markers of his lost limb.

A week later they marched out of the city of El Greco. They carried away from that shrine of silk and steel, whose artisans had forged the swords that subdued the Incas and the Aztecs, a new trophy: a possession which accounted for the length of their stay in Toledo. It was a worn old Toledo sword, an instrument more worthy of their aspirations than the rusted bayonet that had taken the life of Don Félix's seed bull. They had shoveled out half the stables in Toledo to earn the money to buy it. Now with that noble blade proudly resting on Manuel Benítez's shoulder, they set out again in quest of new worlds to conquer.

Their errant footsteps carried them northwest toward Spain's second great bull-breeding area, the vast, treeless spaces stretching out from the university city of Salamanca. Village after village, blindingly white in the summer sun, flowed past their eyes. Like young Buddhist monks with their begging bowls, they beseeched the villagers they passed for a scrap of bread or a bite of *cocido*. Their wanderings carried them across the battlefields where the Duke of Wellington had savored his first victory over Napoleon's troops in 1809, past fields studded with reminders of fresher bloodshed: rusting iron crosses marking the knoll or roadside ditch where some unknown figure had died "for God and Spain" in the summer of 1936.

Their ever-present bundles still hanging over their shoulders, they finally marched past the ocher walls of Salamanca. Their filthy figures were a stark contrast to the privileged youths who paraded its streets in their black academic robes. But bulls, not books, had brought them to this Oxford of the Latin world. They marched past the flowered patios of Salamanca's institutes, past the doorways of its patrician residences—whose portals' stones were as finely chiseled, as ornate almost, as the hand-painted borders of a medieval missal—to the arches of its Plaza Mayor. There their destination was a shabby bar, the café Los Torres, set under one of the arches of the plaza's ninety-arch arcade. Its fat and sweat-slicked owner, Vicente Ortiz, was the patron saint of dirty kids like Juan and Manolo. He gave them the leftovers from his bar and whatever tips he might glean from his clients that could help them in their search for a bull to fight.

"Each evening," Ortiz recalled, "they rolled up in their muletas, those *maletillas,* and lay down on the stones of the plaza to shiver their way through the night, praying for the dawn. In the winter it was really horrible to see their black, shaking forms lying there, because here in Salamanca it is terribly, terribly cold when winter comes. I've seen hundreds of them like that. At seven o'clock, when I opened and the first customers arrived, they crowded inside to get warm and beg for some tip, some indication of where they could go to find a calf to fight. At seven o'clock at night, they were back. They had no chance, those kids. Nobody wanted to know them here. I had a dog then, a boxer. His name was Boris. One night I looked out into the plaza and I saw a *maletilla*, a sad, dejected kid, standing there, all alone. It was raining. He had a newspaper in his hand. He was using it like a muleta, trying to get my dog to charge it, so he could get the practice the breeders couldn't give him. That was my first memory of Manuel Benítez."

That was about the only memory Manolo left behind him in Salamanca that year. The city proved no more indulgent toward him than Toledo and Madrid had been. The only *oportunidad* they found was a chance to pursue their midnight bull baiting in the region's endless fields of brier and scrub oak, and to keep their futile vigils at the gates of the area's great bull breeders.

Their pursuit of the corrida's mirage took them that summer over half of Spain. They existed on the fruits of their petty thieving and, when that failed to nourish them, on whatever they could rip from the fields in which they fought. Sometimes for days the only items in their diet were acorns and grass. They lived in a state of constant fear: of the Guardia Civil, of the ranchers' vaqueros, of the railway police on the freight trains they hopped, of the animals they fought. Filth enveloped them like bark wrapping a tree. For weeks they were never in a toilet. Each had one set of clothes, the dungarees and flannel shirts they wore. They were covered with sores and lice. They rode in cattle cars, in hay wains, in tractor-towed wagons loaded with cow dung. They risked their lives jumping onto freight trains and, once on them, risked them again leaping from car to car, buffeted by the wind, trying to escape the pursuing police. Hungry, hunted, despised by all whose paths they crossed, beaten into dull despair, they sank to a level not far removed from the animal state of the bulls whose pastures they prowled.

Finally autumn came, and with it a new phase in the bullfighting calendar. It was the season of the *capeas*, the capings. The *capea* was the corrida of the poor villages of Castile, and indeed other villages like them throughout most of the rest of Spain, too poor to offer themselves a bullfight, too proud to permit the passing of a village Virgin's feast without some manifestation of the *fiesta brava*'s art. Their season began in the spring but reached its climax in the fall. The village square was fenced off with a handful of poles, some farm trucks, a few donkey carts. Then an aging bull or cow was turned loose in the ring. The bullfighters were any passing *maletillas* brave enough to face the animal inside the ring. If they were good, they were allowed to pass their capes through the crowd, hoping to pick up enough pesetas to keep their bellies full until they got to the next *capea;* if they were not, they were hounded out of town. If they were gored, all they could usually expect was a few squirts of alcohol in their wounds and a hurried escort out of the village. Since most *capeas* were illegal, few communities were prepared to tolerate for long the incriminating presence of a gored youngster inside their village limits.

Plenty of youths were gored, for the *capeas* violated the fundamental rule of the bullfight. Rare were the villages wealthy enough to allow themselves the luxury of killing the bulls put on display. They could afford only to rent them. After the fight, the animals were driven back into their pens and hauled by their owners to another village, another *capea,* and another chance to punch open the bowels of the youngsters desperate enough to stand before their horns. With each passing *capea,* the animals' instincts grew surer, their understanding of the riddle of the cloth more intuitive, until they became viciously dangerous. Every year, their knowing horns took their toll of dead and maimed among the faceless *maletillas* opposing them, leaving them to suffer and to die unapplauded, unrewarded and unknown.*

That fall, Manolo and Juan joined the hordes of hungry youngsters trooping over the countryside, following the bulls from *capea* to *capea.* For two months they slept on the sidewalks or fields of a different village every night. They walked fifteen, twenty, sometimes twenty-five miles a day to get from one village to the next. On occasion, they fought in one dirty square by twilight, then walked all night and most of the next day for no more than the chance to throw their exhausted bodies before the horns of still another bull. They fought with the bulls and they fought with the dozens of other youths swarming from village to village with

---

* Ernest Hemingway in *Death in the Afternoon* refers to one such bull who killed 16 young men and wounded 60 others during a five-year career in the countryside around Valencia.

them. They fought for a cluster of stolen grapes, for the dubious privilege of being first to oppose a bull, for the meager harvest collected by their capes at the end of a good afternoon. On a bad afternoon, when the animals offered them were too savagely dangerous for even Manolo's dumb courage, they left the festive village in shame and haste, sometimes pursued by a pack of urchins pelting them with stones.

It was a bitter, hard school, a world away from the graceful spectacle whose colorful posters of ladies in mantillas and dark men in gold and silver beckoned tourists to Spain. Elegance and style had no place here; only crude courage, instincts almost as primitive as those of the bull, and an unlimited capacity to endure pain, fatigue, hunger and misery. The school of the *capea* taught its graduates very little about the animals they fought; but it taught them a lot about themselves. It taught them above all where the limits of their ambitions lay.

When the last village had offered up its last *capea* and the first fore-taste of winter began to chill the autumn air, Manolo and Juan turned south. The last season in the sun they would pass together ended in Aránjuez, the town where Juan had voluntarily shared a jail cell with his friend. Juan decided to go home to Palma del Río to turn himself in to the Guardia Civil and hasten his conscription into the army. Manolo went north to Madrid to look for another hod to carry on another construction gang. All the beatings they had received together, all the suffering and the hopes they had shared, came down to a hasty handshake and the exchange of the word *"suerte*—luck" by the side of the high road to Andalusia. Each in his own direction, the two dirty, dejected figures walked off, the space between them gradually widening until each had disappeared over the beckoning horizon.

Block 36 of the Marconi Colony is a rabbit warren of cheap workers' flats four miles from Madrid alongside the high road to Andalusia. Its shoddy concrete and cement blocks rise above a barren sheet of dirt, their soulless symmetry epitomizing the wretched dullness of all the world's cheap housing developments. Yet to Encarna Benítez Montés, the girl who had given six months of her wages as a kitchen maid to buy her dead father a coffin, their dreary ranks seemed in the fall of 1956 a rewarding haven at the end of the long road away from Palma del Río.

As Manolo seemed to have done everything wrong in his life, his sister seemed to have done everything right in hers. She had worked ever since that day in 1936 when she plunged her six-year-old hands into her mother's dirty cooking pots in the artillery officers' mess at Pueblo Nuevo del Terrible. From the day she was twelve, she had saved every peseta she could to prepare her flight from Andalusia to Madrid. Her father's death had swept away all her pathetic savings, but she had started over again until she finally had enough to flee Palma. The same ferocious single-minded determination characterized her as she scrubbed floors and scoured dirty sinks in Madrid. Her frantic efforts had one simple goal. It was to provide herself with the weapon her humble birth had denied her, an ample dowry. She had succeeded and with her modest endowment had been able to arrange a solid marriage to a young factory worker whose job's affiliations had opened to her the dull gray doors of Block 36.

One cold night in 1956, Encarna found her brother Manolo standing before her door. She had not seen him since the day she had left Palma vowing never to return. Manolo, she recalled, "just stood there, looking hungry." His abrupt and unexpected arrival filled Encarna with misgivings. Angelita had warned her that "he had become a hopeless bum who only thought about the bulls." She did not cherish the idea of a delinquent brother intruding upon the life she was patiently building for herself. Her concern, however, was groundless. Clutched in her brother's hand was the reason for his visit, a roll of paper. He gently spread it out on her kitchen table, smoothing down its curled edges as though it were some precious water color. It was, in fact, a cheap calendar. On it was the portrait of the idol whose image he had first discovered on the flyspecked walls of Charneca's café, Manolete. He asked Encarna's husband to write upon it the dedication he solemnly dictated to him: "As he was, so shall I be." Then, with his brother-in-law's hand guiding his, he signed his name to that pathetic promise. He wrapped up the calendar with the same show of devotion with which he had unrolled it, and disappeared as abruptly as he had arrived. Sometime later, Encarna learned the use to which her brother had put his calendar. He had sent it as a New Year's present to a girl in Palma del Río named Anita Sánchez.

For Manolo, that winter in Madrid was one of the cruelest seasons of his life. He sank then as low as he would ever sink. Most of the time he was without work and without money. At night he prowled the darkened streets looking for a construction site in which to sleep. When he found a still-open building, he went inside and picked out some corner sheltered from the cutting Castilian wind. Then, wrapped up in an old overcoat, he shivered away a few hours on the cold cement. In the morning he begged the scraps left in the saucers at a handful of bars run by men whose veneration of the bullfight made them particularly indulgent toward young men like Manolo.

Finally he found a laborer's job and, for the first time since he and Juan had quit their construction site, began to work regularly. His sister noted the change with approval. He had a new plan now. He was going to marry Anita in Palma del Río and go to France to get a decent job.

One day, flushed with an evident air of excitement, he arrived at Encarna's flat with a letter. He asked her to read it to him.

"*Querido* Manolo," it began, "we cannot be *novios* any more. You should forget me now. They say you will never do anything good in life, and I cannot wait longer. I must go with other people now and think of marriage. God protect you. Adiós, dear Manolo." It was signed "Anita Sánchez."

That letter was the final vengeance of the man whose traps Manolo had so often evaded in the darkness of Don Félix's fields. José Sánchez had exacted his toll for the slaughter of his employer's seed bull.

When Encarna looked up from her labored reading, she saw on the face of her brother something she had not seen since he had been an infant in Pueblo Neuvo del Terrible. He was crying.

Manolo, heartbroken, quit his job and left Madrid again. It was not to France he headed, however, but to Salamanca and another assault on the breeding ranches. Six weeks later he was back, as broke and hungry as ever.

A few hundred yards northeast of the Las Ventas bullring, on a rise of land looking down on the capital, a new 1,000-flat housing project dominated the skyline of Madrid in that spring of 1957. It employed four hundred workers, and it was the ambitious undertaking of one man, a Madrid café owner named Luis López y López. López was a short, fat man. Packed into the tight Italian silk suits he favored, López looked like an overstuffed sausage threatening to burst its cellophane wrapper.

He had begun his business career working in his father's café. He later took over the café himself, sold it, and bought another. In it, he cultivated a select group of his clients, the men who could, in the early nine-teen-fifties, give him the information he needed to speculate successfully in the opening stages of Madrid's land boom. With his profits from those operations, López had launched himself into the burgeoning construction industry.

LUIS LÓPEZ'S STORY

"EVERY MAN WHO works for me, I know him. I know all their faces. I don't let anything get away from me. So, one day in the spring of 1957, I was up there at Vásquez Melia and I saw a new face. Right away, I noticed him and I'll tell you why. He had long arms. He was mixing mortar in a tub and heaving it up to a mason on the second floor with one fling of his shovel. You don't get many who can do that. I asked my son Luisito who'd hired him, who he was. 'Some bum who just came up from Andalusia,' he said.

"A few days later I saw him again. I came around a corner and there he was playing torero with an empty cement sack. Just because I'm an aficionado I'm not going to let every kid who wants to be a torero play bullfighter on my time. If I did that, we'd still be building these buildings ten years from now. For something like that I usually fired a kid right away, for discipline. There were always plenty of others looking for work. Him, I decided to give a second chance. I remembered those long arms of his.

" 'Listen, kid,' I said, 'you want to be a bullfighter, you go down there to Las Ventas. You want to be a mason, go back to your mortar. I'm not paying you to wave those empty sacks in the air.' He understood. He went back to work.

"Well, a little while later, a couple of weeks maybe, I went to the bullfight at Las Ventas. I have my regular place there, a *barrera de sombra.* As the fifth bull came out of the *toril,* an *espontáneo* jumped into the ring. The kid didn't have any luck. As he jumped, a Guardia Civil grabbed his foot. Instead of landing on his feet in front of the bull, he landed on his hands and knees. The bull slammed him against the *burladero* and everybody screamed. But he was okay. The Guardia picked him up and marched him off to jail.

"I forgot about it until the next day when I saw a picture of the *espontáneo* in the papers. It was the kid with the long arms. What a picture it was. You ought to see it. He has a snarl on his face, a defiance for the world like an animal in a cage. That kid, I told myself, he'd sell his mother to a Moorish whoremaster to become a bullfighter.

"A few days after that, I noticed he hadn't come back to work. I asked Luisito where he was. He was still in jail, he said, because nobody had paid the fine. I suggested we take up a collection to pay the fine and get him out of jail. It didn't work very well. Most of my workers thought he was some kind of nut. I ended up paying most of the five hundred pesetas myself.

"The next time I saw him on the job, I went up to him. 'Look, kid,' I said, 'if you really want to become a bullfighter, I'll help you. We'll see if you've got anything. If you have, maybe I'll become your manager. If you haven't, forget about the bulls. You settle down here and learn to be a good mason.'

"I told him he could come and live in one of the half-finished flats on the project. I had two or three other workers living in there. That way, they sort of served as night watchmen too, and we deducted something from their pay for room and board.

"We took an old wheelbarrow and stripped it down to its wheel and handlebars. Somebody got a set of horns and we tied them to it. That was his bull. Every night, after work, he practiced with it. The other workers kind of adopted him. Half of those masons had wanted to be matadors anyway. They all took turns pushing the cart for him.

"One day I heard about a *capea* in a town outside of Madrid near Jarama where I have a summer place. I knew the mayor over there, so I arranged to get Manolo a tryout. I wanted to see whether he could do anything in front of a real bull or whether he was just a hungry fraud who didn't have the guts to stand up to the horns.

"He didn't know anything. He didn't even know how to hold a cape right. But Jesus, he had one thing: he had courage. My God, he had courage. I was right about that picture. This kid, I figured, was worth a risk. I decided I'd take him under my control and see if I could launch him as a bullfighter. That's not easy. It takes a lot of connections, and sometimes a lot of money. But I had a lot of friends in the game. And I figured that if it cost me money, I might be able to get it back some way.

The manager who gets a bullfighter really going big gets a big piece of the cake. Everybody knows that. Having a percentage of a hot matador in this country is like having a percentage of the graft we have here. So I called him over and I put my arm around his shoulder and I said, 'Manolo, from now on, I'm going to look out for you. I'm going to be your manager.'"

*   *   *

Luis López never smoked cigars and almost never put a hat on his bald and gleaming skull. That made no difference to Manuel Benítez. To him there was no question about it. López was the man with the big cigar and the panama hat, the taurine fairy godmother he'd been waiting for to lift him from his obscurity and place him firmly in the world of the corrida. The very fact that he existed gave Manolo a new confidence, the conviction that now that someone had stepped forward to help him, his destiny was certain to change.

López soon discovered, however, that it was almost as difficult to break into the closed world of the corrida as a manager as it was as a bullfighter. López had an enormous number of friends in that world. He had persuaded himself that by informing them that he had available the services of a new prodigy, he would be deluged with demands for his services. It failed to work out that way. What his friends offered López was a chance to buy a place on a village *cartel* for his prodigy. The price of the privileges they offered ranged from six thousand to twenty thousand pesetas. Spending money in such a manner hardly fitted into the café owner's notion of the economics of being a bullfighter's manager.

While he continued his search for a corrida for his prodigy, he kept him hard at work on his training. He insisted Manolo practice passes with his wheelbarrow bull for hours every evening until his arms hung exhausted at his side. Then he put Manolo on regular duty as his night watchman for a while so he could spend his mornings in the slaughterhouse chopping down a chain of bawling cows with the untutored thrusts of his sword.

The weeks and months dragged by. Manolo continued to shovel up his mortar with a frantic sense of fidelity to his employer. He would later recall López as a man "who didn't give anybody any presents." For the moment, López was hope incarnate. Each time he appeared on the construction site, Manolo rushed up to him to find out whether he'd found him a chance to fight in a regular corrida. The answer was invariably the same: "Not yet."

Then, one day, López walked up to him and, with the smiling solemnity of a banker announcing to a client that his loan application has been approved, informed Manolo that he had finally found him a place on the *cartel* of a regularly organized bullfight.

López's declaration somewhat overstated the importance of his achievement. What he had in fact found for Manolo was a place as a *sobresaliente* in a corrida featuring a *rejoneador* and two unknown matadors in the village of Aranda de Duero, ninety-five miles from Madrid.

It did not, however, alter one basic fact: The dream he had dreamed on the two-peseta bench of the Cine Jeréz was going to come true at last. Manolo was going to appear in a bullring, not as an illegal intruder but as an official participant in the spectacle into which he had been so consistently refused an entry. For the first time his shoulders would bear that solemn and splendid garment he had coveted so long, the matador's suit of lights.

There was, of course, to be no compensation for Manolo's services. Furthermore, to earn the seven hundred pesetas he needed for the rental of a suit of lights, Manolo had to work an extra six hours every night for a week, unloading bricks at the construction site. They were for him nights of feverish anticipation filled with dreamings of the triumph he was going to win in that provincial bullring.

The day before the fight, he went into Madrid to perform a rite notable in the life of a young torero. In a crowded street of a residential neighborhood just off the Puerta del Sol, he pushed his way through a plain, unvarnished doorway and marched down a flight of stairs. A certain hesitation moderated his usually brusque movements. At the bottom of the stairs, behind a set of swinging glass doors, was an establishment long revered by the men of the *fiesta brava:* it was the basement workshop of Santiago Pelayo, the Christian Dior of the corrida.

Inside was a world of flashing rolls of satin: blue, lilac, scarlet, emerald, purple, and white. A dozen heavy magenta-and-yellow fighting capes, standing with their own stiffness, were posted about the floor. Poised over a large work table littered with gold tassels and shreds of

211

satin was the shop's fifty-eight-year-old proprietor. For more than forty years, since he had, as a twelve-year-old boy, delivered a suit of lights to the great Joselito, Santiago Pelayo had devoted his talents to the fabrication of that unique and revered garment, the suit of lights. During that half century, his fingers had stitched up the satin costumes of four generations of matadors.

No other tailor in the world, perhaps, performed a function as specialized as his. The silk from which his suits were made all came from one source, a convent near Barcelona. That silk had only one other use, in the garments worn in another ritual of sacrifice. To perform the sacred offering of the Mass, Spain's cardinals and bishops clad themselves in vestments made from the same silk worn by the nation's matadors. Only two changes had been made in the suit of lights in the fifty years Santiago Pelayo had exercised his trade, and he had been responsible for both of them. He had shortened by an inch the gold and silver tassels bobbing from a matador's vest. And he had developed for Juan Belmonte a special cotton padding of the trousers to give his stumpy legs the smooth appearance nature had denied them. That innovation, like almost everything else Belmonte did, was imitated by his fellow toreros.

It took seven women working eight hours a day for twenty days to make one of Pelayo's suits. Eight years of apprenticeship were necessary to join the ranks of his fifteen seamstresses. In fifty years no hint of mechanization, modernization or compromise had encroached upon that process.

In the back of Pelayo's establishment was the room to which Manolo headed. There, hung in long and colorful rows, were a hundred second-hand suits of lights, discarded by their owners after half a dozen wearings or after a goring had cursed their cloth with bad luck. This was the collection from which Pelayo rented out suits to aspiring young matadors. Their faded fabrics and the scars left by Pelayo's seamstresses in their ceaseless efforts to stitch them back together after a bull's horn had cut them open bore mute testimony to the ineptitude of the young men who came here to rent them.

Manolo made his pick immediately. His choice fell upon a tobacco-and-gold suit, colors his mind somehow associated with good luck.

Manolo put it on the next afternoon in the inn in the town in which López had arranged for his debut. The dingy cell-like room assigned him had one bare light bulb hanging from its ceiling. Its sole piece of furniture was a spindly cane-bottomed chair. On its walls were a cracked mirror and a faded portrait of the Virgin salvaged from some long-outdated calendar. In that half-darkened, melancholy chamber Manolo for the first time became the object of that special and solemn ritual which is the dressing of a matador for a bullfight. No curious aficionado, no inquisitive visitor from the dining room, not even an inn employee, wandered by to watch that usually public ceremony and distract the matador's mind from the trial ahead; there was only Luisito.

López's son, assigned to Manolo as his sword handler, moved wordlessly through the slow and painstaking process of fitting him into his suit of lights. The worn satin trousers were too short, and for several minutes he tugged and strained to stretch them into position, low enough to allow them to be knotted up just below his knees, high enough so they did not slip down below his hip bones. He wound the cummerbund tightly around his waist; as a final precaution, he pinned it to Manolo's trousers. Then he lifted the tobacco-and-gold jacket from the room's one chair and eased it over the shoulders of his young matador.

Manolo straightened up. He turned to look at himself in the mirror. At that sight before him in the glass, he gasped. Bursting into sobs, he fell to his knees under the portrait of the Virgin. He was still kneeling there when López entered the room. Gently, López touched his shoulder.

"We came here to *torear,* not to cry," he said. "Wipe up your tears and let's go to the plaza."

The trio rode to the bullring in the Austin taxi López had rented from a friend to get them to Aranda. As they drove through its gates, López gestured to the posters pasted to its walls. There, in small type, under the names of Sánchez Jiménez and Miguel Carmona, *matadores de novillos,* and José Pepe Mendoza, *rejoneador,* were the words "Sobresaliente: Manuel Benítez, El Niño de Palma del Río." For his first public appearance, López had chosen for him the name of the city from which he had been driven in disgrace.

As he stood in the dank cement passageway, waiting for the *paseo* to begin, emotion overtook Manolo again. When he heard off in the distance, beyond the burst of light ahead of him in the tunnel, the first notes of the trumpet summoning him to the ring, he began to tremble. It was finally here, this moment for which he had waited so long. The feet that had trod so many a moonlit pasture were now going to have their chance on the sand of a bullring. The little group ambled forward, and proudly, Manolo watched the gates of a *plaza de toros* swinging open before him, before his proud figure clad at last in the solemn splendor of a suit of lights.

Watching him march into the ring, López observed "how magnificent he looked, how proudly he held himself, how professionally he swirled his cape as he settled behind his *burladero* ready to fight."

Manuel Benítez, however, was destined to stay behind that *burladero* for the rest of the afternoon. The *rejoneador* dispatched his bull with exemplary ease. The two matadors on the program refused to give the young man so much as a single pass with one of their animals. Cursing and praying for misfortune to overtake them, Manolo watched in despair as one by one they killed the animals assigned them. When the last bull tumbled dead onto the sand, Manolo for the second time this day burst into sobs. His afternoon in Aranda had been nothing but a grotesque masquerade, a brutal assault upon his extravagant hopes.

"All my life," he told López, "I've been followed by bad luck and now it's followed me even down here."

To cheer up his disconsolate matador, López treated him to a dinner of grilled mutton at the inn where Manolo had changed his clothes. Then the three headed back for Madrid in the Austin taxi in which they had set out so proudly eight hours earlier. Ten miles from the capital, the Austin associated itself with the misfortune that had marked Manolo's day. After a few coughs, it shook to a stop, its voyaging finished for some time.

With grunts of despair and anger, López, his son and El Niño de Palma del Río got out of the car. López carefully folded the coat of his suit onto the back seat of the car. Then the three men—an unsuccessful bullfight manager, an unwilling sword handler and an untried bullfighter —resigned themselves to the inevitable in a day of broken dreams. They began to push the taxi back to Madrid.

* * *

The arrival of a small slip of green paper, shortly after the disillusionment at Aranda, put a temporary end to the tauromachian career of Manuel Benítez. The slip of paper, delivered to his sister's home by a member of the Guardia Civil, instructed him to report to the nearest Guardia Civil post for his induction into the Spanish Army.

He came out of the army in 1959, a few weeks before he turned twenty-three years old. By the standards of the world he sought to enter, he was already an old man. Rare are the toreros who have not left their mark upon the corrida at the age of twenty-one. Many, perhaps even a majority, are full-fledged matadors by the time they leave their teens. At the age of Manuel Benítez that spring, a man has either arrived as a bullfighter or slid back into the obscurity and poverty from which he sought to escape. When he was twenty-three, Joselito had already been acclaimed as the greatest matador in history. He was nearing the end of his famous *mano a mano* exhibitions with Juan Belmonte, only three years his senior; a seven-year period of rivalry still hailed as bullfighting's Golden Age. Manuel Benítez's hero, Manolete, was firmly enshrined as his nation's idol at twenty-three. Antonio Ordóñez had performed in 334 bullfights at that age, and Dominguín at twenty-three was publicly acknowledged as Spain's foremost torero. On that May morning in 1959 when Manuel Benítez turned twenty-three, he was an unskilled laborer with a poor employment record. The only thing noteworthy in his dreary personal history was his four sojourns in Spain's jails.

Despite the fiasco of Aranda de Duero, López was still ready to try to thrust his prodigy—and himself along with him—into the lucrative realm of the *fiesta brava*. A few days after Manolo's discharge, López arranged to have his picture published in a Madrid paper along with a brief ad. The ad's text, composed by López, announced the arrival in Madrid of "The Terror of Palma del Río," after "a spectacular series of triumphs in the bullrings of Andalusia." Anxiously, López waited for the replies he expected his inspired prose to produce. He received none.

That his ad should have gone unanswered was not surprising. It was a singularly difficult moment to launch any new enterprise in Spain, even one as seemingly uncomplicated as that proposed by López. Franco's Spain was, in that late spring of 1959, on the edge of bankruptcy. The evils of twenty years of economic mismanagement, chronic incompetence and determined isolation had had their effects. The peseta was selling in the black-market money exchange for hardly half its official value. Spain's central gold and foreign-currency reserves totaled $63,000,000, her debts $67,000,000. Prices had skyrocketed. Goods were scarce, imports had shriveled. The strains of that economic crisis had produced social stress, too, apparent even under the rigid surface of Franco's authoritarian regime. It was, perhaps, the most significant crisis Spain had faced since those turbulent weeks that had preceded the Civil War. Its solutions were for Spain far less dramatic and infinitely less painful than the bloody debacle of 1936; but when history's eye casts its long glance at the story of the Spanish nation, it may well reckon those solutions more important in the evolution of her people than the futile ferocity of her Civil War.

To solve his problems, Franco was forced reluctantly, almost bitterly, to turn for help to the foreigners he had so long despised, the bankers of Wall Street, Paris and London. On July 15, 1959, Spain was bailed out of bankruptcy by a $418,000,000 loan from the International Monetary Fund and a pool of private banks. That loan had its price. Franco was obliged to devalue the peseta and pass control of Spain's economy from his incompetent and corrupt Civil War cronies who had run it for twenty years to a new generation of technocrats.

Most important, he agreed to take two steps he had vowed never to take. He agreed to allow foreign investment into Spain and virtually abolished his rigid import restrictions. And he took his first step toward that institution growing beyond his borders, an institution he had long scorned, the European community of nations. He humbly petitioned for Spain's admission to the Organization for European Economic Cooperation. Six months later he abolished the requirement of visas for Western Europeans visiting Spain.

It was a revolution. For twelve centuries, since the defeat of Charlemagne at Roncesvalles, Spain had lived in splendid isolation behind the fastness of her Pyrenees; Spaniards sallied forth across that mountain barrier only to conquer or be conquered. A dike against the currents of a world she did not trust, the Pyrenees had held her apart from her northern neighbors, kept her immune to their viruses, indifferent to their passions and their progress, unaffected by their strife. Now those mountain gateways to Spain's golden shores had been thrown open. Like water rushing through a breach in a dam, a flood tide of Spain's neighbors would soon come pouring over those passes, exposing her people in one overwhelming rush to all the temptations and values from which Franco had sought to isolate them.

The result of those changes would soon be felt in almost every phase of Spanish life. For the moment, however, the nation's economy sputtered uncertainly. Even the bullfight was not spared the blight afflicting the rest of Spain's national life. Superficially, it appeared to have been stimulated by the famous competition between Antonio Ordóñez and Dominguín. Their rivalry, however, covered only ten bullfights. Only 323 other fights were scheduled for that season, barely a handful more than had been held in the depressed season of 1948 following Manolete's death. The corrida seemed to be living on the memories of its past glories. "Spain," wrote one critic surveying her listless *fiesta brava*, "is looking for a great matador to replace the giants of the past."

LUIS LÓPEZ'S STORY

"THERE WAS NO business anywhere that year and I was getting fed up with the whole routine. It was costing me a lot of time and I wasn't getting anything out of it. I was about to give up on Manolo when I took him one day to a *capea* at Moro de Toledo.

"It was the same story. He was as courageous as ever. Everyone said what guts he had. He'd do anything if he thought it would make the people notice him. He was like some kid standing on the ledge of a building yelling at people to watch him jump off. I don't know what you had to do to get those people to wake up. I think a kid would have to swallow a horn before they'd notice something. After what he did, you asked for a contract for him and all they wanted to know was how much you'd pay to get him on a bullfight *cartel*.

"I had a friend there that day and he said to me, 'Listen. Why waste your time trying to get your kid a bullfight like this? Why don't you do the thing the big way? Run your own bullfight. You have already got a fighter. He won't cost you anything. Go rent yourself a bullring.'

"Well, that was like someone had just turned on a light in a dark room for me. That was the way to do it if you really wanted to get somewhere, promote your own corridas. You can launch your kid and you can make money at the same time.

"This guy had a friend who ran a bullring and he introduced me to him right there at Moro de Toledo. We argued for a while and finally made a deal. I got his ring for a quiet August day for six-thousand pesetas. I picked August 18, 1959. I was really proud because Manolo and I would start the big way. The bullring this guy ran was the bullring at Talavera de la Reina."

*   *   *

The rust-red roofs of the little town of Talavera de la Reina rise at the far end of a thirty-five-arch Roman bridge that spans the Tagus River seventy-two miles southwest of Madrid along the high road to Extremadura. Its artisans produce a blue-and-yellow pottery of considerable renown, and its narrow streets once echoed with the footfalls of French soldiers fleeing before the columns of the Duke of Wellington. Apart from those distinctions, there is little to set Talavera apart from the other cities like it rising from the plains of the Tagus. Just outside its gates, set between a grove of willow trees bordering the Tagus and a thirteenth-century sanctuary of the Virgin of the Prado lies the red-roofed bullring rented by López to launch his prodigy as a bullfighter and himself as an impresario. Physically, the building is as undistinguished as the town it serves. To Spaniards who revere their *fiesta brava,* however, that drab bullring is a shrine, for the ghost of the greatest matador who ever lived haunts its wooden arches. Joselito was killed there on a warm May afternoon in 1920 because he forgot for just a second that the 1,568th bull of his prodigious career had faulty vision.

Manolo dressed for the bullfight in a bare damp room next to the *plaza's* infirmary where the dying Joselito had seen the "green ball," the Gypsy symbol of death, hovering over his wound. The ride out to Talavera from Madrid had been a triumphant procession. The astute López, his eye on his gate receipts, had offered the afternoon off to any of his workers going to the fight. Three bus loads of them had ridden out to Talavera.

Once again, López's son dressed Manolo for the fight. It was, as it had been in Aranda, a hurried, lonely ritual. An unknown girl entered the room as Manolo dressed and offered him a medal "for luck." He fixed it next to Anita Sánchez's first communion medal still hanging faithfully around his neck. When Manolo had finished his prayer, a devotion he uttered facing one of the four bare corners of the room, one of López's friends, a brick contractor named Don Celes, called him to his side.

"Kid," he said to him, "if you don't want to have to go back to your pick and shovel for the rest of your life, this is your chance today."

"Don't worry, Don Celes," Manolo told him, "this is going to be my day."

López had passed up his bullfighter's dressing to watch from the *callejón* as the spectators flowed into the plaza. He was almost as nervous in his debut as a bullfight's impresario as Manolo was in his debut as a matador. It was a hot, energy-draining afternoon. Not even a hint of a breeze stroked the willow trees clustered along the Tagus. Two dark stains of sweat already spread out of the armpits of his tightly cut suit. Tucked into a pocket of that suit was a little notebook, López's master plan for his baptism as an impresario.

In it he had recorded every peseta he had spent on this bullfight: alfalfa for the bulls, 60 pesetas; tips to the Guardia Civil, 500 pesetas; musicians, five of them, 750 pesetas; fee to drag out the dead bulls, 260 pesetas; first-aid supplies, 50 pesetas. The biggest item on his list, of course, was the bulls: 47,000 pesetas. The bullfighters hadn't cost him anything; in fact, he had made a slight profit as far as they were concerned. Manolo had paid for his own suit of lights by working overtime as he had done for the Aranda fight. The manager of the other fighter on the program had made a contribution toward López's expenses in order to get his matador's place on the *cartel*.

López had carefully supervised every detail of the fight. He had set its "popular" prices: 20 to 40 pesetas for a place in the shade, 15 to 25 pesetas for the sun. He had sent two of his construction workers to Talavera ahead of the buses to sit in the booths with the ticket sellers to inspire them with a sense of honesty. He had even invested 1,000 pesetas in "preparing" the press, the first sum of that nature spent on Manolo. It went to Radio Toledo for an interview noteworthy above all for its conciseness. For Manolo's part, it consisted, in fact, of one word, his answer to the question: "Are you scared?" It was "No."

In all, López had invested 65,000 pesetas in the fight. It was, for him, a very considerable sum in that summer of 1959. He had calculated he would need at least 3,200 paying spectators to get it back. Nervously, he studied the people entering the ring, trying to estimate the number flowing in. By fight time, he calculated there were already over 3,000 of

219

them. He was exultant. It did not matter now what his young prodigy did here. His own successful debut as an impresario was assured. Immensely satisfied with himself, López took his place behind the wooden screen in the *callejón* reserved for the management of the bullring and waited for the *paseillo* to begin.

His 750-peseta band struck up a pasodoble, and the two matadors of the day, followed by their one banderillero, marched into the bullring. Manolo, López noticed, had a grin "as big as the bullring" spread all over his face.

It was, indeed, his day. He fought with a savage determination to succeed. His first bull tossed him into the air half a dozen times until his suit of lights was a barnyard brown. Each time he was down, he got back up again. Watching him, Don Celes thought he would "get seasick just from looking at him." The crowd loved it. During his faena, the bull stopped halfway through a charge with his horn hooked under the vest of Manolo's suit of lights. Unconcerned, Manolo tried to get him moving forward again with his muleta. Horrified, López screamed, "No, no, for God's sake, let him get the horn out first! "

With his second animal, he decided to put on a spectacular display with the banderillas. His second pair he broke twice until they were not much longer than a ball-point pen. He jammed them in almost leaning his chest on the bull's skull. The crowd roared its glee. He broke his last pair down to the same length. Don Celes handed him a pair of handkerchiefs to cover his bleeding palms, cut by the jagged ends of the preceding pair. Then he walked out and knelt on the sand before the bull.

The bull bolted at him with a terrible charge. López, horrified, closed his eyes, unable to watch. The crowd screamed. He opened his eyes, expecting to see his prodigy impaled on the bull's horns. Instead, he was dancing happily back to the *callejón,* waving to the applauding crowd.

So it went. Manolo had come a long way to this historic bullring. He was not going to leave these sands unknown and unnoticed. He wanted it desperately, his bullfighter's success and everything that went with it in that rich, well-fed, well-driven, well-housed, well-respected world for which he had lusted so long. There was something almost evil in his fearlessness, in the callousness with which he flaunted his courage before the crowd. But they loved it. He was awarded two ears for his first bull. When the fight was over, his cheering fellow masons stormed into the ring to carry him out of its gates in triumph, up the flowered path with its bronze bust of Joselito staring back toward the bullring in which his genuis had found its reward.

The ride back to Madrid in the rented buses was a wild debauch. López stayed behind to count the receipts, but everyone else scrambled aboard. Manolo was in a state of ecstasy. He raced up and down the aisles of his bus, gulping wine from a dozen different goatskins. He sang, he danced the flamenco, he reenacted the bullfight in the aisles. He was beside himself with joy. He had, after all, won his wager with destiny. He had fought the bulls in public, in a suit of lights, in one of the most storied bullrings in Spain, and he had been a success. Everything he had fought for seemed to be there before him that night, beckoning to him from just a stride beyond his fingertips.

The party went roaring on, after the buses got back to Madrid, at a bar near the housing project; it was called the Gato Negro, the Black Cat. López arrived just after midnight. His face was as white as the immaculate white linen shirt he wore. His stunned expression drew attention to him as soon as he began to stride through his carousing workers. The revelry stilled. The novice impresario had congratulated himself on his success too soon. The two workers he had sent ahead to watch over the ticket sales had arrived in Talavera in time for what had turned out to be a very expensive lunch for Luis López. Their hosts had been the two ticket sellers over whose operations they were supposed to stand guard. Those two had poured, it seemed, half the wine in Talavera down their throats. While López's men had slept off their lunch in a drunken slumber, the ticket sellers had gleefully sold their own, instead of López's, tickets to the corrida and pocketed the receipts. Instead of the profit upon which he had counted, López debut as a bullfight impresario had cost him the staggering sum of fifty thousand pesetas.

The party was over, and so were the tomorrows it was supposed to be celebrating. López bitterly announced that his ventures into the *fiesta brava* as an impresario, as a manager, as anything but a simple spectator, were over.

It took a few moments for the import of that declaration to register on Manolo, who was still celebrating his triumph with a bottle of red wine and a roll of chorizo. His man with the panama hat and the big cigar had left him. He was back where he had begun. He was alone again with his bravery, and that was not enough to buy his way past the doors of a world run more on connections than on courage, more on money than on the manipulations of a muleta.

*   *   *

It was a bitter awakening. With the triumphant *"olés"* of his debut still sounding in his ears, Manolo was forced to return to the despairing routine he thought he had left behind him forever on the sand of Talavera de la Reina's *plaza de toros.* The long hours on the construction project were followed again by his endless round of the country *capeas* with all their desperate risks, their bulls too old and too wise for the chances he took; he strained to keep alive his receding hopes that in one of those sun-baked villages where he risked his life for a fistful of coins, some new benefactor, some new Maecenas in a panama hat with a big cigar, would come forward to replace the disillusioned López.

One of those lost country towns through which his restless feet wandered that fall was called Loeches. It was like all the others, a clump of whitewashed, one-story buildings clustered around a couple of curves on a little-traveled road, circled by a ring of bald clay hills, their surface bleached the color of dead autumn leaves by the sun. At high noon on a summer day in Loeches, with the sun's rays ricocheting off those white walls, a man had to squint, even under a pair of sunglasses, to protect his eyes. The only paved street in Loeches was the blacktopped road that linked it to the world. Its square was a semicircle of open earth, baked rock-hard by the sun, its surface gullied by the winter's rains. The village had five telephones. Seven hundred and fifteen of its 750 dwellings were without running water. It lived, barely, on the output of twelve hand-operated kilns that pressed the clay dug from its barren hills into bricks. Every week the output of those kilns was hauled off to the construction sites of Madrid, for despite the desolation of its existence, Loeches was just fifteen miles east of the Spanish capital.

Once a year, between September 11 and September 14, on the occasion of the feast of the village's *patrona,* Nuestra Señora de las Angustias (Our Lady of Sorrows), Loeches shook itself from its sun-bleached stupor for a few hours of gaiety. On the eve of that feast in September 1959, a ring of thick wooden stakes, spaced two hands apart, was driven around the rim of the village square. Those stakes foretold the arrival of the fiesta.

It would open at exactly half past five in the afternoon of September 11, with a noisy parade of a band hired from a neighboring community. There would be fireworks, dancing, games, and the public procession of the Virgin's statue. But the most important event of the fiesta would take place in the circle of stakes driven into the ground of the village square. They formed the *plaza de toros* of Loeches.

In announcing each year his fiesta's principal attraction, the mayor acted out a little charade with his fellow citizens. He proclaimed a *"sensacional novillada"* featuring the talents of a pair of famous and courageous matadors and six brave bulls from a nearby ranch. It was just for good form, that announcement. The mayor's slim budget made provision for neither *toros* nor toreros.

His limited means obliged him to "rent" his bulls. After the fiesta they were put back in their pens and returned to their owner for use in other *capeas.* The mayor had already had a look at this year's two bulls. One of them, he had noted with a thrill of satisfaction, was seven or eight years old. He was the biggest bull the mayor had ever seen.

His "pair of famous and courageous matadors" would not cost the mayor a peseta. They were neither famous nor limited to two. They were unknown, and they came by the dozens. The first of them were already there, sprawled on Loeches' dirt sidewalks or in the few desiccated vineyards outside the village. They were *maletillas,* and by the time the first animal was released in the square at noon on the second day of the fiesta, there would be, the mayor reckoned, almost fifty of them on hand to amuse the village with their ignorant courage.

Manolo rode out to Loeches in the SEAT of Don Celes, the brick contractor from Madrid who had been with him at Talavera. Few of the *maletillas* there for the opening of the fiesta were that lucky. Among them that September morning was a twenty-three-year-old mechanic named Manuel Gómez. Gómez got up before dawn to walk to Loeches from his workers' barracks in the Madrid slums of Vallecas. He had quit his job for the *capea* season and he did not have in his old blue jeans that morning enough money to buy himself a cup of coffee before he set out on the fifteen-mile march.

It must have been a brutal odyssey, that long journey under a blazing September sun. Gómez would not have minded it. A special passion drove him over the country road to Loeches. Gómez had never been as close to realizing his dreams of becoming a bullfighter as he was that hot September morning. Forty-eight hours earlier, he had been offered a contract to perform in a regular corrida for the first time in his life. There was only one problem which could keep Gómez from fulfilling the contract, and that he was going to remedy in Loeches.

Gómez did not have the money to rent the suit of lights he had to have for that bullfight. He planned to get it by passing his cape among the crowd in Loeches, counting on his courage to earn him the seven hundred pesetas he needed to put on a matador's costume for the first time.

The *capea* began at noon. Almost every one of Loeches' two thousand citizens had crowded into the village square. People stood on the rooftops of the buildings circling the plaza or stationed themselves behind the potted geraniums decorating their windowsills.

In Loeches, the Gates of Fear were the barricaded entry to a blind alley. On a sign from the mayor, those barricades swung open and the first animal galloped onto the hard dirt of the village square. It was the overage animal to which the mayor had thrilled a few days before. Yet even he, a veteran of hundreds of *capeas,* gasped at the sight of that wide-horned, massive beast smashing out his frustration against the stakes of Loeches' improvised bullring.

A wave of panic swept through the *maletillas.* The bull tossed the first youngster who approached him four feet into the air. Fear turned those who followed him into terrified urchins. One after another, they leaped for safety into the village water fountain in the middle of the ring. Soon there were half a dozen of them huddling there, sullen and shivering in the thigh-deep water. The villagers jeered at first; then, their anger rising, they started to pelt the cowering *maletillas* with stones.

Watching, horrified, waiting his turn, Manolo thought, "The bull knows. He knows Latin and Greek and every other language in the world." He was tossed on his first pass. But he got up and managed to maneuver the animal past him three or four times. Then it was the bull's turn. On the next pass he chopped past Manolo's muleta and speared his calf. With one brutal spasm of his neck muscles, the animal jerked him

224

into the air, spun him through a semicircle, then flung him onto the ground. This time Manolo did not get up. His leg was laid open from his knee to his ankle.

They stitched the edges of the wound together in the primitive village first-aid station set up in the town hall next to the mayor's office. Manolo was lucky. There was a doctor in Loeches. He gave Manolo the only anesthetic he had, a gulp of cognac, and began to sew.

Manolo would remember the pain and fever of his ride back to Madrid for a long time. But he would remember even longer the humiliation that lay at the end of it, at the gates of the Toreros' Hospital. The doctor in charge refused to examine him. Even the agony of a leg skewered open by a bull's horn was not enough to open to him the doors of that hospital. Its services were reserved for professional bullfighters, members of the toreros' union. It had no room for the nobodies cut apart in the *capeas* in the forlorn hope that they, too, might someday find a place in that closed corporation which was the corrida. Four years later, as his nation's leading matador and president of the bullfighters' union, he would think back to that afternoon when, fevered, bleeding and unknown, he was turned away from the hospital's door. Then, with his own portrait hanging over those doors, next to that of Sir Alexander Fleming, discoverer of penicillin and patron saint of toreros everywhere, he would order them thrown open to any victim of the *fiesta brava,* and to any Spaniard in need of emergency treatment. Now Don Celes took him to the one hospital that could not refuse him, the enormous Provincial Hospital of Madrid on the Plaza Carlos V.

Manolo's injury had forced a brief halt in the Loeches fiesta. When it resumed, a respectful, almost guilty silence stifled its clamor. Not a single *maletilla* moved toward the ring and the menacing black animal that had gored Manolo. Embarrassed and afraid, they looked at each other in silence, each waiting for someone else to make the first gesture.

Finally one teen-age boy slid through the stakes of the bullring and cited the animal. He was tossed. Another figure stepped through the stakes and, shaking out his cape, called the bull off the fallen boy. The bull charged. With the same unerring instinct he had shown with Manolo, the animal drove past the cape to the body of the frightened youth who held it. This time, however, it was not a calf his horn sliced open.

With one murderous twitch, he drove nine inches of horn into the groin of the youth before him. At the center of the wound, pumping out his blood in uneven spurts, was the boy's torn femoral artery.

As they started to rush the critically injured *maletilla* to a car, the mayor raised his hand. He had a form to fill out first, a police report he would be required to file on the accident. Meticulously, he noted down the victim's name. It was Manuel Gómez, the young mechanic who had walked fifteen miles for the chance to earn with his cape and his courage the seven hundred pesetas he needed to rent his first suit of lights.

MANUEL BENÍTEZ'S STORY

"Two nurses put him on the bed next to mine. They stuck a rubber tube into his arm and hung a bottle over his head. He was asleep but I recognized him. After a while, he woke up. He began to moan. He lay there with his eyes closed, moaning to himself. Pretty soon it got dark, and they turned out the lights in the room. I couldn't sleep. Gómez kept groaning. I tried to talk to him. I said, "Gómez, Gómez, what's the matter?" I knew he couldn't hear me because he didn't answer, just those low groans over and over again.

"It got worse and worse. Sometime in the middle of the night he began to gasp for air. His body seemed to be shaking. Sometimes the sound of his breathing stopped. Then it started again with a dry, rattling sound. It was completely dark. There was only one light, a long way away in a corridor. Everybody was sleeping. I could hear the sounds of people snoring and breathing and the scraping noises old people make when they sleep. Gómez would moan, then gasp and make that rattling sound. I kept calling to him, but he wouldn't answer me. I called for someone to come and help him, but there was no one in the room. No one came. I kept calling his name, softly, 'Gómez, Gómez,' but he never answered. In the dark I could see his bed, and his body shaking under his sheets. Finally, I don't remember when, I gave up calling for help and fell asleep."

*   *   *

226

Outside, the enormous Plaza Carlos V was as deserted as it had been on that winter night, three years earlier, when Manolo Benítez and Juan Horrillo had ridden into Madrid atop a truckload of oranges. As then, the only lights glowing from the buildings around the square were the watch lights shining now for one of them from the massive black bulk of the Provincial Hospital.

Sometime during that night, Manolo blinked awake in the darkness of Ward 19. Through the shadows around him, he saw a black-robed figure leaning over the bed of Manuel Gómez. The man mumbled a few phrases Manolo's fevered brain could not understand. He straightened up and with his finger made the sign of the cross on Gómez's forehead. He reached down and, taking the bedsheet, drew it forward, up over the length of Gómez's body. Then, before lowering it, he closed forever with his thumb the eyes of the young man who had dreamed that afternoon of the rented suit of lights his prowess would win him in Loeches.

It was the hospital chaplain. As the clacking of his leather heels faded away down the darkened corridor, Manolo turned his eyes back to the shrouded body of Gómez lying in the bed beside his. For a long time he lay still in the darkened ward, whose oppressive silence was broken only by the heavy breathing of the other patients, staring at Gómez's body. When dawn came to Ward 19, a somber reality had intruded upon Manuel Benítez's mind. For the first time, he truly understood all the implications of the game he had chosen to play in Don Félix Moreno's moonlit fields.

*   *   *

It was a chill and melancholy fall for Manuel Benítez. By the time he was discharged from the hospital, the *capea* season was almost over. He scrambled off to what capings he could find, to exorcise the image of Manuel Gómez dying in the hospital bed beside him, and prove to himself his courage was still intact. He could well prove it to himself. No one else seemed to care. No one else seemed to heed his pale figure limping after the last cows of another murderous season of *capeas*. The young doctor who had treated him at Loeches noticed him at one of them. He pulled up Manolo's trousers and pointed to his still-unhealed wound.

"You're crazy," the doctor told him.

Manolo shrugged. "I'll kill the bulls or the bulls will kill me," he said.

The only thing that might have killed him that fall, however, was his own despair. The season Manolo had vowed would see him set upon the road to the bullring had come and gone. He had put on a suit of lights and performed creditably in a corrida. He had watched a man die from the wound a bull had given him, and his desire had survived that shock. His desperate ambition burned as brightly as it had the day he set out to chase the mirage of Currito de la Cruz. Only his hope, his instinctive confidence in himself, had gone. He felt now that time had about run out on his dreams. He was not going to be a bullfighter. He would have to learn to be something else.

Whatever that something else was going to be, it was not going to be a mason on Louis López's construction projects. Caught in an economic squeeze, the little contractor felt obliged to cut back on his labor force. Among the workers he decided to lay off was the youth with the long arms whose ambitions had cost him fifty thousand pesetas.

Only one of the men who had stood around him in August at Talavera remained to offer Manolo a hand that fall. It was Don Celes. He had been impressed with his courage. Celes gave him odd jobs to do around his property and kept him nourished with scraps from his bar. He set out on a campaign of his own to find him a manager. Every place he went, everywhere he could find a few knowing aficionados, he looked for an experienced *apoderado,* any *apoderado* to take in a desperate kid.

"I offered his courage like a bouquet of flowers to everybody I could find," he would recall. "Nobody wanted him. He was just another hungry, hopeless Gypsy kid."

*   *   *

The apartment was in an old brick tenement over the Café Armacón on Madrid's Calle Vallehermosa. Every piece of furniture in its sitting room seemed to reek of the rancid odor of half-smoked cigars. Its floor, its few tables, even the mantelpiece over its fireplace, were all littered with a single form of literature indicative of the one consuming interest of the man who lived here; they were the trade journals of the *fiesta brava.*

One winter morning early in 1960, the telephone rang in that apartment. It was well after midday when its summons broke the heavy silence in the sitting room. Several rings passed unnoticed before a fat man in a blue silk dressing gown stumbled sleepily into the sitting room and angrily yanked the receiver from its cradle.

At the other end of that telephone was the last man to whom Don Celes had offered his unwanted bouquet of flowers, the little-esteemed services of Manuel Benítez. He was a sherry salesman named José Rodríguez, and he was a distant relative of the man in the blue silk dressing gown. While Rodríguez talked, the man in the apartment picked a half-smoked cigar from an ashtray and angrily began to chew on it. He had better ways to waste his time, he told his sherry-salesman cousin, than to look over every scruffy delinquent who thought he could fight a bull.

He added, however, that he would, in honor of whichever forgotten aunt or uncle it was whose blood bound them together, offer Rodríguez's prodigy the time needed to consume just one cup of coffee in the café below his flat.

As soon as he hung up the telephone, Rafael Sánchez, "El Pipo," regretted what he considered to be this characteristic display of generosity. "People," reflected the man who had supplied the First Heavy Artillery Regiment during its days at Pueblo Nuevo del Terrible and had slipped an occasional square of chocolate to Ángela Benítez, "are always trying to take advantage of my good nature."

EL PIPO'S STORY

"WHEN THE WAR ended, I was a *milionario*. One million pesetas cash. That war had made me a rich man. I can tell you, there weren't many people in Spain in 1939 who could put their hands on one million pesetas. Now, I've always said you can do two things with money. You can sit around and get constipated looking at it. Or you can spend it. Me, I prefer to spend it.

"My father wanted me to go to work with him in our seafood shops, but me—I had other ideas. I had worked hard for my million pesetas. Nobody was doing me any favors up there. I took my chances along with everybody else. Now it was time to have fun.

"I got it following my friend Manolete. That year my new Studebaker

President was a familiar sight on the roads of Spain. When I'd drive through some of these little Andalusian towns, people would run to their doors just to get a look at that car going by. There wasn't a first-class bullring in Spain that didn't get to know my car that year. Everywhere my friend Manolete went, I went too. I could drive my car right into the *patio de caballos* of any bullring in Spain. All I had to do was blow my horn and the doors would open for me.

"Everybody knew me from my car and my hat. I designed the hat myself with a broad felt brim to keep the sun out of my eyes when I was driving. Rubio, the best hatmaker in Madrid, made them for me, a dozen at a time. It was the good life, those times right after the war.

"We had everything then, Manolete and I, Manolete because he was becoming a famous matador, me because I had money. Things were hard to find then, but we always had the best, the best hotels, the best restaurants, the best nightclubs. There wasn't a flamenco cabaret in Spain that didn't know El Pipo and his wide-brimmed hat and show him right away to the best table. In those days, more often than not, the sun was coming up when I got back to my hotel. But every afternoon I was in my place in the bullring to watch my friend perform.

"It lasted a year, and it was a year I'll never forget. They were golden days. At the end of the year I was broke, ruined. But I didn't care. I had had a good time. Believe me, I'd had fun.

"Since my million was gone, I had to start all over again. I went back to Córdoba and I looked at what was going on around there. 'What,' I asked myself, 'do these people need?' Well, that place was so dirty, Córdoba was so full of vermin and rats, that I said to myself, 'What Córdoba needs is a disinfectant.' I sold my Studebaker and I decided I would become the King of the Disinfectants.

"The trouble was I had everything figured out but one thing. Everybody needed disinfectant all right, but nobody had any money to buy it. You could have put the number of fleas, spiders and beetles the people of Córdoba killed with my disinfectants in one of my hats and still have had some room left over. After a year of that, I was as broke as I was the day I arrived. I sold the business and decided to try my luck with something else in Madrid.

"I opened up a restaurant on the Calle Amor de Dios. I decided to call it El Puerto after those bistros where I had made a fortune during the war in Andalusia. Well, that name was the only thing about it like those bistros. I didn't have any more luck with that restaurant than I had with the disinfectants. I had to sell it to my creditors.

"The day I sold that restaurant, I was a poor man, believe me. There I was, a man who had stayed in the best hotels in Spain, walking the streets of Madrid without enough money in my pocket to buy a cup of coffee.

"Three weeks later, my father died and left me his seafood business. That was the miracle that saved me. As soon as I got back to Córdoba, I decided to expand the business. They used to call my father the King of the Shellfish in Andalusia. Well, before long, they were calling Rafael Sánchez the King of the Shellfish too, but not just in Andalusia. All of Spain was my kingdom then. I did it the big way. I put my shellfish shops all over Spain in Huelva, Cádiz, Seville. I had four of them in Madrid: El Rocío, Las Cancelas, El Regio, Posada del Mar.

"I'd made a lot of friends during those months I'd followed Manolete —generals, ministers, politicians. The people who counted in Spain— Rafael Sánchez knew them all. Those friendships paid off. Thanks to those friends of mine in high places, I got a sort of monopoly on the sale of shellfish. What I did was get the right to handle the packing of all the fresh shellfish coming into the ports of Andalusia. Pretty soon, half the outlets of shellfish in Spain had to supply themselves through me.

"I had an empire, an empire built on shellfish. I made an incredible amount of money, I don't even know how much. It was enough to let me get back to doing what I wanted to do. After a couple of years of the shellfish, I was back on the road with Manolete.

"Those were the golden days of my life. Manolete was at the height of his career. Everybody swarmed around him then—politicians, generals, actresses, artists, foreigners—and me, I was always right there beside him, sharing his existence. Everywhere we went, I gave big banquets in his honor, receptions, flamenco dancing until dawn. It was a blessed period in my existence. But like everything else, it had to have an end.

"As soon as I took my eyes off my business, things started to go bad. The people left in charge started to steal from me. A little I wouldn't have minded, but they had to get greedy and try to grab it all. I woke up one afternoon and found my shellfish empire was falling apart.

"You know how things are. If you're on top, everything goes your way. When you're going down, nothing goes right. Everything went wrong for me. Before long, I was up to my ears in debt. I had to liquidate my empire. There I was, ruined again.

"Things weren't going any better for my friend, either. When Manolete came back from fighting in South America in 1947, he announced he was going to cut the *coleta*. First, nobody believed him. Then, when they did, they got angry. The mob turned against him."

*   *   *

Manolete turned thirty-one on July 4th, 1947. He had been fighting, almost without a letup except for pauses to recover from his gorings, since 1939. During those eight years he had earned almost four million dollars. It was a prodigious sum, particularly in view of the fact it was earned largely during the years Spain was alone, sealed off from a warring Europe, living on the marginal resources of her own war-shattered economy. It was, the matador reckoned, more money than all the male members of his poor Córdoba family put together had earned in five generations. And, he also reckoned, it was time to spend it in peace. The tensions of eight years of fighting bulls had left their marks. He drank too much and slept too little. Returning to Spain from his triumphant tour of South America, he announced his coming retirement.

His mistress had warned him that Spain would not let him go. His "pretty gold uniform," she prophesied, meant "excitement and money to too many people for them ever to let him take it off. They'll kill him first." *

She was right. A chorus of angry disapproval greeted his announcement. Manolete had come to mean too much to Spain. He was more than a bullfighter; he was, to his nation, a symbol, a reminder of its past, a hope for its future and a particularly needed solace in its sorry present. The resentful public that had made him an idol turned on him with savage glee, accusing him of cowardice in quitting the bullring.

Their taunts found their way to that so vulnerable and so Spanish a part of a matador's makeup, his pride. Manolete set out to jam the jeers down the mob's squawking throats with one last, triumphant season. He

* Barnaby Conrad, *Gates of Fear* (New York, Thomas Y. Crowell Company, 1957).

232

did more, he did it better, he did it with more dangerous bulls, than he had ever done it before. And the public that had adored him was indifferent. They wanted more, and more, and more.

He was hooted and jeered by the mob from *plaza* to *plaza,* condemned to suffer the public indignity of their scorn no matter what he did.

"The public keeps demanding more and more of me in every fight," he told an interviewer in San Sebastián, "and it is impossible. I have no more to give."

Later, in that same ring after exhausting himself before an indifferent crowd, he told his great friend and rival, Carlos Arruza, "I know what they want, and one of these afternoons I just might give it to them to keep the bastards happy."

He was seriously gored in Madrid on July 16th. On August 4th, against the pleas of his doctor, he returned to the bullring, weak and physically run down. Shaking with fatigue, the weakness left by his still-fresh wound and the mental strain imposed by the abuse to which he was being subjected, he went from debacle to debacle.

On August 28th he fought in the mining town of Linares, a nondescript community an hour and a half from Córdoba near the northern rim of Andalusia. His fellow matadors were Dominguín and Gitanillo de Triana II, and the animals were the feared and respected "bulls of death," so called because they have been responsible for the deaths of more toreros than any other breed of bulls in Spain: bulls from the *ganadería* of Don Eduardo Miura.

Manolete's second bull, the fifth animal of the afternoon, was small and black. It bore the number 21 on its flanks and it was the 1,004th bull of his career. Its name was Islero. It had one signal defect: it tended to chop with its right horn.

Despite that defect, Manolete managed to draw from the animal a series of beautiful and dangerous passes which won him an enthusiastic ovation from the crowd. His manager begged him to dispatch the animal quickly and perfunctorily, for the bull's defect represented a special danger during the kill. A matador's body must pass over the right horn to escape after the sword has been thrust home.

With a disdainful gesture of his hand, Manolete rejected his manager's advice. Proudly, a sovereign scorn seeming to animate each of his movements, he set out to show the crowd in Linares the full range of his

233

courage and skill, as though to avenge himself here for every insult he had heard that summer.

He leaned over the right horn and deliberately, slowly, pushed the blade in, right up to its hilt, so slowly that it seemed to his sword handler "he was putting it in inch by inch."

It was too slow. The animal jerked up his head and drove his right horn into the matador's thigh. As his banderilleros carried Manolete to the infirmary, the stunned crowd rose to applaud.

EL PIPO'S STORY

"MY ONE REGRET in life is that I wasn't with my friend for his last corrida. As soon as I got the news, I borrowed a Hispano-Suiza and went to get Dr. Guinea Jiménez, the great specialist in bullfight wounds then. We tore off through the night for Linares. Halfway there we stopped at an inn to get some ice for the penicillin we were carrying. Penicillin was a precious thing in Spain in those days. Gitanillo de Triana II was there, come up from Linares to intercept us in Manolete's blue Buick convertible. A rich aficionado in Mexico gave it to him for two *barreras de sombra* to one of his corridas.

"We switched to the Buick and went like hell for Linares. They had him in a room in the little hospital there. He was half conscious. Everybody was there standing around him.

" 'Thank God you're here, Don Luis,' he said to the doctor.

"The doctor told him not to worry. A few minutes later, Manolete told him he couldn't feel anything in his left leg. Jiménez started to massage it.

" 'Be calm, Manolo,' he said, 'and close your eyes.'

" 'They are closed,' Manolete murmured. But they were wide-open, his eyes. I understood then. A few minutes later he grabbed the sheets with his fingers and cried '*Ay, madre.*'

"He stiffened and then it was over. My friend was dead."

*　　*　　*

Manolete had finally given the crowds what he had feared they wanted. In gratitude, they came by the hundreds of thousands to bury

234

him in Córdoba. As they had done with Joselito, those mobs that had hounded him during the last weeks of his life salved their consciences by making a martyr of the man and a legend of his death.

El Pipo, bankrupt once again, chose that inauspicious moment to make his own entry into the world of the *fiesta brava* as a bullfighter's manager. His first ward was a cousin of Manolete's named Rafael Molina. Molina had little of his cousin's skill and none of his courage. El Pipo dropped him for a Mexican called Capetillo who turned out no better. For years Pipo's fortunes rose and fell along with those of a whole series of mediocre matadors. On that winter morning of 1960 when the telephone rang in his Madrid apartment, they were once more at a low ebb.

EL PIPO'S STORY

"Nineteen fifty-nine had been a bad year for me. I'd had a couple of toreros, but they were no good, so I dropped them. The only money I made all year was running a bullfight in Albacete and I damn near had a heart attack doing it, so I wasn't exactly in my glory when winter came.

"Now, the trouble is that in this country every jerk with the money to buy a ticket to the bullring thinks he's an expert on the corrida. So as soon as you have a foot in the *fiesta brava,* they're always bothering you for this or that. They always have some kid they want to stick you with who's going to be another Manolete. You'd think we made Manoletes on the assembly line in Spain. That sherry-selling cousin of mine is an example. I know more about sherry than he knows about the bulls. But just to keep him quiet, just to keep him from bothering me, I agreed to have one cup of coffee with the kid.

"As soon as I walked into the café, I could feel his eyes burning into me. He came up to me and he said, 'You be my manager, and I'll buy you a Mercedes.'

" 'Calm,' I said to him. 'You know how much a Mercedes costs?'

" 'Sure,' he said in that hoarse voice of his, 'a million pesetas.'

"He was disgusting. He was dressed in rags and straw sandals. He was skinny. His hair was too long. I told him to turn around. He made a half circle there in the bar in front of me. I always do that. The first thing I look at in a kid is his arms. His were long. That's a good sign. A muleta handles easier with long arms. I asked him why he wanted to be a bullfighter.

" 'To eat,' he said, 'to get out of my misery.'

" 'Do you like money?' I asked him.

" 'More than you,' he said, 'more than anyone.'

"I asked him how old he was. He said he was twenty-four. I told him he was too old, his shell was already too hard.

" 'Age doesn't count,' he answered, 'it's courage that matters.'

"Then I asked him if he'd ever fought before. 'Sure,' he told me, 'lots of times, at night in the fields. Where else can someone like me fight?'

" 'Listen, kid,' I said to him, 'do you know what color your blood is?'

"He rolled up his trousers. There was a long scar, still unhealed, running down his calf. 'That color,' he said.

" 'Give me a chance, Don Rafael,' he said, 'I promise you won't be sorry.'

"Well, you know, those kids are always the same the first time you see them. The same answers, the same promises. He was a good-looking kid but he was too old. You want to get them when they're sixteen, seventeen years old. I told him I was sorry. I had too much in my hands already. I regretted it because he had something. There was a certain air about him.

"He leaned over to me and blew that vile breath of his into my face. 'Listen, Don Rafael,' he said, 'you don't understand anything. Not about bulls. Not about men.'

"He turned around and walked toward the door. Somewhere inside me, a voice said, 'Rafael Sánchez, you made a mistake.' His hand was already on the doorknob when I called out, 'Hey kid, come back here.' "

*   *   *

El Pipo's first gesture was to offer Manolo a sandwich and a cup of coffee, his first food in twenty-four hours; the second was to tell him to call him every day at noon to find out whether he had been able to locate a tryout for him at a *tienta* in Salamanca.

Weeks dragged by and nothing happened. Manolo in his frustration told El Pipo he was going to march up and down in the Puerta del Sol carrying a sign offering to buy a Mercedes for the first person who offered him an *oportunidad.* Then finally his unbelieving ears heard Pipo announce their coming departure for Salamanca.

Manolo showed up half an hour early for their rendezvous. He was so dirty and smelled so bad that Pipo made him sit alone on the back seat of his borrowed SEAT, as far removed as possible from his own well-groomed and perfumed presence.

Their destination was the ranch of Don Antonio Pérez Tabernero, one of Salamanca's most esteemed breeders. He had turned his *tienta* into a high and festive occasion presided over by two of Spain's leading matadors, Antonio Ordóñez and Curro Romero. El Pipo immediately took his vermin-ridden protégé over to the matadors, elegant in the gray flannel jackets, white lace shirts and leather chaps prescribed for the occasion.

"This kid," he told them with his usual gift for modest prose, "is going to bury both of you one day."

The subject of El Pipo's boast was lamentably bad the first time he was allowed to perform. The second time he was offered a chance, Curro Romero tripped him as he went into the ring, sending him tumbling to the ground to the glee of Pérez Tabernero's guests. Unnerved, he was even worse with the second animal than he had been with the first.

"What did you bring that idiot here for?" Don Antonio asked El Pipo. Mortified, El Pipo asked Don Antonio to excuse him and dragged Manolo out of the breeder's ring.

With a majestic gesture of his arm, he pointed toward the distant highway.

"You see that road?" he asked Manolo. "It goes to Madrid. Get on it and start walking. And if you want my advice, when you get to Madrid, keep on walking. Keep on walking until you get back to Andalusia. Nobody's ever going to make a torero out of you."

His edict of banishment thus duly pronounced, El Pipo returned to the bullring to watch the rest of the *tienta.* It was well after sunset, and after a long and noisy reception at the rancher's hacienda, that El Pipo walked back to his car. To his surprise, he found his banished bullfighter slumped on the back seat, weeping softly. Manolo begged El Pipo not to abandon him, to give him one more chance. El Pipo sighed. It was, in any event, too late now to abandon him that evening. He let Manolo sleep in the car while he spent the night with friends. The next day, El Pipo let him tag along to a second *tienta*.

Manolo leaped into the ring uninvited with the first young cow tested. The *mayoral* had already started toward him to throw him out when Pipo intervened.

"*Tiene afición,* he's legitimate," he said.

Calmer and more sure of himself than he had been the day before, Manolo performed well enough to earn a second chance, and then a third. Before long he was, in his rudimentary way, the attraction of the afternoon. El Pipo watched with growing interest from behind his *burladero*. He had been right. Manolo's arms let him make long, measured passes. There was no hint of fear or nervousness in his gestures now. All afternoon El Pipo stood there watching, his chin resting cupped in his hands on the rim of his *burladero,* his sombrero pulled down to screen his eyes, a cold cigar jutting from his mouth.

When the last cow had been tested and let out to pasture, El Pipo called Manolo to his side. The former King of the Shellfish reached into his pocket and drew out one of his engraved calling cards. On its back he scrawled a few words. Then he handed it to Manolo.

That calling card was the passport to those special preserves that had been closed to him for so long, the breeders' *tientas*. El Pipo told him to stay in Salamanca for the next weeks to practice in every *tienta* he could find. He himself went back to Madrid to contemplate the prospects of the coming season.

Armed with El Pipo's card, Manolo began again his siege of the bull ranches around Salamanca. This time the doors that had been so regularly shut in his face began to open before him. Almost every day he found some *tienta* at which to practice. With the help and the training that had been so long denied him, he began to improve. Before long, he became a well-known figure at those *tientas,* a young man who the ranchers began to declare knowingly "had something."

At night, sleeping in some breeder's shed or rolled up in his muleta in the Plaza Mayor, Manolo began to dream of the life that might soon be his. One worry plagued those dreams. He had a manager he was sure was going to bring a shower of contracts raining down upon him. The arrival of those first contracts would produce a moment of acute embarrassment for Manolo. The few rudimentary bits of learning he had taken from

238

Don Carlos' school had long since wandered from his mind. Not only would he be unable to read the contracts; he would not even be able to sign them. He did not know how to write his own name.

With typical earnestness, he set out to remedy that defect. He got the name of a professor at Salamanca's Salesian college from one of the ranchers, whose finca he had visited. The middle-aged, dignified professor, Antonio Cortez, was astonished to find Manolo's filthy figure on his doorstep one evening begging him to teach him "how to sign." The professor, overcome by the desperation with which he pushed his demand, agreed. Every night for the next six weeks, Manolo presented himself at the professor's door punctually at eleven o'clock.

For the rest of his life, the worthy professor who had never seen a bullfight would remember the image of "that tortured kid, exhausted, filthy, covered with blood and bruises from his latest *tienta,* collapsing in my armchair, pathetically eager for a few scraps of knowledge left over from my teacher's table." Manolo's proudest accomplishment of that season was achieved not in the neighboring fincas but there in the professor's study. Learning first to make a big "M" with a long line flowing from its base to guide his other letters, he soon was able to write "Manuel Benítez El Renco," the four words he dreamed of reading on the wall posters of every city in Spain. He was insatiable in his desire to show off that new skill. Every time he got his hands on a pencil and paper, he traced it out for any audience available.

*　*　*

El Pipo's winter was as uneventful as Manolo's was full. He had every economic reason to make it uneventful. The 350,000 pesetas he had earned in the Albacete corrida had long since disappeared, and the deposed King of the Shellfish was obliged to spend the winter living at the outer limit of his creditors' indulgence. El Pipo appraised the forthcoming season in terms of the theory that by diversifying his efforts, he would maximize his chances of success somewhere. His idea was a simple one: he would introduce several young toreros into the corrida, the way a man might teach puppies to swim. He would toss them all into the water and see who got to shore first. Manolo was just one of the four young men on whom he had his knowing eye.

Whether he could swim or not El Pipo had not decided, but Manolo was the first of his troupe of toreros to pose him a problem. One day at the end of March, a postcard arrived at his home. It came from Salamanca and it was a plea, written on Manolo's behalf, for five hundred pesetas to pay his local debts. He needed the money immediately and if he didn't get it, he was going to be obliged to flee the region.

For El Pipo to reach into his pocket and pass Manolo his calling card was one thing; to reach in and pull out five hundred pesetas was quite another. First of all, he was very unlikely to find them there; five hundred pesetas represented that winter almost as much to the manager as it did to his dirty young torero in Salamanca. It was an investment, a kind of crossing of the financial Rubicon for El Pipo, and he hesitated a long time before making it. Then one afternoon in an impetuous gesture he went out and pawned a gold coin he had brought back from Mexico. He cabled the five hundred pesetas he got for it to Manolo.

A few days later, Manolo was on his doorstep. El Pipo took him into his sitting room and confronted him with a pen and a blank piece of paper. "Sign the paper," El Pipo told him. With an enormous sense of accomplishment, Manolo set upon it for El Pipo the four words that constituted a substantial part of the harvest of his winter in Salamanca: Manuel Benítez El Renco.

El Pipo picked it up and studied it. Preceded by a text he proposed to write himself, that signature would become the price Manolo was going to pay for the answer to his postcard. The piece of paper was going to be his contract with El Pipo. Then after a few moments of reflection, El Pipo announced his first decision taken on behalf of his newly signed protégé. "El Renco" hardly implied the virility the public expected of a matador, he said. Henceforth, he decreed, Manolo would be known as "El Cordobés," the Man from Córdoba.

Manolo looked at him stunned and crestfallen. With those words, all his painstaking efforts in Salamanca had crumbled away to nothing. Sadly he stared at the piece of paper in Pipo's hand and realized he would have to start out all over again to learn how to sign his name.

Manolo found a room with a mason, and El Pipo got him a job as an errand boy in a shellfish shop to keep him alive while he set about looking for a corrida for him.

Mobilizing the full resources of his guile and cunning, the man who had walked in Manolete's shadow now set out to install this miserable and unknown Andalusian orphan upon the maestro's vacant throne. Like some traveling dry-goods salesman, El Pipo began to pound the pavements of Madrid, moving from bullfight bar to bullfight bar in quest of a buyer for the only piece of merchandise he had to sell: the courage of a poor torero. He was a spectacular figure with his ever-present felt sombrero fixed on his head, a cigar, usually dead in deference to his economic misfortunes, clamped between his teeth, an outsized foulard handkerchief flapping from his coat pocket, his person wrapped in a mantle of cheap eau de cologne; El Pipo majestically paced off his daily rounds like an exiled monarch in search of a new court. With the bombastic assertiveness of which he was so uniquely capable, he proclaimed to all who would hear him the virtues of the youth who under his tutelage, he promised, would revolutionize the *fiesta brava*. Serene, confident, giving not the faintest hint of his precarious financial plight, El Pipo set out his well-baited lines and waited for the fish to bite.

Unhappily, however, an unknown matador proved in that season to be a commodity a good deal more difficult to sell than a case of shellfish. His colleagues knew El Pipo too well to take his pompous declarations seriously. This latest genius was just the heir to a whole line of similar *"fenómenos"* the jovial braggart had predicted would turn the bullfighting world upside down—and whose brilliance had barely lasted past a bull or two.

Rebuffed in his efforts to peddle Manolo in Madrid, El Pipo set out on a course that seemed to him eminently logical. He determined to find a fight for Manolo in the land that had spawned him, Andalusia. Packing his bags, El Pipo left for Seville, where the annual feria had just opened, drawing to its storied alleyways the elite of the *fiesta brava*.

Not a man to waste time on the saints when God would do just as well, El Pipo went directly to the moonfaced impresario known as the King of Andalusia, Diodoro Canorea. Canorea controlled, in addition to Seville's bullring, twelve other rings, all the important *plazas* in Andalusia, staged over a hundred and fifty corridas a year, and was, along with Stuyck and two others, one of the four barons who controlled the business end of the *fiesta brava*.

Canorea was all too familiar with the genial mountebank with a cold cigar in his mouth who slid uninvited into his office one April morning in 1960 along with a number of other supplicants and hangers-on. Canorea had even less time than usual to deal with that crowd; the feria was his hectic season. He had no time at all for El Pipo. Not even in his small provincial rings was there a place for his prodigy, Canorea told him. With a gesture, he indicated the horse yard below, crowded with a pack of *maletillas*. There were dozens of youngsters like that, he told El Pipo, in front of every one of his bullrings. Besides, Canorea himself had recently entered the same field as El Pipo. He had selected from the hordes of urchins around his bullrings the half dozen he considered most promising and signed them to management contracts. Any available spots on his *carteles* were going to be filled with his protégés, not El Pipo's.

Thwarted again, El Pipo withdrew to the lobby of the Hotel Colón, an enormous barnlike room which served, during the Seville feria, as the provincial capital of the corrida. There, over endless cups of coffee and glasses of sherry, he tried to find some third-class impresario willing to offer Manolo a chance.

El Pipo knew full well the odds he was up against in the delicate and difficult task of launching a new bullfighter. That year the ten top matadors would divide among them a third of the fights staged in Spain. The two hundred others would fight for what was left, many of them winding up with only half a dozen fights for the entire season. Fewer than a dozen new names would be added to that roster before autumn. Most of those would belong to the protégés of the four major impresarios or the youths in whom they had, through friends or kinsmen, some special interest. Usually the small-town promoters demanded a kickback for placing an unknown fighter on their programs, or almost as often an outright sum of cash. That was the sort of investment that El Pipo would normally have been prepared to take. Cash, unhappily, was a commodity in particularly short supply in El Pipo's life at that moment. Cunning was the only staple he had available in quantity that spring.

Despairing at his failure to find Manolo a contract, Pipo lay one afternoon on the bed of his second-class boardinghouse, prolonging his siesta with the contemplation of his troubles. What he needed, he told himself, was not a bullring but a bullfight. Since he could not find a ring, he would find a town anxious to stage a fight and persuade its mayor to rent one of the portable rings which could rise like a circus tent in any open field.

What town would be more easily persuaded to participate in such a venture than the town that had given birth to his aspiring matador? Trembling with excitement at the brilliance of his idea, El Pipo dressed and rushed to a telephone.

El Pipo's telephone call rang out in a cavernous building that had once been an Arab stable set up against the Moorish walls of Palma del Río. It was Palma's icehouse, and the man who answered was Palma's iceman, Antonio Caro. Caro was the secretary of Palma's *ayuntamiento,* its town council, and as such was responsible for the organization of the few public pleasures Palma del Río was able to afford. His last venture into the *fiesta brava* had been as president of Don Carlos Sánchez's impromptu corrida. That disorderly spectacle had left him with little desire to see any further corridas organized in Palma. He told El Pipo that Palma would have to decline his proposal to run a bullfight for the town.

With all the eloquence of which he was capable, El Pipo described his prodigy as a boy who was already the wonder of Salamanca, the heir to the muletas of Joselito, Belmonte, and Manolete. And, Pipo told him, bringing his sales talk to a climax, that prodigy was a product of Palma del Río.

When Caro heard El Pipo pronounce the prodigy's name, he gasped. The only time the townspeople of Palma had felt any gratitude toward El Renco, he told El Pipo, was the day he had left town for good. No one in Palma, he said, was going to pay a peseta to watch their chronic orange thief fight a bull, and he, as the secretary of the town council, certainly was not going to spend forty thousand pesetas to rent a building for him.

El Pipo insisted, using every bit of salesmanship he could muster. Reluctantly, Caro agreed to present the idea to the town council and call El Pipo back. When he did, his answer was negative. The day Palma's municipal authorities decided to spend any money on Manuel Benítez, he said, they would "buy him a jail, not rent him a bullring."

His answer put El Pipo in desperate straits. He saw his last chance of launching Manolo disappearing. Frantically, he repeated all his arguments to Caro. Then, in an instinctive unthinking gesture, he blurted out that he would pay for the rental of the bullring. Caro wavered. Sensing his prize at his fingertips, El Pipo shouted into the receiver, "And for the bulls, too!"

243

That was too much for Caro. The town council of Palma del Río, he agreed, would officially sponsor the debut of Pipo's prodigy as the highlight of its May fiesta in just two weeks' time.

Relieved and gratified, El Pipo hung up. He slumped happily in a chair in his boardinghouse. Then his face whitened. He had just begun to measure the undertaking to which he had, carried away by his own enthusiasm, committed himself.

"My God," he gasped, "where am I going to get the money?"

*   *   *

Despite the fact it was midday, the pretentiously ornate cut-glass chandelier suspended from the ceiling splattered its light around the room. The curtains and shutters had been closed, not to give the gathering a conspiratorial air but to preserve the cool freshness of the room from the battering heat assaulting the streets outside. The room's occupants were seated around the enormous oval dining table whose somber mahogany planks had borne witness to all the triumphs and tragedies of the Sánchez family. The wedding banquets of the young had been heaped upon these boards, and the ritual offering of coffee and sweets set out here for friends come to mourn their dead. Every major decision of the Sánchez family had been debated, weighed and finally taken in this room, and now, ranged attentively around the table, the kinsmen of Rafael Sánchez, El Pipo, solemnly pondered another.

Everybody was there. There was El Pipo's brother, director of the family's shellfish shop on the Calle de la Plata. Uncle José, the first man installed in the chain of shops set up by the family in Andalusia before the war, was there. El Pipo's three married daughters were there with their husbands. Aunts, uncles, cousins, all the profuse progeny of the Sánchez clan, had assembled at the call of their tribal chieftain, sitting at the head of the table, mopping the sweat from his nervous brow with his multicolored foulard.

El Pipo had been talking for almost ten minutes. His monologue had been a summary of the rising and falling tides of fortune in his erratic career. His emphasis had been placed understandably on its high points rather than its less glorious moments such as the one through which he was now passing. El Pipo had been generous with his wealth during those high points in his career; and it was largely upon these people seated around him that the benefits of that generosity had fallen.

Now, he explained to them, he was preparing to make the last dramatic roll of the dice of his life. He was going to make it on a young mason who wanted to be a matador. Repeating the solemn promise he had uttered to half the impresarios of Spain, El Pipo assured his assembled family that his unknown mason would one day revolutionize the corrida. He, Rafael Sánchez, was going to launch him, and to do it he needed two hundred thousand pesetas. That sum represented the price of one day's rent for a portable bullring and six of the cheapest bulls the ranges of Andalusia could furnish. Whether the youth on whose fate he proposed to wager this sum was a good torero or a bad one, he did not know and he did not care, he said. He was certain of only one thing: that one day, because of his blind bravery, this boy's earnings would spill out of all the banks of Córdoba.

As he finished his little speech, El Pipo let his eyes wander dramatically around the room, catching in turn those of each of his assembled kinsmen. Before him, in the middle of the table, resting on the lace cloth set out for this occasion, was an empty cardboard shoe box. His eyes came back finally to that shoe box and contemplated its outlines for a second. Then El Pipo turned to his eldest daughter, Rosa. He pointed to her left hand. There, sparkling on one of her fingers, was an emerald ring. El Pipo had brought it to her from a trip to South America with Manolete. Now, with a grave and serious voice, he asked her to give it back to him.

El Pipo had chosen his eldest daughter for his first request with the instinctive psychology of an auctioneer. He knew she could not refuse him anything. "Papá," she said in a half whisper, "you're crazy." But she twisted the ring from her finger and passed it to him.

He rolled it briefly between his fingers, so that its green stone sparkled under the chandelier, making sure all present savored the value of her gesture. Then he dropped it with a ceremonious *plunk* into his cardboard shoe box. He raised his eyes and surveyed the stunned faces around him. This time his hungry glance fell upon the white cuffs of his brother's shirt. Holding them together was a pair of gold-and-pearl hand-worked cuff links. Those cuff links, too, were products of El Pipo's generosity in better times. He pointed a pudgy finger at them.

"The cuff links, Pepe," he said. "I need the cuff links. Don't worry, you'll get them back."

His brother shook his head in dismay. Then he silently unclipped the cuff links and tossed them into the box.

And so, around the table, Pipo's fingers went their greedy way, summoning forth a brooch from an aging aunt, a pearl necklace from a daughter, a tie clasp from a son-in-law. At some whose ascetic attire failed to glitter with the wonders of El Pipo's munificence, he stopped and thought. Inevitably, his mind found some bauble, some souvenir, once generously offered, which he now reclaimed. Its owner was politely sent off to fetch it from his home. One by one, the relatives thus designated left and then filed back to deposit their contributions on the pile of jewelry rising up in the shoe box.

Finally it was almost full with its bizarre load of coins, religious medals, rings, bracelets, wristwatches and necklaces. Then El Pipo let out a long sigh, unstrapped his own wristwatch, and with a majestic gesture laid it in the box. From a finger of his right hand he laboriously pulled an enormous gold ring; its seal consisted of two S's flanking a pair of dogs attacking a wild boar. That ring had belonged to El Pipo's father and his grandfather. It was, in a sense, his bishop's ring, his formal seal of office as the head of the Sánchez family. With a last ceremonial gesture, he stretched out his arm and dropped the ring into the shoe box with the rest of the family jewels. El Pipo stood up. He made a stiff half-bow, and in a few words he thanked his relatives for their votes of confidence deposited, however reluctantly, into the box before him.

He scooped up his treasure chest and fitted it snugly under his arm. Then, in a cloud of cigar smoke, he strode off to the pawnshop, prepared at last to rent a bullring for the prodigy whose services he had been unable to foist upon any reputable *plaza de toros* in Spain.

*   *   *

The streets of Palma del Río had never seen anything like it. It was an old French Citroën pickup truck, and fixed to its roof was a pair of enormous loudspeakers. As it crept along Palma's streets at the pace of an exhausted mule, a din that seemed to rattle the beaded curtains along its route burst forth from those microphones. It was the voice of El Pipo,

246

announcing with his inexhaustible supply of superlatives the special treat that awaited the citizens of Palma del Río May 15 in the culminating event of their feria: the world debut of a young matador destined to become the toast of the *fiesta brava*. Already, he promised, he was "the sensation of all the *tientas* of Spain." And, he declared, he was a beloved son of that famous cradle of bullfighting, Palma del Río. "Palmeños," he proclaimed in a voice that could almost have shaken the oranges from the trees on the other side of the Guadalquivir, "you must all come to applaud. It will be the corrida of a lifetime."

The reactions produced by El Pipo's subsequent revelation of the prodigy's name ranged from indifference to hilarity. On the Calle Pacheco where Sergeant Mauleón's authorization had been needed for the exile's return, the dominant reaction was contempt. Don Carlos Sánchez was pleased, and hastily made a note to remind the man who had taken over his impresario's role how fitting and welcome a gesture it would be if he could divert some of the corrida's proceeds to his parish charities. Don Félix's *mayoral,* José Sánchez, viewed the news with alarm. His eldest daughter had not yet found a mate worthy of her hand and he wanted no relapse in her resolution to forget the young man he still regarded as an incurable delinquent. Charneca, the bartender, was surprised. He had not thought that the boy who had stared up at his calendar portraits of Manolete could ever reach the bullring. He could only marvel at what furious determination had finally taken him there.

For Antonio Caro, the iceman, the whole project had become a nightmare. Half the town council was still furious at the thought that the honorable institution they represented could bestow the blessing of its patronage upon the bullfighting debut of a thief with four jail sentences to his name. And El Pipo's credit was turning out to be as poor as his voice was loud.

When the proprietors of the portable ring Caro had rented learned that it was El Pipo and not the town council that was organizing the fight, they threatened to tear the ring down if they weren't given cash in advance. They knew from experience how swiftly El Pipo could total up a bullfight's box office and how quickly he could get out of town if it failed to live up to his expectations.

Angelita Benítez learned of her brother's return in a letter written by one of his friends. When it was read to her, she burst into tears. She had never really believed his threats to become a bullfighter. To her, his pursuit of the corrida had always been something that he chose to avoid work. She had wanted his return more than almost anything else in the world; almost anything except his return under the circumstances that were bringing him back.

Manolo rode down to Palma in an aging SEAT belonging to one of the other young prodigies El Pipo had decided to launch that year. The young man was the least talented of El Pipo's prospects, but he had a car and he had already advanced his manager twenty thousand pesetas to cover the first expenses of the season. In El Pipo's current economic dilemma, such tangible assets counted for considerably more than valor in the bullring.

Don Celes, the brick contractor, saw Manolo off. As a parting gift he gave him a sweater and a pair of blue jeans belonging to his son. As he climbed into the car, Manolo embraced him. "I swear, Don Celes," he said, "I'll never pick up the pick and shovel again."

For Manolo, the return to his hometown was a moment of enormous satisfaction. He had come back as he had said he would, riding in a car. He was coming back to do what a cynical community had never believed he could do: fight a bull in a regular corrida, in a suit of lights, for the edification of those people who had considered him unfit to live among them. The first thing he saw when he rode past the yoked arrows of Ferdinand and Isabella that marked the entry to Palma del Río was his own picture, his portrait in a suit of lights, plastered to a wall of his hometown. Over it was one of El Pipo's preferred phrases: "Alone with Danger."

El Pipo's first order to him was to "make himself seen" along with the other matador El Pipo had engaged to complete the program for the corrida: Juan Horrillo. Together the two friends wandered the *calles* of their hometown, Manolo for the first time in four years. A few, a very few, people were glad to see them. Indifference and contempt were the usual reactions stirred by their presence in Palma's cafés and street corners. Manolo quickly understood that his picture pasted to the walls of Palma was not going to turn him overnight into a hero for these townspeople to whom he was still a juvenile delinquent.

His reputation did nothing to boost the credit rating of his manager either. El Pipo, nursing along the harvest of his family's jewelry, parted with each of his precious pesetas with an almost visible anguish. An aura of craftiness seemed to precede him as surely as the heavy aroma of the eau de cologne with which he regularly doused himself. He was obliged to pay for all his purchases in cash, whittling steadily away at the bundles of banknotes he had brought away from the pawnbroker's.

El Pipo was far too experienced in the art of the corrida to make the same mistake López had made at Talavera. He installed as ticket sellers two of his kinsmen, men he knew had sizable pieces of jewelry resting in his name in Córdoba's pawnshop. To fill the role of the one banderillero required by law for the program, El Pipo engaged a hanger-on at his brother's bar, a fifty-year-old veteran of the bullfight who had begun his career five years before Manolo was born. El Pipo hammered down his banderillero's claims for compensation for the afternoon's work to a single demand: a solid meal after the bullfight was over.

After a long and patient search El Pipo found the animals for his corrida on the ranch of Don Francisco Amián. There were, first, five bulls Amián had been unable to sell elsewhere. Then, to meet El Pipo's rigid economic specifications, the rancher added to them an enormous seven-year-old cow destined for the slaughterhouse. Custom demanded payment for the animals when they left for the ring. El Pipo, however, hoped to postpone that moment of reckoning until he had been able to sell the animals for meat. He sent his fifty-year-old banderillero to fetch them with the truckers and to explain to the rancher that El Pipo was held up in Córdoba and would be along later to pay.

The rancher did not fall for the ploy. He posted one of his vaqueros, rifle in hand, at the ranch gate with orders that the truck was not to budge until he had been paid for his bulls.

Antonio Caro, the iceman, took Manolo to Córdoba to rent a suit of lights for the fight. He chose one in pale blue and gold. On the way back, the iceman was struck by Manolo's stubborn, almost sullen silence. In an effort to draw him into conversation, Caro asked him why he wanted so much to be a bullfighter.

"Because I'm fed up with being hungry," Manolo snapped, and lasped back into silence.

Angelita had married since his departure from Palma and there was no place for Manolo in the two-room hut into which she and her husband had moved. Manolo spent the night in a room El Pipo found for him behind Caro's icehouse. His blue-and-gold suit was laid out over a box beside his cot. All night, unable to sleep, he stared at that suit caught in the moonlight coming through his shack's one open window. Time and time again he reached out to stroke its satin surface as though he were caressing the fur of a kitten. Half a dozen times he got up and in the darkness slipped on the blue jacket as though to reassure himself that it was really there.

Closing his eyes to savor more intensely the joy he felt with that suit hugging his body, he pictured the scene of the morrow, that glorious moment of vindication when he, "the good-for-nothing the Guardia Civil were always beating up," would step into the bullring before his townsmen, trembling with pride in his blue-and-gold suit of lights, when he could prove at last that he had been right and they had been wrong; that something more than the instincts of a common thief had lain behind his stolen oranges and his throttled chickens.

* * *

A young girl walked toward Palma del Río through the damp stillness of the morning. Along the way she stopped from time to time to pluck a handful of wildflowers from the fields alongside the road. By the time she had reached the shrine of the Virgin, her arms were filled with her spring bouquet. With loving care Anita Sánchez arranged them on the Virgin's altar. She was the only member of her family who would not attend the bullfight. Now she quietly begged the Virgin's favor for the young man who had come back to honor the promise he had made to her with his back covered by the bruises of her father's clubs: *"Voy a ser torero."*

* * *

The blue-and-gold suit of lights was now laid out on the bed from which Manolo had stolen his sister's blanket to make his first crude muleta. On the table beside it was a newly purchased image of the Blessed Virgin flanked by a pair of fluted tin dishes into which two candles had been set. Angelita had taken those candles to Mass this morning for Don Carlos Sánchez's blessing. She had given her brother this room, in which she and her husband slept, to dress for the corrida. She waited in the other room crying softly with Tía Carmen, her father's sister.

Already a crowd of noisy youngsters clustered in the dirt alleyway outside the hovel, waiting to give her brother an escort of honor to Palma's portable bullring. El Pipo, perspiring and nervous, pushed his way through the beaded curtain separating the house from the street, nodded brusquely to Angelita, and entered the room where Manolo was already dressing.

There was no joviality in El Pipo's mien now. He had too much invested in this corrida to smile. There would be no second chance if today's bullfight failed—not for his bullfighter and not for El Pipo. Grimly he told Manolo to "get so close to those bulls the people will think you're wearing them for a coat." If he was hurt, he said, "get up and go on until you pass out."

Antonio Columpio, the banderillero El Pipo had hired for the afternoon, was knotting up the trousers of his matador when he heard his reply.

"Listen, Don Rafael," Manolo said, "I'll walk over my own guts if I have to kill my bulls." Then, laughing, he went back to his dressing.

In the next room Angelita heard his laughter. She was kneeling now against a chair, despairingly mumbling the rosary. That sound distressed her. She had always heard that bullfighters were supposed to be quiet and serious before a fight. If he wasn't that, she thought, "at least, he should be silent and praying," as she was. A few minutes later, with a rattling of the beaded curtains, he stepped out of the bedroom.

ANGELITA BENÍTEZ'S STORY

"I SHRIEKED when I saw him. He had a smile as big as the room over his face. My knees started to shake. He came over and took me in his arms and he kissed me.

"I never thought he would come to anything. I never believed all those things he said. And there he was, just as he said he would be, he was a torero now, he was finally the 'somebody' he always wanted to be. Me, I cried. All I could think of was him, my baby brother, standing before those horns. I never cried any tears for him when he was a boy any more bitter than the tears I cried that afternoon.

251

"He put his arms around me and we walked to the door. The whole town was out there waiting for him, yelling and pushing. I felt faint. 'Please, please, Manolo,' I begged, 'don't go!'

"He bent down and he kissed me again, on the eyes this time.

" 'Don't cry, Angelita,' he said. He put his hand on his suit and he said, 'Tonight, either I'll buy you a house or I'll dress you in mourning.' "

CHAPTER SEVEN

Madrid:
THE FAENA

THE CROWDED stands of Las Ventas were silent and expectant. From them a stillness seemed to have seeped over Spain, softening the clamor of her exuberant existence. For a few moments, in the fading brightness of this May afternoon, the rhythm of the nation's life hung suspended, paused attendant upon the deeds of one man. Traffic and commerce had almost ceased, policemen had abandoned their posts, telephones went unanswered. Caudillo and convict, Minister and peasant, landowner and charwoman, banker and factory worker, twenty million men and women, almost two out of every three Spaniards, waited before the flickering gray screens of television sets, united by the electronic miracle that reached into the bullring of Las Ventas as Spain had not been united for any single event since 1939.

It was an extraordinary moment, this instant that destiny had accorded the young man from Palma del Río. Only one other man would draw to his figure in the vast, impersonal amphitheater of a nation's television a greater proportion of his countrymen, and it would be his tragic fortune to do so from his coffin as a martyred President. The United States burying John F. Kennedy; England bestowing a crown upon her Queen; Italy mourning good Pope John; France watching Charles de Gaulle beg for help in the midst of a generals' rebellion in Algiers; only the telecasts of those events could be compared, in the na-

253

tions which had known them, with the impact the spectacle now unfolding on the rain-soaked soil of Madrid's Plaza de Toros had had on Spain. Rarely had any single performer been called upon to display his art before an audience as vast as those forty million eyes now following the slender figure of El Cordobés as it slid, alone, across the gray field of the television screen.

In the flowered patio of a little house in Palma del Río, the appearance of that figure stirred a chorus of anxious voices summoning Angelita Benítez. Too nervous to watch the preliminaries to this culminating moment in her brother's career, she had instead spent the past ten minutes pacing her patio, trying desperately to remember the words of a prayer. Furiously blessing herself, she allowed two kinsmen to guide her back into her darkened room and her seat of honor before her new television set.

Not far away, in the cement ranks of the housing development to which her father had retired, another woman settled nervously before her television set. Upon her back was the sky-blue suit she had made for this day and the feria of Palma del Río. Anita Sánchez too murmured a hasty prayer for the young man gliding across her television screen, the unruly orphan into whose hand she had once slipped her first communion medal with the pledge that she would be his forever.

A respectful silence filled the crowded café on Córdoba's Calle de la Plata. Leaning past his half-filled glass of beer, a stocky spectator followed the matador's shuffling walk with an intense gaze. He knew that walk well. Once he had ordered it down the *calles* of Palma del Río with the drumbeats of his club. Retired now from the Guardia Civil, Rafael Mauleón, "Tomato Face," had traded the authority of his sergeant's stripes for the respectable office of an accountant's assistant in an automobile spare-parts firm. For nothing in the world would he, the man who had imposed on Manuel Benítez the most humiliating experience of his life, have missed this chance to stand witness at his greatest triumph.

El Cordobés' footsteps carried him to the patch of sand just below the box from which Police Commissioner de Quiros looked down upon the ring, solemn and unsmiling. There a brief but important ceremony awaited him, since this fight represented the official confirmation of his *alternativa*, his formal entry into the archives of the *fiesta brava* as a *matador de toros*.

254

Manolo had taken his *alternativa* in the bullring of the city whose name he bore, Córdoba. That ceremony had seemed to the eager followers of the corrida heavy with portent and symbolism. He had received his *alternativa* at the hands of Antonio Bienvenida, the oldest matador in Spain. No torero could have been more unlike the ill-disciplined young revolutionary he had welcomed to the ranks of his ancient profession than that stern and graceful dean of toreros. Bienvenida had begun fighting bulls the year El Cordobés was born. He was, on that day he had offered Manuel Benítez the tools of his trade, forty-one years old. He had extended the muleta and the sword in the *alternativa* to thirty-six men, more than any other matador in history. Above all else, he represented a concept of the bullfight radically opposed to that of the angry young men to whom he had given the *alternativa.* He was a classic bullfighter, a man seeking to create beauty through the grace and elegance of his gestures. The young man with the unruly hair before him in Córdoba scorned all that. There was no pattern and little elegance in what he did. He broke the rules and laughed at the traditions. But he gave the crowd something it valued more than beauty—emotion. He scared it; and the crowd that had walked to see Bienvenida ran to see El Cordobés. When Bienvenida had embraced El Cordobés and slipped his scarlet muleta into his hands, it was as though the seals of office of the *fiesta brava* had been passed from one generation to another. And to many in the bullring that day, the ceremony had seemed to foretell other changes, the imminent passing of the seals of office from one generation to another in fields unrelated to the *fiesta brava,* an event which would carry with it profound implications for the Spanish nation.

The ceremony in Madrid was offered by the senior matador on the program, Pedro Martínez, Pedrés, only four years older than El Cordobés. By tradition, the bull Impulsivo, the first animal of the day, should have been his as the senior torero on the program. Now, with a symbolic exchange of muletas and swords, he offered that animal to El Cordobés.

El Cordobés nodded briefly to President de Quiros. Then he turned, and raising his black *montera,* he extended it toward the crowded stands of Las Ventas. With a pivot, he swung about in a little circle, his extended hat describing a still-wider arc, a gesture that dedicated the life of Impulsivo to the thousands of spectators piled on the cement ranks of the bullring and, by extension, to the millions of impatient Spaniards waiting by their television sets.

A round of grateful applause greeted his gesture. El Cordobés casually dropped his hat onto the wet sand. Carefully he stretched out his muleta and started across the ring. Watching him go from his president's box, Police Commissioner de Quiros nervously reviewed again his decision to let this fight take place. Aware of the tension in the stands around him, he was reassured. As he had felt forty minutes earlier, so he felt now. There had been no choice. He had been a prisoner of the fame of the young man starting into the bullring.

In the *callejón* below him, Don Livinio Stuyck, poised behind the wooden screen reserved for him, drew a large Cuban cigar from his pocket and lit it. It was, for the impresario of Las Ventas, a moment of profound satisfaction. San Isidro had not failed him. Rain could not stop now the debut of the youngster he had once turned away from the gates of his bullring.

Not far from the red brick stands of Las Ventas, on a shady side street, the corridors of a small green-shuttered building were, like those of so many other buildings in Spain that day, silent and empty. Every nurse and attendant and every one of the patients of Madrid's Toreros' Hospital were gathered around an enormous television set placed in the hospital's recreation room. Every patient, that is, except one. Alone in his room, Robustiano Fernández, the scrap-metal scavenger gored in a country corrida in Extremadura, struggled toward consciousness through the anesthetic still numbing his brain. He had spent three hours on Dr. Máximo de la Torre's operating table. Now, in his dazed state, he did not know for a few instants where he was or what time it was. His window was open and his first waking impression was that of the dull roar of a crowd drifting through that window. Then, in the hall beyond him, he heard another sound, the rasping voice of an announcer proclaiming that the faena was about to begin.

That word faena, alive with so many associations for Fernández, yanked the injured banderillero back into reality and above all the reality of his own life. Groaning gently, he tried to raise his head and shoulders from his bed. His anesthetized muscles failed him, and his head fell back onto his pillow. He called for help, but in the silent corridors of the hospital there was no one to come to his side. Summoning his will for another effort, he thrust back his elbows to support himself and forced his head up until his chin rested on his chest.

His eyes swept down over the sheet below his waist. At the end of that white expanse, his eyes fell on the point thrust into the sheet's surface by the toes of his right leg. Beside that little mound, in the place where his left foot should have been, there was nothing; from there to his torso there was nothing but the flat whiteness of the sheet. Half hysterical, Fernández thrust one arm forward and tried, with his fingers, to touch that empty stretch of sheet, as though somehow those fingers might be able to withdraw from its folds his missing member. Then, as the awareness of what had happened to him penetrated to his mind, he fell back onto his pillow.

Outside, the rumble of the distant crowd, reaching up even to his room, grew louder. Half of Spain was yelling for what Robustiano Fernández had wanted to be. He turned his head to his pillow and began to weep bitterly for what he had now become.

$$* \quad * \quad *$$

El Cordobés stalked carefully forward, his eyes fixed on the black and motionless hulk of Impulsivo waiting for him at the other side of the ring. He did not hear the slow murmur of the crowd that accompanied each of his steps. Of that packed amphitheater circling around him, he saw only the sand and the animal poised upon it, fixing him with its steady gaze. In those instants all his thoughts lay concentrated on that handsome black animal he must now put to death, a product, as he was, of the soil of Andalusia.

He had brought him to this conflict just as he had wanted to. Impulsivo had proved his bravery against José Sigüenza's pic, but he had escaped that trial intact. The banderillas had awakened his ardor. To El Cordobés he seemed, for an instant, an ideal bull—"a bull for glory," he thought with a fleeting smile.

His confidence was not justified. The stabs of José's pic and the blood they had drained from Impulsivo's body had not—as they sometimes could do—improved his faulty vision, nor altered his tendency to chop with his left horn. Both abnormalities represented clear dangers to a man determined to ride out of Las Ventas on a stretcher or the shoulders of

257

the mob, just as real as the danger he could feel through his slippers' thin soles: the cold and heavy sand on the surface below him. The rain had stopped now, but, beyond the rim of the bullring, he could see an ominous black mass of cloud building up on the horizon. He was fighting the bull before him in difficult circumstances. But, he realized, he might be fighting his second bull in impossible ones. If he was going to impress the demanding public of Madrid, it was going to have to be now with Impulsivo.

Normally, El Cordobés would have been tempted to begin his faena with one of the special gestures that had become the hallmarks of his style, citing the bull from afar, spinning about while he charged to pass him with his back to the animal's horns, or on his knees. He had vowed, however, to give the Madrid public a straightforward, unadorned display of his skill and his courage. He was not going to allow his critics to accuse him of using tricks to deceive them.

As he had done with his cape, so would he do now with his muleta. He would fight Impulsivo in the most remote, the most dangerous spot in the bullring, its center. There, should he stumble or be caught by Impulsivo, he was a hundred feet from help, a hundred feet of soggy sand to be covered by men encumbered with seven-pound capes as they ran. Their rescuing rush would take perhaps ten seconds, ten seconds in which he would be helpless under the searching horns of Impulsivo.

El Cordobés led the bull to the center of the ring with two quick, functional movements of his cloth. Then, straightening up with a proud shake of his shoulders, he planted his feet in the ground, announcing with that gesture his determination to conduct his entire faena there, in the center of the ring. An approving mumble rose from the crowd.

He stretched out his muleta to its full scarlet spread. Slowly, almost imperceptibly, he set its folds flowing with the gesturings of his wrists, fixing Impulsivo's eyes to that cloth. He swung it casually forward a few inches; then with a snap of his wrist he jerked it to a stop and drew it slowly back. In the silence of that instant, twenty-six thousand people could hear the voice that had echoed through a hundred moonlit pastures bark: "Hey, *toro!*"

Impulsivo's massive head seemed to twitch. Then, with one clean motion, he answered the scarlet summons of the cloth before him.

The bull covered the fifteen feet separating him from El Cordobés' cloth in three smooth strides. El Cordobés awaited him as frozen in his stance as a marble statue. Only his hands, clamped to his muleta, moved. His feet and legs were pressed so tightly together he could almost feel his thighs pushing against each other.

As the bull reached for his muleta, held chest-high, El Cordobés drew it slowly up and away, raising the bull's massive skull with it, so that head and horns floated past him at the level of his armpits. Indifferently, he watched those horns glide by under his eyes, then stab at the air as Impulsivo burst from under the muleta, trying to spear the illusion El Cordobés had just snatched away.

The matador did an about-face with a series of quick, flatfooted steps and brought Impulsivo back past him again, from the other side this time. Those passes were called *pases por alto,* high passes, and they represented a deliberate choice on El Cordobés' part. They had a game to play together, those two products of Andalusia's soil, and the high passes prepared Impulsivo to play it.

He was a different animal now from the black mass of unthinking energy that had hurtled from the Gates of Fear ten minutes earlier. Then he had been ready to throw himself at any object that caught his attention. His charges had been instinctive, the spontaneous reaction of a beast whose capacities had never been challenged or tested. He had been wounded now. The blood that had spilled out of the holes cut by José Sigüenza's pic was already beginning to mat and dry on his black hide, but the holes were raw and painful, as painful as the memories they had left. The pic had, as it was supposed to, battered some of the prideful bearing from Impulsivo's carriage. His head, carried so high when he had entered the ring, was borne less proudly now; his ponderous skull was a burden to his weakened shoulder muscles.

Above all, his savage, unspoiled animal confidence had been shaken. He had been deceived by the infuriating, unseizable lure of the cape. He was wary now, and his charges were no longer wild gestures but conscious attacks, the deliberate search for some solid substance he could impale upon his horns.

He was infinitely more dangerous than he had been when he entered the ring. As Impulsivo's attacks became more selective, his posture more defensive, the matador was obliged to risk more to provoke the animal's charge. It was one of the paradoxes of this strange rite that while death

259

was the bull's inescapable end, time was on his side. With each pass, with each minute ticking by, he learned a little more, until finally, if too much time, or too many passes, went by, he learned it all. Then he, too, could kill.

The three high passes El Cordobés gave Impulsivo were designed to boost his confidence, to sharpen his desire to charge. They were straightforward, open passes, refreshing, almost, for the wounded animal.

As they ended, El Cordobés gave him a moment to draw his breath. Then, with infinite care, he began to move again toward his bull. His muleta he carried in his right hand, its folds hung lower now, his arm hanging away from his shoulder so that the cloth fell away from just below his hips. Eight feet, seven feet, six feet, slowly his delicate steps drew him closer to the animal, closer to an invisible frontier over which he must not cross. It was that point beyond which Impulsivo would charge automatically. At the beginning of the fight it had been thirty yards, perhaps, from the animal; now it was not much farther away than the length of a small car. Later it would be only a foot or two from his gray horns, a distance so small that any miscalculation on El Cordobés' part could bring the horns slashing into his flesh.

That invisible frontier marked the bull's "territory." It varied with every bull and with almost every minute of the fight, but the consequences of violating it remained constant. Once a man had crossed that line, the bull would charge, not in reaction to the man's summons but in his own defense. Then it would be the animal and not the man who commanded the fight.

As he inched his way forward toward Impulsivo's waiting horns, feeling his way toward that frontier like a man groping for a wall in the dark, El Cordobés kept his attention riveted upon one thing. It was not on those menacing gray spikes but on the only guide he had to the intelligence behind them, the dull black-brown eyes of Impulsivo.

They were the key to the bullfight, those eyes, the key to everything he hoped to accomplish in this bullring. It was there that he would see the warning that would tell him to stop, that his advancing feet had drawn abreast of the invisible line drawn in the sand of Las Ventas, dividing the bull's world from his.

He could not describe that warning, the change that came over those glistening black-brown ovals at that instant. He could only read it. It was the only warning a matador got that an attack was coming, and if experience had not taught him to read it, the bulls would drive him out of the ring. Sometimes, El Cordobés knew, "you see those eyes swing off the muleta and look at you." Then there was just one recourse: "to shake the muleta as hard as you can to get them back where they belong, because if you don't, there'll be a horn stuck in your gut in a few seconds."

He stopped now, six feet from Impulsivo, sensing that he was about to trespass into the bull's world. Carefully he slid his body about until he stood profiled before the bull, his body exposed to the animal's gaze, his right hand grasping both the pummel of his sword and the stick of his muleta, the sword thrust under its folds to give extra width to the scarlet serge. It was lower now, much lower, and its edges trailed over the sand as El Cordobés drew it toward the bull's nose.

Behind his *burladero,* his cape clutched in his hands, ready to run to his matador's aid, Paco Ruiz watched with tense fascination. "The bull's going to play, the bull's going to play," the banderillero told himself. "Manolo is going to have his triumph in Madrid."

And, almost in recognition of Paco's thoughts, Impulsivo surged forward, his head low, tearing for the scrap of cloth El Cordobés drew along before his horns with tantalizing slowness. The bull swiveled about as soon as he had passed, searching for the illusory target just snatched away from him. It was there waiting, barely two feet from his horns. El Cordobés was there, too, profiled beside it, an invader in the realm of Impulsivo; but the man had contrived to center the bull's eyes on only one thing now, the piece of cloth. The matador shook it, in one brusque, dancing gesture, and Impulsivo charged again, frantically trying to catch that fleeting image on the tips of his horns. Again the bull passed and spun, and again there the cloth was before him, barely a foot away now with, beside it, the man he could not see because that man had riveted his gaze to the cloth. Another flick of El Cordobés' wrist, and obediently Impulsivo lurched for the muleta, this time to the accompaniment of a thunderous burst of *"olé's"* from the stands.

It was not enough. El Cordobés beckoned him back with his demanding cloth. Again Impulsivo charged, his nose almost touching the sand now, his massive bulk pulled forward as though it were chained to that flaring red rag only inches from his skull. Once, twice, three times, El Cordobés pulled the bull around his body, stirring him back to movement with a snap of his wrists each time his forward motion faltered, drawing him closer each time in a tightening coil until, finally on the last circle, the bull was almost a part of him, until his black hide rubbed up against him, smearing his gold-and-tobacco suit with the blood left from José's pic; and El Cordobés, tottering on the wet sand, had to hold onto the spine of the animal pressing up against him to keep his balance. Then, with another final flick of his wrist, he sent the bull shooting away from him like a spring shooting out of its socket.

The crowd was in an uproar. A frantic wave of *"olé's"* beat down into the ring. El Cordobés strode away from Impulsivo, leaving the bewildered animal to gasp for breath. An enormous smile lit up the matador's face. Looking out at him, Paco Ruiz relaxed for a second and a huge smile broke over his face, too. "He's going to make it," Paco thought. "He's going to ride out the gate *en hombros.*"

The matador moved back to the spot on which he had just given Impulsivo his three right-hand passes. As he spread out his muleta for a new series of passes, he felt a raindrop strike his head, then another and another. The storm clouds he had spotted marching out to his rendezvous with Impulsivo were unleashing their burden earlier than he had expected. In a few seconds, a steady, beating rain was pouring down again on Las Ventas. Wiping the raindrops and his hair from his face with a gesture of his hand, El Cordobés started again, three more right-hand passes this time, each one accompanied by a new and thunderous burst of *"olé's"* from the packed stands.

With each pass he twisted Impulsivo closer to him until, after the last one, the tobacco-and-gold of his suit of lights was a dark mass of blood, flecked with the sand kicked up from the arena's floor by the animal's hoofs. Again he ended his series with a high breast pass that sent the animal shooting out and away from him. Satisfied, he stepped back to let his bull catch his breath.

Peering anxiously from his *burladero,* Paco Ruiz wondered what his matador was going to do next. He did not have to wait long to find out. To his horror, he saw him shift the muleta to his left hand. Paco's fingers tightened in fear on the rim of the cape he clutched to his chest. Proud and provocative, his matador began his march back toward Impulsivo, the folds of his muleta trailing now at his left side.

With that one gesture, the shifting of his muleta from his right hand to

262

his left, El Cordobés had cut in half the size of the lure he was offering to Impulsivo. His sword no longer stretched open the folds of his cloth. It was less than a yard wide now, barely wider than the full sweep of those flaring, vicious horns that would shortly try to shred it apart. It was, this left-handed pass he was about to attempt, the classic muleta pass of the bullfight, one of its most beautiful and one of its most dangerous. Few passes exposed the matador's body more, staking out more clearly to the animal the alternatives offered his horns, man or muleta. The measure of the danger it involved could be found in the fact that usually four passes out of five a matador makes during a faena are done with the right hand.

Watching El Cordobés stalk toward Impulsivo, his back arched, his harsh voice calling to the animal, Paco felt a bead of sweat sliding down his backbone. He knew the risks his matador was taking with this gesture. In any other ring, in almost any other circumstances, he would have refused to take them. Today he had no choice. Madrid, Paco realized, "had to have its *naturales.*" This howling, demanding public, living now in a constant roar, would accept no less.

That meant El Cordobés would have to bring Impulsivo's dangerous left horn scraping close to his body with each left-handed pass he tried. During the agonizing seconds each of those passes would encompass, an element of sheer chance would enter the combat El Cordobés was waging. For, during those seconds, Impulsivo's unseeing left eye would sweep along El Cordobés' body too. There would be no lure there to pull that eye along the course the matador had selected for the bull, only a blur: a blur that did not separate man from muleta. Then the bull could gore blindly in the same manner as the bull who had killed the incomparable Joselito in Talavera de la Reina.

Softly, El Cordobés called the animal to his cloth. He was barely four feet from Impulsivo's horns now. Only one thing at that instant lay between those horns and his exposed body. It was the control, the command his left wrist could give to the folds of his beckoning cloth muleta. He advanced the muleta toward those dull, black-brown eyes, a tentative, probing gesture, groping toward the instant of attack. When it came, he withdrew the cloth, keeping it low toward the sand, retreating just before the horns. El Cordobés swayed with the charge, his left arm flowing along ahead of the horns, keeping the muleta always there a few tantalizing inches from their lips. With cool purpose, he brought those horns along past his body, then, leaning, allowed his body to bend and follow the curve of the bull's charge until with a quick flicking of his wrist directed to the bull's good right eye, he sent Impulsivo safely away, slanting off to the right.

Five times he repeated that pass, each time drawing Impulsivo closer, until finally on the last two passes the bull's horns slashed past only an inch or two from his groin, and a mere twitch of the animal's head could have torn open his bowels. When the fifth pass was finished and the animal, guided by the movements of El Cordobés' wrist, slid off safely to the right, an enormous sigh of relief burst from Paco Ruiz's lungs.

Las Ventas was a roaring tunnel of noise. Half the crowd was on its feet, shouting its admiration. In thousands of bars and cafés around Spain, people yelled, screamed, pounded each other on their backs, spilled their drinks, let themselves be swept away with the exhilaration stirred by the sight they had just witnessed.

Standing in the middle of the ring, letting the cries of the crowd pour over him, El Cordobés was transfigured by the emotion of that moment. He was covered with blood and mud. But the roar of the crowd made him feel "almost drunk with joy." At that moment, "filled up with the fantastic force the *ole's* give you," he felt capable of doing anything in the world he wanted to do.

It was not always like that. El Cordobés knew as well as any other matador that an exulting crowd could turn viciously upon a man who failed to meet their demands, and it was a frightening experience. At such times, standing in the middle of the ring, El Cordobés "could hear every insult, every curse, pouring down from the stands." The reaction it produced in the matador was "like chopping down a green tree and drying it all of a sudden. It drains your soul out of you."

Now, buoyed by this wildly enthusiastic crowd, El Cordobés switched the muleta back to his right hand and stalked toward Impulsivo again. He started a new series of right-handed passes, the best he had yet done. Once, twice, three times, the bull charged past him, coming so close El Cordobés felt the air his rush displaced brushing his face. With each pass he heard the wild, clamoring call of the crowd ringing down from the stands. Each of those bursts of noise was as irresistible a lure to him as his cloth was to the bull. With each one he went on again, to try to bring

Impulsivo past him one more time. Finally he brought the bull around him in a tightening circle, once, twice, twisting him around his erect body like a ribbon around a maypole, Impulsivo furiously, blindly panting after his elusive red flag. At the end of that circling pass, the flat of his searching horns bumped up against El Cordobés' legs, forcing the matador to struggle for an instant to stay on his feet.

El Cordobés walked away to another delirious roar from the crowd, leaving Impulsivo staring dumbly at his retreating figure as though his simple animal brain were trying to understand why his horns could find no more solid a target for their blows than air.

Paco Ruiz was exultant. "He's done it," he thought, "he has won." El Cordobés had kept his promise. Now, when this bullfight was over, Paco knew, the great gates of Las Ventas would swing apart to let him ride from the bullring in triumph on the shoulders of his admirers. What he had done here, in the rain, with a bull whose vision was faulty, who had not been sufficiently piced, was more than any public could dare hope for. It was time to kill now, and Paco turned to search out the figure of El Cordobés' sword handler ready to pass him the *estoque,* the steel sword with which he would end the life of the bull Impulsivo.

As he did, he heard a new, approving roar rise from the crowd. Turning his eyes back to the ring, he saw to his astonishment the figure of his matador marching back toward the bull. Unable to control himself, Paco stepped out from behind his *burladero* as though to sprint to the middle of the ring to pull him back. "No, no, Manolo!" he screamed. "That's enough!"

El Cordobés turned at the sound of his frightened yell. With a brutal gesture, he waved him back behind his *burladero.* As he reluctantly retreated to cover, Paco could hear another voice yelling out to El Cordobés from across the plaza. It came from his fellow banderillero, Pepín Garrido. He, too, was adding his frantic warning to Paco's.

The young man in the middle of the ring was not heeding their warnings or anyone else's. The only voice to which he responded came from somewhere within his own exhilarated soul. He swept his hair back from his forehead. Then, snapping the folds of his muleta, he called Impulsivo to the left again, exposing his stomach once again to the blind left eye and the hooking left horn.

With each pass he now gave Impulsivo, El Cordobés ran a new risk, a

265

risk of upsetting a fine equation, a balancing of the many forces of the bullfight. If a matador gives his bull too few passes, his animal will not be trained to take the lure of his cloth, and so, when the moment comes to kill, and the bull must follow that cloth if the man is to go in over his right horn and get away safely, the bull will refuse to do so. Then the animal may catch his executioner on his horns. But if the man gives the bull too many passes, the animal will begin to understand: he will learn the difference between man and muleta. Already, with each pass, Impulsivo's massive skull was beginning to sway tentatively left and right, probing for some solid substance to satisfy his wrath.

The rain was beating down steadily now. El Cordobés' muleta was wet and heavy, its bright folds spattered with dirt. The center of the ring was pocked with Impulsivo's hoofprints as though a whole herd of bulls had been driven over that site. His own feet were soaking wet, his pink stockings stained with dampness above his ankles. Every step he took on the slick sand had to be sure and precise or he risked a fall.

Paco Ruiz cursed each time Manolo forced the animal past him. Each of those left-handed passes seemed to bring Impulsivo closer than the one that had preceded it, yet he knew it was impossible. Every time that horn thrust by, Paco's throat tightened until Manolo, with his incredible dexterity, caught the animal's right eye by a movement of the muleta and sent him safely away. So close did those passes seem that Paco swore Manolo had to feel the tip of the horn scraping along his thighs.

El Cordobés felt nothing of the sort. Out there alone in the middle of the ring, he could hear the beseeching cries of his banderilleros begging him to stop. But he could not stop. Each cracking round of *"olé's"* drove him on, fighting to wrench one more pass from an animal from whom he had already extracted too many.

Las Ventas, as it had been for moments, was a roaring cavern of noise. Yet, in that wildly howling mob, a sense of concern began to rise in a few seasoned minds. From his privileged seat above the Gates of Fear, Francisco Galindo, the *mayoral* of Don José Benítez Cubero, had watched the spectacle with pride and relief. Bull number 25 had borne with honor the blue-and-white colors of the ranch Galindo served. He had followed the cloth, despite his faulty vision, with a fierce, unhampered bravery. But it could not go on. Staring at the spectacle before him, Galindo thought to himself that El Cordobés "had gone beyond the bull. He had given him more muleta than he could take."

Trying to accomplish the impossible feat of licking the paper of one of his hand-rolled cigarettes without taking his eyes from the man in the center of the ring, Don Juan Espinosa Carmona, the chaplain of the bullring, had the same thought. For several moments his anxious mind had turned over a nonstop invocation to the Virgin for the impetuous youth who had this afternoon stirred his feelings as no matador had done for two decades.

Thirty ranks below him, unnoticed in the yelling crowd, a man slipped from a stool set alongside the rim of the *callejón*. While the crowd went crazy, Dr. Máximo de la Torre hobbled anxiously toward his infirmary.

Theirs, however, were only a few warning voices in a sea of exultation. All Las Ventas, it seemed, was on its feet yelling, shouting. So was half of Spain, pulled into the bullring by a television cable. Cafés, bars and restaurants all over the country were in a pandemonium. Everywhere —in clubs, schools, stores, homes—people pushed and shoved, fighting for a glimpse of the screen, demanding, "What's he doing? What's he doing?"

Those instants were the fulfillment of everything El Cordobés had ever wanted, the solace for every beating he had ever taken, the balm for every hunger pain he had ever known. He was, in the center of that bullring, the very quintessence of a "somebody." Twenty million people were calling his name, and yet he—he—was alone in a world of his own with a bull spinning around him.

At that moment El Cordobés was crazy with happiness. He was "on a cloud" where absolutely nothing else in the world counted beyond the incredible sensation he was living. Again he pulled the bull around him, using his body as pivot, dragging Impulsivo's head with him as though it were fixed by some magic force to his muleta. Slipping and sliding on the wet sand, he kept the bull coming, the animal's hot, heaving flanks rubbing his, until he himself was dizzy and slightly nauseated from their wild whirling circle. He had forgotten everything—prudence, the warnings of his banderilleros, the bull's vision—everything but the exhilarating, exalting thing he was doing.

His astonishing display had long reduced the men in the half-darkened sitting room of Don José Benítez Cubero's ranch house, 288 miles from Madrid, to an awed and nervous silence. Now in the room there was no sound except the voice of the announcer rising from the television set and the heavy breathing of the men around it. Don José leaned forward, staring at the screen, his fingernails digging nervously into the arms of his black leather easy chair. His pride in his animal's performance had long since been satisfied. He wanted only one thing now: to see this fight end well, without a tragedy for its matador. Twice in the last few moments he had said to himself, "He's mad, he's mad." It seemed impossible that his bull could have any more passes left in him, and yet El Cordobés forced him on and on.

Suddenly Don José stiffened. He had seen the sign he had been waiting for, the sign he knew had to come, a gesture at the end of this last pass El Cordobés had forced from his bull. At the end of that pass, as El Cordobés flicked his muleta to send the bull out and away from his body, Impulsivo's horn had stabbed inward, deliberately tossing back the folds of the muleta. He knows, Don José thought; he's learned the rules. He's after the man.

Don José half rose from his seat. His anxious voice filled the dark and hushed room, calling out a warning: a warning directed not to these silent men around him, but meant to carry somehow over 288 miles to the man standing alone in the center of the Las Ventas bullring with one of his bulls.

"*Mátalo, hombre, mátalo!*" he yelled. "Kill him, man, kill him!"

CHAPTER EIGHT

THE CRAZY SUMMER

Six pairs of gleaming black leather boots clacked together in the guardroom of the whitewashed building on the Calle Pacheco. White gloves clutched in his hand, his bicorn hat tucked under his arm, his air as severe and worthy as any general mustering his troops for parade, Sergeant Rafael Mauleón passed the men of his little garrison in review. Not a button, not a belt buckle, escaped the sergeant's vigilant eye. When he had finished, he barked a brusque command. His troop turned and, as proud and martial as the advancing guard in the opera *Carmen,* marched forth from Palma del Río's Guardia Civil barracks.

The harbingers of the event summoning them from their austere headquarters this May afternoon in 1960 were the posters covering every wall and lamppost in Palma. In blaring black letters, they promised at five o'clock this afternoon a spectacle it had not been Palma del Río's privilege to witness in over thirty years, a real bullfight. As the principal participant in that historic event, those posters announced the name of the young man who had once been the prime target of Sergeant Mauleón's wrath, Manuel Benítez, El Cordobés.

By a strange shift of destiny, "Tomato Face" and his men would form today a kind of guard of honor for the former delinquent whose fleeing figure they had pursued through half the pastures of Palma del Río. In just thirty minutes, in the wooden bullring rented in his honor, their polished patent-leather hats and gray-green uniforms would symbolize peace and public order at the tumultuous ceremony marking the return of Manuel Benítez.

It had been years since an event had excited so much interest and so much sarcasm in Palma. In this late afternoon, from the town's narrow streets and sun-baked plazas, from its flowered patios and squalid hovels, Palmeños by the hundreds were already marching toward the bullring at the end of town. Picking their way proudly through their ranks, already filling the broad sweep of the Avenida del Generalísimo, were the carriages of Palma's wealthy. Don Félix Moreno, his head crowned by a felt sombrero, rode among them like some stern but paternal monarch surrounded by his subjects. Sweating and puffing in the hot sun, "Tomato Face" extended the breeder a respectful nod as he marched his men past the rich landowner's ornate carriage. Several yards behind the sergeant's guard, discreet and unnoticed in her black mantilla, was his wife. She remembered well the hungry face of the prisoner to whom she had once tossed the leftovers from her husband's table; today she was going to the *plaza de toros* to see that face again, marked this time, she hoped, not with pain but with a conqueror's grin.

Don Carlos Sánchez, clothed in the good cassock he wore only for occasions as solemn as the annual presentation of his respects to the bishop of his diocese, also hurried toward the plaza. Three days of soul-searching thought had preceded his decision to join this crowd marching off to watch the young man whose runny nose he had wiped so often years ago. One thought had finally eased his conscience and prompted his decision. It was that "God forbid, the services of a priest might be needed in the bullring." Adolfo Santaflor, the carpenter who had given Manolo the sticks to stiffen his first muleta, was there. So were José Sánchez the unforgiving *mayoral;* Don Rafael, the doctor without medicine of the cruel years after the war; Luis Palo, the stationmaster who had found Manolo's bloody trophies hung on the nails of his Seville-Córdoba timetable; Antonio and Miguel, the water sellers of the Calle Belén: all were there walking along in the tide of Palmeños flowing toward the bullring.

Of all the crowd drifting to the flag-decked ring, no man was happier than the lone passenger of an old taxi. Almost a decade had passed since

Pedro Charneca had first met the young man whose name now covered the walls of Palma del Río. Hung from the doors of the fat barkeep's taxi was a hand-lettered sign: his tribute to the constancy of the faith of the boy who had once stood and stared at his revered calendar portraits of Manolete. "Manolo," it proclaimed, "you shall be the greatest matador in Spain."

The excited young man who, in his aged blue suit of lights, had just left his sister's house, marched already down the road toward that rash promise. Surrounded by a horde of urchins as he had been on that infamous evening when "Tomato Face" drove him down the *calles* of Palma, hastened along his way by smiles of encouragement and scowls of disapproval, he calmly strode through the *calles* of the town that had cast him from its gates as a pariah. Beside him, awkward in his first suit of lights, marched the companion of so many of his misfortunes and his adventures, Juan Horrillo. Behind them strode the lone banderillero of their makeshift *cuadrilla,* Antonio Columpio, the veteran of the *fiesta brava* who had undertaken this engagement for no greater reward than the promise of a good dinner after the corrida.

The man who had promised him that dinner was already at the plaza. His head elegantly crowned by one of his beige sombreros, a cigar clutched between his teeth, El Pipo studied the animals for which he had pawned his family's jewelry, the beasts upon whose race and nobility his fortunes and those of his unknown prodigy now hung. They were a miserable lot. There was an ill-assorted group of bulls, dull-coated, scrawny, without character, and a seven-year-old cow with an enormous set of horns, a lot of animals more suitable, El Pipo reflected, for the slaughterhouse than the bullring.

El Pipo threw away his cigar in disgust. The success of his gamble clearly rested on one thing: the courage and skill of the untidy youth he had decided, against his better instincts, to manage. It would require either madness or genius, El Pipo thought, for his protégé to draw from these animals a corrida worthy of their joint aspirations.

He was leaving nothing, however, to chance. Unable because of his strained financial circumstances to purchase the presence and benevolence of a few journalists to report in glowing prose his matador's debut, El Pipo had done the next best thing. He had assigned to himself for the afternoon the function of special correspondent in Palma del Río of the

Spanish news agency CITRA. In his pocket was the carefully prepared article he proposed to telephone this evening, no matter what happened, to the agency's bureau in Córdoba, proclaiming the birth of a new genius of the *fiesta brava* under the sky of Andalusia.

The entry of the matadors into the ring was marked by a round of good-natured applause. It was followed by a lower-pitched, less benevolent sound, a ripple of laughter rising largely from the shady side of the ring. That laughter was symptomatic of the prejudice with which many crowded into this portable ring were prepared to judge the performance of the town's former juvenile delinquent.

Grave and solemn at the side of Antonio Caro—Palma's iceman, who had been chosen to preside over this corrida—El Pipo drew a white handkerchief from his pocket. His investment of two hundred thousand pesetas in the spectacle about to begin had earned him the right to serve as Caro's *asesor,* his technical adviser. At the sight of El Pipo's handkerchief, the trumpeter in the four-piece band he had hired for the afternoon rose and with a brief bugle call opened the corrida.

The first animal to charge into the ring was the enormous seven-year-old cow. Her name was Almendrita—Little Almond. El Pipo had prudently made certain this monster would not be unleashed on his protégé.

Another novice matador, his legs trembling, his arms twitching with nervous tics, stepped into the ring. To Juan Horrillo, Little Almond's horns seemed wider than the branches of an almond tree. He was certain he and Manolo had already given this beast an education in the rules of the corrida in some moonlit pasture. He felt he would never have the courage to confront the cow waiting for him in the ring. And yet he knew she was his to fight and kill, "that filthy beast, before all those Palmeños with their dirty stares, looking like I would have to hang myself up on those horns before they would be happy."

Behind him, he could hear Manolo hissing, "Go ahead, Juan, don't worry, I'll watch you." Encouraged, he tried to go forward. But at each step, Horrillo felt his legs folding under him as though they were made of rubber. The arena began to spin around his eyes "like a merry-go-round." Many in the crowd, sensing what they had come for, began to jeer. Still Horrillo couldn't move.

"I was paralyzed," he could recall. "I trembled all over. Those insults kept coming out, and still I couldn't take a step. They began to throw stones and bottles at me. They started to yell *"Fuera, fuera"*—out, out. God, I hated it. And there was Almendrita in the middle of the ring staring at me with those murderous eyes of hers. Suddenly it happened. She came for me. I did a terrible thing then, an unforgivable thing. I dropped my muleta and ran. I ran as fast as I could for the *barrera,* as fast as I ever ran from the Guardia Civil. When I got there, I jumped the *barrera* and fell into the *callejón.* As I lay there, shaking, they spat on me. I could hear them all screaming, whistling. It was horrible. I don't know how long I lay there listening, but I knew one thing: for me, everything was finished. I could never put on the suit of lights again."

It was indeed over for Horrillo. Never again would he put his foot into a bullring. But for Manolo, it was just beginning. While El Pipo stared aghast, he stepped into the ring. He spread open his cape, and, tossing his hair from his forehead with a jerk of his head, he began to march toward Almendrita.

ANTONIO COLUMPIO'S STORY

"IN THIRTY YEARS in the bullring, I thought I'd seen everything. Well, I was wrong. That crazy kid walking up to that cow was going to smack me with some emotions I didn't even know existed. After all those cries, all those whistles, the crowd began to quiet down. They were stunned, those people. A couple of minutes before, they were yelling 'Bums, clowns, go back to jail!' Now, now, they had their eyes and their mouths wide open. Oh sure, it wasn't to yell *'olé'* yet. It was more like they were waiting to see the lion eat the lion tamer. Because, believe me, that Almendrita was a bitch of a cow. To fight her, to get something out of her, you had to have an experience Manuel Benítez certainly did not have in those days.

"My God, when I saw that kid try to cite her with his cape five meters from her nose, my old *peon's* blood almost froze. 'Not so close, not so close,' I yelled. I got ready to go out to help him. He shook his cape and yelled *'Vaca, vaca.'* Almendrita lowered her head and charged. Somehow, he got her by. I kept my eyes glued to him from the *callejón.* After the first pass, he got her back and started her by again. This time it didn't work. She caught him with the flat of her horn in the gut. The blow

273

tossed him into the air. He landed like a sack of corn, but somehow he got up before the cow could get him. I had started out to the ring but as soon as he got up, he ordered me back with a wave of his hand. And he went on. He was crazy. His hair was all over his head. He yelled, he screamed, he swore, he ran around. But he got that cow back and forth, back and forth. Maybe he didn't know how he did it. It was everything except bullfighting, but it gave you such an emotion he had every eye in the *plaza* on him. I heard the first *'olé,'* then they began to come on in waves as he got crazier and crazier. Pretty soon he was wrapping that cow around him like an overcoat. I got so excited watching, I bit off one of my teeth on the collar of my cape. When he finished, the ring exploded in applause. Ah, it was a sight, all those hostile people shouting out their joy, their admiration. They got Manolo so stirred up he decided to go on. He paid for it. Almendrita caught him another whack in the flat of his stomach with her horn. This time he didn't get up so fast. I ran out to him with my cape and took the animal off him. Out of the corner of my eye I could see El Pipo. One instant he was waving to Manolo to get up. The next he was covering his eyes in despair as though he was watching a galleon full of gold sink. Manolo finally got up. Before I could stop him, he ran back to Almendrita, waving his cape. I yelled, 'Cut it out, that's enough!' He wouldn't listen. He had gone half mad. He was back at the cow. The whole crowd was just one big *'olé'* then. Even the Guardia Civil men in the *callejón* behind me were yelling. Even Don Félix Moreno. It was incredible.

"But those Palmeños, they hadn't seen anything yet. He had some surprises waiting for them—some surprises you don't see very often in any bullring, anyplace. The bugle blew to change the *tercio*. It was time for the banderillas now. Manolo came strolling back to the barrier, trailing his cape behind him. He took the two banderillas I gave him and showed them to the public. Then he took them and broke them in half on the edge of the ring. Then he broke them in half again. By the time he had finished, they weren't any bigger than a pencil.

"With that big smile of his, he started to sneak along the edge of the ring like a cat to the spot where Almendrita was waiting. Five or six meters from the horn he stopped. The crowd gasped when they saw what he was doing. He turned his back toward the wall and knelt down. 'He's trying to kill himself,' I said. I slipped behind the *burladero* closest to him. The animal was so close, I didn't even dare shout to him to stop. Put in the sticks like that, kneeling down, with your back to the wall, sticks no bigger than a pencil, I can tell you there isn't anything much more dangerous you can do in bullfighting. It takes an incredible precision and you have to be dumb with courage to do it. The slightest error, the slightest twist in his charge, and—*op*—you've got a horn in your eye or your mouth. Or stuck through your lung. They don't have any surgeons to take care of those wounds. Nobody stops a hemorrhage in your lungs. It's fatal.

"You couldn't hear a sound in the bullring. I had the feeling everybody there was holding his breath like they thought any noise at all would cause a tragedy. Manolo raised his arms with those tiny sticks stuck in his palms. He stuck out his chest and yelled '*Vaca, venga!*' Almendrita shook her head. '*Vaca, vaca!*' he shouted again. The cow hesitated. Then, *whoosh,* she charged. For one second it looked like she would get him. I did the only thing I could to help. I flicked the corner of my cape from behind the *burladero,* trying to get the cow's eye. That sudden flash of color bent her charge just enough. As her horns went by his face, he spun and stuck his sticks right where they belonged.

"After that, they were ready to tear the ring down. Everybody was standing up, yelling, applauding, stamping their feet. Manolo was glowing. He wiped the sweat from his forehead with the back of his hand. He gave me a quick wink of thanks. With his two hands he made a gesture of thanks to the crowd. They were wild. Even Almendrita had her head hanging down, looking at him stupefied. Me, I was shaking like a leaf."

*   *   *

A courageous but crude display with his muleta, a proficient kill, and it was over. In ten brief minutes the ghost of the *campo,* the "chronic delinquent" in the files of the Guardia Civil, had redeemed an adolescence of misbehavior. As Manolo stepped, sweating and triumphant, from the ring, even Sergeant Mauleón offered him congratulations with his outstretched hand.

"Ah, *hombre,*" Manolo said, taking it with a wan smile, "it was not always so gentle, this hand." Then he turned to stare with pride at the stunned and happy faces looking down at him. In offering to his fellow

275

townsmen that most precious gift, the cold thrill of danger lived vicariously, he had kept the vow spoken by a dried creek bed almost ten years before: *"Voy a ser torero."*

The person to whom he had uttered those words had not heard the ovation pouring down on him, the *"olé's"* ringing from the throats that had once laughed at his pretensions. Anita Sánchez had spent the moments of the corrida alone, kneeling in the shadows of the Ermita where once she had kept a weekly rendezvous with the little-loved adolescent who had come home to risk his life in a rented bullring.

At the other end of Palma, another woman, too, had spent those moments in prayer. Her heart burdened with this new anguish, Angelita Benítez had punctuated her prayers by prowling restlessly through the restricted confines of her home. Suddenly she heard a noise outside. She ran to the window.

ANGELITA BENÍTEZ'S STORY

"THERE WAS A big cloud of dust coming down the *calle* and a whole lot of people running. They were all shouting and yelling. I recognized Don Carlos running with them from his black cassock. 'Oh my God, oh my God,' I thought, 'something has happened to Manolo and he's coming to tell me.' Then I saw Charneca. Then I saw *him*. He was up there on the shoulders of grown people I didn't even know, my little brother Manolo. And there were all those kids like he had been before running in front of him, yelling to tell everybody he was coming.

"I couldn't believe it. My brother Manolo, the one they said would never come to anything, the one they said was a thief and the Guardia Civil was always hitting, my brother Manolo who had made me cry so much, and there he was, on the shoulders of those men with the whole town running after him.

"He was smiling and shouting and waving the ears and the tail they had cut for him. My God, he seemed happy. I ran out to meet him. All of a sudden as I got close to him, I saw blood on his stomach. I screamed when I saw it. Don Carlos saw me crying and he ran up to me. 'No, no, Angelita,' he cried, 'it's the bull's blood, not his!'

"He jumped down when he got to the house and came to me. I tried to hold back my tears, but I couldn't. It was too much for me. He took me in his arms and I started to shake. I don't know how long he held me like that. Everybody was watching us. Ana Horrillo, Juan's mother—she was crying, too. The other women there, too. Then Manolo said, 'Come on, Angelita, help me get undressed. I'm hot.'

"Manolo waved goodbye to the crowd. They all yelled. Then we went into the room where he had dressed. He took out an old handkerchief all tied up in a knot. He opened it up. It was filled with money, all dirty bills and coins. Manolo started to count them. Then he counted out one thousand pesetas and put them together. He handed them to me.

" 'Here,' he said, 'this is the first one thousand pesetas I give you.' "

*   *   *

Despite his first caress of success, Manuel Benítez was still an incredibly long way from the goal he sought. That goal could only be reached through other afternoons of triumph, in places like Seville, Barcelona, and Madrid. His triumph may have salved his pride, but it had done nothing for his renown. Palma del Río was just an infinitely small drop of water in the tauromachian ocean, a distant outpost where two ears and a tail were symbolic trophies without any real meaning. The history of the *fiesta brava* is studded with the record of local "prodigies," the echoes of whose sensational debuts got no farther than a hometown café.

No one was more aware of that reality than El Pipo. Two things had mattered this afternoon for El Pipo. He had gotten his money back and his hopes confirmed. He would go on. The echoes of the *"olé's"* in his rented bullring had barely died when his busy brain set to work deciding how.

EL PIPO'S STORY

"YOU SELL A bullfighter the way you sell soap powder. There are lots of different soaps and there are lots of different bullfighters. The one that wins is not always the best product but the one whose promoter knows how to sell it the best. Me, I knew right away this kid was worth gold. Not because he was a great torero. He seemed to know about as much about the rules of bullfighting as he did about the rules of cricket. As far as art was concerned, he was a sorry spectacle. But don't talk to me about art in the bullring. Art you can get in the Prado. In the bullring you want something else. In the bullring, one thing interests me: it's a kid who can excite a crowd. Show me a kid who can make a crowd's hair stand up in the bullring, and I'll show you a kid who can make money as a matador. Manuel Benítez, he wanted that Mercedes of his so badly, he wanted so much to become, like he was always saying, 'a man in a panama hat with a big cigar,' that he was ready for any crazy stunt. And these crazy stunts, he could do them whenever he wanted to because he didn't know the disease that sometimes gets into the guts of the greatest matadors and paralyzes them: fear.

"I saw the way those people in Palma reacted to Manuel Benítez. It was all there—anguish, joy, surprise. Ah, and fright. It was above all fright. He scared them. That crazy courage of his gave them goose pimples. And that is what gets people into the bullring, and don't ever let anybody tell you anything else.

"So I saw what I had to sell: courage, the desperate courage of a kid. That was my fortune. With a little luck, I said to myself, by the end of the summer I'll be a millionaire again, and him, too. As long as he doesn't get himself half killed doing one of those crazy stunts of his. Already I was turning around all kinds of slogans for him in my head. Pretty soon I'd have his picture on the walls of half the villages in Andalusia with slogans like 'Sunday I have a rendezvous with death. Come see me.'

"For the moment, the problem was to strike the iron while it was still hot and repeat the success of Palma fast, someplace else. It wasn't easy. I got my money back out of the Palma fight. But my family was after me to take it to the pawnbroker's and retrieve their jewelry. They understood nothing about the ambitions of men. They wanted their jewels back when I had in my hands the most beautiful jewel in the world, the courage of a kid. Now I had to try to take the kid down to Córdoba. That was where it would really begin.

"I went to see the old rascal who ran the ring in those days. He had a *novillada* coming up with some South American nobody had ever heard of. I knew how to get him.

" 'How much are you paying the cheapest matador on the *cartel?*' I asked him.

" 'Twenty thousand pesetas,' he said.

" *'De acuerdo,'* I said. 'I'll give you my kid for ten.' "

*   *   *

The house was, in its way, a shrine. It lay between the railroad station
and the gray concrete walls of the *plaza de toros* of Córdoba, and rare
were the Córdoba citizens walking between those two points who did not
pause for an instant in front of 20 Avenida de Cervantes. On the afternoon of his first corrida in the city whose name he would henceforth link
to his, Manuel Benítez stopped on his way from the station to stare up at
its rose-covered iron grille. Beyond the grille, framed by a pair of banana
trees that seemed to serve as sentinels, he could see the white stucco
arches of the house. At the curb beside him was a black Jaguar. Once a
day, always at the same hour, the occupant of the house emerged from
its rose-covered gates and got into the car. The drive that followed was
as ordered as any ritual could be. Its itinerary was inevitably the same
and its duration a precise twenty-five minutes.

The drive over, the lonely figure stepped from the car and retreated
once again into the silence and solitude of the big house. She was an old
woman, almost blind, always dressed in black, allegedly one of the richest women in Spain. Besides her factories and her estates, she was un-
doubtedly the only person in the world who could claim to be the principal shareholder of her own subway system, the subways of Madrid. Yet
she derived almost no benefit from her immense fortune. She lived clois-
tered with her memories of the son who had deeded it to her.

Once, when in his red-velvet-draped bedroom in that house he dressed
for his bullfights, thousands clustered before its gates, and the shaded
avenue leading from the house to the *plaza de toros* of Córdoba was for
him an avenue of triumph. Now, thirteen years after Manolete's death,
those streets were deserted and the corrida of the day had excited little
more interest than a second-run movie. The stands of the bullring of the
caliphs, so often jammed for Manolete, would be half empty for the local
debut of the boy who had once idolized his portrait on an old calendar.
To Manolo, gazing at his hero's home, it did not matter. He would draw
the crowds to the ring one day, he knew, because the same furious ambition burned in him that had once burned in the sad-faced occupant of
20 Avenida de Cervantes.

279

Ending his reverie, Manolo marched off to the little hotel room on the alley of the Avenida del Gran Capitán, where his sole admirer awaited him in his felt sombrero with his ever-present cigar.

El Pipo was concerned. The ceremony of the drawing of the bulls for the day's corrida had not augured well for his young matador. His two more experienced partners of the day's program had insisted on rigging the draw and assigning to their unknown colleague the two animals they themselves deemed too dangerous for their talents. At El Pipo's announcement of the news, El Cordobés only laughed.

"Don't worry yourself, Don Rafael," he said. "If one of those bulls puts a hole in my stomach, I'll cover it with my hand and go on."

El Cordobés' suit for the day had been shipped down from Madrid. Córdoba's sole vendor of matadors' costumes, Francisco Prieto, had refused to rent Manolo a second suit after getting back the one he had given him for Palma. He told Manolo he wasn't going to rent his suits to someone who already had the reputation of spending more time in the air than on the sand of the bullring.

Prieto would remember for a long time the young man's haughty reply. "Tomorrow, Señor Prieto," he said, "every matador in Spain will want to wear my costumes because they'll bring luck. And I'll be so rich, I'll be able to throw them away after every corrida."

For the moment, the boastful young matador and his manager were so short of cash that they could not rent a fiacre to get to the plaza. After a brief prayer before an image of the *patrona* of Palma, Manolo left the hotel on foot. It was the first time in the memory of most Córdoba citizens that a matador had ever gone to the *plaza de toros* on foot like a humble spectator.

His little stroll was not the only humiliation awaiting Manolo that afternoon. Streaming from the side streets along his route came a flow of youngsters to escort him to the plaza gates with their excited cries. Standing before those gates, Manolo whispered to El Pipo, "Don Rafael, throw them some coins." El Pipo looked at him, then gave a helpless shrug of his shoulders. His pockets were so empty he could not find in them a single peseta to throw to these urchins who had escorted his matador to the bullring.

Manolo had drawn for his first bull of the day a stocky rust-red animal with horns like bicycle handlebars. When the time came for his faena, he nodded to the president. Then, a great smile on his face, he strolled along the *callejón* until he came to the young man serving that afternoon as his sword handler. Manolo stretched his black hat toward his friend, condemned now by his fear to remain forever on the other side of that wooden barrier. "To you, Horrillo," he said, "my first bull, for all the chickens we stole and all the hurts we shared together." He spun about. With a snap of his wrists he flipped his *montera* over his head into the *callejón*. Then he strode off to meet his bull.

The stands of Córdoba's old bullring were only half full. But the spectators who were there that afternoon can still recall with awe the Córdoba debut of the young man who had once been a prisoner in their city jail. Antonio Columpio, the aging banderillero still at El Cordobés' side, was sure the matador would go straight from the bullring to the cemetery. Pepín Garrido, serving that day as a banderillero for one of the other matadors on the bill, told himself this was "the first and probably the last time" he would be able to see El Cordobés. Manolo was tossed at least half a dozen times. But each time, bruised and aching, he staggered to his feet.

Watching from a sunny side seat, Andrés Jurado, the mechanic of the local Mercedes agency, promised himself that "if this kid gets out of here alive today, I'll go see every one of his corridas." A strange twist of Jurado's destiny would make it impossible for him to keep that promise. In not too many months, the young matador's passionate attachment to that symbol of material success, a Mercedes, would bring him to Jurado's employer, from whom he would get his car and Jurado along with it as his chauffeur. Together, they would travel more than a hundred thousand miles, four times the distance around the globe, going from corrida to corrida. Jurado would almost never have a chance to see those corridas. While his matador fought, he would be condemned to sleep to refresh himself for the night's drive.

Now his future employer ran the full gamut of hair-raising stunts that had won so much success in Palma. He passed the bull on his knees, with his chest exposed, from the left, from the right, in all the ways a torero was supposed to pass a bull and in some he was not. And the crowd sat up, then went wild with joy and fright.

The flat of the bull's horn whacked him time and time again, but the *patrona* of Palma del Río was watching over her orphan son that afternoon. Kicked, whacked, tossed repeatedly into the air, he got up every time, and the only blood spilled was that of his adversary. When it came time to kill, Manolo's determination to succeed was so intense he forgot to let go of his sword. As the sword sank in, the bull gave an enormous upward thrust of his neck muscles. There followed an extraordinary spectacle: Manolo pinwheeling through the air, his hand still clutching the sword that had gone in, and then out, of the bull. Seconds after Manolo tumbled to the ground, the bull rolled over, dead.

Manolo had walked to the bullring, but he was carried out aloft, by a new group of admirers. At his hotel he peeled off his clothes and fell exhausted on the bed. His body was a mass of welts and bruises inflicted by the bulls he had just killed. As he lay there, El Pipo entered the room. Under his arm was a little package wrapped in an old newspaper. He undid it. It contained a slim stack of banknotes. With a triumphant gesture, El Pipo tossed them in the air so they floated down like a shower of confetti on his matador's naked body. Manolo looked at him, his fatigue-dulled eyes too tired to register surprise.

"They're yours, kid," said El Pipo. "From this afternoon."

Then, before Manolo could move, he added, "But if you want another bullfight, you've got to give them back to me to keep things going."

Manolo reached down a weary hand and peeled off one of the banknotes stuck to his sweating body. Listlessly he pushed the others to the floor. Then, without a word, he rolled over and turned his face to the wall. As he did, El Pipo got down on his hands and knees. One by one, he picked up the sweat-soiled bills, smoothed them out and put them back into a neat little stack.

The next morning, Manuel Benítez invested the sole banknote he had been able to extract from his manager in a railroad ticket to Palma del Río. He had a promise to keep there. Under his arms he too carried a package wrapped in an old newspaper. It contained a treasure of a different sort from El Pipo's, a treasure he had promised to bring to his friend Pedro Charneca. He strode into Charneca's café with a radiant grin and tossed his package on the bar.

"Here are the groceries you ordered," he said. No gift could have pleased the stout barman more. Inside were the ears and the tail of the first bull his young friend had killed in the bullring of the city of the caliphs.

*   *   *

El Pipo's personal stock rose sharply following his protégé's triumph in Córdoba. The Córdoba newspaper noted that "if God helps Manuel Benítez—and God helped him every minute this afternoon—he will become a great torero. One can learn to fight and to kill well. What one can't learn is what he has, a brave heart."

The echoes of the ovations Manolo had received in Córdoba and Palma, however, were still too fresh to have reached the ears of the men to whom El Pipo now proposed to address himself. So the manager climbed into an old taxi and took to the road again as a traveling salesman. His destination was invariably some town or village shortly to celebrate an annual feria with a corrida or two. There, in his booming voice, he tried to persuade the local impresarios that he had under his management the newest star in the firmament of the *fiesta brava*.

*   *   *

The baroque spires of the town of Écija rise at the foot of a ring of rolling hills set along the main road from Córdoba to Seville. There, in the freshness of an August morning a quarter of a century past, the Nationalist columns had set out to subdue Palma the Red. Alongside the sluggish waters of the Genil, on the ruins of a Roman amphitheater, the whitewashed walls of Écija's *plaza de toros* sparkle in the sun.

Not far from the ring, under the arcades of the principal square of Écija, a man marched regularly up to an iron café table every noon, sat down and unfolded his morning paper. Jesús Jiménez Torres' day was beginning. Of all the occupations discharged by the people of Écija, his was perhaps the most colorful. Torres was the impresario of the bullring of a town of 49,762 people.

JESÚS JIMÉNEZ TORRES' STORY

"FIFTY THOUSAND PEOPLE, that's a big city, no? Well, just try and get two thousand five hundred of them into my bullring. It takes genius, believe me, genius. Talk to me about the *fiesta brava* that burns

283

in the heart of every Spaniard. Madrid, Seville, Pamplona, maybe. But here, in this wasteland, you really need a bag of tricks to get those people stirred up. Here we hardly know what a tourist is. The only time a tourist stops here, it's to ask directions. Can you imagine a foreigner coming to Écija to see a bullfight?

"Too bad, too, because the tourists eat it up, the corrida. They'll pay anything for a ticket. Whether they come to see a pretty show or see a matador get gored, it's all the same. They don't know anything. It's the local color they're buying.

"But when you've got to bring in the real aficionados, it's something else. They don't come for nothing. Sure, they'll come out to see a good matador. Some of them, anyway. But a good matador costs money. So I have to raise the prices. If the fight is awful—and that happens, because the corrida, it's a lottery—well, the people around here who paid two hundred pesetas for a ticket, you should see the hell they raise. They sit there in the boiling sun and they think about their two hundred pesetas. Then they think about how hot it is. Then they think about how bad the bullfight is. Then they reach for a Coke bottle to throw at the matador, and the fight begins.

"To put on a bullfight here costs, minimum, a hundred and fifty thousand pesetas. You need at least two thousand people to get your money back. At that price, you pay your matadors nothing. I get dozens, hundreds maybe, of *maletillas* around here every season begging for a chance on one of my *carteles*. They get on only one way. They have to buy at least two hundred and fifty tickets from me. Sure, they can't pay for them themselves. They have to sell them. No sale, no corrida.

"But the best way to get people in here is with your own brain. When I want to get attention for my fights, I use the village dwarf. We call him 'the Flea.' Sometimes I dress him up in a miniature suit of lights. One day I hired a truck with a loudspeaker and drove around announcing that a big bicycle race was following behind me. Everybody rushed to the roadside to see. Five minutes later there was the Flea on a little boy's bike dressed like a bicycle racer throwing away handbills for my Sunday bullfight.

"Ah, what you have to do to make a single peseta around here! Sometimes, when I know my matadors are no good, I put on a little sideshow to warm up the crowd. For example, you put a greased pole in the center of the ring with a big ham on top of it. Then you tell the kids the first one to the top gets the ham. While they're running for it, you let a little bull into the ring. There's always some kid caught up there on the pole, trying to hang on to his ham with the bull waiting for him down below.

"This is the real *fiesta brava* here, in places like this, not that showy stuff they see in the big cities. I tell you it's small-town impresarios like me that keep the corrida alive in Spain. Without us the *fiesta* would be a spectacle for rich Spaniards and foreigners.

"Anyway, that day when I saw the big felt hat of El Pipo riding up to my café in his taxicab, I said to myself, 'Here comes the King of the Shellfish trying to put over another one of his big deals.'

"El Pipo was hung up in those days. He was broke. Nothing had been going right for him. There are, as we say in Spain, full boats and empty boats. Well, that year El Pipo's boat was about as empty as a boat can be.

"He wanted to talk to me about his El Cordobés. 'A *fenómeno,*' he kept saying, 'a *fenómeno,* you'll see, he's going to bury them all.'

"Well, that song, I'd been hearing it from El Pipo for years. To me his El Cordobés was just another one of those kids he'd been promising every year would revolutionize bullfighting. I already had my corrida set for Sunday, two matadors and four bulls. I couldn't afford any more. But El Pipo kept insisting.

"Finally I said, 'You give him to me for a thousand pesetas?'

" '*De acuerdo,*' he said.

" 'And you guarantee the cost of the bulls if I lose money?'

" '*De acuerdo,*' he said.

" 'And you sell three hundred tickets?'

"To my amazement, he said '*de acuerdo*' again. 'Well,' I thought to myself, he really must believe in this one. And El Pipo was right. For once, he wasn't lying. This time it was a *fenómeno,* a real one, that he brought me."

* * *

Rarely had the organization of a bullfight caused Jesús Torres such agony. At noon on the day of the corrida neither El Pipo's *fenómeno* nor his representatives had shown up in Écija to participate in the drawing for the bulls. The *fenómeno* was, at that instant, bouncing down the back roads to Écija in a cloud of dust. For the youth who would one day be the richest torero in Spain, the matador's car that day was not an old Rolls-Royce, a Hispano-Suiza or the traditional Chrysler with a sword trunk strapped to its roof. It was the rusting baggage rack of the motorcycle of Palma's garage owner, persuaded to give Manolo a lift to Écija by the supplications of his favorite bartender, Pedro Charneca.

His progress had been slowed by the appearance of a rabbit at the side of the road. At that sight, Manolo's vagabond instincts had gotten the best of him. He asked the garage keeper to stop. Leaping off the motorcycle, he began to chase the rabbit. Finally he stunned it with a well-aimed stone and brought it back to the motorcycle.

Half an hour later, triumphantly brandishing his rabbit from his backfiring motorcycle, the young man El Pipo had promised would revolutionize the corrida made his entry into Écija. Torres gaped in astonishment at the unkempt youth whose picture he had hung on the gates of his bullring with the extravagant announcement that he was the newest sensation of the bullfight. To Torres, he looked "more like an escaped convict than a torero." He got a second shock when he watched his bullfighter eat the lunch he had set out for him in the simple dining room of Écija's Hotel Central. Ignoring the rule that urges a matador to eat lightly the day of a corrida so his stomach will be empty if he is gored, Manolo gulped down food "as though he hadn't eaten for three days," and until, Torres thought, his face was "as purple as a bishop's cloak."

Those concerns were, however, only minor ones to the impresario. His real problem was at his bullring's box office. Rare were the corridas the ingenious Torres had promoted that had aroused so little interest among his townsmen. He had, in addition to El Pipo's allotment, sold exactly four hundred tickets for the corrida, a total so laughably small he was faced with a major fiasco. Despairingly, Torres began to use the ingenious resources of his mind to find some pretext to cancel the corrida.

As he pondered his dilemma, he heard the sputtering backfire of a Vespa, then another, and another, coming from the street outside. He ran to the window. The noises that had interrupted his musings had roused the town from its torpor. People lurched from their siestas to see what was happening outside.

What was happening was, in a sense, a reversal of the invasion of

1936. A whole column of motorbikes, motor scooters, motorcycles and bicycles came roaring into Écija from Palma del Río. Behind them rolled a chain of old farm trucks, spilling over with an excited, howling horde of Palmeños. They yelled, they laughed, they sang, they shouted, as the stunned townspeople of Écija gaped up at them. The wooden sides of their trucks were hung with dust-covered signs extolling the virtues of the young matador who had just finished devouring a six-course meal in the Hotel Central.

Swept up by the noise, the cries, the air of excitement radiating from the trucks lurching by, the people of Écija began to fall in behind their neighbors' raucous cavalcade. First there were dozens, then scores, then hundreds and even thousands, all straggling along after that bizarre parade marching off to the *plaza de toros* of Écija. Riding in the van of the lead truck, as proud and impassive as any conquistador poised in the prow of his galleon, was the man responsible for this curious procession. An enormous straw sombrero clamped upon his head, Pedro Charneca led his townsmen on to the bullring to applaud his young friend in his confrontation with the two black bulls of Écija.

By the time the bugles blew to begin the fight, the day was saved. Charneca's parade had performed a little miracle of the loaves and the fishes. Instead of the four hundred people Jesús Jiménez Torres had predicted for his corrida, almost four thousand curious aficionados had swarmed into his bullring. A few minutes later, with a grateful gesture of his black *montera,* El Cordobés dedicated his first bull to his friend. "To you, Charneca," he said. "You helped me get here today. I swear to you that after the next bull I dedicate to you, we will ride away from the bullring together in my own car."

*   *   *

And so began what would become known as the crazy summer of Manuel Benítez. The courage of a hungry young man married to the commercial acumen and shrewdness of El Pipo would produce before that summer was over one of the most spectacular successes in the history of the *fiesta brava*. Before the chills of autumn would strike the city of Córdoba, all of Andalusia, and soon after all of Spain, would be alive to the appeal of the young man destined to become the idol of the modern era of the bullfight. The family jewels of El Pipo would have found their way back to the hands of their owners, each accompanied by a further manifestation of the generosity of the King of the Shellfish. And El Cordobés would be earning for a single corrida 200,000 pesetas ($3,300), enough money to buy with every twenty minutes he spent in the bullring another example of the treasure he had lusted after for most of his twenty-four years: an automobile.

*   *   *

El Pipo ran his tauromachian revolution from a nondescript little Córdoba alleyway called the Calle de la Plata, the street of silver. Once the gold and silver of the Aztecs and Incas had found their way into that little alley to be transformed by the nimble fingers of the artisans whose stands lined its length into jewelry to excite the royal houses of all Europe. Now only the dust-covered windows of a handful of pawnbrokers' shops gave an intimation of what had once been that alley's proud vocation. Its distinction rested instead on a miserable café, the Café Ivory. It was the gathering place of the aficionados of Córdoba. A score among them were always present in permanent assembly on its terrace and before its little bar: bull breeders passing through town, retired banderilleros and picadors, ill shaven, staring dreamily into their chronically empty coffee cups, unemployed matadors with their drawn and baleful countenances.

The social arbiter of their world was a fifty-year-old shoeshine boy named Curro, a former banderillero who had lost his matador when a bull nailed the unfortunate torero's chest to the *barrera* of the Madrid bullring. From morning until night, Curro glided through the crowd on the terrace of the Café Ivory, and there was no surer measure of a man's standing in that world than the effusiveness of Curro's greeting and the determination with which he spit-polished a client's boots to a high gloss. Before many weeks had passed, no shoes on the terrace of the Café Ivory gleamed more brightly than those belonging to that superb and majestic figure, El Pipo. His head shaded by his famous hat, his cigars now inevitably lit, El Pipo held court among its tables. No longer was he obliged to scurry about the country towns like a drummer, begging for a favor from the local impresario. Now they came to him.

288

El Pipo's first decision of the summer had been a bit of genius. He had found the proper package for his soap. Courage was, after all, a fairly common commodity in a nation that made a cult of that quality. His problem had been to give that courage, and the man who displayed it, a special cachet. One afternoon he decreed that Manuel Benítez would henceforth be "the torero of the poor."

With that initial decision taken, El Pipo set out to build a legend around his prodigy: a legend that would place Manolo not in the center of the bullring but in the center of the thoughts of his fellow Andalusians; a legend that would draw to the plazas people who had never before visited a bullring; a legend that drew its significance from the roots common to Manolo and so many of his countrymen—poverty.

To launch that legend, El Pipo drafted in his own modest hand the text for an illustrated brochure on his matador's life. Rarely has the rich hyperbole of the *fiesta brava* touched heights equal to those attained by El Pipo in his pamphlet, called simply "The Torero of the Poor." It heralded the birth "on a strip of deep-green velvet in the heart of the land of Andalusia of an inestimably precious stone named Manuel Benítez, El Cordobés. Sprung from the heart of the people, a blossom born of the native soil, body and blood of the Spain of our legendary days, this rough diamond has found to polish him a genial lapidary, a product of the people as well, Rafael Sánchez, El Pipo."

From there El Pipo went on to relate Manolo in one way or another to almost every significant achievement in Spanish history and culture: the eviction of the Napoleonic oppressors, the paintings of Goya, the nobility of Don Quixote. His tract culminated by noting "the mounting passion of Spain for the vagabond of her highways, continually renewing his blood offering upon the high altar of the *fiesta brava*." To the unfortunate Juan Horrillo fell the task of distributing the tract, working his way alone now through the villages where he and Manolo had wandered a few years earlier.

To give a concrete dimension to his legend, El Pipo decreed that Manolo would henceforth engage in public displays of charity to show that in his glory he would not forget his own. El Pipo's idea of charity, however, was a very special one. One morning in Córdoba, he took a local news photographer on a walk. "Watch what that torero's going to do," he said as soon as he spotted his carefully planted matador.

In a loud voice Manolo gave a shoeshine boy three hundred pesetas so he could "put away those brushes for three days." The photographer took a picture. When he had disappeared, El Pipo turned to the shoeshine boy to get his money back. To his horror, the boy had taken his little stunt seriously and disappeared with El Pipo's three hundred pesetas. Not even Manolo escaped the results of his manager's frugality. One day El Pipo arranged to have his matador's picture taken eating prawns, the first he had ever tasted, in his brother's shellfish shop. Manolo was able to eat exactly one prawn, the one required for the photo, before El Pipo took the plate away from him and put it safely back behind his brother's counter.

Whenever they visited a village together, El Pipo sought out its most prominent beggar for a demonstration of his matador's charity. In Andújar he arranged to have his matador offer a cripple a wheelchair so he could "come see the corrida." El Pipo was so immensely pleased with the success of his stunt that he reclaimed the wheelchair after the fight was over so he could repeat the gesture elsewhere. In Posada he invited a dozen of the town's poor to a banquet honoring his matador in a friend's restaurant. As soon as the newsmen had left, El Pipo ordered the sumptuous buffet he had set out for their benefit swept from the table and replaced by the simplest meal the restaurant offered.

His ingenuity would reach its highest point the following year in Barcelona. After a triumphant return from the bullring, El Pipo ordered his matador to the balcony outside his window. There El Cordobés began to autograph 100-peseta notes and toss them to the crowd gathered below. A near riot broke out, finally forcing the police to intervene. The next day the story was carried in every paper in Spain. El Pipo was enormously pleased, almost as pleased as he was by the fact the men he had hired for the task had managed to recover close to two thirds of the banknotes El Cordobés had tossed from the balcony.

Nor did El Pipo limit to the material world the charisma he constructed for his matador. One day he hired a woman in Palma del Río to announce that her son had been cured of a grave illness after touching the matador's hand. Later, riding to a country corrida, El Pipo noticed a group of peasants laboring in a field. He ordered their taxi to a halt, summoned his matador to follow him, and marched up to the workers. With the ease of an accomplished politician he launched into a long speech in praise of his matador, culminating with the exhortation: "You see this young man? When he's rich and famous one day, he'll free you all from your slavery. Come on, touch his hand. It'll bring you luck." El Cordobés, bewildered by this latest crazy antic of his manager, suddenly saw them move timidly forward to caress his arm.

In the taxi El Cordobés angrily protested. "Never mind," grunted El Pipo, "you'll see. They'll all be at the bullfight this afternoon." And a few hours later, surveying the line before the bullring box office, El Pipo noted with pleasure that he had been right.

As the effects of El Pipo's extravagant publicity began to be felt, the demands for his matador's services grew. Over dirty roads, over pot-holed routes no tourist ever takes, by bus or wheezing taxi, under a pounding summer sun, Manolo and his manager traveled from town to town, from portable bullring to portable bullring, Manolo offering to his countrymen the prodigious spectacle of his courage, El Pipo counting up with pleasure the growing crowds turning out to see him.

Manolo's fee for those early corridas was twenty thousand pesetas, but he saw little of it. Most of it went to his manager to pay their expenses and to fuel his publicity campaign. With some of the first pesetas he managed to wrest from his manager, he invested in a strange talisman. It was a ham, an enormous mountain ham such as the hovel on the Calle Belén had never seen. That ham became his constant companion, his pride, a kind of reassuring presence to remind him that the world in which he was now moving was not a dream.

"I walked into the hotels with my ham," he could later recall. "I hung it up in the window, and every time I was hungry I cut off a slice. It made me feel good just to look at it. It was wonderful to think I was rich enough to buy myself a whole ham and to cut off a slice whenever I was hungry, night or day. There are people who like to travel with a friend. Me, in those days, I only wanted to travel with my ham. It was more than a friend for me, it was something that took away your hunger, that you could eat little by little. And when it was all finished, and there was nothing left but the bone, well, I bought another one, and to me it was still the same ham."

He was soon destined to be joined by a second companion, an injured sparrow he rescued from the roadside. It became, briefly, his good-luck symbol, and everywhere the novice killer of bulls went, the sparrow went too, perched on his shoulder. The bird was, alas, a short-lived mascot destined to last barely the lifetime of a couple of hams before falling victim to a hotelkeeper's cat.

Another possession would, however, shortly replace the ham and the crippled sparrow in his affection. It was a car. He came upon it one evening in the town of Andújar as his admirers carried him in triumph from their portable bullring. With a yell, he ordered them to stop. He leaped to the ground and, carelessly tossing aside the two ears and a tail he had just been waving, began to argue with its owner. The car was a small green Renault "four-horse" whose wheels had already covered almost twice the distance around the globe. Its paint was peeling and its springs thrust up through its upholstery. Those defects did not matter to Manolo. After years of hardship, that little car represented the perfect incarnation of his new success.

Sweat pouring from his face, Manolo rushed to his manager and without a word ripped their fees for the day's corrida from his hands. While the crowd watched in glee, the matador in his blood-smeared suit of lights furiously began to slam banknotes onto the car's roof. "There," he yelled, when his pile was high enough, "fifty thousand pesetas. This car is mine."

Since Manolo lacked a driver's license, he was forced to make, then and there, a second acquisition. He hired a chauffeur: the youth from whom he had just bought the car. His battered little automobile became for Manolo "the most beautiful toy in the world." It was material proof that he had arrived. "Now," he thought, "I can finally drive up to Don Félix's finca and ride in by the big gate."

Without even waiting to get out of his suit of lights he climbed into his new car and set out for Palma del Río. There, toward two o'clock in the morning, he raced through the sleepy *calles* of his hometown, down to a whitewashed building with green shutters whose silhouette he knew well. Like a fraternity boy on an initiation stunt, the matador tooted his horn until finally a light snapped on in the window. When he saw an angry face peering from the window, Manolo let out a raucous laugh and raced off into the night. For the last time, Manuel Benítez had roused his old enemy, Sergeant Mauleón, from a good night's sleep.

*   *   *

Priego, Lucena, Andújar, Bélmez, Cardeña: little towns and big villages, hanging from the rocky terraces of the sierra or clustered on bold rises in the valley, blindingly white in the summer sun—they represented a series of bullrings bearing witness that hectic season to the rise of a new phenomenon.

"They were," El Pipo could recall, "afternoons of triumph and tragedy. It was unbearably hot. There were always two or three people for every seat. Those portable bullrings seemed to sway with the crowds. Sometimes the stands were ready to collapse. People screamed and women fainted. Sometimes the bulls got into the stands. Sometimes they broke out of their corrals. The Guardia Civil began to shoot. It was incredible. It was panic, folly."

That panic was often caused by El Pipo's hands. His matador was not going to perform, if he could help it, in half-filled *plazas*. To get them filled, to bring the crowds milling around outside, El Pipo resorted to a number of expedients. A favorite was to offer the parish priest a block of tickets to sell for the benefit of his charities. Then El Pipo printed a second batch of tickets to compensate for those he had given the priest and he sold them, too. When he could, he sold two or three tickets for every seat the bullring held, to be sure of a wild mob scene at fight time.

El Pipo carefully orchestrated the growing air of excitement thus produced in the press and radio through the journalists whose favors he regularly purchased. Their efforts he supplemented with his own growing publicity campaign. "People who suffer from weak hearts and nerves are asked to stay away from the corridas of El Cordobés because of the emotions his art produces," proclaimed one paper. "When is the King of Courage coming to Córdoba?" asked another. "The tension is mounting," "the *afición* is boiling hot," "the truth about bullfighting begins today," "the day of the year," "the event of the century"; with such headlines and ads, El Pipo built and maintained a state of permanent suspense he would soon seek to create throughout Spain with stunts such as putting his matador's name up in lights in Barcelona or proclaiming that the Bilbao bullring had been set on fire by the sparks produced by a crowd clapping for El Cordobés.

Whenever possible in those early corridas, El Pipo installed himself as president or *asesor* of the bullfight to encourage the award of the ears and the tail to his matador. But even such foresight on El Pipo's part could not assure his matador regular possession of the corrida's trophies.

To hedge against those days when fortune failed to favor Manolo, El Pipo sent off his banderillero, Antonio Columpio, to the butcher's to buy a black tail and a set of black ears which became a part of their luggage. When El Cordobés was not awarded the ears of his bulls, El Pipo rushed him from the ring to have his picture taken outside, waving Columpio's butchershop trophies. The tactic worked quite well until one day in Bélmez when Manolo was spotted waving his black butchershop tail— after having killed two rust-red bulls.

El Pipo's fine capacity for chicanery would reach its high point the following season in Granada. There he persuaded a surgeon to extend with his scalpel the edges of a goring received one afternoon by his matador. As soon as the wound had been stretched to gory but superficial dimensions, El Pipo summoned a photographer to record it in all its artificial horror. When his matador returned to the ring a few days later, El Pipo had the photographer's picture published all over Spain as graphic evidence of his matador's physical and mental toughness.

None of El Pipo's efforts that summer, however, were more important in the manager's mind than one devoted to protecting the most valuable asset he possessed, his matador's health. Manolo was already on his way to realizing the destiny El Pipo had predicted for him. Only one thing could stop his progress to that goal: a bad goring which would put him out of action for weeks or months. Serious gorings are the occupational hazards of the toreros' craft; the risk of one was present every time Manolo stepped into a bullring. El Pipo could, however, minimize those risks, and minimize them he did.

As he was fond of saying, "When you're poor and unknown, you've got to get along with the crumbs the others don't want. But once you start to be somebody, its your turn to eat the cake and leave the crumbs to the others." As his prodigy's successes began to follow one another, and the impresarios started to crowd his table at the Café Ivory, El Pipo began to eat into the cake. No longer was he compelled to accept whatever bulls the impresarios foisted upon him. Now he was often able to impose the bulls he wanted on them.

The bulls El Pipo wanted were *toros cómodos,* bulls as amenable as a bull can ever be. He went into the *campo* to select them himself. Whenever possible, he chose animals whose horns curled inward instead of flaring outward and heightening the chance of their goring a matador in a pass. He also chose animals with long necks so Manolo could more easily get their heads down at the moment of the kill.

Beyond that initial selection, El Pipo tried to see to it that his matador got the best two bulls of each lot of six bulls. Since El Cordobés rapidly became the star attraction in the countryside around Córdoba, El Pipo was usually able to choose the matadors who would appear with him. El Pipo did not give his blessing to a young man without exacting a price. The price was his deferring to El Cordobés during the *sorteo* so that El Pipo's matador wound up with the bulls he wanted him to have.

Having made certain his matador was assigned the bulls he had chosen for him, El Pipo set out whenever he could to see that those animals did not enter the bullring brimming over with excess zeal or energy. There were several stratagems he could use. The simplest was to keep the animals penned up, in the boxes in which they had been shipped to the ring, until just before the fight began. The brutal summer heat, the frustrations of captivity, and a calculated lack of nourishment all combined to send them into the ring in a weak and diminished state.

There were other ways as well. As El Pipo knew, "nothing slowed up a bull better than dropping a few sandbags on his back before the fight." El Pipo's favorite technique, however, and the one he most often employed, was the classic fraud of the modern bullfight. It was directed toward the weapon with which the bull defended himself, his horns. They were shaved.

The object of the shaving was not to reduce the danger represented by the horns themselves. In fact, less than an inch was snipped from their tips, and once cut, the horns were filed back to their original sharpness. The reason behind the shaving was much more subtle than that. The bull's horn is a living organ equipped with its own cellular and nervous system. It bears the same relationship to the bull that whiskers bear to a cat. It is a kind of radar thanks to which the bull perceives and judges distances in the world around him. When the tips of his horns are cut, the animal's delicate sense of distance is distorted and his horn thrusts lack the precision and exactness that is usually associated with them.

Shaving became so common a practice in the years after the war that it was finally outlawed by the Spanish state. Manolete was often accused of using it. A special laboratory was established by the security police to detect shaved horns, and fines of up to thirty thousand pesetas were ordered for breeders who allowed the practice. A well-shaved horn, however, is an extremely difficult thing to detect. The law largely ended the abuse in the cities and first-class corridas, but it continued to flourish in the countryside where local police and veterinarians were more receptive to the whispered offer of a bribe.

In the small-town corridas of Andalusia where El Pipo practiced horn shaving in 1960, his own notoriety and that of his matador were not yet sufficient to draw the vigilant eye of the security police upon them. The artisan assigned the task of shaving the horns was El Pipo's veteran banderillero. Columpio's thirty-five years in the bullring had given him an expert's knowledge of almost every aspect of the corrida, and he was considered one of the most accomplished bull barbers in Andalusia.

The operation usually took place the night before the corrida on the ranch where the bulls awaited shipment to the ring. The timing was important because the bull regained his lost sense of distance within twenty-four hours after the shaving. Columpio slipped discreetly to the spot where the animals awaited shipment along with a couple of the ranch's vaqueros hired for the occasion. One by one the bulls were run into a wooden box used to hold them when they were sick so they could be treated efficiently. The cage was speckled with portholes to give a veterinarian safe access to the animals, and two of those portholes were designed to give passage to the horns. A winch held the animal's head firmly in place while the shaving was performed.

Occasionally, when a zealous rancher refused to accommodate El Pipo in his demands, Columpio shaved the crated animals on the way to the bullring, crouching in the van of the truck carrying them to the plaza. Wherever he performed his task, the banderillero inevitably slipped a set of souvenirs of his work into his pocket. Later he was obliged to pass those mementos discreetly to El Pipo as proof that his job had been carried out.

All of El Pipo's chicanery, however, all of his blatant publicity and his barbered bulls, could carry the manager and his protégé only so far. A bull's horn, shaved or not, can still gore. The horns of the bull that killed Manolete had been shaved; that did not stop the animal from driving one of them nine inches into the maestro's groin. Where El Pipo's hoop-la and his gimmickry ended, something else had to take over and that was the courage of his matador.

Courage was, still, the powder in the soap package El Pipo was peddling, the senseless courage of a young man desperate for success. Without that, he had nothing to sell. And courage is what his matador displayed in reckless abundance that summer, running again and again his foolish risks until, as those hot weeks dragged by, even his cynical manager began to gasp in wonder at the chances he took.

Over and over again El Cordobés planted his tiny banderillas kneeling before the bull. He planted them standing with his back to the *barrera,* refusing to budge from that incredibly dangerous position until the bull was on him and he had only a fraction of a second in which to escape a frightful goring. He planted them after kneeling with his back to the bull, whirling about at the last second.

With his muleta he performed faenas that left terrified crowds begging him to stop. He performed chest passes forcing his bulls almost to scrape his rib cage with their horns. He passed them on his knees, again and again bringing their horns whistling by an inch or two from his eyes, his skull, his mouth. He passed them with his back to the *barrera,* he passed them kneeling up against that wooden barrier with no margin for escape, so that the slightest deviation in a bull's charge would nail him to that wall like a butterfly pinned to a board.

Riding to a corrida in Andújar, he turned to Columpio and announced he was going to do something that afternoon no one had ever done in the bullring before. Sure that he had seen everything in his long career, the old banderillero regarded him with a skeptical stare. He was wrong.

While his gray-haired banderillero stared aghast, El Cordobés broke his banderillas down to pencil length, marched up to his bull waiting in the middle of the ring, then turned his back to him. Slowly he paced his way backwards toward the bull. As the bull charged, he stopped. In the second before the animal's horns reached his back, he stuck out his right leg to catch his eye and divert his charge. As the animal swerved, he snatched it back, spun and slammed his banderillas into its back. His stunned banderillero joined the crowd in their wild applause.

Later in Pozoblanco, El Cordobés gave his old banderillero even more reason to applaud. That afternoon he stalked to the middle of the ring, folded his muleta and stood stock-still three yards from the bull's horns. The bull moved up to study this strange presence. Not a muscle in Manolo's body budged. At that moment, Columpio noted, "you could hear a fly buzzing in the arena." Then, very slowly, Manolo turned around and sat down on the sand, right under the bull's horns, barely a foot and a half from his muzzle. With the deliberate gestures of a trapeze artist performing without a net a hundred feet in the air, he stretched slowly forward, took one of his feet in his hands, and carefully removed his slipper. At every instant he could feel the hot, damp breath of the bull on his back. Methodically, perfectly in control of himself, he repeated the gesture with his other slipper.

When he had finished, he took a slipper in each hand, stood up, and with very, very slow steps turned around until he was facing the bull barefoot. He caressed each of his horns with the slippers. Then standing there before the animal, moving at the exquisitely languid pace of a slow-motion film, he put the shoes back on. He bent over and gently drew his muleta up from the sand. Then, with a swift snap of his wrist, he thrust its vibrating folds before the bull's eyes. The animal burst at the cloth with one violent thrust.

A roar such as Antonio Columpio had never heard burst from the stands. Everybody, he recalled, "was standing up screaming, jumping," while the banderillero assured himself that if he hadn't died of a heart attack during those long moments, he never would.

Most often, the displays put on by El Cordobés had nothing to do with the noble art of the bullring as it had been taught by the masters of Seville and Ronda. His faenas were often raw, crude, brusque affairs without the pattern and rhythm of the classical bullfight. A sense of savagery inhabited the ring whenever he fought; the confrontation seemed to be between a savage animal and a savage man. But whether he wore his hair too long, whether he slapped a reluctant bull's nose with his sword, whether he held his cape improperly or kept his feet together when they should have been apart, one thing stood out above all else: his reckless courage and his willingness to take chances no one else would take. Already he gave rise to hysterical admiration and bitter criticism. Admirers and critics had one thing in common, however. They all ran to see him fight.

Soon El Pipo no longer had to oversell his *plazas* to get out a crowd. They came anyway, drawn by the growing magic of El Cordobés' name. His corridas began with a wild mob fighting for places in the bullring, and ended with another wild mob hysterically acclaiming the matador. Rabbits, ducks, chickens, chunks of sausage, goatskins of wine, poured

298

down on the exhausted torero during the delirious demonstrations that usually followed his fights in the small towns. In the cities it was hats, shoes, mantillas, flowers, a scrap ripped from a dress by a nearly hysterical woman.

The season that had begun with a gamble ended in a rising crescendo of acclaim. Like a storm building strength as it moved along, El Cordobés moved from corrida to corrida, generating a new wave of excitement in each town through which he passed. In August he returned to Palma del Río to fight for the first time with picadors. Antonio Caro, the iceman who had proclaimed three months earlier that the town would rather buy him a jail than rent him a bullring, now rushed out to rent the biggest portable bullring in Spain. And El Cordobés, the boy who had been handed a fistful of dirty bills knotted up in an old handkerchief for his first fight, now asked for and got "green money," a clean new stack of 1,000-peseta notes for his fee. The day of the fight, Pedro Charneca ceremoniously took down the calendar portraits of Manolete from the walls of his bar and carefully put them away in an old trunk. Proclaiming "Manolete belongs to the dead, El Cordobés to the living," he replaced them with a series of pictures of the young man who would henceforth be the idol of his clients and the inspiration of the young vagabonds wandering home from Don Félix's fields.

A few days later Manolo fought in Écija. Jesús Jiménez Torres, the impresario who had reluctantly hired him for a thousand pesetas, had to beg El Pipo to bring him back for a hundred thousand. In Córdoba, heralded as "alone before danger," he fought four bulls in an afternoon while the press announced "the train for Seville will not leave until after the corrida is over." "El Cordobés' on a bullring's *cartel* is enough to sell out any *plaza de toros* in Andalusia," a Córdoba paper proclaimed. As September came, and the season of fall festivals, he fought in a bewildering series of fights all month long. In Bélmez one wild afternoon, he cut eight ears, two tails and one hoof from four bulls and was paraded through the town for two hours on the shoulders of his admirers. In Priego his appearance caused a traffic jam that blocked the town's main street for hours. In Jaén he fought in a driving rainstorm.

"The season will never end this year," wrote a Córdoba journalist. "Every town wants to have a bullfight with El Cordobés. If things go on, the Banco d'España will belong to him."

But it did end, finally, in a drenching rain squall in Córdoba. The bullring of the caliphs, which had been half empty for his first appearance in the city whose name he bore, was overflowing with excited spectators. When the last bull tumbled dead to the sand and the crowd rose to offer the matador a sanding ovation, a proud *señorial* figure advanced on the president's box. With a gesture, he indicated he was ready to offer El Cordobés and the crowd the last bull remaining in the corrals of the bullring, the animal traditionally held in reserve in case one of the bulls on the program turns out to be defective.

No gesture could have provided a more fitting close to the first season in the career of El Cordobés. The man who had offered him his last bull of the year was the man who had so often sought to ban him from his *tientas* and his vast estates, the man whose seed bull he had slaughtered with a thrust of his Civil War bayonet. It was Don Félix Moreno.

ANGELITA BENÍTEZ'S STORY

"I WAS ALONE in the house doing the cleaning. He drove up in that green car he'd bought. 'Come on, come on, come out right away!' he cried. 'I've got something I want to show you.' He acted so excited I thought he was taking me to Madrid. I ran out to his car with my apron on and soap on my hands.

"It was raining that day and the streets were all mud. He drove to another place where there was pavement and there was no mud. He stopped and he said, 'Come on, come on with me.' He walked into a big house.

"There were no lights on in it. We took a candle and we felt our way around in the dark, from room to room, touching the walls with our hands. 'I wanted to buy you a house,' he said, 'because you don't have a house.' He had bought it already. He had come one day and done all that and didn't tell me.

"Me, I'm tranquil. I'm not one of those people who break down with emotion under things. I've had too much in my life for that. If someone says they are going to do something for me, I say 'thank you.' If they don't do it, well, I forget it because people are like that, I know. Him, he was serious. He promised me he'd buy me a house that day he fought his bulls here. I believed him because he said he would.

"But that day I couldn't stop myself. I couldn't believe it. Right away as we started to walk through the house I began to cry. I liked the bedrooms. We never had those. We all slept in one room all our lives. There was water, a faucet to get your water from. We never had water in a house before. There was a little patio where I could hang out my laundry.

"But what impressed me most, it was big, very big. I kept saying over and over, *'Que grande, que grande.'* A house that big, I worked in a house that big when I was young, scrubbing tiles, but houses like that weren't for poor people like us to live in.

"Manolo, he was very pleased with himself, very happy. At the door, he blew out the candle and he took the keys from his pocket. He gave them to me.

" 'Well,' he said, 'there's the house I promised I'd buy you.' "

*   *   *

And so, in the rain, there on the doorstep of the house he had just bought for his sister, the crazy summer of Manuel Benítez came to an end. It had been an extravagant success. He had begun it as a chicken thief and ended it as a hero. The road to the world of Currito de la Cruz lay open at long last before his adventuring feet.

The next afternoon Angelita Benítez, her husband and her four children moved into the house her brother had bought her. For her, too, a new life was beginning. But in her new house and the new life it symbolized, one thought would remain to haunt the nights of Angelita Benítez. Never could she forget how her brother had earned the money to buy that house; nor the fact that some sunny afternoon, in some distant bullring, in some unnoted city, her brother might fulfill the rest of the prediction he had made the day he vowed to buy her a house or dress her in mourning.

CHAPTER NINE

Madrid:
THE
MOMENT
OF TRUTH

THE ONLY SOUND in the immense arena seemed to be the muted splash of the raindrops striking the sand. There was no smile on the face of El Cordobés now. His stare solemn, his features drawn, his mouth dry, he advanced with mechanical steps toward Impulsivo. A cold liquid, rain or sweat, slid off his neck and ran down inside his collar toward his waist. At this instant El Cordobés, like so many other matadors, felt the soft, sapping fingers of fear feeling their way along the edges of his being. His Toledo steel blade clutched in his right hand, he marched out to kill the black animal planted like a dark statue on the sand before him.

And so it had come, the last ritual act of the corrida, the moment of truth. It was the instant for which Impulsivo had been born under the branches of a paradise tree on a distant December night. He was going to die now, and his ritual sacrifice would culminate this renewal of the unique spectacle that is the *fiesta brava.* The ritual of the sacrifice had been set for generations, since the days of Spain's first great matadors. El Cordobés' first gesture would be to fix Impulsivo in position for the kill, with the bull's forefeet clamped together and his head lowered. That position was essential if El Cordobés was to kill properly, for only with his forefeet together would Impulsivo's shoulder joints spread apart, stretching open the space the size of a man's palm into which the matador would have to drive his sword. Legend likes to pretend that making that sword thrust is like driving a knife into butter; but a bull is not made of butter. He is made of bone and sinew, and more than one matador has snapped his wrist trying to drive his sword down into those black depths awaiting El Cordobés.

Not for nothing had the act ahead of him been labeled "the moment of truth." No single action of the corrida, no action, perhaps, in any other spectacle created by man's imagination, offered dangers as great as those inherent in the gesture El Cordobés was about to accomplish. Eight out of ten of the most serious gorings received in the bullring came at this instant. Weakened by the brutal puncture of the pic, dazed by the deceptions of El Cordobés' turbulent faena, Impulsivo seemed numb and passive before the oncoming matador. He was not. His animal strength was largely intact, his murderous instincts heightened, if anything, by the frustrations to which he had been subjected. Now, at the moment of his impending death, Impulsivo remained perfectly capable of killing the man who proposed to take his life. In that fact lay the justification for this final action of the corrida.

The lore of the bullfight holds that "the hand that kills is the hand that holds the muleta," not the right hand that holds the sword. Even at this final instant, the deception of the cloth is practiced to lure the bull to his death. As the matador lunges for the bull to drive in his sword, he must keep the bull's eyes fixed on the muleta. At the instant of the truth, the torero crosses his left hand under his right to pull the bull's head and horns away from him, off to his right. The bull must follow that lure, for to kill well, taking the risks that act requires, the matador's body must pass over the bull's right horn as he drives in his sword. For that second he lays open to the right horn one of the most vulnerable parts of his body, a small triangle of flesh in the upper thigh. There, just below a thin layer of muscle, lie two of the vital canals of the human body, the femoral vein and artery.

El Cordobés calmly planted himself a few feet from the saliva-covered muzzle of Impulsivo. After the spectacular faena he had just completed, only this last gesture now lay before him. In a few seconds, when the bull would have crumpled to the sand from a good kill, a wild wave of enthusiasm would shake the bullring from this public he had come here to conquer. He could see before him, moving slightly with the bull's labored breathing, two black velvet triangles, Impulsivo's ears. Soon, he was certain, a sea of white handkerchiefs would order those triumphant symbols cut for him, to crown his debut in this most prestigious of bullrings. Only the kill separated him from that triumphant moment.

Manolo had little taste for this last gesture. Like many masters of the muleta, he was an inept handler of the sword. Since a severe goring in his right shoulder in Bilbao, he had been unable to raise his right arm high enough to sight his sword properly for the kill. That, coupled with the instinctive nervousness he felt at this moment, often led him to a bad kill. Perhaps he was afraid that might happen now, or perhaps he was unable to resist a desire for one last clamorous burst of applause. Whatever the reason, he ignored the warnings of Impulsivo's searching horns. Snapping out the folds of his muleta, he called the bull to him in a last defiant assault on his animal intelligence.

Crouched behind their *burladeros,* Paco and Pepín watched horrified at his gesture. From the stands behind them came not a burst of applause but a murmur of awe and apprehension. Somewhere up in that wall of faces, Don Juan Espinosa Carmona, the bullring chaplain, nervously began to twist the beads of his rosary in his cassock pocket. A few feet from Paco and Pepín, watching from his own *burladero,* Don Livinio Stuyck regarded with dismay the scene unfolding before him. None of the stupefied spectators behind him was as disturbed by this last bold gesture of El Cordobés as Don Livinio was. If El Cordobés' luck failed him, it would not be just the matador who would suffer the consequences of that failure. Don Livinio and the other impresarios like him in Spain would suffer too, in their wallets. The commercial empires they had built upon his name for the weeks ahead would crumble. Every drop of blood El Cordobés might lose in a goring could cost them thousands of pesetas in unsold tickets should their favorite matador be forced to abandon the bullring for a hospital bed.

Impulsivo dove forward once again at the bewitching summons of the scarlet cloth. Manolo, his feet fixed together, his left arm gracefully extended, pulled him past his body in a *natural,* the bull's dangerous left horn almost scraping his thigh as he glided past. No frantic warning, no plea for caution, could stop him. He was at that instant, he could later recall, "crazy happy." He was hypnotized by his own success with this animal, unable to think of anything else but that splendid, drunken feeling of power each movement, each pass of the bull, gave him. He spun around, tossed the hair from his head, and shook out his cloth again. Again, at the last moment, with a commanding jerk of his wrist, he forced the bull's searching horn out and away from his body.

Paco and Pepín screamed for him to stop. A murmur of anguish from the crowd greeted each of his passes as though somehow those thousands felt the jab of a horn entering their own skins. Before the television sets, millions stopped talking, drinking, cheering, stunned into silence by the somber beauty of El Cordobés' dangerous ballet. The heavy sword dangling in his right hand, his left clutching his dirty, bloodstained muleta, El Cordobés started a third *natural.* This time, hypnotized by the scarlet lure, Impulsivo refused to leave its folds. Man and animal swept into an extraordinary round pass, Impulsivo spinning around El Cordobés' pivoting feet in a tightening circle. Like the hub of a wheel the matador spun, struggling for his footing, forcing the bull's heaving flanks up against his thighs, fighting to keep his control of the animal. The crowd roared and Impulsivo continued into a second, tighter circle. Confidently, then anxiously, then almost desperately, El Cordobés shook his cloth to draw out the animal, to unwind the coil squeezing about him. Impulsivo refused to come.

And so it happened. Impulsivo's horns found what they had been looking for so long. El Cordobés felt a brutal bump on his thigh. For a second he started to stumble. Desperately, he tried to grab the animal's spine in an attempt to stay on his feet. He could not. His feet slid out from under him on the wet sand and he fell helpless to the ground.

Impulsivo spun about and hurled himself in vengeful fury at the figure writhing on the ground below his horns. His back on the sand, his head half raised, El Cordobés watched helplessly as the bull bore down on him, his heavy gray horns slashing the air as he came. In a split second he remembered where he was, in the middle of the bullring, as far as he could possibly be from the protecting capes that might have lured the bull from his body. He felt the horns beating his body, searching. Then he screamed in agony. With one vicious lunge Impulsivo had found that vulnerable patch of skin which El Cordobés would have exposed to his horns at the instant of the kill.

His face contorted with pain, El Cordobés reached down and grabbed at the horn, inches deep in his thigh, as though with that gesture he could somehow thrust the horn of a thousand-pound bull out of his body. His head spun with pain. He screamed for help, wondering when his *peones* would come to his side. Thrusting against that horn with both hands, feeling his strength ebb away, all alone, El Cordobés had a "horrible impression of impotence." He could feel Impulsivo's breath washing over him, the terrible pain in his leg, then nothing at all. He fainted.

The help he had screamed for was running desperately over the soggy expanse of sand separating El Cordobés from the edge of the bullring. Never would Paco Ruiz forget "that horrible vision before me as I ran like a madman across the mud the terrible pain twisting Manolo's face as that left horn ripped open his thigh." One image stabbed through Paco's mind, the image of Manolete dying. "The femoral," he cried, "my God, the femoral."

El Cordobés' first recollection as he regained consciousness was of "the yellow-and-magenta capes of my *peones* spinning over my head like big flower petals as they took the bull away." Their whirling colors were a blur in his mind mingled with "the sight of the bull's black snout, his smell, the shouts of my *peones*, the screams of the crowd, and that pain that was everywhere in my body." In the circle of faces above him, he recognized Paco. *"Me ha dado fuerte*—he gave me a bad one," he murmured. During those instants, El Cordobés thought, "My life is running out through the hole in my leg." He saw for a last time the swirling yellow and magenta of a cape dancing over his head. Then he fainted again.

Five red-shirted ring attendants hoisted El Cordobés' inert figure to their shoulders. While his *peones* kept Impulsivo's attention, they began to carry him out of the ring. Instants before, when the horns of Impulsivo had found their way into his flesh, thousands of people in Las Ventas, millions more around their television sets, had leaped to their feet, screaming in a common burst of fright. Now, their faces numbed with shock or fear, they watched as the television camera followed the matador's limp body out of the bullring. From the stands, from windows, balconies and café doors, everywhere, a commiserating murmur followed his progress. It was as though the memory of an older nightmare had jolted the minds of thousands of onlookers, the memory that had panicked Paco: the specter of Manolete dying in Linares.

Before El Cordobés arrived, the corridor leading to the infirmary was packed with confused, shouting people, offering their blood, their tears, their prayers or their curious stares. In the *callejón,* policemen, photographers and reporters pushed and shoved, blocking the matador's route to help. From their *burladeros* and *barrera* seats, the representatives of Spain's great impresarios stared down, trying to get an appraising look at the wound, trying to assess in an instant the damage Impulsivo's horns had done to their hopeful projects for the days, weeks and months to come.

As the attendants swung El Cordobés into the *callejón,* his sword handler, Paco Fernández, stepped forward. In his hand was an elastic tourniquet, a device that never left his pocket during a bullfight. Paco twisted it around his matador's thigh in a desperate effort to stem the blood pouring out of his wound. When the pale, unconscious matador's body passed down the *callejón,* women along the *barrera* dropped flowers on him and men made the sign of the cross or reached down as though to touch the blood-soaked silk suit of lights passing below them. Drawing their nightsticks, the police pushed back the clog of photographers and spectators jamming the *callejón.* Caught in that crowd, Don Juan Espinosa Carmona could only wave a hurried blessing as the young matador's figure swept past him. With a final lunge, the attendants burst past the last spectators into the beckoning doors of the infirmary.

The infirmary, too, was filled with hangers-on. In their midst, the two male nurses on guard had already slipped into their white smocks. One of them quickly yanked the cover from the ancient operating table, a gift of Ricardo Torres, "Bombita," a great matador at the turn of the century. The other went to the refrigerator. From it he drew two flasks of type-O blood, donated earlier in the day by a pair of aficionados in return for a precious present, a *barrera de sombra* seat for the day's bullfight. Swiftly he suspended them, their rubber tubes already inserted in their caps, in the metal containers waiting for them beside the operating table.

As the attendants carried El Cordobés toward the operating table, the infirmary anesthetist bolted his rubber mask to a pair of metal cylinders, one containing pure oxygen, the other a nitrogen compound. Furious at the sight of the gawkers crowding his infirmary, Dr. Máximo de la Torre screamed *"Fuera*—out" and waved to the police. While they cleared the room, he turned his eyes back to the pale and bloody figure on his operating table. Manolo opened his eyes, and the sight of Dr. de la Torre brought a faint smile to his face. "Doctor," he murmured, repeating the phrase he had uttered to Paco, *"me ha dado fuerte."* Behind him the door of the infirmary slammed shut.

*   *   *

The slamming of that door, and the drama that preceded it, had stunned Spain. People ran from house to house, shouted at each other across streets, made friends with strangers in bars and cafés, to compare the emotions those instants had given them. In Palma del Río, Angelita Benítez had risen screaming from her seat at the sight of Impulsivo's horn goring her brother. Never again would she permit herself to watch a bullfight. Convinced her brother had fulfilled the rest of the prediction he had kept in buying her house, she collapsed.

Don Carlos Sánchez stood silent before his television set. At the instant of the goring, a strange thought had crossed the aging priest's mind. "He has honored the blood of his people," Don Carlos thought. El Cordobés had seen the danger in the oncoming horns and refused to step away from it. His display of courage before so many millions of his countrymen had, it seemed to Don Carlos, avenged many a shame suffered by his poor family. With that thought Don Carlos walked into his church to begin a prayerful vigil for the life of Manuel Benítez.

Outside, the feria of Palma del Río had come to a stop. Children stopped playing, the merry-go-round ground to a halt, even the tongues of the fortunetellers fell silent. Pedro Charneca, tears in his eyes, rushed from the home of the midwife to his bar. He, too, had seen trouble coming. "He's going to get it, he's going to get it," he had mumbled as he watched Manolo's last passes, glumly certain he would not back away from the danger he had invited.

On the telephone he had installed in his bar at such great expense, Charneca called Madrid for news. Already the square before his bar was black with people. Until three o'clock in the morning they would remain there. And until three o'clock the faithful Charneca would telephone Madrid every fifteen minutes for news of his young friend, news he would promptly shout to the crowd outside.

Not far away, Anita Sánchez wept quietly in her darkened bedroom. In a few moments she would get up and remove the blue dress she had made for this occasion. For Anita, as for the rest of Palma, there would be no feria this year.

Everywhere people shared the consternation of the townsfolk of Palma del Río. In Córdoba a busload of bewildered American tourists arriving at the doorsteps of a great hotel were greeted by a bellboy who shouted at them, *"muy grave*—it's very bad." The Ivory Bar was as solemn as a wake. Curro, the banderillero-turned-shoeshine boy, had tears in his eyes. "Tomato Face" and Horrillo listened almost side by side to the radio reports from Madrid.

Under an enormous cut-glass chandelier, his face a melancholy mask, another man stared glumly at his television set. El Pipo was not, with his cigar and his felt sombrero, in his accustomed place in the *callejón* of Las Ventas. His discovery had a new manager now, and the returns upon which El Pipo had counted as the reward for his shrewdness were going to other hands. Alone in the dining room where he had once requisitioned his family's jewelry to rent a bullring for the future idol of Spain, El Pipo allowed himself a moment of bitter reflection. It was he, Rafael Sánchez, the King of the Shellfish, who had first recognized the genius in Manuel Benítez and thrust him upon an indifferent public. To the imagination of Rafael Sánchez, El Cordobés remained essentially what he had held him to be in that wild summer of 1960, the reflection of his own genius. It was not just El Cordobés that the horns of Impulsivo had kept from riding in triumph from the great gates of the Madrid bullring; they had prevented El Pipo, too, from savoring the thrill of that last, great triumph.

They had shared many thrills in the turbulent months that had followed that crazy summer of 1960. At the end of that summer, in the town of Jaén, El Pipo had offered to one of the bullfight world's major impresarios, the aging Pedro Balañá, an exhibition of his matador's art that was so breathtaking in its boldness Balañá had exclaimed, "Rafael, your torero is going to give goose pimples to all Spain."

Balañá's cry had given goose pimples to El Pipo. He knew well it was worth millions of pesetas. Balañá owned the bullrings of Barcelona, Palma de Majorca and a half-dozen other major cities, possessions that made his empire one of the most flourishing enterprises in the *fiesta brava*. The following February, El Pipo had taken his protégé north to Barcelona. After four days, after four successive triumphs before a public loath to acknowledge idols it had not helped create itself, El Cordobés rode out the great door of the Plaza Monumental on the shoulders of his newly won Catalonian admirers. The greatest bullrings in Spain now lay open before the resourceful manager and his torero.

Sixty-seven times that second summer, Manolo put on his suit of lights, killing 133 bulls, cutting 212 ears, creating in every corner of Spain the same wild frenzy he had stirred in his native Andalusia the summer before. For each one of those fights he was paid the sum of two hundred thousand pesetas, almost as much as his idol Manolete had received for his corridas in the last summer of his life.

One evening the following winter, in a hotel room in Madrid, the jovial manager marked a figure on a book of matches and casually passed the matchbook to El Cordobés. That astronomical sum represented the total earnings El Pipo had estimated for his matador for their third season together. El Cordobés' eyes lost their way in the string of zeroes trailing out from that figure. It was sixteen million pesetas, more than a quarter of a million dollars. El Pipo gently suggested a three-way division of that enormous sum: one third for the matador, one third for himself, one third for expenses and a publicity campaign El Pipo proposed to undertake. El Pipo's arithmetic reflected his desire to get the golden eggs out from under the chicken without any unnecessary delay. He knew how uncertain and short-lived a matador's career could be.

Manolo declined El Pipo's offer. He was persuaded the lion's share of the third allotted to publicity would find its way into El Pipo's yawning pockets. The inevitable rupture came early the next season in Barcelona. El Pipo sent his male secretary to the matador's room with an ultimatum a few minutes before a corrida: either El Cordobés would agree to a fifty-fifty split of his earnings or they were through. The young secretary, watching El Cordobés dress for his corrida, lost his nerve. He was unable to deliver the ultimatum. Finally a furious El Pipo telephoned the room to ask his secretary if he had given his message to the matador. El Cordobés heard his angry tones pouring through the receiver. He grabbed the telephone from the quaking secretary and in an angry rush of Andalusian curses told the King of the Shellfish he was a "crook" and no longer his manager.

El Pipo had forgotten that while it might have been his commercial skills that had launched El Cordobés, it was his matador's appeal that had kept him in the public eye. That season, El Cordobés' success had surpassed that which he had enjoyed under El Pipo's tutelage. By the time it was over, he was the highest-paid matador in Spain.

The most powerful managers and impresarios in the country fought each other to take El Pipo's place as his *apoderado.* Their representatives stalked the corridors of his hotels like private detectives to whisper him their employers' latest propositions. The unlettered youth asked only one question of the representatives of the men who had so often driven him away from the doors of their bullrings: "How much?"

The answer was provided in February 1963 by a dour Basque impresario, Pablo Chopera. It was a guaranteed fee of 525,000 pesetas per corrida, more than $4,000 for each bull he killed, over $400 for every minute of each one of his faenas, an extraordinary figure which made the illiterate orphan the highest-paid performer in history.

And so he had it all now. He rode to his bullfights in a white Mercedes. He could, as he had promised an uncooperative Córdoba tailor, throw away his suits of lights after each one of his corridas. But above all, the distant prophecy of El Pipo had come true. By the millions, the pesetas earned by the unruly ghost of the *campo* now flooded into the banks of Madrid and Córdoba. Laboriously tracing out the only words he knew how to write, the awkward scratches a priest in Salamanca had taught him to make, Manolo had begun to sign the checks that invested his fortune in the only goods his poor peasant mind might covet: brown earth and rock.

He could steal the oranges from his own trees now, and fight his own bulls in the lost corners of his own vast estates. He raised his own breed of fighting bulls, and when he sent those animals to fight in the cities whose jails he had once known, he could see his name upon their bullrings' walls with the proud title of "Don Manuel Benítez."

None of his acquisitions, however, was more symbolic than the one he had made in a draw of land in the mountains just north of the city whose name he bore. There, in a grove of scrub oak and wild olive trees, were the darkened ruins of an ancient farmhouse. A Nationalist outpost in the summer of 1936, it had served briefly as a Guardia Civil barracks before being abandoned and taken over by a solitary shepherd and his flock. One stormy night during the season of their wanderings, Manuel Benítez and Juan Horrillo had knocked on the door of the ruin. The old shepherd, instead of driving them away, invited them inside. He let them dry their clothes by the fire and gave them some milk to drink. The next morning when they left, Manolo promised the old shepherd that one day when he was rich and famous, he would come back to buy those ruins and build there his house. The old shepherd and his flock had long since disappeared, but Manolo had kept his word. He had bought that ruin, and while he had crisscrossed Spain going from corrida to corrida, an army of workers had transformed the ruin into a pink-and-white plaster mansion complete with its own bullring, its stables and, on the slopes where the shepherd's lambs had played, an enormous swimming pool. On its gates, beside a representation of the flat-brimmed Cordoba hat that had become Manolo's symbol, were the words: HACIENDA MANUEL BENÍTEZ EL CORDOBÉS, the wrought-iron realization of the dream of the young man now fading into unconsciousness on Dr. Máximo de la Torre's operating table, the youth who had a few moments before felt his life running away through a hole in his leg.

*　　*　　*

On the sand of Las Ventas a last rite still remained to be accomplished. There was no forgiveness for Impulsivo because he had disabled his human foe. He was condemned to die by the ineluctable law of the corrida at the hands of the man who had, a few minutes before, confirmed El Cordobés' ascension to the rank of *matador de toros*. His own steel sword in his hand, Pedrés advanced on Impulsivo.

No flourish, no excess of skill, was expected of him in this gesture he prepared to accomplish in the name of his wounded colleague. The animal before him had gored, and aiming his sword for its thrust, Pedrés could see the still-wet stains left by El Cordobés' blood on the end of his left horn. Impulsivo knew now where the object he was looking for was, and he was even more dangerous than he had been a few minutes before when he had gored El Cordobés. No one now asked from Pedrés anything more than a swift and prudent kill.

The eyes of Don José Benítez Cubero followed with rapt attention the matador's arm as it began its forward movement. A flash of its black on the gray television screen, a quick lurch, and the matador's hand drove like a boxer's fist over the horns toward the waiting ball of muscle below his head. The blade buckled for an instant, then, finding its path, shuddered its way into the black mass of Impulsivo until only its red handle remained above his hide. Pedrés let go and swiftly slipped to the side, away from the animal.

The white-haired bull breeder lived that instant with a poignant intensity. Five years of savage existence, generations of careful breeding, had reached their destined end. Mortally wounded, his beautiful black animal waged a last, hopeless struggle for the life fleeing his limbs. He staggered, drew himself together, staggered again. The swirling capes of Paco and Pepín dizzied him, further forcing him to twist and turn, forcing the sword in his body to hasten his end. His proud, heavy head hung down now, shaking as he coughed up his blood, his tongue hanging from his open mouth. He sagged down on his knees as though to symbolize the sacrifice of which he had just been the object. Then his rear legs collapsed and his massive form sank to the ground. He tossed his head in a last dying look at the foreign world around him. His eyes filled with tears. Then Impulsivo rolled over on his side, dead, the fate for which he had been born under his faraway paradise tree fulfilled.

As the bull rolled over, an appreciative roar rose from the stands. They blossomed with a waving field of white handkerchiefs, beseeching his ears for the matador who now lay unconscious on an operating table while a surgeon struggled to save his life.

*   *   *

The skilled fingers of Dr. Máximo de la Torre felt their way into the thigh of Manuel Benítez with deft and sure movements. The surgeon's first gesture had been to order an antitetanus injection for the wounded matador. His second had been an order to his anesthetist. He could not wait for a slow-working anesthetic to take effect. The wound before him was too serious. He had ordered a heavy dose of sodium pentothal injected into the matador's veins.

Now, as his fingers worked down deeper into El Cordobés' thigh, Dr. de la Torre could see the face of the half-conscious matador contort in

313

pain. He himself winced at the sight. But he could not stop. Already his advancing fingers were taking stock of the damage done by Impulsivo's horns, a long succession of torn nerves, perforated tissues, gashed muscles. Behind them was an enormous blood clot, and as his sensitive fingertips began to probe its outlines, Manolo's face constricted in pain again. At the center of that clot lay the vessel Dr. de la Torre's fingers were looking for, the vessel on whose preservation Manuel Benítez's life depended, his femoral artery. His face drawn, the doctor began to work his fingers along the artery. Its collateral blood vessels and nerves were shredded apart. He continued his probe. Then an air of relief swept his face. The femoral was intact. Impulsivo's horn had missed that vital canal by just five millimeters.

The doctor withdrew his fingers. The hole before him punched by Impulsivo's horn was eight inches deep. With an electric vacuum he began to pump up the blood pouring from the wound. Then with a stroke of his scalpel he opened both edges of the wound to be sure no trajectory of the horn escaped his searching fingers. Slowly he repicked his way along the trajectories left by the horn, cleaning the wound of foreign material. It was a fruitful search. Soon on the white cloth beside him Dr. de la Torre had laid out scraps of silk, fragments broken off from Impulsivo's horn, even a gold thread from Manolo's suit of lights.

The only sounds in the room were the uneven breathing of the matador and the occasional command of the surgeon calling for an instrument or the pulsebeat and blood pressure of his patient. The onrush of blood from the wound resisted Dr. de la Torre's efforts as he tried to tie together one by one the blood vessels torn off the femoral artery. Manolo's blood pressure dropped alarmingly, and Dr. de la Torre ordered a transfusion. Worried now that El Cordobés might fade away into deep shock or an irreversible coma, the surgeon demanded at quickening intervals his pulse rate and blood pressure. A second flask of blood began to flow into the matador's veins.

After seventy minutes, the doctor's work was done. The unconscious man's chances now rested on his own ability to resist the shock a serious goring invariably brought on. The blinking light of an ambulance pushed through the crowds outside to the door of the infirmary. As Manolo's unconscious body was wheeled into it, a man rushed up and laid an object on his stretcher. Paco Ruiz would not allow his matador to leave this plaza, which Manolo had made so many sacrifices and so many desperate efforts to enter, without the trophy awarded him by the public he had come here to conquer, the ear of the bull Impulsivo. It was an extraordinary gesture because the tradition of the bullfight demands that its trophies be awarded only to a matador who has completed his task by killing his bulls.

As the ambulance drew away, the exhausted Dr. de la Torre came to the infirmary door. In his hand was a piece of paper on which he had just written three words, his appreciation of the state of El Cordobés. Soberly, he handed the paper to the newsmen gathered at the door. It read: *"Prognóstico muy grave."*

*   *   *

Thousands of anxious *Madrileños* dogged the curbs along the ambulance's short route to the Toreros' Hospital. A troop of mounted police had to open a path for it among the shoving mob blocking the gates of the bullring. From the roof of a nearby bus, a television camera recorded the scene for millions of Spaniards still fixed before their television screens. Its light blinking, its siren wailing, the ambulance slid out of Las Ventas toward the hospital, realizing El Cordobés' pledge that he would leave that ring on the shoulders of the crowd or on a hospital stretcher.

At any time it is a sad sight when a man who has entered a bullring radiant in his suit of lights leaves it unconscious in an ambulance. This day that spectacle was accompanied by a special sorrow, for the man in the ambulance was more than just a famous torero capable of arousing emotions few men in the history of the *fiesta brava* had been able to stir. For hundreds of men and women, El Cordobés was the prolongation of the myth El Pipo had built around him in that crazy summer of 1960, the symbol of the success for which the poor and oppressed of many a Spanish village and town hungered. He was to many the product of a new Spain, a nation beginning to feel even in the ordered ritual of its national *fiesta brava* the stirring breath of the winds of change. As his triumphs were theirs, so, too, were his sufferings. That on this May evening he should be riding out of the gates of the arched temple of the corrida in an ambulance instead of on the shoulders of the crowd was more than a drama. It was a tragedy reaching down into their own lives.

Protected by a wall of policemen, the ambulance stopped before the green wrought-iron gates of the Toreros' Hospital. As the unconscious matador's stretcher was lifted from the ambulance, a respectful silence fell over the crowd surrounding the hospital. Flash bulbs popped and a few hushed voices called *"Suerte*—luck, Manolo." Then, his hair spilling over his head in disorder, El Cordobés was carried into the hospital to which he had been refused admission just five years and five months earlier.

A respectful guard of honor lined the hallways as his stretcher rolled into the hospital. In their striped pajamas, in wheelchairs, on crutches, supported by nurses, the hospital patients silently watched the figure of the most illustrious member of their fraternity roll by.

Robustiano Fernández, the first patient of Dr. de la Torre this day, still dazed by the shock of the operation that had taken his leg, heard the commotion in the corridor outside. Raising himself on his elbow, he watched as El Cordobés' figure was wheeled past his door. The little procession stopped just three doors from his. There in Room 9 of the second floor of the Toreros' Hospital, El Cordobés began his struggle to recover from the brutal wound in his thigh.

Outside, the crowd surrounding the clinic grew steadily. *Maletillas* tried to scramble over its iron grilles. Two of them managed to sneak into a macabre hiding place, the morgue, in their efforts to catch a glimpse of their wounded hero. A horde of reporters, photographers, television cameramen, as well as radio cars, blocked each of the hospital exits. Unable to find any other subject for their attentions, they began to photograph El Cordobés' bloodstained suit of lights and his muddy shoes as though they were holy relics. The hospital's switchboard operator, a matador forced to leave the bullring after a terrible goring in Caracas, had to call for extra police reinforcements to control the crowds. Soon a flow of cars began to deliver a stream of distinguished callers at the hospital's gates: other matadors, artists, the mayor of Madrid, the Chief of Police, newspaper owners, celebrities, all anxiously demanding news of the wounded torero. The hospital's switchboard was swamped with telephone calls. Telegrams began to arrive by the dozens, then by the hundreds and thousands.

Outside the matador's door, guarded by two husky male nurses, his

316

close friends and relatives gathered: Paco and Pepín, both weeping softly, Carmela and Encarna, his two sisters, and Chopera, the manager who had negotiated his fabulous contract for Las Ventas.

Nor was the vigil for El Cordobés confined to the gates of the Toreros' Hospital. On the boulevards of Barcelona, under the arcade of Salamanca's Plaza Mayor, in the old city of Seville, people huddled around radios anxious for news. In Córdoba the churches were full of people praying for the life of the young man who had adopted their city as his; the tiny chapel of the Carmelites was crowded with women reciting the rosary before an image particularly revered by the toreros of Córdoba, the portrait of Christ falling under the weight of his cross on the road to Golgotha. In Lima, Caracas, Mexico City, radio stations interrupted their programs to give the news of the matador's goring.

Shortly before midnight a rumor passed through the crowd outside: El Cordobés was dead. A stunned hush stilled the chatter, followed by a relieved babble when the rumor was denied.

Not long thereafter, a faint voice began to murmur in Room 9. Fevered and dizzy, El Cordobés began to stir into consciousness. "*Agua, dame agua*—water, give me water," he asked. Then he called for Paco Ruiz. When he recognized the face of his banderillero leaning over his bed, he murmured, "Is the bull dead?"

Paco nodded. Then he drew from his pocket an object he had recovered from the matador's stretcher.

"Manolo," he said, showing it to him, "here is the ear."

Forty-eight hours later, El Cordobés was out of danger. But the drama his goring stirred continued unabated. Not since the death of Manolete had a matador's misfortune so monopolized the attention of the Spanish press and radio. Every paper in Spain carried enormous front-page stories of his goring. Those reports were accompanied by pictures of the matador writhing in agony under Impulsivo's horns and reports even more clinically detailed than those reserved in the United States for a Presidential heart attack or operation. Even papers as remote from the world of the corrida as *The New York Times, The Times* of London, *Le Figaro* of Paris, and *Mainichi* of Tokyo carried accounts of the incident.

Outside the hospital, the crowd continued to keep its vigil. Solicitous visitors left religious medals for the matador, homemade remedies, de-

317

vices to ward off the evil eye, pies, chickens, cakes. The telephone switchboard was jammed with calls. A pair of French girls who had flown to Madrid to be near their idol joined the hospital's overworked operator. Cables, some addressed simply to "El Cordobés, Spain," continued to pour in. They came from movie stars, waiters, noblemen, factory hands, policemen. Daily, as El Cordobés struggled to regain his strength, the press continued to publish lengthy reports of his progress, exhausting, in their search for detail, even the fruitful imagination of the city's most resourceful newsmen.

By a strange coincidence, one man was destined to benefit from that enormous ration of attention heaped on the wounded matador in Room 9. Wandering through the halls of the hospital one day, a newsman glanced into a room three doors away from that of the man he had come to interview. The room's sole occupant was staring out the window, weeping softly to himself. It was Robustiano Fernández. Curious, the newsman walked into his room.

And so the scrap-metal scavenger was able to escape briefly the obscurity he had so long sought to flee. The reporter published his story, and Robustiano's smiling face adorned at last the pages of a newspaper —although the story recounted, alas, not his triumphs but his tragedy. Even that sad publicity had its fruits. "The torero dies, but the man lives," concluded the article, and to help the man live, a fund was launched.

Its harvest was small, not much more than the man in Room 9 could earn in a few minutes in the bullring. But it was enough to buy Robustiano Fernández a bit of hope, a reassurance that all had not ended for him on Dr. de la Torre's operating table. It was a two-room flat in a cheap tenement on the outskirts of Madrid. One sunny morning, alone and unnoticed, Robustiano Fernández hobbled away from the Toreros' Hospital to that flat. There he began his new life as a one-legged scrap-metal scavenger, returning forever to the obscurity from which he had so briefly emerged, a sad and unremarked symbol of the corrida's failures.

*   *   *

El Cordobés left the hospital on crutches eleven days after he had entered it, every move of his pale figure witnessed by a cheering crowd and dozens of photographers.

Eleven days later, against the advice of his doctors and the pleas of his friends, he dragged his emaciated body into the bullring of the coastal town of Marbella. There—his wound still raw, his weakened limbs shaking with strain—he cut four ears and a tail from two bulls of the ranch of Antonio Martínez Elisaute to prove to Spain and to the world that his courage had not spilled out through the hole torn in his thigh by the bull Impulsivo. The strain of the corrida tore open the scar of his wound. It did not matter. He could go on now, up that long road he had taken one distant night in a darkened movie house. The next afternoon, in another bullring, in another city, he had a new rendezvous with a pair of brave bulls in the dying sunlight of a summer day.

Epilogue

WHIPPED BY THE cold wind off the sierras, a ballet of bright orange sparks danced upward into the night sky from the campfire. Three adolescents huddled around its coals, concentrating their efforts on a message one of them tried to print in charcoal on a swatch of cloth he had cut from his shirttail. Scattered around them were the acorns which, with the grass underneath their feet, had constituted their sole nourishment for three days. When their sign was finished, they stood up, stretched their joints, aching with the winter cold, and slipped through the darkness to a wrought-iron gate a few yards away. There they patiently tied their sign to its black bars, right next to the flat-brimmed Córdoba hat that was the symbol of the owner of the estate stretching away from those gates. Then they stepped back to inspect their handiwork.

For those shivering, half-starved youths, that iron grille marked the door to a promised land, a kind of shrine symbolizing the world they craved to enter. They were *maletillas*. To them and the thousands like them swarming the roads of Spain like a plague of locusts, the man who lived behind those iron gates was a new Currito de la Cruz; it was his legend that had driven them onto the highways in their frayed sandals and faded blue jeans, and his success they desperately hoped might one day be theirs. Antonio Carbello, "Mejita," was the last of a family of sixteen children only five of whom had survived childhood. Juan Esposito Garido, "El Carabinero," was the fourth son of a blind beggar, a dour bitter youth hobbled by a misshapen leg, the souvenir left from a three-hour beating by the Guardia Civil of his village. Constantino "El Grande" didn't even know who his parents were. He had been left, a half-starved infant, on the doorsteps of a convent in Huelva.

Stamping their feet to shake off the cold, trying to forget the hunger knotting their stomachs, they stared enviously at the lights in the hacienda and waited for its owner to emerge.

Suddenly, through the darkness beyond the outlines of the empty swimming pool, past the whitewashed walls of the stables, a pair of headlights stabbed through the night. With a contented rumble, a cream-colored XKE Jaguar, one of the three in Spain, slid down the long drive toward the gates. At that sight, the three *maletillas* rushed to the iron grille. They swarmed over the car, peering into its windows at the man inside, a silk foulard carefully knotted around his neck, a custom-tailored cashmere sports jacket resting on his shoulders. One of them rushed to the gates and tore down the sign they had so carefully drafted. It read, "We congratulate you on your great success in Mexico. Like you we want to know glory. We beg you to give us a chance." He passed it to the man inside the car. With that pathetic gesture, the three *maletillas* begged in their turn for an *oportunidad* at the gates of the finca of El Cordobés.

Manolo stared at their sign. Gently he told the three youths to go to his kitchen to get something to eat. Then, in a shower of flying gravel, he disappeared into the night.

A quick turn to the right and there, spread below him, a gray-white splotch in the moonlight, was the city of the caliphs, his city now, Córdoba. Down there in that city was the rendezvous that had brought him out into this winter's night, his first in his home since his return from Mexico. Nothing could keep him from it. He honored it faithfully every night he was here.

No cabaret artist, however, no flamenco dancer, no restaurant owner, waited for El Cordobés in Córdoba. It was instead a priest, a simple parish priest to whom El Cordobés had cried in despair one day, "Padre, make a man out of me. Teach me how to read and write." For the richest matador in the history of the corrida, a man whose fame rivaled that of

322

the ruler of his country, could not read the message on the sign handed him by a *maletilla* at the gates of his finca.

Padre Juan Arroyo had met El Cordobés in a crowded hotel room in Córdoba one summer day as the matador dressed for a bullfight. It was not a sacred mission that had brought the priest there, but a pasodoble he had written in the young torero's honor. It was called "The Smile of El Cordobés" and it soon became one of the most popular songs in Spain. Since the afternoon he had first played it on his accordion for the young matador, a friendship had arisen between the bullfighter and the priest. For two hours every night when he was in Córdoba, Padre Arroyo's sparsely furnished sitting room became Manuel Benítez's classroom and his worn blue-velvet armchair the seat in which the matador tried to grasp the learning that would make him "a man."

In a plain schoolboy's notebook, the hand that had killed over a thousand bulls patiently copied down the phrases set out for him by the priest: *"Yo soy Manuel Benítez*—I am Manuel Benítez"; *"Me gusta mucho torear*—I like to fight bulls very much."

A special eccentricity accompanied his reading lesson. The priest taught Manolo how to read from a textbook in handwritten rather than printed script. The most urgent need Manolo had for reading was to decipher the contracts daily thrust upon him; their key financial clauses were invariably written by hand.

The reading and writing lesson over, the priest turned to a new subject. Sometimes it was arithmetic. Sometimes it was French, a language El Cordobés had shown a pathetic eagerness to master. To help him, Padre Arroyo had compiled a simple vocabulary of the language of Voltaire. In his selection the priest had displayed a worldly awareness of his pupil's interests. The first word on his list was *Bonjour*. The second was *mademoiselle*.

The lesson ended with a less rigorously scholastic exercise. Padre Arroyo drew a red leather-bound volume from his library shelves. It title was *Maxims and Thoughts,* and from its pages the priest selected a nightly thought to rouse the mind of his pupil. One night it was "Do not let your body become the tomb of your soul"—Pythagorus; another, "To live for others is not just a stern duty, it is happiness"—Auguste Comte; or, "Friendship is the beauty of virtue"—Kant. The young man who had known so little of the world beyond its hunger, the bars of its prisons and the misery of its cities tried to understand concepts as foreign to his existence as "virtue," "the soul" and "beauty." Prodded by the priest, roused by his questions, Manolo stretched open his eyes and discovered in this modest room a new abstract world of which he had never been aware.

Those were not the only discoveries the most famous torero in Spain made in the blue velvet armchair. One day, prompted by a program he had seen on television, he told the priest he was fascinated by space. But, he added, he could not understand one thing.

"Why," he asked, "do the astronauts go round and round in circles?"

The astonished priest brought a schoolboy's globe into his room. Patiently he explained its significance to the idol of the land that had sent Christopher Columbus across the seas. As El Cordobés' enraptured mind grasped the thoughts laid before him, he muttered the same phrase he had uttered on that moonlit night he had discovered the mystery of the muleta: *"Fenomenal, fenomenal, fenomenal."* Like an excited schoolboy, he spun the globe, caressing with his delighted fingers the continents his ancestors had discovered five centuries earlier. It was a voyage of discovery, there in the priest's sitting room, for Manuel Benítez, too. For, until that instant, on this winter evening of the mid-1960's, the most celebrated matador in the world had not known that the earth was round.

* * *

Those few hours of reflection in a priest's sitting room are about the only quiet moments in the life of El Cordobés now. No man is alone less than a great matador, and solitude is a luxury the young man who once prowled the open *campo* now neither enjoys nor wants. Wherever he goes, he is surrounded like some Arab sheik by his suite of hangers-on; their very presence is a kind of drug to reassure him of his importance and his popularity. Flatterers, parasites, servants, profiteers of all sorts— they fill the salon of his hacienda, his hotel rooms, the *callejones* of his bullrings. Impresarios trying to make a deal, bullfight critics in search of a handout, bull breeders, friends, girls in search of quick adventure, young toreros in search of help, perfect strangers knocking on his door just to gape at him—they intrude in almost every moment of his existence, permanent reminders of the fact he is at last a somebody, a man whose name is known among the millions.

He who just seven years ago could go three days without food because he lacked the funds to buy a bowl of coffee now quite literally does not know how much money he has. When he opened his first bank account, the bank manager asked him how much he wanted to deposit.

"I don't know," he answered. "How many kilos do you want?" Now his fortune is evaluated at at least 500,000,000 pesetas, the equivalent of about $8,300,000. More than a hundred and fifty people depend on him for their livelihood. His face and name appear on products as numerous and diverse as wine, ashtrays, postcards, beer mugs, penknives playing cards, cigars, dolls, plaster statuettes, pennants and 14-carat-gold pins.

El Cordobés, who used the first pesetas he earned before the horns of a bull to buy his sister a house, owns his own construction company now. From the windows of their barracks, the Guardia Civil of Córdoba can admire its most notable realization: a seven-story luxury hotel from whose summit burns, in enormous letters, the name of the man whose first lodging place in their city was their jail. With its Turkish bath, its swimming pool, its rooftop nightclub, and its 105 rooms, each decorated with a painting produced by the matador's hand, the new hotel El Cordobés is one of the most modern hostelries in tourist-conscious Spain.

In addition to his Jaguar, his garage houses a French Alpine sports car, a Land Rover, and a fleet of the Mercedes' after which he lusted for so long. Sometimes he climbs into one of those cars and drives it crashing across the open fields, each protesting creak, each wincing gear, an affirmation of the extravagant wealth now in his hands. Another vehicle, however, has replaced the Mercedes in Manolo's mind as the symbol of success. It is his newest and proudest possession, an $80,000 six-passenger Piper Aztec, named "El Cordobés" and duly blessed by the faithful Padre Arroyo. El Cordobés has become the first matador in history to fly to his corridas in his own plane.

To pilot it, he has his own aerial chauffeur, an F-86F pilot hired away from the Spanish Air Force. But usually it is Manolo himself who flies it, forcing his pilot to clamp his hands on his head. Nothing pleases the man who walked over half of Spain more than rushing away from a corrida in France to fly to Madrid so he can eat fried eggs and chorizo in his sister's

325

apartment and contemplate in happy amazement the transportation miracle that got him there.

No *maletilla* ever goes away hungry from his door, no beggar without a coin in his palm. The fiestas he gives on his ranch are the occasion for the poor peasants of the neighborhood to fill their stomachs—and pockets—with food. When he opened his private bullring on his second estate recently, his one thousand guests included two hundred *maletillas* for whom he provided a truckload of ham and montilla. He provided Don Carlos Sánchez with the equipment and furniture for a large new boys' trade school in Palma del Río. Few matadors have fought for charity as often as El Cordobés has. Yet he can complain with understandable bitterness that "whenever anyone knocks on my door, it's to ask for something."

No aspect of El Cordobés' personality is more publicized than his extroverted, gregarious nature. He is in life what he is in the bullring, an impulsive, carefree savage being with a seemingly indestructible capacity to drink, laugh, play the guitar, sing, and dance the flamenco all night. He is almost inevitably warm and hospitable to strangers; and he bears himself with the dignity and simple courtesy that seem to be the birthright of all Spaniards no matter how humble their origins. Yet he is essentially a reserved and withdrawn young man, quick to offer his hand and his smile, but keeping the rest for himself and a few intimate friends.

His yesterdays were hard and bitter, and he does not like to let them crowd in upon the present. He knows where he came from, and he is never going back there now; but the dark and hungry shadows of his youth have taught him to be wary and defensive. He is too proud to be ashamed of his hungry years, and quick to remark that "poverty is not an insult." But he does not often let his mind drift back to those days, and he has little patience with those who would try to lead it there. He is where he is now, in his fabulous present, where the memories of past injustices and misery have little place. His body and spirit were schooled by the clubs of the Guardia Civil and the shivering nights on the construction projects of Madrid, and Don Manuel Benítez is a realist.

"You have to be rich to protest," he declares. "Money is the only thing people listen to." He has made his private peace with the regime responsible for so much of the misery in his family's life. During Spain's recent Constitutional referendum, his smiling face on wall posters exhorted the masses to "Vote '*Sí*' like El Cordobés."

His life is marked above all by an extraordinary sense of spontaneity, the heritage, probably, of the years he and Juan Horrillo roamed the countryside like a pair of stray animals. He leads his life from minute to minute, a happy slave to his passing whims. His lack of punctuality has even offended a nation that has made an art of not knowing what time it is; recently, he turned up late for one of his fights in the prestigious feria of Seville.

Despite his spontaneity, many of his public gestures are carefully calculated. He knows what his admirers want and expect of him. Having learned from El Pipo the importance of standing out in a crowd, he often makes a point of wearing a white sombrero. His long hair and carefully casual slouch are now as much a part of his public posture as of his private preference. He fights, between Spain and his South American tours, close to a hundred fights a year: two hundred bulls; two hundred times he must step into the bullring and expose himself to injury. In 1965 he fought in 111 corridas in Spain alone, breaking a record held by Juan Belmonte since before the Civil War. In August of that year, he fought thirty-two times in thirty-one days, killing 64 bulls, cutting 53 ears and 11 tails, traveling six thousand miles to do it.

Such grueling marathons have left their marks. His body bears the traces now of over twenty gorings. Two of them almost killed him, and if the scars on his body were laid end to end, they would stretch three times around his waist. They are not the only wounds he has received. Twice he has been operated on for his bad shoulder. There are other marks that don't show, the ones that come from the strain and tension of facing the bulls and the demanding crowds day after day. To stand before the horns of a bull and risk one's life as a young and desperate youngster is one thing; to do it at thirty-two with eight million dollars in the bank is another.

El Cordobés drinks too much under the strain now, and like Manolete in the last year of his life, it is not red wine he drinks but Scotch whisky. In the season, he has to knock himself to sleep with pills he has brought, thirty tubes at a time, from Mexico. The next morning, to shake himself from the stupor they induce, he needs other pills.

In Málaga, in Murcia, in Zaragoza, the journalists following him have seen him so exhausted, his nerves so worn, that they have predicted tragedy ahead if he does not care for his health. But as he was that rainy May afternoon in 1964 when he looked up at the howling stands of Las

327

Ventas, so El Cordobés is a prisoner now of his own fame, of the glory he so desperately sought, of the contracts that follow one on another in a rhythm never before equaled in the life of a torero.

He tried to break that rhythm, but it was the rhythm that broke him. It happened at four o'clock in the morning one winter night in the pine-paneled bedroom of his newest hacienda. El Cordobés sat up trembling in his bed. He had just had a nightmare, a dream of an enormous black bull driving a hole in his body. As he had on the sand of Las Ventas under the horns of Impulsivo, El Cordobés had seen his life running away through that imaginary hole. He woke up his chauffeur, drove to Córdoba and called Madrid to announce he was retiring from the bull-ring.

Six days later, like a parade of mourners following a hearse, a line of dark limousines drove up to the gate of El Cordobés' finca. From those cars stepped the half-dozen men who rule the bullfight: Don Livinio Stuyck, the man who had brought El Cordobés to Madrid; Pedro Balañá, son of the man who predicted to El Pipo that his torero would "give all Spain goose pimples"; Diodoro Canorea, whose rings had once had no room for the youth who was going to "revolutionize the *fiesta brava.*"

Thanks to television, tourism and the young man they had come to visit, their *fiesta brava* was enjoying a prosperity unparalleled in its history. More people paid more money to see more bullfights than ever before. The institution that had been able to produce only 333 bullfights in 1959 now produced over 1,000 a year. Those men had erected twelve new bullrings in less than five years. Their big ferias had grown bigger and their season longer, their own importance more significant and their bank accounts appreciably grander.

And now because a volatile young man who could barely read and write had had a nightmare, their little world had started to unravel. As soon as the news of the matador's retirement was announced, people had rushed to the Maestranza in Seville to demand their money back for their subscription seats to the city's April feria. The proprietor of the largest hotel in the seacoast resort of Castellón de la Plana lamented that without El Cordobés his city would have "no feria and no tourists." One wide-eyed economist estimated that the matador's retirement would cost Spain's hotels, taxicab drivers, ticket scalpers, and restaurant owners six million dollars in lost revenues. To Spain's distraught impresarios, the one hundred corridas the matador would no longer fight represented, probably, over five million dollars in receipts.

With grim and solemn faces they marched into the office of El Cordobés. The matador greeted them in an open sports shirt, below a bust of Manolete and the toga-draped figure of another former Córdoba resident, the Roman philosopher Seneca. For three quarters of an hour, these men whose *plazas* had once had no place on their programs for a hungry mason named Benítez begged El Cordobés to go back to the bullring and save their season from the disaster that menaced it. Finally —aware, perhaps, that his bad dream might cost him two million dollars in lawsuits—El Cordobés agreed. He signed his name to a declaration the seven men before him had drawn up, reversing his decision because "of the harm [it brought] to Spain's tauromachian enterprises, the public and the *fiesta brava.*"

And so he went back, back to the bulls and the crowds, the long trips and the sleeping pills, the horns and the strains he had sought to escape. His season is a swirl of passing towns and faces, strange hotel rooms and frantic sprints through the crowds to his airplane. Some days he does not even remember the name of the town he is fighting in or the ring he will be heading to the next afternoon. All he knows is that each day, for one half hour of danger, he earns one million pesetas: $8,250 for each bull he kills, $800 for each minute he performs.

His real wealth, however, is his courage, and that he squanders every afternoon of his season. That daring has made El Cordobés the most celebrated and controversial Spaniard of his generation. Venerated as a demigod by millions of Spaniards, he is loathed by millions of others. He has been called a fraud, a clown, an outrage, a show-off, an intruder who has turned the corrida into a savage ritual without grace and beauty. To his admirers he has given emotion back to an institution that had become an effete spectacle, and returned it to its origins, a lusty combat between a man and an animal. El Cordobés, the dean of Spain's bullfight critics maintains, is a rejection of "all this Hemingway mysticism that deformed the *fiesta.*"

No man is more scornful of the attacks directed against him than the matador himself. "I say to them," he proclaims, " 'Come down there in the arena with me.' When they have felt the horns go by their heads and their lungs, when they have seen them inches from their eyes, then I'll

329

take them seriously. Let them know that I could fight like Manolete or Ordóñez. But then I'd be another Manolete, another Ordóñez. What I want to be is what I am, El Cordobés, the only El Cordobés."

Perhaps it is true, as his critics claim, that El Cordobés represents a vulgarization of a certain image of the corrida. But the vulgar breath that El Cordobés has brought to the sand of the bullring is just a zephyr of a wind blowing over all Spain. It is sad, perhaps, but it is also inevitable. The Spain of clacking castenets, the flamenco, and the *paseo,* the pure, noble, and romanticized Spain of Hemingway and Montherlant, is slowly disappearing before the oncoming tide of another civilization. It is a civilization of neon lights, Formica tabletops, low-cost housing, easy credit terms and standardization. But it is also a civilization of fuller stomachs and the awakening aspirations of a long-thwarted people. It does not matter what judgment the critics of the corrida pass upon El Cordobés' art. His acclaim arises elsewhere, on the vast, sunny stretches of the bullring that is Spain. To the masses there, it does not matter whether he is a good torero or a bad torero; he is their torero, and they applaud across his frail and defiant silhouette the harbinger of a new, a better life.

* * *

The apartment is blatantly new. Its walls are hung with the tinted color portraits of a host of matadors. In the dark hallways beyond the room there is a continual coming and going, of maids in dark green dresses, of lean and furtive men talking in low mumbles, as though this were the anteroom of a gambling parlor or some other illicit establishment. A bar stands in one corner and behind it a thin, sad-faced young man quietly polishes sherry glasses.

He is not a bartender, that boy. His name is José Fuentes, and he is a matador, the newest prodigy of the apartment's owner, El Pipo. Here, in these polished surroundings, amid his stream of callers, the King of the Shellfish pursues the last ambition of his life, to find a new *"fenómeno,"* a new idol to revolutionize the *fiesta brava* and make the crowds forget the last hero he cast to the heights of the corrida.

He is heavier now and the furrows on his brow are deeper, but El Pipo too has become a legend in Spain. One day recently in Córdoba, a luckless *maletilla* threatened to leap from a window ledge four stories above the city's main street if someone did not offer him an *"oportunidad."* The fire department ran an aerial ladder up to his perch, and from it priests, policemen and passersby tried to coax him down. Then a fat fireman had a genial inspiration. He doffed his uniform, put on a wide felt sombrero, stuck an enormous cigar in his mouth, and began to ascend the wavering ladder. When the despairing *maletilla* saw that familiar symbol climbing up to him from the sidewalk below, he reached out, pulled the ladder to his ledge, and began to climb down. He had been persuaded that the King of the Shellfish had come to offer him, too, the *oportunidad* he had so long sought.

*   *   *

Angelita Benítez has moved into a new house now, the second her matador brother has bought her. All Palma del Río knows that house as "the house of El Cordobés." For Angelita, life has changed very little since the afternoon her brother honored his promise and took her away from her hovel. She has never been to Madrid; nor is she ever likely to go. But her eldest son will not go as she did, as her father did, to spend his strength in the Morenos' fields. He is studying for another role, one he will discharge in the enterprises of his millionaire uncle. He is going to be an accountant. Angelita's own waking hours are a never-ending round of washing, polishing, cooking, scrubbing, the reactions of a lifetime of routine she cannot, in her new life, shed. But there is a dark well of bitter memories not too far below the surface of Angelita's personality.

"Nobody wanted to know us when we were poor and starving," she says. "Now that my brother is rich and famous, people who wouldn't spit on us then think they're our friends." Every day now there is a stream of people begging at her door, a pair of hungry women, a man who wants fifty thousand pesetas for an operation—because he is "an aficionado."

But her real concerns are those that creep over her at night when darkness has stilled the cranes nesting in the rooftops of Palma del Río stretching past her bedroom window. Then, in a nightly invocation to the *patrona,* she begs her, as she has begged her for years, to take her brother away from the bulls, away from the threat she has felt hovering

331

over her shoulders since the day he promised to buy her a house or dress her in mourning.

*   *   *

Not far away, in a more modest dwelling in a block of new apartments on the Calle Averroës, another woman, too, thinks often of El Cordobés. In one room of that apartment, on the sewing maching the matador bought her, Anita Sánchez designs and runs up dresses for the young women of Palma. She is a poised girl, sad and quiet, still darkly attractive.

"When I talk about Manolo now," she said, "it is all a dream. I don't even recognize myself when I talk about it. I hate this little town," she adds. "I am suffocating to death here. I would like to go away to Madrid, to Barcelona, anywhere, to find a new life."

For, in the ingrown little community in which she dwells, a mark hangs upon her head. She was "El Cordobés' *novia,*" and the men she might marry look at Anita Sánchez and pass her by.

*   *   *

Juan Horrillo is married and the father of three children. He lives in an apartment Manolo bought him in a new section of Palma del Río. But he remains as an adult what he was as an adolescent: a child of the *campo,* careless, happy-go-lucky, totally incapable of submitting himself to any form of discipline. Sometimes he disappears for days, even weeks. He works when he needs money or when he feels like it. When he doesn't, he does what he wants to do. The day he was to sign the papers for the house Manolo offered him, he failed to show up for their meeting. On the way, he had met a woman who offered him some *migas* and he spent the day with her instead. When a furious Manolo asked him where he had been, he replied, "Ay, *hombre,* yesterday wasn't a day to buy a house. It was a day to eat *migas.*"

Manolo tried to make Horrillo the manager of his first finca. But Horrillo's indifferent attitude toward his responsibilities was too much even for Manolo's undemanding nature. Now, when Horrillo needs money, he earns it by squirting the air of the city of the caliphs into the tires of passing tourists. Sometimes the millionaire and the gas-station attendant roam about together in the matador's Mercedes, over the roads they wandered as youths. Occasionally, on these trips, they stop and, with a bizarre gesture, try go recapture the exultation of the days when they were inseparable friends: they sneak into the fields and steal a few oranges.

*   *   *

Don Carlos Sánchez remains where he has been for thirty years, in the sacristy of Our Lady of the Assumption, quietly administering his parish, recording in his fine and labored hand the skeletal history of a town's existence: the births, marriages and deaths of another generation of Palmeños.

Not far away, Charneca's bar remains triumphantly unchanged, as untidy and cluttered as ever, its owner, a trifle fatter, firmly ensconced for the rest of his lifetime on the throne he so enjoys, that of the first aficionado of Palma del Río.

Don Félix Moreno rests in his family mausoleum in the cemetery of San Juan Bautista, brought there with military honors, his coffin followed to his last resting place by the relatives of not a few of the men whose bodies lie only a few yards from his in the common trench that was the price for slaking their appetites on the flesh of his precious Saltillo bulls.

*   *   *

Physically, little seems to have changed in Palma in the decade since Manuel Benítez was driven from its gates. A new manual training school and a brick kiln have been built, and new apartment houses ring one side of the town, their white rectangular forms looking down on the lower, older dwellings hugging its crowded streets. Don Félix's great estate has been divided up among his sons. But the bells of Our Lady of the Assumption still toll the passing of a Palmeño. The town's Moorish walls still tower above the clots of children playing at torero and the old men sleeping in the sun. A foreign car can still attract a crowd, and Palma's burned-out churches still stand as gaunt and silent reminders of a violent past.

333

Those signs are deceptive, however. Change has fallen upon Palma del Río, and few are the aspects of the town's life that have not felt its hand. The streets that were muddy gulches in 1945 are all paved now. There is electric light for all. Progress will soon assign Miguel and Antonio, the water vendors of the Calle Belén, to a new occupation. A new construction project is shortly to deliver pure drinking water to the homes of Palma del Río.

But the most significant change of all is in the fields of the river valley rolling away from Palma's walls. Gone at last are the old Arab waterwheels that furnished the water for Palma's fields from the days of the caliphs until the Civil War. Now an enormous irrigation scheme has turned those fields into a fertile plain beyond the dreaming of even Don Félix Moreno's well-tutored mind. Thirty thousand acres have been watered by that scheme, and thanks largely to its effect, the amount of cultivated land in Palma has increased tenfold since the war.

The orange crop, which a decade ago was barely large enough to feed the town and satisfy Manuel Benítez's acquisitive fingers, today totals 16,500 tons a year and the oranges of Palma del Río find their way to the marketplaces of Paris, Amsterdam and Frankfurt. The *campo* through which the sandaled feet of Manuel Benítez used to roam is filled with a white sea of cotton now; the bulls he sought have been driven to more distant and arid pastures. That cotton, the new wealth of the river valley, fills hundreds of trucks each year, which head north to the textile mills of Barcelona. More and more, it is a puffing tractor instead of a team of oxen that rises over that valley.

The most significant change has been social. Palma is still dominated by five great families, the heirs of Don Félix Moreno and the other landowners of the prewar era. But since 1958 a middle class that now has importance both socially and numerically has grown up. It is composed of the new small landholders installed by the government on some of the land reclaimed by irrigation: skilled workers, mechanics, shopkeepers, a growing number of clerks and office workers, the foremen and managers of the orange and cotton cooperatives.

The daily line-up in the Plaza de Trabajadores, where Manuel Benítez's father's generation went to beg the alms of a day's work, still exists; but irrigation has cut the long season of unemployment, and for his sweat a field hand now gets ten times what the Benítez children earned in the fields of Don Félix a decade ago.

A new range of economic activities, the inevitable by-products of Palma's first steps toward prosperity, has sprung up in the town. In the springtime when El Cordobés put on his first suit of lights, Palma del Río did not have a single gas station. Today it has six. The town whose automotive resources in 1936 were limited to two taxis and a handful of cars, now has 1,000 motorcycles and motorbikes, 400 cars and 250 trucks. In 1958 the town's leading motorcycle shop sold one machine a year; last year it sold 156.

The town that watched El Cordobés gored by Impulsivo on barely a dozen television sets now has five hundred television aerials intruding upon the cranes nesting on its tiled rooftops. The poorest hovel in Palma now contains a domestic device unknown twenty years ago: the electric iron that has consigned to memory the old irons heated on Palma's wood stoves. The baby carriages that a decade ago were the luxury of the wealthy now clog the town's streets. Rare is the girl in Palma so poor that she does not have a chest of drawers, a table and a set of chairs as her dowry on her wedding day. As a symbol of prosperity's first gracious breath, Palma has a toy store now. In its window is an object of luxury, a plaything worth what the father of Manuel Benítez earned with a hundred and fifty days of labor: a doll that bats its eyes, cries, and costs 950 pesetas.

Those first fruits of change have hardly made a paradise of the cruel land that drove Manuel Benítez, and countless others before him, to seek their salvations before the horns of a brave bull. There is still poverty in Palma del Río and there are still hovels inside its walls where hunger is not a stranger. But there is less poverty and less hunger now than there was when Manuel Benítez was stealing oranges to help feed his family, and slowly, very slowly, the pools of Andalusian poverty from which the Belmontes, the Manoletes and El Cordobés sprang are drying up.

* * *

The changes that have swept Palma in the decade since a discredited Manuel Benítez shuffled off to its railroad station are a small reflection of the far greater changes that have overtaken Spain as a whole in the same period. The central fact of Spanish life in the last ten years has been an economic expansion unparalleled in any other similar period in her history.

335

The nation that produced its first motorcar in 1954 turns out 150,000 a year now. Half a million TV sets a year now flow from her factories. Wages have risen, and despite the pressures of inflation, Spain's workers have begun to share in the prosperity their nation enjoys.

Censorship has eased enormously. Movie censors now acknowledge that sex exists. Hundreds of books, barred until four years ago, are now on sale: Marx, Sartre, Joyce, Hemingway.

The society that relegated women to a restricted social role a decade ago now has female bartenders and taxicab drivers, and a Madrid gas station is equipped with girl attendants in James Bond-inspired black-leather motorcycle suits. The birth control pill was long more easily obtained in Catholic Spain than in neighboring France.

Inevitably, that progress has brought in its wake a growing demand for an easing of the rigid political regime under which it has been wrought. Spain is now undergoing a "revolution of rising expectations," and Franco's government finds itself at that "most dangerous moment" defined by Alexis de Tocqueville when a heavy-handed government tries to reform itself.

Beset by student unrest, labor agitation, a growing group of young clergymen at odds with their own hierarchy, and a rising generation for whom the Civil War was "a bloody squabbling between selfish men who tore Spain apart to slake their own vanity," the Franco regime is caught in a dilemma of its own making. It must find a way to accommodate the pressures upon it for political change without sweeping away the institutions with which it has governed Spain for three decades.

To date the search has produced a great deal of surface agitation and very little change. Even the central dilemma before Spain, the problem of Franco's succession, remains unsolved while the Caudillo himself, in what his detractors maintain is the sole manifestation of his sense of humor, reminds the nation of the longevity for which his family is known.

And so, as the government has debated, the disaffection has grown, the strikes become more open, the student unrest more violent, the young priests more vocal, the younger generation more dissatisfied. Thus far, unfortunately, the only real answer the beset regime has found to their demands is the one that has greeted all its foes for almost thirty years, the one the Guardia Civil of Palma del Río gave to a young *maletilla* fleeing his misery: the swinging of a policeman's club.

336

*   *   *

An icy winter wind swept the mournful plain of Castile. Migrating birds fled south through a sky heavy with snow clouds. The flood of cars of the millions of tourists of still another year had gone back across the Pyrenees, leaving behind their millions of pesetas and their memories of a sunburned paradise. Winter had emptied Spain.

A strange silence wrapped the cement spirals of those arenas where prancing men in their suits of lights had passed a season in the sun, killing black bulls before the screaming crowds. The *fiesta brava,* like the rest of Spain's tourist industry, rested, marking time before a new *temporada.*

And yet on the cold roads of Castile, on the wind-whipped roofs of swaying freight cars, a horde of ragged *maletillas* converged on the brick walls of Madrid's second bullring to join in an extraordinary congress, the congress of the *maletillas* of Spain. A hundred, two hundred, a thousand, they poured into Madrid. They ranged in age from fourteen to forty-two, from dwarfs to giants, from superb athletes to semicripples. They bore names as bizarre as "Little Banana," "The Gypsy Pharaoh," and "The Desperado." But they had one thing in common: they were desperately poor. For every boy from Barcelona, there were ten from Andalusia, for every one from Bilbao, a dozen from Extremadura.

They came in answer to a call launched by a brother of matador Luis Miguel González, Dominguín. *"Maletillas,* here is your chance!" he proclaimed.

They camped on the sand of the bullring and at night cooked over open fires the remains of the cows on which they had practiced during the day. Gradually the less proficient of them were weeded out and Dominguín's brother finally selected a half dozen of the most promising to inaugurate his *maletillas'* festival, wearing suits of lights before a real crowd. To dramatize their appearance, he organized a brief television program called *"Oportunidad"*—a chance. The program recounted the history of each *maletilla* he had selected to perform, the pathetic circumstances that had led him to the bullring. His program was an enormous success, and one day, soon thereafter, the Director General of Spanish television came to call.

"All these stories of misery and despair are just tricks," Dominguín's

337

brother was told. "All this business about social conditions giving rise to the *maletillas*. You must talk of the romance of the corrida, of the heroic blood of our nation, of our cult of courage and our scorn of death that flow through their veins. That is the real, the imperishable, legend of the corrida, and it is your duty to maintain that legend."

*   *   *

Twelve miles east of the Andalusian city of Jaén, at the foot of the Monte Mágina, the massive walls of the castle of Arroyo Vil rise above a silver-green carpet of ten-centuries-old olive trees. Once a year, at the New Year's holidays, the owners of that vast estate, the count and countess of Argillo, invite their second son, his wife and his parents-in-law to a country fiesta whose program has been fixed by long tradition. From ten in the morning until six there is hunting for Spanish red partridge, interrupted by a lunch of fried eggs and bacon, *serrano* ham and montilla served in the open fields. After a rest until midnight, there is Mass in the palace chapel, a banquet and flamenco dancing until dawn. It is a quiet family gathering, distinguished from the dozens of others like it on Spain's other great estates only by the nature of the in-laws the count and the countess welcome to their castle gates. The father-in-law of their second son is General Francisco Franco.

The very nature of that occasion makes it one of the most private and intimate moments in Franco's year. Few are the guests invited past the gates of Arroyo Vil who are not members of one of the two families. Last year, in defiance of that custom, a special guest was invited to occupy the place of honor at the right of Señora Franco and share the hunting blind of the Caudillo of Spain. It was Manuel Benítez, El Cordobés.

For forty-eight hours the former orange thief of Palma del Río lived intimately with the man whose prison camps had been responsible for his father's death. Franco's newest plaything was an 8-millimeter movie camera, and—like any excited tourist outside a bullring—Franco used it to photograph the famous matador. El Cordobés killed an honorable thirty-five partridges, danced the flamenco for Franco's daughter and discussed the problems of olive growing with his hosts. Then the two most famous men in Spain, the thirty-one-year-old son of a Loyalist

338

soldier and the man who had stepped from a British plane to take command of modern history's bloodiest civil war, posed side by side: two generations, two Spains, two worlds, captured in the photograph of an old man approaching the end of his life and his powers, and the unruly matador who unconsciously symbolized so many of his restless nation's aspirations.

GLOSSARY OF
BULLFIGHTING TERMS

AFICIÓN: Love for bullfighting; also aficionados as a group.

AFICIONADO: One who loves and understands bullfighting.

ALGUACIL: The mounted constable, wearing a sixteenth-century costume from the time of Philip II, who precedes the bullfighters as they parade into the ring. He performs the ceremony of requesting the key to the *toril* from the president, transmits the president's orders to the bullfighters, and cuts and gives to the matadors any ears awarded by the president. There are usually two *alguaciles* at corridas in large bullrings.

ALTERNATIVA: The ceremony in which a *matador de novillos* becomes a *matador de toros*. (See "Matador.") In this ceremony the senior matador on the program cedes the killing of the first bull to the young aspirant. After this bull is killed, the senior matador takes the second bull, and the other matador on the program the third. They then alternate in the usual way, with the senior matador taking the fourth bull, the other matador the fifth, and the initiate the sixth. The *alternativa* may take place in any recognized bullring in Spain, but before it is officially accepted it must be "confirmed" in a second similar ceremony in the Plaza Monumental in Madrid or the Plaza México in Mexico City.

ANANDADA: The upper roofed gallery of the bullring; also a seat in this gallery.

APODERADO: The manager of a matador.

341

APODO: The professional nickname of a bullfighter.

ASESOR: The president's technical adviser at a corrida. He is usually a retired matador.

ASTIFINO: Of a bull having thin sharp horns; also a bull with such horns.

AVISO: The warning trumpet call that tells the matador to kill the bull. If the bull is not killed ten minutes after the beginning of the faena, the first *aviso* is given. Three minutes later a second warning may be issued, and two minutes later a third. If by this time the matador fails to kill his bull, he must retire and a group of steers is brought in to herd the bull out of the ring.

BANDERILLA: The barbed stick, wrapped in colored paper, placed in pairs in the bull's withers in the second part of the corrida. The stick is 29½ inches long, including the 2½-inch steel barb.

BANDERILLERO: The man who places the banderillas. A matador usually employs three banderilleros, but sometimes places the banderillas himself.

BANDERILLERO de confianza: Literally, banderillero of confidence; the matador's chief banderillero. Traditionally one of a matador's three banderilleros is closer to him than the other members of the *cuadrilla*. Usually an older man, he is the matador's adviser in the ring and often a close personal associate. As a rule he represents his matador at the *sorteo* on the morning of a fight.

BARRERA: The red wooden fence that surrounds the arena; also a seat in the first rows of the stands. *Barreras de sol* are on the sunny side of the ring, *barreras de sombra* on the shady side.

BRAVA, bravo: Brave, fierce.

BURLADERO: A shield of wooden planks in front of a *barrera* opening, behind which bullfighters may run to safety when pursued. Also, when positioned inside the *barrera*, *burladeros* are the places reserved for the bullfight officials, the police and the press, and sanctuaries behind which the occupants of the *callejón* may retreat if the bull jumps the *barrera*.

CALLEJÓN: The passageway between the *barrera* of a bullring and the grandstand.

CAPEA: Literally, a caping. An informal bullfight or bull-baiting contest, usually in a small town, in which amateurs are allowed to take part.

CARTEL: The poster announcing a bullfight and its program; also the program of a bullfight.

CASTOREÑO: The picador's wide-brimmed beaver hat.

COLETA: A pigtail, the badge of the matador's profession. *Cortar la coleta*, to cut the pigtail, formerly meant to retire. Nowadays a bullfighter wears a false *coleta*.

CORRIDA: A running of the bulls, a bullfight. The usual corrida consists of the killing of six bulls by three matadors, the senior matador killing the first and fourth, the second matador the second and fifth, and the junior matador the third and sixth. See also *"Alternativa."*

CUADRILLA: The matador's team composed of one picador for each bull he will fight in a corrida, and one more banderillero than the number of bulls allotted to him on the program.

DEHESA: Pastureland; any place where bulls are cared for when young.

ESPONTÁNEO: A young man who "spontaneously" jumps into the arena during a bullfight and tries to cape the bull in the hope of attracting the attention of a manager or an impresario.

ESTOQUE: The matador's steel sword, used only in the kill. Its average blade is 33 inches long and tapers from ⅞ of an inch to ¼ of an inch in width. It has a slight downward curve at the end, beginning about 12 inches from the tip. Because its weight is difficult for the matador to support at the end of his wrist during the long faena, it has become the custom for the matador to use an *espada,* a lightweight sword often made of wood, until the moment for the kill has arrived. The custom was introduced by Manolete after his wrist was injured in an automobile accident.

ESTRIBO: The wooden ledge circling the base of the fence on the inside of the arena, about 18 inches high. Its purpose is to help a man vault from the ring.

FAENA: The work done by the matador with the muleta during the last part of the bullfight.

FENÓMENO: Phenomenon. A young bullfighter who shows unusual aptitude for his profession; also, sarcastically, a bullfighter whose publicity is not justified by his performance in the ring.

FERIA: A fair. Almost every Spanish town has an annual fair at which at least one corrida takes place.

FIESTA: A holiday or holiday period; a celebration.

FIESTA BRAVA: The bullfight.

GANADERÍA: A ranch; in particular, a ranch where fighting bulls are raised.

HERRADERO: The branding of the calves on a ranch.

HOMBROS: Shoulders. To leave the bullring *en hombros* is to leave it on the shoulders of the crowd.

MALETILLA: Literally, little suitcase. A youngster who aspires to be a bullfighter. He is so called because of the bundle of belongings he carries with him on the road.

MANO A MANO: Literally, hand to hand. Applied to corridas in which only two matadors, instead of the usual three, take part: contests between rivals in which each tries to outdo the other in skill and daring.

MANSO: Literally, tame. When applied to a bull in the ring, it means cowardly. Domestic cattle are called *mansos.*

MATADOR: The bullfighter who kills the bull. Matadors are officially classified in two categories. A *matador de toros* has taken his *alternativa* and is qualified to fight full-grown bulls: four-year-old animals weighing at least 900 pounds. A *matador de novillos* is a professional matador who has not yet taken his *alternativa* and theoretically fights only with three-year-old bulls, although he sometimes fights with older animals who have been rejected by *matadores de toros*.

MAYORAL: The foreman of a ranch, who often accompanies the bulls from the ranch to the ring.

MONTERA: The cloth hat worn by the matador and his banderilleros.

MORILLO: The bull's hump of neck muscle.

MOZO DE ESTOQUES: The sword handler, who cares for the matador's equipment and serves as his personal servant.

MULETA: The heart-shaped scarlet wool cape, with a wooden stick for support, used by the matador in the faena.

NATURAL: The basic left-handed pass with the muleta.

NOVILLADA: An apprentice bullfight, theoretically with *novillos* but sometimes with older bulls who have been rejected by *matadores de toros*.

NOVILLERO: A professional matador who has not taken the *alternativa*.

NOVILLO: A young bull, about three years old, fought in *novilladas*.

OLÉ!: Bravo!

PASE: A pass. Any work done with the cape or muleta in which the man remains stationary as the bull passes.

PASE POR ALTO: A high right-handed muleta pass in which the sword spreads the cloth and the bull is drawn across the matador's chest.

PASEILLO: Same as *paseo*.

PASEO: Procession; the processional entrance of the bullfighters into the ring.

PASODOBLE: A piece of music in quick march time: the type of music played in the arena before the fight begins and during the *paseo*, also often during a good faena.

PATIO DE CABALLOS: Horse yard: where the picadors' horses are kept in the *plaza de toros*.

PEÓN: Slang for a banderillero.

PIC: The picador's lance: the *pica* or *vara*. It is a wooden shaft 8 feet long that ends in a pyramid-shaped steel point.

PICADOR: The mounted lancer who pics the bull's neck muscles so that the bull's head will be lowered for the kill.

PLAZA DE TOROS: The bullring.

PRESIDENT: The supreme authority in the bullring for a specific corrida. He is usually a town official and is advised by an *asesor*. He sits in a high box from which he signals his orders by waving different-colored handkerchiefs.

PUERTA DE ARRASTRE: The doorway through which the dead bulls are dragged out of the ring. It is also the doorway through which the bullfighters enter. Also called *puerta de cuadrillas*.

QUERENCIA: The part of the ring in which the bull feels at home. He often chooses, apparently arbitrarily, a place in the ring that he considers his territory, and he will leave it only to charge the man, after which he will return to it.

REJONEADOR: A bullfighter on horseback. He rides a highly trained horse from whose back he kills the bull with a *rejón,* or javelin.

SOBRESALIENTE: A substitute. When two matadors are scheduled to fight in a corrida, a *sobresaliente* is hired to kill the bulls in case both matadors are wounded and unable to continue. He is usually a *novillero* or an aspirant matador who takes part in the *paseo* with the matadors and is allowed—and expected—to work with the bull with his cape.

SOL: Literally, sun. The sunny part of the grandstand of a bullring, where the seats are cheaper.

SOMBRA: Literally, shade. The shady part of the grandstand of a bullring, where the seats are more expensive.

SORTEO: The drawing of lots for the bulls at a corrida. It usually takes place at noon on the day of the corrida.

SUIT OF LIGHTS: The costume worn by matadors and banderilleros. It is made of silk heavily encrusted with embroidery, and weighs about 25 pounds.

TEMPORADA: The bullfighting season.

TENDIDO: The section of seats behind the *barrera* seats; also a seat in this section.

TERCIO: Literally, third; one of the three main acts of the bullfight: the picing, the placing of banderillas, and the killing of the bull.

TIENTA: A testing of calves for bravery on a bull-breeding ranch.

TORERO: A professional bullfighter. Although banderilleros, picadors and matadors are all toreros, the word is often used to mean a matador only.

TORIL: The enclosure in which the bulls are kept before they enter the ring.

TORO: A fighting bull. *Los toros* is the phrase used by Spanish-speaking people for either bullfighting as a whole or a bullfight.

VAQUERO: A herder of fighting bulls on a ranch.

VERÓNICA: The basic pass with the cape.

ZAPATILLAS: The matador's heelless slippers.

ACKNOWLEDGMENTS

As it must be evident, the preparation of *Or I'll Dress You in Mourning* would have been an extremely difficult task without the wholehearted cooperation of Manuel Benítez, "El Cordobés." From our first meeting in Córdoba in January 1965 until we left him almost a year later in a Madrid hospital recuperating from his first shoulder operation, he was unfailingly pleasant, courteous and cooperative, receiving us at his finca as regular members of his entourage, allowing us to share with him his long voyages from corrida to corrida, the dusty *callejones* of the *plazas de toros* through which he passed, the carefree moments of life on his ranch, riding through the *campo,* watching him practice on his young cows, reveling and singing by night. It was an experience upon which we look back with particular delight.

Not only did Manolo open to us the doors of his hacienda but he also introduced us to his family and friends, without whose help this book would have been impossible. To all of them we owe a special word of thanks: to his sisters, Angelita, Encarna and Carmela Benítez, for reviewing the often painful memories of their youth; To Pedro Charneca for his humor and his wisdom; to Don Carlos Sánchez, the parish priest of Palma del Río; to Juan Horrillo, who traveled with us over many of the same roads he had once wandered with Manuel Benítez; to Anita Sánchez; to Rafael Sánchez ("El Pipo"), who so patiently reconstructed the events of the "Crazy Summer" when he introduced Manuel Benítez to the world of the *fiesta brava.*

347

We have tried to relate the story of Palma del Río, the birthplace of the matador—its convulsions during the Civil War, its suffering in the years afterward—with objectivity and honesty. In recounting the events that took place in the town during those days we are not attempting to make a judgment, but to give an exposition from which that judgment may be made. It is not possible for us to thank publicly all the people who helped us in this endeavor without exposing them to risk or embarrassment; some of them we had to interview at night, in moving cars, to protect their anonymity then, and we cannot violate it now. If, however, it falls to them to read this book, they will know that to them, too, we offer our thanks.

The members of El Cordobés' *cuadrilla* were not only helpful friends but excellent companions: Paco Ruiz, Pepín Garrido, the *banderilleros;* José Sigüenza, the picador; Paco Fernandez, Manolo's sword handler; Andrés Jurado, his chauffeur; and Luis Gonzales, his estate manager—to all of them go our thanks.

Beyond them are dozens of others, key people among the scores we interviewed to prepare *Or I'll Dress You in Mourning,* to whom we owe a special debt. To men like Don Livinio Stuyck, director of the Madrid bullring, José Maria Jardon, Antonio Bienvenida, the dean of Spain's matadors, Dr. Máximo de la Torre, Lozano Sevilla, the Spanish television bullfight commentator, the bullfight critics of *El Pueblo,* ABC and *Dígame;* Padre Arroyo, the matador's patient tutor; Luis Lopez y Lopez and Dr. Antonio Ortiz Clot, the surgeon of the bullring of Córdoba; Antonio Columpio, the *banderillero* of Manolo's early fights; Don José Benítez Cubero, the breeder who raised Impulsivo, and Don Eduardo Miura, who invited us to visit his distinguished ranch; José and Antonio de la Cova, Alonso Moreno—to all of these we extend our thanks. Bernadette Moro and Eugenio Suarez were invaluable in helping us reconstruct the atmosphere in Madrid the day of El Cordobés' *alternativa.* Wendy Gordon was an invaluable aide during our long days in Palma del Río and a researcher of extraordinary insights.

In the tedious, long and often dreary task of assembling all our material, typing and retyping our manuscripts, we were extraordinarily well served by a devoted team of assistants. First among them was Mlle Dominique Conchon, who labored by our side for months, cheering us with her unfailing good humor, kind, gentle, endowed with the patience of a legion of Jobs, without whose help *Or I'll Dress You in Mourning* would surely never have been finished on schedule. She was assisted at various times by a number of others to whom we also express our gratitude and good wishes: Manuela Andreota, already exposed to our working habits during the preparation of *Is Paris Burning?*, Marie-Benoite Allizon who brought to Saint Tropez a breath of the fresh air of the Alps she loves so well, Annie Phillips, who did so much to get our project off to a successful start.

The authors also want to address their special thanks to John Marks, author of *To the Bullfight,* and Claude Popelin, author of *Le Taureau et son Combat,* for having carefully screened respectively the English and French manuscripts of *Or I'll Dress You in Mourning* for technical errors. To them all, and to the many others whom space or discretion will not allow us to cite, our thanks.

And, a final word of thanks to our editor, and above all, our friend Anthony Schulte, of Simon and Schuster, for his patience, his understanding and his good counsel.

Les Bignoles
Valderian, Ramatuelle
May 11, 1967

ABOUT THE AUTHORS

LARRY COLLINS, thirty-eight years old, was born and raised in West Hartford, Connecticut, and is a graduate of Yale University. He was for more than ten years a foreign correspondent in North Africa, the Middle East and Europe, first for UPI and then for *Newsweek,* for which he was Paris bureau chief. He is married and has one son and now lives in Paris. *Or I'll Dress You in Mourning* is his second book.

DOMINIQUE LAPIERRE is thirty-six years old and was for many years a senior reporter and editor for *Paris-Match.* He is the author of several earlier books published in France, some of them based on his knowledge of the United States, where he attended Lafayette College and where his father served with the French diplomatic service. He met Larry Collins in 1955, when Collins was in the U. S. Army and he was an interpreter at SHAPE Headquarters. Ten years later their friendship led to the publication of the international bestseller *Is Paris Burning?*

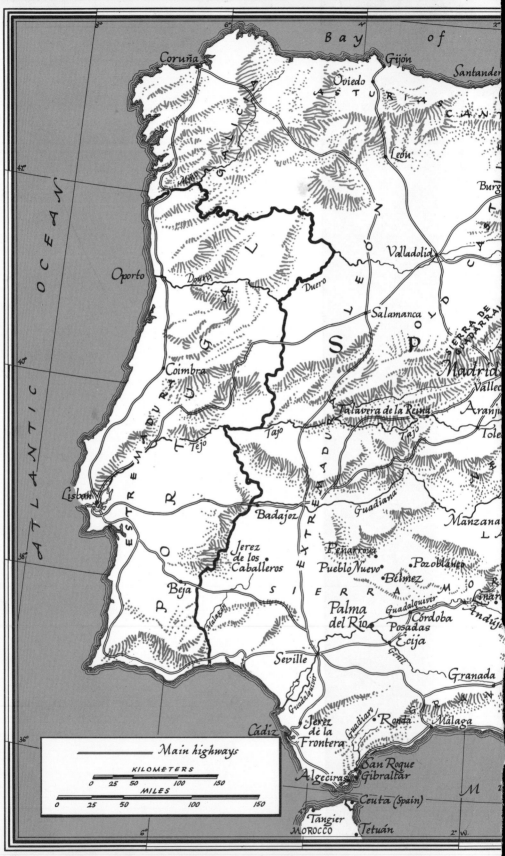